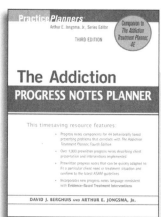

The Veterans and
Active Duty Military Psychotherapy
Progress Notes Planner

PracticePlanners® Series

Treatment Planners

The Complete Adult Psychotherapy Treatment Planner, Fourth Edition
The Child Psychotherapy Treatment Planner, Fourth Edition
The Adolescent Psychotherapy Treatment Planner, Fourth Edition
The Addiction Treatment Planner, Fourth Edition
The Continuum of Care Treatment Planner
The Couples Psychotherapy Treatment Planner
The Employee Assistance Treatment Planner
The Pastoral Counseling Treatment Planner
The Older Adult Psychotherapy Treatment Planner
The Behavioral Medicine Treatment Planner
The Group Therapy Treatment Planner
The Gay and Lesbian Psychotherapy Treatment Planner
The Family Therapy Treatment Planner
The Severe and Persistent Mental Illness Treatment Planner, Second Edition
The Mental Retardation and Developmental Disability Treatment Planner
The Social Work and Human Services Treatment Planner
The Crisis Counseling and Traumatic Events Treatment Planner
The Personality Disorders Treatment Planner
The Rehabilitation Psychology Treatment Planner
The Special Education Treatment Planner
The Juvenile Justice and Residential Care Treatment Planner
The School Counseling and School Social Work Treatment Planner
The Sexual Abuse Victim and Sexual Offender Treatment Planner
The Probation and Parole Treatment Planner
The Psychopharmacology Treatment Planner
The Speech-Language Pathology Treatment Planner
The Suicide and Homicide Treatment Planner
The College Student Counseling Treatment Planner
The Parenting Skills Treatment Planner
The Early Childhood Intervention Treatment Planner
The Co-Occurring Disorders Treatment Planner
The Complete Women's Psychotherapy Treatment Planner
The Veterans and Active Duty Military Psychotherapy Treatment Planner

Progress Notes Planners

The Child Psychotherapy Progress Notes Planner, Third Edition
The Adolescent Psychotherapy Progress Notes Planner, Third Edition
The Adult Psychotherapy Progress Notes Planner, Third Edition
The Addiction Progress Notes Planner, Third Edition
The Severe and Persistent Mental Illness Progress Notes Planner, Second Edition
The Couples Psychotherapy Progress Notes Planner
The Family Therapy Progress Notes Planner
The Veterans and Active Duty Military Psychotherapy Progress Notes Planner

Homework Planners

Brief Couples Therapy Homework Planner
Brief Family Therapy Homework Planner
Grief Counseling Homework Planner
Group Therapy Homework Planner
Divorce Counseling Homework Planner
School Counseling and School Social Work Homework Planner
Child Therapy Activity and Homework Planner
Addiction Treatment Homework Planner, Fourth Edition
Adolescent Psychotherapy Homework Planner II
Adolescent Psychotherapy Homework Planner, Second Edition
Adult Psychotherapy Homework Planner, Second Edition
Child Psychotherapy Homework Planner, Second Edition
Parenting Skills Homework Planner

Client Education Handout Planners

Adult Client Education Handout Planner
Child and Adolescent Client Education Handout Planner
Couples and Family Client Education Handout Planner

Complete Planners

The Complete Depression Treatment and Homework Planner
The Complete Anxiety Treatment and Homework Planner

Practice*Planners*®

The Veterans and Active Duty Military Psychotherapy Progress Notes Planner

David J. Berghuis

Arthur E. Jongsma, Jr.

WILEY

JOHN WILEY & SONS, INC.

Library of Congress Cataloging-in-Publication Data

Berghuis, David J.
  The veterans and active duty military psychotherapy progress notes planner / by David J. Berghuis, Arthur E. Jongsma, Jr.
    p. cm. -- (Practiceplanners series)
  Includes bibliographical references.
  ISBN 978-0-470-44097-1 (pbk.)
  1. Veterans--Mental health--United States--Handbooks, manuals, etc. 2. Soldiers--Mental health--United States--Handbooks, manuals, etc. 3. Psychotherapy--Planning--Handbooks, manuals, etc. 4. Psychology, Military--Handbooks, manuals, etc. I. Jongsma, Arthur E., 1943- II. Title.
  UH629.3.B47 2010

616.85'212--dc22

2009031714

Printed in the United States of America

10 9 8 7 6 5 4 3 2 1

To all those who have given life and limb to hold up the
lamp of liberty around the world.

– A.E.J.

With love and wishes for safety and success to my nephew,
Lance Corporal Peter Van Dyken, United States Marine Corps.
Your service makes your family proud.

– D.J.B.

CONTENTS

PRACTICE*PLANNERS*® SERIES PREFACE

Accountability is an important dimension of the practice of psychotherapy. Treatment programs, public agencies, clinics, and practitioners must justify and document their treatment plans to outside review entities in order to be reimbursed for services. The books and software in the Practice*Planners*® series are designed to help practitioners fulfill these documentation requirements efficiently and professionally.

The Practice*Planners*® series includes a wide array of treatment planning books including not only the original *Complete Adult Psychotherapy Treatment Planner*, *Child Psychotherapy Treatment Planner*, and *Adolescent Psychotherapy Treatment Planner*, all now in their fourth editions, but also *Treatment Planners* targeted to specialty areas of practice, including:

- Addictions
- Co-occurring disorders
- Behavioral medicine
- College students
- Couples therapy
- Crisis counseling
- Early childhood education
- Employee assistance
- Family therapy
- Gays and lesbians
- Group therapy
- Juvenile justice and residential care
- Mental retardation and developmental disability
- Neuropsychology

- Older adults
- Parenting skills
- Pastoral counseling
- Personality disorders
- Probation and parole
- Psychopharmacology
- Rehabilitation psychology
- School counseling
- Severe and persistent mental illness
- Sexual abuse victims and offenders
- Social work and human services
- Special education
- Speech-Language pathology
- Suicide and homicide risk assessment
- Veterans and active military duty
- Women's issues

In addition, there are three branches of companion books that can be used in conjunction with the *Treatment Planners*, or on their own:

- **Progress Notes Planners** provide a menu of progress statements that elaborate on the client's symptom presentation and the provider's therapeutic intervention. Each *Progress Notes Planner* statement is directly integrated with the behavioral definitions and therapeutic interventions from its companion *Treatment Planner*.

- **Homework Planners** include homework assignments designed around each presenting problem (such as anxiety, depression, chemical dependence, anger management, eating disorders, or panic disorder) that is the focus of a chapter in its corresponding *Treatment Planner*.

- *Client Education Handout Planners* provide brochures and handouts to help educate and inform clients on presenting problems and mental health issues as well as life skills techniques. The handouts are included on CD-ROMs for easy printing from your computer and are ideal for use in waiting rooms, at presentations, as newsletters, or as information for clients struggling with mental illness issues. The topics covered by these handouts correspond to the presenting problems in the *Treatment Planners*.

The series also includes:

- **Thera*Scribe*®,** the #1-selling treatment planning and clinical record-keeping software system for mental health professionals. Thera*Scribe*® allows the user to import the data from any of the *Treatment Planner*, *Progress Notes Planner*, or *Homework Planner* books into the software's expandable database to simply point and click to create a detailed, organized, individualized, and customized treatment plan along with optional integrated progress notes and homework assignments.

Adjunctive books, such as *The Psychotherapy Documentation Primer* and *The Clinical Documentation Sourcebook*, contain forms and resources to aid the clinician in mental health practice management.

The goal of our series is to provide practitioners with the resources they need in order to provide high quality care in the era of accountability. To put it simply: We seek to help you spend more time on patients and less time on paperwork.

ARTHUR E. JONGSMA, JR.
Grand Rapids, Michigan

PROGRESS NOTES INTRODUCTION

ABOUT PRACTICE*PLANNERS*® PROGRESS NOTES

Progress notes are not only the primary source for documenting the therapeutic process but also one of the main factors in determining the veteran's/service member's eligibility for reimbursable treatment. The purpose of the *Progress Notes Planner* series is to assist the practitioner in easily and quickly constructing progress notes that are thoroughly unified with the veteran's/service member's treatment plan.

Each *Progress Notes Planner*:

- Saves you hours of time-consuming paperwork.
- Offers the freedom to develop customized progress notes.
- Features over 1,000 prewritten progress notes summarizing patient presentation and treatment delivered.
- Provides an array of treatment approaches that correspond with the behavioral problems and *DSM-IV* diagnostic categories in the corresponding companion *Treatment Planner*.
- Offers sample progress notes that conform to the requirements of most third-party payors and accrediting agencies, including JCAHO, COA, CARF, and NCQA.

HOW TO USE THIS *PROGRESS NOTES PLANNER*

This *Progress Notes Planner* provides a menu of sentences that can be selected for constructing progress notes based on the behavioral definitions (or client's symptom presentation) and therapeutic interventions from its companion *Treatment Planner*. All progress notes must be tied to the client's treatment plan—session notes should elaborate on the problems, symptoms, and interventions contained in the plan.

Each chapter title is a reflection of the veteran's/service member's potential presenting problem. The first section of the chapter, "Veteran/Service Member Presentation," provides a detailed menu of statements that may describe how that presenting problem manifested itself in behavioral signs and symptoms. The numbers in parentheses within the "Veteran/Service Member Presentation" section correspond to the numbers of the "Behavioral Definitions" from the *Treatment Planner*.

The second section of each chapter, "Interventions Implemented," provides a menu of statements related to the action that was taken within the session to assist the client in making progress. The numbering of the items in the "Interventions Implemented" section follows exactly the numbering of "Therapeutic Intervention" items in the corresponding *Treatment Planner*.

All item lists begin with a few keywords. These words are meant to convey the theme or content of the sentences that are contained in that listing. The clinician may peruse the list of keywords to find content that matches the client's presentation and the clinician's intervention.

It is expected that the clinician may modify the prewritten statements contained in this book to fit the exact circumstances of the client's presentation and treatment. To maintain complete client records, in addition to progress note statements that may be selected and individualized from this book, the date, time, and length of a session; those present during the session; the provider; provider's credentials; and a signature must be entered in the client's record.

A FINAL NOTE ABOUT PROGRESS NOTES AND HIPAA

Federal regulations under the Health Insurance Portability and Accountability Act (HIPAA) govern the privacy of a client's psychotherapy notes as well as other protected health information (PHI). PHI and psychotherapy notes must be kept secure, and the client must sign a specific authorization to release this confidential information to anyone beyond the client's therapist or treatment team. Further, psychotherapy notes receive other special treatment under HIPAA; for example, they may not be altered after they are initially drafted. Instead, the clinician must create and file formal amendments to the notes if he or she wishes to expand, delete, or otherwise change them. Our Thera*Scribe TM* software provides functionality to help clinicians maintain the proper rules concerning handling PHI, by giving the ability to lock progress notes once they are created, to acknowledge client consent for the release of PHI, and to track amendments to psychotherapy notes over time.

Does the information contained in this book, when entered into a client's record as a progress note, qualify as a "psychotherapy note" and therefore merit confidential protection under HIPAA regulations? If the progress note that is created by selecting sentences from the database contained in this book is kept in a location separate from the client's PHI data, then the note could qualify as psychotherapy note data that is more protected than general PHI. However, because the sentences contained in this book convey generic information regarding the client's progress, the clinician may decide to keep the notes mixed in with the client's PHI and not consider it psychotherapy note data. In short, how you treat the information (separated from or integrated with PHI) can determine if this progress note planner data is psychotherapy note information. If you modify or edit these generic sentences to reflect more personal information about the client or if you add sentences that contain confidential information, the argument for keeping these notes separate from PHI and treating them as psychotherapy notes becomes stronger. For some therapists, our sentences alone reflect enough personal information to qualify as psychotherapy notes, and they will keep these notes separate from the client's PHI and require specific authorization from the client to share them with a clearly identified recipient for a clearly identified purpose.

ADJUSTMENT TO KILLING

VETERAN/SERVICE MEMBER PRESENTATION

1. Negative Emotional Reaction to Killing (1)*

A. The veteran/service member displays frequent and intense emotions related to killing another human.

B. The veteran/service member displays guilt, remorse, and shame about his/her participation in killing another human.

C. The veteran/service member displays sadness about his/her involvement in killing another human.

D. The veteran/service member displays anger about his/her involvement in killing another human.

E. As treatment has progressed, the veteran's/service member's emotional reactions to killing have become less frequent and less intense.

F. The veteran/service member reports that he/she has come to be at peace with his/her military involvement related to taking the life of another person.

2. Ruminations about Killing (2)

A. The veteran/service member reports constant ruminations about his/her participation in killing another human.

B. The veteran/service member reports that he/she has frequent thoughts about his/her participation in killing another human.

C. As treatment has progressed, the veteran's/service member's ruminations about killing and harming others have decreased.

3. Avoids Future Killing Situations (3)

A. The service member avoids activities that might lead to having to kill another human again.

B. The service member has avoided combat missions in an effort to keep from having to kill another human.

C. The service member has broken military protocol and defied orders in order to avoid situations that might lead to killing another human.

D. As treatment has progressed, the service member has been willing to accept his/her duty that may involve taking of another human life.

4. Avoids Reminders of Killing (4)

A. The service member avoids activities that serve as reminders of killing.

B. The service member has declined activities such as shooting a weapon during training because of the association with his/her experiences of killing another human.

---

*The numbers in parentheses correlate to the number of the Behavioral Definition statement in the companion chapter with the same title in *The Veterans and Active Duty Military Psychotherapy Treatment Planner* (Moore and Jongsma) by John Wiley & Sons, 2009.

C. As treatment has progressed, the service member's anxiety with activities that remind him/her of taking the life of another has decreased.

D. The service member reports that he/she is able to engage in all expected activities, regardless of whether these serve as a reminder of his/her experience related to killing another human.

5. Spiritual and Moral Conflicts (5)

A. The service member reports that he/she has been experiencing spiritual and moral conflicts related to killing others.

B. The service member is contemplating conscientious objector status.

C. The service member is struggling to reconcile his/her religious beliefs with his/her expectations and actions within the military.

D. As treatment has progressed, the service member has resolved his/her spiritual and moral conflicts.

6. Sleep Disturbance (6)

A. Since the traumatic killing event occurred, the veteran/service member has experienced a desire to sleep much more than normal.

B. Since the traumatic killing event occurred, the veteran/service member has found it very difficult to initiate and maintain sleep.

C. Since the traumatic killing event occurred, the veteran/service member has had a fear of sleeping.

D. The veteran's/service member's sleep disturbance has terminated and he/she has returned to a normal sleep pattern.

7. Alcohol/Drug Abuse (7)

A. Since the traumatic experience, the veteran/service member has engaged in a pattern of alcohol and/or drug abuse as a maladaptive coping mechanism.

B. The veteran's/service member's alcohol and/or drug abuse has diminished as he/she has worked through the traumatic killing event.

C. The veteran/service member reported no longer engaging in any alcohol or drug abuse.

8. Suicidal Thoughts (8)

A. The veteran/service member reported experiencing suicidal thoughts since the onset of posttraumatic stress disorder (PTSD).

B. The veteran's/service member's suicidal thoughts have become less intense and less frequent.

C. The veteran/service member reported no longer experiencing any suicidal thoughts.

INTERVENTIONS IMPLEMENTED

1. Assess Emotions (1)[*]

A. The veteran/service member was assessed in regard to the different types of emotions associated with killing another human.

---

[*]The numbers in parentheses correlate to the number of the Therapeutic Intervention statement in the companion chapter with the same title in *The Veterans and Active Duty Military Psychotherapy Treatment Planner* (Moore and Jongsma) by John Wiley & Sons, 2009.

B. Active listening, support, and empathy were provided during the clinical interview as the veteran/service member described his/her feelings of shame, guilt, anxiety, anger, and fear.

C. The veteran/service member was provided with support as he/she was quite emotional and forthcoming about his/her reaction to killing another human.

D. The veteran/service member was quite stoic and denied any significant emotions associated with killing another human, and was encouraged to express his/her emotions as they become more apparent.

2. Assess Severity of Emotional Impact (2)

A. The impact of the emotions on the veteran's/service member's current functioning was assessed through the use of clinical interview techniques.

B. The level of impact of the veteran's/service member's emotional functioning on his/her current functioning was assessed though the use of psychological testing.

C. It was reflected to the veteran/service member that he/she experiences a mild impact of the emotional reaction to killing on his/her current functioning.

D. It was reflected to the veteran/service member that he/she experiences a moderate impact of the emotional reaction to killing on his/her current functioning.

E. It was reflected to the veteran/service member that he/she experiences a severe impact of the emotional reaction to killing on his/her current functioning.

3. Teach about Negative Emotion Awareness (3)

A. The veteran/service member was taught techniques about how to become more aware of negative emotions.

B. The veteran/service member was taught to scan his/her body for physiological cues linked to his/her emotions.

C. The veteran/service member was provided with examples of physiological cues linked to his/her emotions (e.g., a tightening in the stomach to signal anxiety; balled fists to signal anger).

D. The veteran/service member was reinforced for his/her clear understanding of the physiological cues linked to negative emotions.

E. The veteran/service member has struggled to identify his/her negative emotions and was provided with remedial feedback about how to monitor for such emotions.

4. Assist with Labeling of Emotions (4)

A. The veteran/service member was assisted with correctly labeling his/her emotions.

B. The veteran/service member was supported as he/she sought to correctly label his/her emotions.

C. The veteran/service member was directed to use more descriptive terms for his/her emotions (e.g., breaking "mad" down into more descriptive terms such as "enraged," "frustrated," or "irritated").

D. The veteran/service member struggled to correctly label his/her emotions and was provided with remedial feedback in this area.

5. Explain Thoughts Impacting Emotions (5)

A. The veteran/service member was taught about the concepts of how thoughts impact emotions.

B. The veteran/service member was provided with several examples of the connections between cognition and feelings.

C. The veteran/service member was reinforced as he/she displayed a clear understanding of how thoughts impact emotions.

D. The veteran/service member provided specific examples of how his/her thoughts impact his/her emotions.

E. The veteran/service member struggled to understand the concept of how thoughts impact emotions, and was provided with remedial feedback in this area.

6. Teach about Automatic Thoughts (6)

A. The veteran/service member was taught the role of distorted thinking in precipitating emotional responses.

B. The veteran/service member was assisted in identifying the distorted schemas and related automatic thoughts that mediate PTSD responses.

C. The veteran/service member was reinforced as he/she verbalized an understanding of the cognitive beliefs and messages that mediate his/her PTSD responses.

D. The veteran/service member was assisted in replacing distorted messages with positive, realistic cognitions.

E. The veteran/service member failed to identify his/her distorted thoughts and cognitions and was provided with tentative examples in this area.

7. Assign Automatic Thought Record/Journal (7)

A. The veteran/service member was requested to keep a daily journal that lists each situation associated with automatic thoughts.

B. The Socratic method was used to challenge the veteran's/service member's dysfunctional thoughts and replace them with positive, reality-based thoughts.

C. The veteran/service member was reinforced for instances of successful replacement of negative automatic thoughts with more realistic, positive thinking.

D. The veteran/service member has not kept his/her record of automatic thoughts and was redirected to do so.

8. Teach about Cognitive Errors (8)

A. The veteran/service member was taught about common cognitive errors.

B. The veteran/service member was taught about cognitive errors such as judging, catastrophizing, labeling, all-or-nothing thinking, self-blaming, etc.

C. The veteran/service member was assisted in connecting his/her cognitive errors to his/her thoughts about the traumatic events.

D. The veteran/service member was assigned "Negative Thoughts Trigger Negative Feelings" from the *Adult Psychotherapy Homework Planner*, 2nd ed. (Jongsma).

E. The veteran/service member was reinforced for his/her understanding about cognitive errors.

F. The veteran/service member struggled to identify his/her cognitive errors and was provided with remedial feedback in this area.

9. Conduct Behavioral Experiments (9)

A. The veteran/service member was encouraged to do "behavioral experiments" in which negative automatic thoughts are treated as hypotheses/predictions and are tested against reality-based alternative hypotheses.

B. The veteran's/service member's automatic negative thoughts were tested against the veteran's/service member's past, present, and/or future experiences.

C. The veteran/service member was directed to talk with other veteran/service members about their thoughts and beliefs about killing.

D. The veteran/service member was assisted in processing the outcome of his/her behavioral experiences.

E. The veteran/service member was encouraged by his/her experience of the more reality-based hypotheses/predictions; this progress was reinforced.

F. The veteran/service member continues to focus on negative automatic thoughts and was redirected toward the behavioral evidence of the more reality-based alternative hypotheses.

10. Replace Negative Thoughts with Adaptive Thoughts (10)

A. The veteran/service member was assisted with replacing negative thoughts with more adaptive thoughts.

B. The veteran/service member was assisted in developing more adaptive thoughts through his/her experience of reality testing experiments, therapeutic computation, and sporadic questioning.

C. The veteran/service member was reinforced for developing more adaptive thoughts to replace his/her negative ruminations.

D. The veteran/service member has struggled to replace negative thoughts and ruminations with more adaptive thoughts, and was provided with more specific examples in this area.

11. Reinforce Positive Self-Talk (11)

A. The veteran/service member was reinforced for any successful replacement of distorted negative thinking with positive, reality-based cognitive messages.

B. It was noted that the veteran/service member has been engaging in positive, reality-based thinking that has enhanced his/her self-confidence and increased adaptive action.

C. The veteran/service member was assigned to complete the "Positive Self-Talk" assignment from the *Adult Psychotherapy Homework Planner,* 2nd ed. (Jongsma).

12. Review Possible Outcomes for Future Missions (12)

A. In an effort to reduce anxiety and prepare emotionally for future combat/training missions, the service member was requested to identify the possible scenarios regarding future missions.

B. The service member was asked to theorize about the worst-case scenarios regarding future missions.

C. The service member was requested to identify the best-case scenarios regarding future missions.

D. The service member was asked to identify the most likely case scenarios regarding future missions.

E. The service member was assisted in comparing and contrasting the likely scenarios regarding future missions.

13. Instill Confidence in Capability (13)

A. In an effort to instill a sense of confidence and capability in the veteran/service member, his/her past training and successful performance were reviewed and processed.

B. The veteran/service member was reinforced as he/she identified his/her experience of past training and successful performance.

C. The veteran/service member struggled to identify his/her past successes and was provided with specific examples in this area.

14. Teach Relaxation Techniques (14)

A. The veteran/service member was trained in a variety of relaxation techniques to reduce anxiety.

B. The veteran/service member was taught about the use of deep muscle relaxation.

C. The veteran/service member was taught about the use of visual imagery.

D. The veteran/service member was taught about deep breathing exercises.

E. The veteran/service member has regularly used relaxation techniques, and their benefits were reviewed.

F. The veteran/service member has not regularly used relaxation techniques and was redirected to do so.

15. Use Imaginal Exposure (15)

A. The veteran/service member was asked to describe a traumatic experience at an increasing, but client-chosen, level of detail.

B. The veteran/service member was asked to continue to describe his/her traumatic experience at his/her own chosen level of detail until the associated anxiety reduces and stabilizes.

C. The veteran/service member was provided with recordings of the session and was asked to listen to it between sessions.

D. The veteran/service member was reinforced for his/her progress in imaginal exposure.

E. The veteran/service member was assisted in problem-solving obstacles to his/her imaginal exposure.

16. Assess Sleep Pattern (16)

A. The exact nature of the veteran's/service member's sleep disturbance was assessed, including his/her bedtime routine, activity level while awake, nutritional habits, napping practice, actual sleep time, rhythm of time for being awake versus sleeping, and so on.

B. The effect of the killing incident on the veteran's/service member's sleep pattern was assessed.

C. The assessment of the veteran's/service member's sleep disturbance found a chronic history of this problem, which becomes exacerbated at times of high stress.

D. The assessment of the veteran's/service member's sleep disturbance found that he/she does not practice behavioral habits that are conducive to a good sleep-wake routine.

17. Instruct on Sleep Hygiene (17)

A. The veteran/service member was instructed on appropriate sleep hygiene practices.

B. The veteran/service member was advised about restricting excessive liquid intake, spicy late-night snacks, or heavy evening meals.

C. The veteran/service member was encouraged to exercise regularly but not directly before bedtime.

D. The veteran/service member was taught about minimizing or avoiding caffeine, alcohol, tobacco, or other stimulant intake.

E. The veteran/service member was directed to use the "Sleep Pattern Record" from the *Adult Psychotherapy Homework Planner,* 2nd ed. (Jongsma).

F. The veteran/service member was reinforced for his/her regular use of sleep hygiene techniques.

G. The veteran/service member has not regularly used sleep hygiene practices and was redirected to do so.

18. Refer for Physician Evaluation (18)

A. The veteran/service member was referred to his/her physician to rule out any physical and/or pharmacological causes for his/her sleep disturbance.

B. The veteran/service member was referred to his/her physician to evaluate whether psychotropic medications might be helpful to induce sleep.

C. The veteran/service member was referred for sleep lab studies.

D. The physician has indicated that physical organic causes for the veteran's/service member's sleep disturbance have been found, and a regimen of treatment for these problems has been initiated.

E. The physician ruled out any physical/organic or medication side effect as the cause for the veteran's/service member's sleep disturbance.

F. The physician has ordered sleep-enhancing medications to help the veteran/service member return to a normal sleep pattern.

G. The veteran/service member has not followed through on the referral to his/her physician and was redirected to complete this task.

19. Monitor Medication Compliance (19)

A. The veteran/service member was noted to be consistently taking the antidepressant medication and stated that it was effective at increasing normal sleep routines.

B. The veteran/service member reported taking the antidepressant medication on a consistent basis but has not noted any positive effect on his/her sleep; he/she was directed to review this with the prescribing clinician.

C. The veteran/service member reported not consistently taking his/her antidepressant prescription and was encouraged to do so.

20. Normalize Spiritual and Moral Conflicts (20)

A. The veteran/service member was provided with empathetic listening as he/she verbalized his/her current spiritual and moral conflicts.

B. The veteran/service member was advised that his/her spiritual and moral conflicts are quite typical for an individual in his/her situation.

C. The veteran/service member was reinforced as he/she appeared more at ease with his/her emotional struggles.

21. Refer to Chaplain (21)

A. The veteran/service member was referred to a chaplain.

B. The veteran/service member was referred to spiritual and moral leaders associated with the military.

C. The veteran/service member has followed up on the referral to his/her chaplain, and the benefits of this opportunity were reviewed.

D. The veteran/service member has not contacted his/her chaplain and was reminded to do so.

22. Assign Reading Material about Killing (22)

A. The veteran/service member was assigned to read the book *On Killing* (Lieutenant Colonel Dave Grossman).

B. The veteran/service member has read the assigned material about killing in the military, and his/her reaction to the material was processed.

C. The veteran/service member has not read the assigned material on killing and was redirected to do so.

23. Normalize Apprehension and Anxiety (23)

A. Active listening was used as the service member talked about his/her apprehension and anxiety about going on future combat/training missions.

B. The service member's apprehension and anxiety about future combat/training missions was normalized.

C. Specific examples of how others have struggled with similar apprehension and anxiety about future combat/training missions were reviewed.

24. Acknowledge Weapon Discomfort (24)

A. The service member's discomfort with maintaining a weapon was acknowledged.

B. The service member was assisted in exploring his/her reasons behind the discomfort with maintaining a weapon.

C. Active listening and support were provided as the service member talked about his/her discomfort with maintaining a weapon.

D. The service member was very stoic about his/her discomfort with maintaining a weapon and was urged to talk about this as he/she feels more comfortable.

25. Encourage Continued Weapons Practice (25)

A. The service member was encouraged to participate in shooting range practice.

B. The service member was encouraged to continue to spend time and cleaning his/her weapon.

C. The service member has continued difficult practices regarding weapon use, and his/her experience was processed.

D. The service member continues to avoid anything to do with weapons and was provided with additional treatment in this area.

26. Teach about Impact of Conflicted Thoughts (26)

A. The veteran/service member was taught about how conflicted thoughts can affect emotions.

B. The veteran/service member was taught about how conflicted thoughts can affect physiological functioning.

C. The veteran/service member was assisted in applying the effects of conflicted thoughts to his/her experience.

D. The veteran/service member was supported as he/she identified the effects that his/her conflicted thoughts have had on his/her emotional and physiological functioning.

E. The veteran/service member denied any impact of his/her conflicted thoughts on emotional and physiological functioning and was urged to remain open to these concepts.

27. Refer for Substance Use Evaluation (27)

A. The veteran/service member was asked to describe his/her use of alcohol and/or drugs as a means of escape from negative emotions.

B. The veteran/service member was referred for an in-depth substance abuse evaluation.

C. The veteran/service member was supported as he/she acknowledged that he/she has abused alcohol and/or drugs as a means of coping with the negative consequences associated with the traumatic killing event.

D. The veteran/service member was quite defensive about giving information regarding his/her substance abuse history and minimized any such behavior; this was reflected to him/her and he/she was urged to be more open.

28. Refer for Medical Evaluation (28)

A. The veteran/service member was referred for a medical evaluation because substance dependence is suspected.

B. The veteran/service member has received the medical evaluation, but no substance dependence was identified.

C. The veteran/service member has received the medical evaluation, and substance dependence is confirmed.

29. Refer to Chemical Dependence Treatment (29)

A. The veteran/service member was referred for chemical dependence treatment.

B. The veteran/service member consented to chemical dependence treatment referral, as he/she has acknowledged it as a significant problem.

C. The veteran/service member refused to accept a referral for chemical dependence treatment and continued to deny that substance abuse is a problem.

D. The veteran/service member was reinforced for following through on obtaining chemical dependence treatment.

E. The veteran's/service member's treatment focus was switched to his/her chemical dependence problem.

30. Tell the Story of the Killing (30)

A. The veteran/service member was gently encouraged to tell the entire story of the traumatic event.

B. The veteran/service member was given the opportunity to share what he/she recalls about the traumatic event.

C. Today's therapy session explored the sequence of events before, during, and after the traumatic event.

31. List Regrets (31)

A. The veteran/service member was asked to develop a list of all the regrets he/she has concerning the killing.

B. The veteran/service member was provided with empathetic listening and assistance in verbalizing his/her thoughts about the regrets that he/she has concerning the killing.

C. The veteran/service member was assisted in processing the list of regrets related to the killing in which he/she has participated.

32. Use Rational Emotive Approach (32)

A. A rational emotive approach was used to confront the veteran's/service member's statements of responsibility for the killing.

B. The veteran/service member was encouraged to consider the reality-based facts surrounding the killing and his/her distortion of those facts in accepting responsibility for the loss irrationally.

C. The veteran/service member was reinforced as he/she has decreased his/her statements and feelings of being responsible for the killing.

33. Treat/Explain Regarding Grief (33)

A. The veteran's/service member's experience was treated as one of grieving.

B. The veteran/service member was assisted in understanding the stages of grief.

C. The veteran/service member was assisted in identifying his/her current stage of grief.

D. The veteran/service member was taught about how to cope with, manage, and move through the stages of grief.

34. Assess Suicide Risk (34)

A. The veteran's/service member's experience of suicidal urges and his/her history of suicidal behavior were explored.

B. It was noted that the veteran/service member has stated that he/she does experience suicidal urges but feels that they are clearly under his/her control and that there is no risk of engagement in suicidal behavior.

C. The veteran/service member identified suicidal urges as being present but contracted to contact others if the urges became strong.

D. Because the veteran's/service member's suicidal urges were assessed to be very serious, immediate referral to a more intensive supervised level of care was made.

E. Due to the veteran's/service member's suicidal urges and his/her unwillingness to voluntarily admit himself/herself to a more intensive, supervised level of care, involuntary commitment procedures were begun.

F. The service member's chain of command was notified of the service member's suicide ideation and was asked to form a 24-hour suicide watch until the service member's crisis subsides.

35. Restrict Access to Weapons (35)

A. Support and supervisory people were contacted and told to remove weapons from the living environment of the veteran/service member.

B. A recommendation was made to the service member's chain of command that the service member be limited to low risk training.

C. The veteran/service member understood and agreed with the actions taken to restrict his/her access to weapons that he/she could use for self-injury.

36. Encourage Time with Supports (36)

A. The veteran/service member was encouraged to spend more time with family and friends.

B. The veteran's/service member's tendency to isolate himself/herself was monitored.

C. The veteran/service member was reinforced for his/her regular involvement with friends and family.

D. The veteran/service member has not regularly maintained involvement with extended family and was reminded to do so.

ADJUSTMENT TO THE MILITARY CULTURE

SERVICE MEMBER PRESENTATION

1. Difficulty Following Rules and Orders (1)*

A. The service member reported difficulty adjusting to following the many rules of the military culture.

B. The service member has difficulty accepting orders from others.

C. The service member's problems with following rules and orders have resulted in disciplinary action.

D. As treatment has progressed, the service member has adjusted to following rules, orders, and other military expectations, and this progress has been reinforced.

2. Emotional Reaction to Loss of Independence (2)

A. The service member focused on his/her sense of loss of autonomy and independence as he/she has entered the military culture.

B. The service member reports sadness, frustration, anxiety, and hopelessness due to the loss of autonomy and independence.

C. The service member has displayed erratic behavior due to his/her negative reaction to the loss of autonomy and independence.

D. As treatment has progressed, the service member has become more stable in his/her reaction to the loss of autonomy and independence.

E. The service member is now much more accepting of the loss of independence in the military culture.

3. Reprimands (3)

A. The service member identified a persistent pattern of insubordination, misconduct, disrespect, and failure to follow orders.

B. The service member does not regularly adhere to military customs and courtesies.

C. The service member has been reprimanded often for his/her failure to comply with military expectations.

D. The service member is at risk for serious reprimands for failure to follow military expectations.

E. As treatment as progressed, the service member reports increased compliance with following orders and accepting military expectations.

F. The service member has not been recently reprimanded for any insubordination, misconduct, disrespect, or failure to follow orders/expectations.

4. Failure to Meet Standards (4)

A. The service member has failed to meet the minimum standards set by the military.

---

*The numbers in parentheses correlate to the number of the Behavioral Definition statement in the companion chapter with the same title in *The Veterans and Active Duty Military Psychotherapy Treatment Planner* (Moore and Jongsma) by John Wiley & Sons, 2009.

B. The service member has failed to meet the minimum standards for physical fitness as expected by the military.

C. The service member has failed to meet the basic academic expectations of the military.

D. The service member has failed to meet the basic professional standards set by the military.

E. As treatment has progress, the service member has improved his/her performance in meeting military standards.

F. The service member meets all minimum physical fitness, academic, and professional standards.

5. Negative Effects of Decreased Sleep (5)

A. The service member reported a pattern of decreased sleep.

B. The service member's mental functioning has decreased as a result of his/her decreased level of sleep.

C. The service member's physical functioning has suffered because of his/her lack of sleep.

D. The service member's mental and physical functioning has improved as sleep has increased.

6. Absent Without Leave (6)

A. The service member has decided to go absent without leave as a means to escape the stress of military life.

B. The service member went absent without leave and is now being disciplined.

C. Although the service member has been tempted to go absent without leave, he/she has seen the problems this may create and has declined to do so.

D. The service member acknowledged the poor judgment associated with going absent without leave.

7. Desires to Leave Military (7)

A. The service member reported a desire to leave the military and return to civilian life.

B. The service member has initiated proceedings to leave the military.

C. As treatment has progressed, the service member reports greater certainty in regard to his/her decision about remaining in the military.

D. The service member has made a clear decision to leave the military.

E. The service member has reversed his/her thinking and has made a clear decision to remain in the military.

8. Homesickness and Isolation (8)

A. The service member reports strong feelings of homesickness.

B. The service member reports strong feelings of isolation and difficulty connecting with any other service members.

C. The service member reports a better connection to others within the military.

D. The service member's feelings of homesickness have significantly decreased.

INTERVENTIONS IMPLEMENTED

1. Explore Current Stressors (1)*

A. The service member's current military stressors were reviewed.

B. The service member was helped to make a connection between current stressors and feelings of frustration, hopelessness, depression, and anxiety.

C. The service member was reinforced for his/her acknowledgment of stressors and emotions.

D. The service member reported decreased feelings of hopelessness, depression, and anxiety, and this progress was reinforced.

2. Rank Order Stressors (2)

A. The service member was assigned to create a list of stressors contributing to his/her current situation.

B. The service member was asked to rank order the stressors from the most troubling to the least troubling.

C. The service member has completed his/her rank order list of stressors, and these were processed in the session.

D. The service member has not completed his/her rank order list of stressors and was redirected to do so.

3. Identify Similar Situations and Outcomes (3)

A. The service member was assisted in identifying several dissatisfying situations in the past that were similar to his/her current circumstance and feeling.

B. The service member was asked to identify the outcomes of the similar situations in his/her past.

C. Reasons behind both negative and positive outcomes of similar past situations were processed.

4. List Emotions (4)

A. The service member was assigned to create a list of the various emotions caused by his/her challenges in adjusting to the military culture.

B. The service member was offered a list of emotions from which to select his/her typical emotions when challenged by adjustment to the military culture.

C. The service member has identified a variety of emotions regarding his/her challenges to adjusting in the military culture, and these were accepted and processed.

D. The service member had difficulty naming emotions caused by his/her challenges in adjusting to the military culture and was provided with additional feedback in this area.

5. Explore Stigma about Emotions (5)

A. Stigma that may be associated with identifying and accepting emotions was explored with the service member.

B. Beliefs contrary to identifying and accepting emotions (e.g., "emotions make you weak") were reviewed and processed with the service member.

C. The service member acknowledged beliefs that tend to minimize and invalidate emotions, and these were processed.

---

*The numbers in parentheses correlate to the number of the Therapeutic Intervention statement in the companion chapter with the same title in *The Veterans and Active Duty Military Psychotherapy Treatment Planner* (Moore and Jongsma) by John Wiley & Sons, 2009.

D. The service member denied any beliefs that would minimize or invalidate the identification and expression of emotions, and he/she was provided with beliefs for which he/she should be monitoring.

6. Identify Military Positives (6)

A. The service member was assigned to develop a list of what he/she likes about serving in the military.

B. The service member has created a list of reasons why he/she likes serving in the military, and this was processed within the session.

C. The service member has struggled to identify a list of what he/she likes about serving in the military and was provided with specific examples in this area.

D. The service member has not attempted to develop a list of what he/she likes about serving in the military and was redirected to do so.

7. Switch Role Play (7)

A. A role-play situation was facilitated in which the service member and the therapist switch roles, and the service member was required to convince the therapist that the military can be a positive environment.

B. As a result of the switched role play, the service member has identified ways in which the military can be a positive environment; this progress was reinforced.

C. The service member has struggled to identify ways in which the military can be a positive environment, and he/she was urged to identify possible options in this area.

8. Encourage Acting as Model Service Member (8)

A. The service member was encouraged to act or role-play (as if) he/she were a model/squared-away service member while at work.

B. The service member has attempted to present himself/herself as a model service member, and his/her experience was processed.

C. The service member has not attempted to act as if he/she were a model/squared-away service member and was redirected to practice this for a time-limited period.

9. Brainstorm Stress Management Techniques (9)

A. The service member was assisted in brainstorming healthy ways of coping with stress and improving mood.

B. The service member was encouraged to use progressive muscle relaxation techniques.

C. The service member was encouraged to replace negative thoughts with positive ones.

D. The service member has identified several healthy ways of coping with stress and improving his/her mood; his/her response and progress were monitored.

E. The service member has struggled to identify healthy ways to improve his/her mood and was provided with additional feedback in this area.

10. Teach Anger Management Techniques (10)

A. The service member was taught techniques for managing anger.

B. The service member was taught deep breathing techniques.

C. The service member was taught about taking a time-out.

D. The service member has used anger management techniques to control his/her level of frustration.

E. Through the use of the identified anger management techniques, the service member has significantly decreased his/her impulsive actions.

F. The service member has struggled to learn and utilize anger management techniques and was provided with remedial instruction in this area.

11. Apply Problem-Solving Processes (11)

A. The service member was taught how to apply the seven-step military problem-solving process to his/her current situation.

B. The service member was taught about recognizing and defining the problem as well as gathering facts and making assumptions.

C. The service member was taught about defining end states or goals and establishing criteria for success.

D. The service member was taught about developing possible solutions and analyzing and comparing possible solutions.

E. The service member was taught about selecting and implementing a solution as well as analyzing the solution for effectiveness.

F. The service member displayed a clear understanding of how to use the seven-step military problem-solving process to his/her current situation and was reinforced for this.

G. The service member struggled about how to apply the seven-step military problem-solving process to his/her current situation and was provided with remedial assistance in this area.

12. Apply Problem-Solving Process (12)

A. The service member was asked to identify a current problem on which to apply the problem-solving process.

B. The service member was assisted in identifying how he/she would utilize the problem-solving process for the identified problem.

C. The service member was assisted in developing an action plan for real-world implementation.

D. The service member was assisted in reviewing and processing the outcome of his/her problem-solving process.

13. Teach Assertiveness (13)

A. Role-playing techniques were used to teach the service member various methods for being more assertive in personal and professional situations.

B. The empty-chair technique was used to teach the service member about assertiveness.

C. Role-reversal techniques were used to practice and learn about assertiveness in personal and professional situations.

D. The service member has displayed increased understanding about assertiveness in professional and personal situations; this progress was reinforced.

E. The service member has struggled to learn about increased assertiveness and was provided with remedial feedback in this area.

14. Assign Books on Assertiveness (14)

A. The service member was assigned to read books on assertiveness.

B. The service member was assigned to read *The Complete Idiot's Guide to Assertiveness* (Davidson).

C. The service member was assigned to read *How to Grow a Backbone: Ten Strategies for Gaining Power and Influence at Work* (Marshall).

D. The service member has read the assigned information on assertiveness, and the content was processed and applied to current life problems.

E. The service member has not read the assigned information on assertiveness and was redirected to do so.

15. Develop Pleasant Activities (15)

A. The service member was encouraged to develop activities that he/she enjoys.

B. The service member was encouraged to include activities that can be done with others or alone, if desired (i.e., hiking, fishing, and biking).

C. The service member was assigned "Identify and Schedule Pleasant Activities" from the *Adult Psychotherapy Homework Planner,* 2nd ed. (Jongsma).

D. The service member completed the homework assignment, and the content was processed within the session.

E. The service member has completed the assignments for developing activities, and this list was processed.

F. The service member has engaged in desired activities, and his/her experience was processed.

G. The service member has not developed or used any list of activities in which he/she can participate with others or alone and was redirected to do so.

16. Set Strict Boundaries for Time Off (16)

A. The service member was assisted in setting clear and strict boundaries when he/she has time off from work.

B. The service member was encouraged to identify the circumstances under which he/she is willing or not willing to accept additional work.

C. The service member has set clear boundaries for his/her time off from work, and his/her implementation of this was reviewed and processed.

D. The service member has struggled to maintain his/her clear boundaries about time off from work and was assisted in problem-solving these struggles.

17. Encourage Non-Military Related Activities (17)

A. The service member was encouraged to participle in non–military-related outings/activities that promote a sense of connectedness to others in the community.

B. Examples of activities that promote a sense of connectedness were provided to the service member, including attending church socials, volunteering at an animal shelter, etc.

C. The service member has begun involvement in non–military-related outings and activities, and his/her experience was processed.

D. The service member has not sought out nonmilitary activities that promote connectedness with the community and was reminded about this important resource.

18. Encourage Friendships (18)

A. The service member was encouraged to develop friendships with current and past service members.

B. The service member was encouraged to seek out social supports who understand the challenges of being in the military.

C. The service member has talked on a social basis with others who understand the challenges of being in the military, and his/her experience was processed.

D. The service member has not sought out friendships with current or past service members and was reminded to do so.

19. Encourage VFW Activities (19)

A. The service member was encouraged to attend an activity at a local Veterans of Foreign Wars (VFW) organization.

B. The service member was provided with specific information about the availability of VFW activities.

C. The service member has attended an activity at a local VFW post, and his/her experience was processed.

D. The service member has not attended a VFW activity and was redirected to do so.

20. Connect with Chaplain (20)

A. The service member was encouraged to talk with his/her unit chaplain about his/her problems adjusting to the military culture.

B. The service member has talked to the unit chaplain about his/her problems, and his/her experiences were processed.

C. The service member did not feel that his/her needs were met through the contact with the unit chaplain and was provided an alternative spiritual resource with whom to share.

D. The service member has not contacted the chaplain and was redirected to do so.

21. Assist in Contact with Base/Post Services (21)

A. The service member was assisted in making contact with local base/post services that help service members adjust to military life.

B. The service member was encouraged to get involved with base/post services, such as the single soldiers' club.

C. The service member has made contact with the local base/post services that help service members adjust to military life, and his/her experience was processed.

D. The service member has not made contact with a base/post services and was redirected to do so.

22. Encourage Talking with Superiors (22)

A. The service member was encouraged to talk about his/her difficulty adjusting to military culture with his/her squad leader, platoon sergeant, first sergeant, or others in the chain of command whom he/she trusts.

B. The service member has talked with his/her chain of command about the current situation, and the experience was processed.

C. The service member has not informed the chain of command about his/her current adjustment difficulties and was reminded that this will be an important step.

23. Include Family (23)

A. The service member's significant other was included in joint sessions to deal with problems that are impacting all parties involved.

B. The service member's family was included with joint sessions to deal with problems that are impacting all parties involved.

C. The service member reported better support from his/her family members, and this progress was reviewed.

24. Encourage Physical Fitness Instruction (24)

A. The service member was encouraged to meet with a certified instructor at his/her local base/post in order to develop a physical fitness training plan.

B. The service member has started a physical fitness training regimen, and his/her experience was processed.

C. The service member reports better adjustment as he/she experiences better physical fitness; this progress was highlighted.

D. The service member has not coordinated involvement with a certified instructor at his/her local base/post and was reminded to do so.

25. Reinforce Physical Fitness Gains (25)

A. The service member was noted to have made significant physical fitness gains.

B. Encouragement was provided to the service member in regard to his/her physical fitness program.

C. Positive feedback was provided to the service member for his/her physical fitness gains.

26. Teach Imagery Techniques (26)

A. The service member was taught imagery techniques that can improve his/her performance on the required physical fitness test.

B. The service member was taught how to imagine success versus failure at fitness tasks.

C. The service member has regularly used imagery techniques, and his/her experience was processed.

D. The service member has not used the imagery techniques and was reminded about how these can be helpful.

27. Teach about the Need for Authority (27)

A. The service member was taught about the need for authority and chain of command to promote order and safety in the face of threat and chaos during an attack.

B. The service member was reinforced for his/her acceptance of the need for authority and chain of command.

C. The service member was assisted in identifying how the authority and chain-of-command issues need to occur during training, deployment, and all other times within the military, not just during the threat and chaos of an attack.

D. The service member has shown increased adjustment since his/her acceptance of the need for authority and chain of command, and this was reinforced.

E. The service member continues to resist the need for authority and chain of command and was provided with additional feedback.

28. Explore History of Resistance to Authority (28)

A. The service member's civilian patterns of resistance to authority were reviewed.

B. Distinctions were drawn between the resistance to authority within civilian life and the need for authority and chain of command within the military setting.

C. The service member was encouraged to develop new reactions to authority within the military setting.

D. The service member was encouraged to view civilian resistance to authority as appropriate at that time but submission to authority as appropriate for this time.

29. List Negative Consequences for Resistance to Authority (29)

A. The service member was asked to list the negative consequences that will occur if a pattern of resistance to authority continues.

B. The service member was assisted in developing a list of negative consequences for resistance, including lack of promotion, possible confinement, disciplinary assignments, etc.

C. The service member has listed the negative consequences that will occur if the pattern of resistance to authority continues, and this list was processed.

D. The service member has not listed the negative consequences that will occur if a pattern of resistance to authority continues, and this resistance was processed.

30. Explore Isolation and Homesickness (30)

A. The service member's feeling of isolation was queried and processed.

B. The service member was asked about his/her feelings of homesickness.

C. The service member identified significant feelings of isolation and homesickness, and these were accepted.

D. The service member denied any pattern of homesickness or isolation, and he/she was reminded to monitor for this.

31. Role-Play Establishing Social Contact (31)

A. Role-play situations were used for the service member to practice reaching out to others to establish social contact.

B. The service member was assigned "Restoring Socialization Comfort" from the *Adult Psychotherapy Homework Planner,* 2nd ed. (Jongsma).

C. The service member completed the homework assignment, and the content was processed within the session.

D. The service member has developed a greater comfort with reaching out to others to establish social contact, and this was reinforced.

E. The service member continues to struggle with how to reach out to others to establish social contact and was provided with remedial feedback in this area.

AMPUTATION, LOSS OF MOBILITY, DISFIGUREMENT

VETERAN/SERVICE MEMBER PRESENTATION

1. Loss of Limb(s) (1)*

A. The veteran/service member has experienced a partial loss of limb during a combat or training mission or from an accident.

B. The veteran/service member has experienced a complete loss of limb during a combat or training mission or from an accident.

C. The veteran/service member has had multiple limb loss.

2. Significant Physical Limitations (2)

A. The veteran/service member has significant physical limitations due to limb loss.

B. The veteran/service member has a loss of mobility due to his/her limb loss.

C. The veteran/service member has decreased range of motion due to his/her limb loss.

D. As treatment has progressed, the veteran/service member has begun to improve in regard to his/her physical limitations.

E. The veteran/service member has maximized his/her movement or range of motion subsequent to limb loss.

3. Burns (3)

A. The veteran/service member has experienced significant body burns during a combat or training mission or from an accident.

B. The veteran/service member has begun the process of recovery from significant burns that occurred during a combat or training mission or from an accident.

C. The veteran/service member has displayed maximum improvement in regard to his/her significant body burns.

4. Psychological Distress (4)

A. The veteran/service member reports clinically significant psychological distress resulting from his/her loss of mobility, disfigurement, and social and occupational functioning.

B. The veteran/service member reports that he/she is quite depressed about his/her physical problems and the subsequent loss in functioning.

C. The veteran/service member reports significant anxiety about his/her future functioning subsequent to his/her injury.

D. The veteran/service member reports significant social anxiety regarding how he/she appears to others.

E. As treatment has progressed, the veteran's/service member's psychological distress has decreased.

---

*The numbers in parentheses correlate to the number of the Behavioral Definition statement in the companion chapter with the same title in *The Veterans and Active Duty Military Psychotherapy Treatment Planner* (Moore and Jongsma) by John Wiley & Sons, 2009.

5. Hopelessness about Work (5)

A. The veteran/service member verbalizes feelings of hopelessness regarding future occupational opportunities.

B. The veteran/service member is uncertain about how his/her injury may affect his/her future ability to work.

C. The veteran/service member reports feelings of anxiety and depression secondary to his/her outlook for future occupational opportunities.

D. The veteran/service member reports that his/her feelings of anxiety and depression related to loss regarding his/her future work opportunities have decreased.

6. Decreased Life Satisfaction (6)

A. The veteran/service member reports experiencing feelings of hopelessness and worthlessness regarding how he/she will function subsequent to his/her injury.

B. The veteran/service member reports that he/she no longer enjoys previously satisfying experiences.

C. The veteran/service member has made comments about his/her ability to go on.

D. The veteran/service member reports that his/her satisfaction with life has improved.

E. The veteran/service member has a very positive outlook on his/her life despite his/her injury.

7. Marital/Family Conflicts (7)

A. The veteran/service member reports frequent and continual arguing with his/her partner.

B. The veteran/service member describes a lack of communication within his/her family.

C. The veteran/service member describes multiple marriage and family conflicts, resulting in arguments and estrangement.

D. As treatment has progressed, the veteran/service member reports decreased marital and family conflicts.

8. Suicidal Ideation (8)

A. The veteran/service member reported recurrent suicidal ideation but denied having any specific plan to implement suicidal urges.

B. The veteran/service member reported experiencing ongoing suicidal ideation and has developed a specific plan for suicide.

C. The veteran/service member has made a suicide attempt.

D. The veteran/service member stated that his/her suicidal urges have diminished and he/she has no interest in implementing any suicide plan.

E. The veteran/service member reports no suicide urges.

INTERVENTIONS IMPLEMENTED

1. Discuss Injury (1)*

A. The veteran/service member was encouraged to discuss his/her injury as much as he/she feels comfortable.

---

*The numbers in parentheses correlate to the number of the Therapeutic Intervention statement in the companion chapter with the same title in *The Veterans and Active Duty Military Psychotherapy Treatment Planner* (Moore and Jongsma) by John Wiley & Sons, 2009.

B. The veteran/service member was provided with support and encouragement as he/she discussed his/her injury.

C. A specific focus was provided in regard to potential posttraumatic stress disorder symptoms that may occur while describing the incident.

D. The veteran/service member was allowed to proceed at his/her own pace in regard to discussing the injury.

2. Assess Injury Impact (2)

A. The type, intensity, and frequency of the veteran's/service member's ongoing, injury-related symptoms were assessed.

B. The impact of the veteran's/service member's injury on his/her social, occupational, and interpersonal functioning was assessed.

C. The impact of the veteran's/service member's injury on his/her functioning was assessed to be rather mild.

D. The impact of the veteran's/service member's injury on his/her functioning was assessed to be moderate.

E. The impact of the veteran's/service member's injury on his/her functioning was assessed to be severe.

3. Identify Emotions (3)

A. The veteran/service member was helped to identify, clarify, and express his/her feelings associated with the injury.

B. The veteran/service member denied any significant emotional reaction to his/her injury; this was accepted at face value.

C. The veteran/service member denied any significant emotional reaction to his/her injury but was urged to be aware of his/her potential emotional reactions.

D. The veteran/service member was openly supported as he/she expressed his/her feelings regarding the injury.

E. The veteran's/service member's emotions were processed within the session..

4. Assign Feelings Log Journal (4)

A. The veteran/service member was asked to keep a feelings journal in which he/she would record the time of day, where and what he/she was doing, the severity of the negative feelings, and what seemed to exacerbate them.

B. The veteran/service member was assigned to use the "Pain and Stress Journal" in the *Adult Psychotherapy Homework Planner,* 2nd ed. (Jongsma).

C. The veteran/service member has followed through on completing the feelings journal, and his/her journal was reviewed.

D. The material from the veteran's/service member's pain journal was processed to assist him/her in developing insight into triggers for and the nature of his/her pain.

E. Interventions were discussed that could help the veteran/service member alleviate the frequency, duration, and severity of his/her pain.

F. The veteran/service member reported that he/she has not kept a pain journal and was redirected to do so.

5. Refer for Medication Review (5)

A. The veteran/service member was referred to a physician who specializes in chronic pain management to obtain a medication review.

B. The veteran/service member has followed through with attending an appointment with a physician who reviewed his/her medications; the results of this evaluation were discussed.

C. The veteran/service member has begun taking the new medications prescribed by the physician to regulate the pain, and his/her reaction to the medication was reviewed.

D. The veteran/service member has not followed through with a referral to a physician for a medication review and was redirected to do so.

E. Contact was made with the veteran's/service member's physician, who evaluated pain control medications.

F. The veteran's/service member's physician was given a progress report regarding his/her chronic pain management.

G. The veteran's/service member's physician indicated that no further medication options were available to manage his/her pain; these findings have been reviewed with the veteran/service member.

6. Monitor Medication Compliance (6)

A. As the veteran/service member has taken the medication prescribed by his/her physician, the effectiveness and side effects of the medication were monitored.

B. The veteran/service member reported that the medication has been beneficial in managing his/her pain and mood; the benefits of this progress were reviewed.

C. The veteran/service member reported that the medication has not been beneficial; this was relayed to the prescribing clinician.

D. The veteran/service member was assessed for side effects from his/her medication.

E. The veteran/service member has not consistently taken the prescribed medication and was redirected to do so.

7. Educate about Treatment Importance (7)

A. The veteran/service member was educated about the importance of attending all assigned medical appointments.

B. The veteran/service member was encouraged to follow through on all medical treatment recommendations.

C. The veteran/service member was encouraged to take his/her medication as prescribed.

D. The veteran/service member was encouraged to change bandages as indicated.

E. The veteran/service member was supported for his/her compliance with treatment and recommendations.

F. The veteran/service member has not complied with his/her treatment recommendations and was redirected to do so.

8. Teach about Grief (8)

A. The process of grieving was taught to the veteran/service member.

B. An emphasis was placed that grief is not related just to the death of a loved one but can be applied to the veteran's/service member's injury.

C. The veteran/service member has been resistant to grief concepts and was provided with additional feedback.

9. Teach about Stages of Grief (9)

A. The veteran/service member was taught about the five stages of grief.

B. The veteran/service member was taught about denial, anger, bargaining, depression, and acceptance.

C. It was emphasized to the veteran/service member that grief is not an all-or-none or stepwise progression.

D. The veteran/service member was assisted in identifying his/her grief stage.

E. The veteran/service member displayed a fair understanding of his/her stages of grief and was reinforced for this.

F. Remedial information was provided to the veteran/service member as he/she seems to have difficulty understanding the grief stages.

10. Challenge for a Positive Focus (10)

A. The veteran/service member was challenged to focus his/her thoughts on the positive aspects of life rather than on the losses associated with his/her medical condition.

B. The veteran/service member was referred to the *Grief Recovery Handbook: The Action Program for Moving Beyond Death, Divorce and Other Losses* (James and Friedman).

C. When the veteran/service member focused on the positive aspects of his/her life, immediate reinforcement was provided.

D. The veteran/service member remains preoccupied with the losses associated with his/her medical condition and was reminded about the need to focus on the positive aspects of his/her life.

11. Educate about Grief Differences (11)

A. The veteran/service member was educated about how grief is dealt with differently by different people.

B. The impact of culture on the veteran's/service member's grief was explored.

C. The veteran/service member was reminded that different people grieve for different periods of time.

12. Refer for Occupational Therapy Services (12)

A. A referral was provided to the veteran/service member for occupational therapy services.

B. The veteran's/service member's use of occupational therapy services was monitored and reinforced.

C. The veteran/service member was reinforced for his/her regular involvement in occupational therapy services.

D. The veteran/service member has not consistently applied himself/herself to occupational therapy services and was redirected to do so.

13. Educate about Occupational Therapy Benefits (13)

A. The veteran/service member was educated about how occupational therapy will assist in his/her functioning at a higher level.

B. The benefits of occupational therapy in his/her employment opportunities were reviewed.

C. The benefits of occupational therapy for the veteran's/service member's everyday life were reviewed.

14. Refer for Physical Therapy Services (14)

A. A referral was provided for to the veteran/service member for physical therapy services.

B. The veteran's/service member's use of physical therapy services was monitored and reinforced.

C. The veteran/service member was reinforced for his/her regular involvement in physical therapy services.

D. The veteran/service member has not consistently applied himself/herself to physical therapy services and was redirected to do so.

15. Educate about Physical Therapy Benefits (15)

A. The veteran/service member was educated about how physical therapy will assist in his/her functioning at a higher level.

B. The benefits of physical therapy in his/her employment opportunities were reviewed.

C. The veteran/service member was assisted in identifying how physical therapy will help to increase mobility, strength, and physical stamina, improving his/her life's satisfaction.

D. The benefits of physical therapy for the veteran's/service member's everyday life were reviewed.

16. Provide Family Therapy (16)

A. Family therapy was provided to the veteran/service member and family members in order to overcome the hurt associated with the loss.

B. A focus was made on strengthening the family support system to help the veteran/service member overcome the effects of his/her injury.

C. The family system seems to be strengthened through the use of family therapy.

D. Despite family therapy services, the veteran/service member does not receive a great deal of support and help from the family system; this struggle was processed.

17. Encourage Support Groups (17)

A. The veteran/service member was encouraged to investigate various support groups that focus on his/her disability/injury.

B. The veteran/service member was provided with specific information about how to link to various support groups.

C. The veteran/service member was encouraged to seek information over the Internet in regard to support groups, including these Web links: www.amputee-coalition.org; www.americanamputee.org/library/supportgroups.asps; http://burnsurvivor.com.

D. The veteran/service member has begun involvement in support groups, and his/her experience was processed.

E. The veteran/service member has not begun involvement in support groups and was reminded to do so.

18. Discuss Physical Deformity Acceptance (18)

A. A discussion held with the veteran/service member about how physical deformities can be difficult to accept but that most people do adjust with time.

B. The veteran/service member was supported as he/she expressed his/her own difficulty accepting his/her physical deformities.

C. The veteran/service member was supported as he/she described how others have not been accepting of his/her physical deformities.

D. The veteran/service member was supported as he/she identified how his/her adjustment to his/her physical deformities has improved over time.

19. Assign Readings on the Journey of Recovery (19)

A. The veteran/service member was assigned to read about others' journeys through recovery.

B. The veteran/service member was assigned *Tiny Dancer: The Incredible True Story of a Young Burn Victim's Journey from Afghanistan* (Flacco).

C. The veteran/service member has read about others' journeys through recovery, and the content of these readings was processed.

D. The veteran/service member has not read about others' recovery and was redirected to do so.

20. Develop Ability Identity (20)

A. The veteran/service member was assisted in developing his/her identity as someone with numerous abilities.

B. The veteran/service member was encouraged to emphasize his/her abilities over his/her disabilities/limitations.

C. The veteran/service member was supported and reinforced whenever he/she emphasized his/her abilities over his/her disabilities.

D. The veteran/service member was occasionally redirected in regard to his/her emphasis on disabilities over abilities.

21. Read about Inspiration for Ability (21)

A. The veteran/service member was assigned to read materials about inspiring stories of individuals emphasizing their abilities over their disabilities.

B. The veteran/service member was assigned to read *To the Left of Inspiration: Adventures in Living with Disabilities* (Schneider).

C. The veteran/service member has read the assigned materials on inspiration for abilities over disabilities, and the content was processed.

D. The veteran/service member has not read the assigned material on inspiration for abilities over disabilities and was redirected to do so.

22. Identify Discouraging Schemata (22)

A. The veteran/service member was assisted in developing an awareness of his/her automatic thoughts that reflect discouraging schemata.

B. The veteran/service member was assisted in developing an awareness of his/her distorted cognitive messages that reinforce hopelessness and helplessness.

C. The veteran/service member was helped to identify several cognitive messages that occur on a regular basis and feed feelings of depression.

D. The veteran/service member recalled several instances of engaging in negative self-talk that precipitated feelings of helplessness, hopelessness, and depression; these were processed.

23. Assign Daily Journal (23)

A. The veteran/service member was assigned a homework exercise in which he/she journals automatic thoughts associated with discouraging feelings.

B. The veteran/service member was assigned "Negative Thoughts Trigger Negative Feelings" in the *Adult Psychotherapy Homework Planner,* 2nd ed. (Jongsma).

C. The veteran/service member was assigned "Daily Record of Dysfunctional Thoughts" from *Cognitive Therapy of Depression* (Beck, Rush, Shaw, and Emery).

D. The veteran/service member was assigned to develop positive alternatives for his/her negative self-talk.

E. The veteran/service member was challenged in his/her depressive thinking patterns and urged to replace them with reality-based thoughts.

F. The veteran's/service member's modification of negative self-talk was reviewed and reinforced

G. The veteran/service member has struggled to change his/her negative self-talk into positive alternatives and was provided with remedial assistance in this area.

24. Conduct Behavioral Experiments (24)

A. The veteran/service member was encouraged to do "behavioral experiments" in which discouraging automatic thoughts are treated as hypotheses/predictions and are tested against reality-based alternative hypotheses.

B. The veteran's/service member's automatic discouraging thoughts were tested against his/her past, present, and/or future experiences.

C. The veteran/service member was assisted in processing the outcome of his/her behavioral experiences.

D. The veteran/service member was encouraged by his/her experience of the more reality-based hypotheses/predictions; this progress was reinforced.

E. The veteran/service member continues to focus on discouraging automatic thoughts and was redirected toward the behavioral evidence of the more reality-based alternative hypotheses.

25. Reinforce Positive Self-Talk (25)

A. The veteran/service member was reinforced for any successful replacement of distorted negative thinking with positive, reality-based cognitive messages.

B. It was noted that the veteran/service member has been engaging in positive, reality-based thinking that has enhanced his/her self-confidence and increased adaptive action.

C. The veteran/service member was assigned to complete the "Positive Self-Talk" assignment from the *Adult Psychotherapy Homework Planner,* 2nd ed. (Jongsma).

26. Provide Information on Wheelchair Games (26)

A. The veteran/service member was provided with information about the ability to participate in National Veteran's Wheelchair Games.

B. The veteran/service member was provided with the following Web site: www. wheelchairgames.va.gov.

C. The veteran/service member was encouraged to participate in the National Veteran's Wheelchair Games.

D. The veteran/service member has investigated the use of the National Veteran's Wheelchair Games, and his/her thoughts about this were processed.

E. The veteran/service member has not investigated the National Veteran's Wheelchair games information and was redirected to do so.

27. Explore Remaining in Military (27)

A. The service member was asked to discuss his/her thoughts and feelings about remaining in the military.

B. The service member was supported as he/she expressed his/her thoughts and feelings about remaining in the military.

C. The service member has decided to attempt to remain in the military, and this was supported and encouraged.

D. The service member has decided to leave the military, and he/she was supported in this decision.

28. Develop Plan for Remaining in Military (28)

A. The service member was instructed to talk with his/her chain of command about developing a plan for remaining in the military.

B. The service member was instructed to talk with his/her primary care provider about developing a plan for remaining in the military.

C. The service member was instructed to talk with his/her case manager about developing a plan for remaining in the military.

D. The service member has discussed the opportunities for remaining in the military, and a specific plan has been developed.

E. The service member has not developed a specific plan for remaining in the military and was urged to make specific decisions in this are.

29. Refer to Center for the Intrepid (29)

A. The service member was instructed to request a referral from his/her primary care provided to the Center for the Intrepid at Brooke Army Medical Center in San Antonio, Texas.

B. The service member was reinforced for making a request for a referral to the Center for the Intrepid, Brooke Army Medical Center in San Antonio, Texas.

C. The service member has not sought out a referral to the Center for the Intrepid and was redirected to do so.

30. Participate in Medical Separation Appointments (30)

A. The service member was urged to attend all appointments with medical staff who are evaluating his/her physical states relative to medical separation from the military.

B. The service member has been resistant to keeping appointments with the medical staff and was urged to do so.

C. The service member was reinforced for his/her cooperation with the medical staff.

31. Facilitate Veterans Affairs Representative Meeting (31)

A. A Veterans Affairs representative from the appropriate geographical region was contacted.

B. The veteran has been put in contact with the appropriate Veterans Affairs representative.

32. Provide Veterans Affairs Benefits Information (32)

A. The veteran was provided with the appropriate information in regard to his/her Veterans Affairs benefits.

B. The veteran was referred to a Web site for Veterans Affairs: www.vba.va.gov/vba.

33. Emphasize Importance of Veterans Affairs Meetings (33)

A. The importance of attending all Veterans Affairs medical appointments was stressed to the veteran.

B. The importance of attending compensation evaluations was stressed to the veteran.

C. The importance of attending regular health care appointments was stressed to the veteran.

D. The veteran has attended all scheduled appointments and was reinforced for this.

E. The veteran has not attended all scheduled appointments and was reminded to do so.

ANGER MANAGEMENT AND DOMESTIC VIOLENCE

VETERAN/SERVICE MEMBER PRESENTATION

1. Explosive, Destructive Outbursts (1)[*]

A. The veteran/service member described a history of loss of temper in which he/she has destroyed property during fits of rage.

B. The veteran/service member described a history of loss of temper that dates back to childhood, involving verbal outbursts as well as property destruction.

C. As therapy has progressed, the veteran/service member has reported increased control over his/her temper and a significant reduction in incidents of poor anger management.

D. The veteran/service member has had no recent incidents of intimidating verbal assaults or explosive outbursts that have resulted in destruction of property.

2. Explosive, Assaultive Outbursts (1)

A. The veteran/service member described a history of loss of anger control to the point of physical assault on others who were the targets of his/her anger.

B. The veteran/service member has been arrested for assaultive attacks on others when he/she has lost control of his/her temper.

C. The veteran/service member has used assaultive acts as well as threats and intimidation to control others.

D. The veteran/service member has made a commitment to control his/her temper and terminate all assaultive behavior.

E. There have been no recent incidents of assaultive attacks on anyone, in spite of the veteran/service member having experienced periods of anger.

3. Overactive Irritability (2)

A. The veteran/service member described a history of reacting too angrily to rather insignificant irritants in his/her daily life.

B. The veteran/service member indicated that he/she recognizes that he/she becomes too angry in the face of rather minor frustrations and irritants.

C. Minor irritants have resulted in explosive, angry outbursts that have led to destruction of property and/or striking out physically at others.

D. The veteran/service member has made significant progress at increasing frustration tolerance and reducing explosive overreactivity to minor irritants.

4. Physical and Emotional Abuse against Significant Other (3)

A. The veteran/service member acknowledges having engaged in emotional abuse of his/her significant other.

---

[*]The numbers in parentheses correlate to the number of the Behavioral Definition statement in the companion chapter with the same title in *The Veterans and Active Duty Military Psychotherapy Treatment Planner* (Moore and Jongsma) by John Wiley & Sons, 2009.

B. The veteran/service member acknowledges having engaged in physical abuse of his/her significant other.

C. As treatment has progressed, the veteran/service member has stopped abusing his/her significant other.

5. Harsh Judgment Statements (4)

A. The veteran/service member exhibited frequent incidents of being harshly critical of others.

B. The veteran's/service member's family members reported that he/she reacts very quickly with angry, critical, and demeaning language toward them.

C. The veteran/service member reported that he/she has been more successful at controlling critical and intimidating statements made to or about others.

D. The veteran/service member reported that there have been no recent incidents of harsh, critical, and intimidating statements made to or about others.

6. Angry/Tense Body Language (5)

A. The veteran/service member presented with verbalizations of anger as well as tense, rigid muscles and glaring facial expressions.

B. The veteran/service member expressed his/her anger with bodily signs of muscle tension, clenched fists, and refusal to make eye contact.

C. The veteran/service member appeared more relaxed, less angry, and did not exhibit physical signs of aggression.

D. The veteran's/service member's family reported that he/she has been more relaxed within the home setting and has not shown glaring looks or pounded his/her fist on the table.

7. Passive-Aggressive Behavior (6)

A. The veteran/service member described a history of passive-aggressive behavior in which he/she would not comply with directions, would complain about authority figures behind their backs, and would not meet expected behavioral norms.

B. The veteran's/service member's family confirmed a pattern of the veteran's/service member's passive-aggressive behavior in which he/she would make promises of doing something but not follow through.

C. The veteran/service member acknowledged that he/she tends to express anger indirectly through social withdrawal or uncooperative behavior rather than using assertiveness to express feelings directly.

D. The veteran/service member has reported an increase in assertively expressing thoughts and feelings and terminating passive-aggressive behavior patterns.

8. Challenging Authority (7)

A. The veteran's/service member's history shows a consistent pattern of challenging or disrespectful treatment of authority figures.

B. The veteran/service member acknowledged that he/she becomes angry quickly when someone in authority gives direction to him/her.

C. The veteran's/service member's disrespectful treatment of authority has often erupted in explosive, aggressive outbursts.

D. The veteran/service member has made progress in controlling his/her overreactivity to taking direction from those in authority and is responding with more acts of cooperation.

9. Verbal Abuse (8)

A. The veteran/service member acknowledged that he/she frequently engages in verbal abuse of others as a means of expressing anger or frustration with them.

B. Significant others in the veteran's/service member's family have indicated that they have been hurt by his/her frequent verbal abuse toward them.

C. The veteran/service member has shown little empathy toward others for the pain that he/she has caused because of his/her verbal abuse of them.

D. The veteran/service member has become more aware of his/her pattern of verbal abuse of others and is becoming more sensitive to the negative impact of this behavior on them.

E. There have been no recent incidents of verbal abuse of others by the veteran/service member.

10. Rationalization of Abuse (9)

A. The veteran/service member rationalizes his/her abuse toward others.

B. The veteran/service member identified reasons why his/her victim "deserved" abusive behavior.

C. The veteran/service member tended to minimize his/her abuse toward others.

D. As treatment has progressed, the veteran/service member has become more accepting of his/her responsibility for the abuse of others.

11. Blaming (10)

A. The veteran/service member blames others for his/her aggressive and abusive behavior.

B. The veteran/service member tends to identify minor concerns that he/she sees as legitimizing abusive behavior.

C. As treatment has progressed, the veteran/service member has discontinued blaming others for his/her aggressive and abusive behavior.

INTERVENTIONS IMPLEMENTED

1. Assess Anger Dynamics (1)[*]

A. The veteran/service member was assessed for various stimuli that have triggered his/her anger.

B. The veteran/service member was assisted in identifying situations, people, and thoughts that have triggered his/her anger.

C. The veteran/service member was assisted in identifying the thoughts, feelings, and actions that have characterized his/her anger responses.

[*]The numbers in parentheses correlate to the number of the Therapeutic Intervention statement in the companion chapter with the same title in *The Veterans and Active Duty Military Psychotherapy Treatment Planner* (Moore and Jongsma) by John Wiley & Sons, 2009.

2. Refer for Physical Examination (2)

A. The veteran/service member was referred to a physician for a complete physical examination to rule out organic contributors (e.g., brain damage, tumor, elevated testosterone levels) to his/her anger.

B. The veteran/service member has complied with the physical examination, and the results were shared with him/her.

C. The physical examination has identified organic contributors to poor anger control, and treatment was suggested.

D. The physical examiner has not identified any organic contributors to poor anger control, and this was reported to the veteran/service member.

E. The veteran/service member has not complied with the physical examination to assess organic contributors and was redirected to do so.

3. Refer for Medication Evaluation (3)

A. The veteran/service member was referred to a physician to evaluate him/her for psychotropic medication to reduce anger symptoms.

B. The veteran/service member has completed an evaluation by the physician and has begun taking medication.

C. The veteran/service member has resisted the referral to a physician and does not want to take any medication to reduce anger symptoms; his/her concerns were processed.

4. Monitor Medication Compliance (4)

A. The veteran's/service member's compliance with the physician's prescription for psychotropic medication was monitored for the medication's effectiveness and side effects.

B. The veteran/service member reported that the medication has been beneficial to him/her in reducing his/her experience of anger symptoms; the benefits of this progress were reviewed.

C. The veteran/service member reported that the medication does not seem to be helpful in reducing anger symptoms; this was reported to the prescribing clinician.

D. The therapist conferred with the physician to discuss the veteran's/service member's reaction to the psychotropic medication, and adjustments were made to the prescription by the physician.

5. Assign Anger Journal (5)

A. The veteran/service member was assigned to keep a daily journal in which he/she will document persons or situations that cause anger, irritation, or disappointment.

B. The veteran/service member was assigned the homework exercise "Anger Journal" in the *Adult Psychotherapy Homework Planner,* 2nd ed. (Jongsma).

C. The veteran/service member has kept a journal of anger-producing situations, and this material was processed within the session.

D. The veteran/service member has become more aware of the causes for and targets of his/her anger as a result of journaling these experiences on a daily basis; the benefits of this insight were reflected to him/her.

E. The veteran/service member has not kept an anger journal and was redirected to do so.

6. List Targets of/Causes for Anger (6)

A. The veteran/service member was assigned to list as many of the causes for and targets of his/her anger that he/she is aware of.

B. The veteran's/service member's list of targets of and causes for anger was processed in order to increase his/her awareness of anger management issues.

C. The veteran/service member has indicated a greater sensitivity to his/her angry feelings and the causes for them as a result of the focus on these issues.

D. The veteran/service member has not been able to develop a comprehensive list of causes for and targets of anger and was provided with tentative examples in this area.

7. Identify Anger (7)

A. The veteran/service member was assisted in becoming more aware of the frequency with which he/she experiences anger and the signs of it in his/her life.

B. Situations were reviewed in which the veteran/service member experienced anger but refused to acknowledge it or minimized the experience.

C. The veteran/service member has acknowledged that he/she is frequently angry and has problems with anger management and was provided with positive feedback about this progress.

8. Identify Anger Expression Models (8)

A. The veteran/service member was assisted in identifying key figures in his/her life who have provided examples to him/her of how to positively or negatively express anger.

B. The veteran/service member was reinforced as he/she identified several key figures who have been negative role models in expressing anger explosively and destructively.

C. The veteran/service member was supported and reinforced as he/she acknowledged that he/she manages his/her anger in the same way as an explosive parent figure had done when he/she was growing up.

D. The veteran/service member was encouraged to identify positive role models throughout his/her life whom he/she could respect for their management of angry feelings.

E. The veteran/service member was supported as he/she acknowledged that others have been influential in teaching him/her destructive patterns of anger management.

F. The veteran/service member failed to identify key figures in his/her life who have provided examples to him/her as to how to positively express his/her anger and was questioned more specifically in this area.

9. List Negative Anger Impact (9)

A. The veteran/service member was assisted in listing ways that his/her explosive expression of anger has negatively impacted his/her life.

B. The veteran/service member was supported as he/she identified many negative consequences that have resulted from his/her poor anger management.

C. It was reflected to the veteran/service member that his/her denial about the negative impact of his/her anger has decreased and he/she has verbalized an increased awareness of the negative impact of his/her behavior.

D. The veteran/service member has been guarded about identifying the negative impact of his/her anger and was provided with specific examples of how his/her anger has negatively impacted his/her life and relationships (e.g., injuring others or self, legal conflicts, loss of respect from self or others, destruction of property).

10. Identify Bodily Impact of Anger (10)

A. The veteran/service member was taught the negative impact that anger can have on bodily functions and systems.

B. The veteran/service member indicated an increased awareness of the stress of his/her anger on such things as heart, brain, and blood pressure; this awareness was applied to his/her own functioning.

C. The veteran/service member was reinforced as he/she has tried to reduce the frequency with which he/she experiences anger in order to reduce the negative impact that anger has on bodily systems.

11. Reconceptualize Anger (11)

A. The veteran/service member was assisted in reconceptualizing anger as involving different components that go through predictable phases.

B. The veteran/service member was taught about the different components of anger, including cognitive, physiological, affective, and behavioral components.

C. The veteran/service member was taught how to better discriminate between relaxation and tension.

D. The veteran/service member was taught about the predictable phases of anger, including demanding expectations that are not met, leading to increased arousal and anger, which leads to acting out.

E. The veteran/service member displayed a clear understanding of the ways to conceptualize anger and was provided with positive reinforcement.

F. The veteran/service member has struggled to understand the ways to conceptualize anger and was provided with remedial feedback in this area.

12. Identify Positive Consequences of Anger Management (12)

A. The veteran/service member was asked to identify the positive consequences he/she has experienced in managing his/her anger.

B. The veteran/service member was assisted in identifying positive consequences of managing anger (e.g., respect from others and self, cooperation from others, improved physical health).

C. The veteran/service member was asked to agree to learn new ways to conceptualize and manage anger.

13. Teach Calming Techniques (13)

A. The veteran/service member was taught deep muscle relaxation, rhythmic breathing, and positive imagery as ways to reduce muscle tension when feelings of anger are experienced.

B. The veteran/service member has implemented the relaxation techniques and reported decreased reactivity when experiencing anger; the benefits of these techniques were underscored.

C. The veteran/service member has not implemented the relaxation techniques and continues to feel quite stressed in the face of anger; he/she was encouraged to use the techniques.

14. Assign Use of Calming Techniques (14)

A. The veteran/service member was assigned implementation of calming techniques in his/her daily life when facing anger trigger situations.

B. The veteran/service member related situations in which he/she has appropriately used calming techniques when facing anger trigger situations; this progress was reinforced.

C. The veteran/service member describes situations in which he/she has not used calming techniques, and these failures were reviewed and redirected.

15. Explore Self-Talk (15)

A. The veteran's/service member's self-talk that mediates his/her angry feelings was explored.

B. The veteran/service member was assessed for self-talk, such as demanding expectations reflected in "should," "must," or "have to" statements.

C. The veteran/service member was assisted in identifying and challenging his/her biases and in generating alternative self-talk that corrects for the biases.

D. The veteran/service member was taught how to use correcting self-talk to facilitate a more flexible and temperate response to frustration.

16. Assign Self-Talk Homework (16)

A. The veteran/service member was assigned a homework exercise in which he/she identifies angry self-talk and generates alternatives that help moderate angry reactions.

B. The veteran's/service member's use of constructive self-talk alternatives was reviewed within the session.

C. The veteran/service member was reinforced for his/her success in changing angry self-talk to more moderate alternatives.

D. The veteran/service member was provided with corrective feedback to help improve his/her use of alternative self-talk to moderate his/her angry reactions.

17. Assign Thought-Stopping Technique (17)

A. The veteran/service member was directed to implement a thought-stopping technique on a daily basis between sessions.

B. The veteran/service member was assigned the homework exercise "Making Use of the Thought-Stopping Technique" in the *Adult Psychotherapy Homework Planner,* 2nd ed. (Jongsma).

C. The veteran's/service member's use of the thought-stopping technique was reviewed.

D. The veteran/service member was provided with positive feedback for his/her successful use of the thought-stopping technique.

E. The veteran/service member was provided with corrective feedback to help improve his/her use of the thought-stopping technique.

18. Teach Assertive Communication (18)

A. The veteran/service member was taught about assertive communication through instruction, modeling, and role-playing.

B. The veteran/service member was referred to an assertiveness training class.

C. The veteran/service member displayed increased assertiveness and was provided with positive feedback in this area.

D. The veteran/service member has not increased his/her level of assertiveness and was provided with additional feedback in this area.

19. Conduct Conjoint Session for Assertiveness (19)

A. The veteran/service member was asked to invite his/her significant other for a conjoint session.

B. The veteran/service member and his/her significant other were seen together in order to help implement assertiveness, problem-solving, and conflict resolution skills.

C. The veteran/service member was reinforced for his/her increased use of assertiveness, problem-solving, and conflict resolution skills with his/her significant other.

D. The veteran's/service member's significant other was urged to assist the veteran/service member in his/her use of assertiveness, problem-solving, and conflict resolution skills.

E. The veteran/service member has not regularly used assertiveness, problem-solving, and conflict resolution skills with his/her significant other and was assisted in identifying barriers to this success.

20. Teach Conflict Resolution Skills (20)

A. The veteran/service member was taught conflict resolution skills through modeling, role-playing, and behavioral rehearsal.

B. The veteran/service member was taught about empathy and active listening.

C. The veteran/service member was taught about "I messages," respectful communication, assertiveness without aggression, and compromise.

D. The veteran/service member was reinforced for his/her clear understanding of conflict resolution skills.

E. The veteran/service member displayed a poor understanding of conflict resolution skills and was provided with remedial feedback.

21. Construct Strategy for Managing Anger (21)

A. The veteran/service member was assisted in constructing a veteran/service member–tailored strategy for managing his/her anger.

B. The veteran/service member was encouraged to combine somatic, cognitive, communication, problem-solving, and conflict resolution skills relevant to his/her needs.

C. The veteran/service member was reinforced for his/her comprehensive anger management strategy.

D. The veteran/service member was redirected to develop a more comprehensive anger management strategy.

22. Select Challenging Situations for Managing Anger (22)

A. The veteran/service member was provided with situations in which he/she may be increasingly challenged to apply his/her new strategies for managing anger.

B. The veteran/service member was asked to identify his/her likely upcoming challenging situations for managing anger.

C. The veteran/service member was urged to use his/her strategies for managing anger in successively more difficult situations.

23. Consolidate Anger Management Skills (23)

A. Techniques were used to help the veteran/service member consolidate his/her new anger management skills.

B. Techniques such as relaxation, imagery, behavioral rehearsal, modeling, role-playing, or in vivo exposure/behavioral experiences were used to help the veteran/service member consolidate the use of his/her new anger management skills.

C. The veteran's/service member's use of techniques to consolidate his/her anger management skills were reviewed and reinforced.

24. Monitor/Decrease Outbursts (24)

A. The veteran/service member was asked to monitor his/her angry outbursts toward the goal of decreasing their frequency, intensity, and duration.

B. The veteran/service member was urged to use his/her new anger management skills to decrease the frequency, intensity, and duration of his/her angry outbursts.

C. The veteran/service member was assigned the homework exercise "Alternatives to Destructive Anger" in the *Adult Psychotherapy Homework Planner,* 2nd ed. (Jongsma).

D. The veteran's/service member's progress in decreasing his/her angry outbursts was reviewed.

E. The veteran/service member was reinforced for his/her success at decreasing the frequency, intensity, and duration of his/her angry outbursts.

F. The veteran/service member has not decreased the frequency, intensity, or duration of angry outbursts, and corrective feedback was provided.

25. Refer to Domestic Violence Program (25)

A. The veteran/service member was referred to a structured domestic violence program.

B. The veteran/service member is focusing on issues of power and control, gender roles, and beliefs that create and maintain violence within the structured domestic violence program.

C. The veteran/service member has engaged in the domestic violence program, and his/her progress was noted and reinforced.

D. The veteran/service member has not regularly participated in the structured domestic violence program and was redirected to do so.

26. Encourage Disclosure (26)

A. The veteran/service member was encouraged to discuss his/her anger management goals with trusted persons who are likely to support his/her change.

B. The veteran/service member was assisted in identifying individuals who are likely to support his/her change.

C. The veteran/service member has reviewed his/her anger management goals with trusted persons, and their responses were processed.

D. The veteran/service member has not discussed his/her anger management goals and was redirected to do so.

27. Differentiate between Lapse and Relapse (27)

A. A discussion was held with the veteran/service member regarding the distinction between a lapse and a relapse.

B. A lapse was associated with an initial and reversible return of angry outbursts.

C. A relapse was associated with the decision to return to the old pattern of anger.

D. The veteran/service member was provided with support and encouragement as he/she displayed an understanding of the difference between a lapse and a relapse.

E. The veteran/service member struggled to understand the difference between a lapse and a relapse and was provided with remedial feedback in this area.

28. Discuss Management of Lapse Risk Situations (28)

A. The veteran/service member was assisted in identifying future situations or circumstances in which lapses could occur.

B. The session focused on rehearsing the management of future situations or circumstances in which lapses could occur.

C. The veteran/service member was reinforced for his/her appropriate use of lapse management skills.

D. The veteran/service member was redirected in regard to his/her poor use of lapse management skills.

29. Encourage Routine Use of Strategies (29)

A. The veteran/service member was instructed to routinely use the strategies that he/she has learned in therapy (e.g., calming, adaptive self-talk, assertion, and/or conflict resolution).

B. The veteran/service member was urged to find ways to build his/her new strategies into his/her life as much as possible.

C. The veteran/service member was reinforced as he/she reported ways in which he/she has incorporated copying strategies into his/her life and routine.

D. The veteran/service member was redirected about ways to incorporate his/her new strategies into his/her routine and life.

30. Develop a "Coping Card" (30)

A. The veteran/service member was provided with a "coping card" on which specific coping strategies were listed.

B. The veteran/service member was assisted in developing his/her "coping card" in order to list his/her helpful coping strategies.

C. The veteran/service member was encouraged to use his/her "coping card" when struggling with anger-producing situations.

31. Schedule "Maintenance" Sessions (31)

A. The veteran/service member was assisted in scheduling "maintenance" sessions to help maintain therapeutic gains and adjust to life without angry outbursts.

B. Positive feedback was provided to the veteran/service member for his/her maintenance of therapeutic gains.

C. The veteran/service member has displayed an increase in anger symptoms and was provided with additional relapse prevention strategies.

32. Assign Reading Material (32)

A. The veteran/service member was assigned to read material that educates him/her about anger and its management.

B. The veteran/service member was directed to read *Overcoming Situational and General Anger: Client Manual* (Deffenbacher and McKay).

C. The veteran/service member was directed to read *Of Course You're Angry* (Rosselini and Worden).

D. The veteran/service member was directed to read *The Anger Control Workbook* (McKay).

E. The veteran/service member has read the assigned material on anger management, and key concepts were reviewed.

F. The veteran/service member has not read the assigned material on anger management and was redirected to do so.

33. Teach Forgiveness (33)

A. The veteran/service member was taught about the process of forgiveness and encouraged to begin to implement this process as a means of letting go of his/her feelings of strong anger.

B. The veteran/service member focused on the perpetrators of pain from the past, and he/she was encouraged to target them for forgiveness.

C. The advantages of implementing forgiveness versus holding on to vengeful anger were processed with the veteran/service member.

D. Positive feedback was provided as the veteran/service member has committed himself/herself to attempting to begin the process of forgiveness with the perpetrators of pain.

E. The veteran/service member has not been able to begin the process of forgiveness of the perpetrators of his/her pain and was urged to start this process as he/she feels able to.

34. Assign Books on Forgiveness (34)

A. The veteran/service member was assigned to read books on forgiveness.

B. The veteran/service member was assigned to read the book *Forgive and Forget* (Smedes) to increase his/her sensitivity to the process of forgiveness.

C. The veteran/service member has read the book on forgiveness, and key concepts were processed within the session.

D. The veteran/service member acknowledged that holding on to angry feelings has distinct disadvantages over his/her beginning the process of forgiveness; he/she was urged to start this process.

E. The veteran/service member has not followed through with completing the reading assignment about forgiveness and was encouraged to do so.

35. Assign Forgiveness Letter (35)

A. The veteran/service member was asked to write a letter of forgiveness to the target of his/her anger as a step toward letting go of that anger.

B. The veteran/service member has followed through with writing a letter of forgiveness to the perpetrator of pain from his/her past, and this was processed within the session.

C. The veteran/service member has not followed through with writing the forgiveness letter and was noted to be very resistive to letting go of his/her feelings of angry revenge.

D. Writing and processing the letter of forgiveness have reduced the veteran's/service member's feelings of anger and increased his/her capacity to control its expression.

ANTISOCIAL BEHAVIOR IN THE MILITARY

SERVICE MEMBER PRESENTATION

1. Adolescent Antisocial History (1)[*]

A. The service member confirmed that his/her history of rule breaking, lying, physical aggression, and/or disrespect for others and the law began when he/she was a teenager.

B. The service member reported that he/she was often incarcerated within the juvenile justice system for illegal activities.

C. The service member acknowledged that his/her substance abuse paralleled his/her antisocial behavior dating back to adolescence.

2. Dysfunctional Childhood History (1)

A. The service member described instances from his/her childhood in which severe and abusive punishment resulted whenever a parent laid blame on him/her for some perceived negative behavior.

B. The service member described a history of experiences in which he/she was unfairly blamed for others' behavior, leading to feelings of resentment of authority and a pattern of lying to avoid punishment.

C. The service member provided examples from his/her own childhood of instances when parental figures consistently projected blame for their behavior onto others, causing the service member to learn and practice this same behavior.

D. The service member began to verbalize some insight into how previous instances of pain in childhood are causing current attitudes of detachment from the concerns of others and a focus on self-protection and self-interest.

E. The service member began to understand how his/her attitudes of aggression are the result of having learned to accept and normalize aggression during childhood abusive experiences.

3. Failure to Conform to Military Norms (2)

A. The service member displays a failure to conform to military norms.

B. The service member often fails to follow orders or respect superiors.

C. The service member often fails to adhere to military customs and traditions.

D. As treatment has progressed, the service member has gained a greater ability to conform to military expectations.

4. Aggressive/Argumentative (3)

A. The service member presented in a hostile, angry, and uncooperative manner.

B. The service member was intimidating in his/her style of interaction.

---

[*]The numbers in parentheses correlate to the number of the Behavioral Definition statement in the companion chapter with the same title in *The Veterans and Active Duty Military Psychotherapy Treatment Planner* (Moore and Jongsma) by John Wiley & Sons, 2009.

C. The service member is trying to interact in a more cooperative manner within social and employment settings.

D. The service member is showing less irritability and argumentativeness within therapy sessions.

5. Authority Conflicts (3)

A. The service member acknowledged a history of irritability, aggression, and argumentativeness when interacting with authority figures.

B. The service member's history of conflict with acceptance of authority and has led to employment instability and legal problems.

C. The service member is beginning to accept direction from authority figures, recognizing his/her need to resist challenging such directives.

6. Lack of Remorse (4)

A. The service member, after describing his/her pattern of aggression or disrespect for others' feelings, showed no remorse for his/her behavior.

B. The service member projected blame for his/her hurtful behavior onto others, saying there was no alternative.

C. The service member is beginning to develop some sensitivity to the feelings of others and to recognize that he/she has hurt others.

D. The service member reported feelings of remorse and guilt over previous behaviors that were hurtful to others.

7. Blaming/Projecting (5)

A. The service member showed an attitude of blaming others for his/her problems.

B. The service member refused to take responsibility for his/her own behavior and decisions; instead, he/she pointed at the behavior of others as the cause for his/her decisions and actions.

C. The service member blamed interpersonal conflicts on others without taking any responsibility for the problem.

D. The service member is beginning to accept responsibility for his/her own behavior and to make fewer statements of projection of responsibility for his/her actions onto others.

E. The service member is gradually accepting more responsibility for his/her behavior and increasing the frequency of such statements.

8. Lying (6)

A. The service member reported a pattern of lying to cover up his/her responsibility for actions with little shame or anxiety attached to this pattern of lying.

B. The service member seemed to be lying within the session.

C. The service member acknowledged that his/her lying produced conflicts within relationships and distrust from others.

D. The service member has committed himself/herself to attempting to be more honest in his/her interpersonal relationships.

9. Verbal/Physical Aggression (7)

A. The service member reported physical encounters that have injured others or have threatened serious injury to others.

B. The service member showed little or no remorse for causing pain to others.

C. The service member projected blame for his/her aggressive encounters onto others.

D. The service member has a violent history and continues to interact with others in a very intimidating, aggressive style.

E. The service member has shown progress in controlling his/her aggressive patterns and seems to be trying to interact with more assertiveness than aggression.

10. Recklessness/Thrill Seeking (8)

A. The service member reported having engaged in reckless, adventure-seeking behaviors, showing a high need for excitement, having fun, and living on the edge.

B. The service member described a series of reckless actions but showed no consideration for the consequences of such actions.

C. The service member has begun to control his/her reckless impulses and reported that he/she is trying to think of the consequences before acting recklessly.

11. Sexual Promiscuity (9)

A. The service member reported a history of repeated sexual encounters with partners with whom there is little or no emotional attachment.

B. The service member's described sexual behaviors are focused on self-gratification only and reflect no interest in the needs or welfare of the partner.

C. The service member acknowledged that his/her sexual behavior has no basis in respect or expression of commitment to a long-term relationship.

D. The service member reported that he/she would like to develop a relationship in which sexual intimacy was a reflection of commitment and caring rather than merely sexual release.

12. Disciplinary Actions (10)

A. The service member has received multiple disciplinary actions for disruptive and disrespectful behavior.

B. The service member is at risk for being discharged due to his/her disruptive and disrespectful behavior.

C. As treatment has progressed, the service member has become more respectful in his/her behavior.

13. Possible Dishonorable Discharge (11)

A. The service member has reported that his/her superiors have threatened to dishonorably discharge him/her from the military.

B. The service member noted that dishonorable discharge is a significant possibility due to his/her antisocial behavior.

C. As treatment has progressed, the service member has become less likely to be dishonorably discharged.

14. Personality Disorder (12)

A. The service member has had visits with military behavioral health professionals in regard to antisocial personality disorder concerns.

B. The service member may be separated from the military due to a diagnosis of a personality disorder.

C. As treatment has progressed, the service member has been able to manage his/her behavior and is not being considered for a diagnosis of a personality disorder.

15. Not a Productive Team Member (13)

A. The service member has been noted to fail as productive unit team member.

B. The team members have indicated that the service member fails to contribute to the unit goals.

C. As treatment has progressed, the service member has been noted to be a productive, efficient unit team member.

INTERVENTIONS IMPLEMENTED

1. Take History/Confront Denial (1)*

A. The service member's history of illegal activities was collected.

B. The service member was confronted consistently on his/her attempts to utilize minimizations, denial, or projection of the blame onto others for behavior for which he/she was responsible.

C. The service member's history was explored for instances of unkind, insensitive behavior that trampled on the feelings and rights of others.

2. List Antisocial Consequences (2)

A. The service member was asked to list the negative consequences that have accrued to him/her due to his/her antisocial behavior.

B. The service member was confronted with the fact that his/her antisocial behavior results in others losing respect for him/her, loss of freedom for him/her due to legal consequences, and loss of self-respect.

C. The service member was consistently reminded of the pain that others suffer as a result of his/her antisocial behavior.

D. The service member was asked to list others who have been negatively impacted by his/her antisocial behavior and the specific pain that they have suffered.

E. Examples were provided to the service member of how others are affected by his/her behavior, such as comrades being undeservedly punished for someone else's behavior or others being put at risk in hostile environments.

F. The service member was confronted with the fear, disappointment, loss of trust, and loss of respect that result in others as a consequence of his/her lack of sensitivity and self-centered behavior.

G. The service member was provided with positive feedback as he/she was able to accept the consequences of his/her antisocial behavior.

*The numbers in parentheses correlate to the number of the Therapeutic Intervention statement in the companion chapter with the same title in *The Veterans and Active Duty Military Psychotherapy Treatment Planner* (Moore and Jongsma) by John Wiley & Sons, 2009.

3. Identify Trust as Basis for Relationships (3)

A. The service member was reminded that his/her behavior of broken promises, insensitivity, and trampling on the rights of others results in broken relationships as others lose trust in him/her.

B. The service member was consistently reminded that any meaningful relationships within the military are based on trust that the other person will show respect and honor and will always be there to "watch their back."

C. The service member's behavior pattern was reviewed to understand how he/she treated others with a lack of respect and a lack of kindness and how these actions resulted in the loss of trust in the relationship.

D. Support and encouragement were provided to the service member as he/she identified how his/her behavior has caused a lack of trust in the relationship.

E. The service member denied any connection between his/her behavior and the loss of trust in the relationship and was provided with tentative examples in this area.

4. Confront Lawlessness (4)

A. The service member's pattern of unlawful behavior was reviewed, and he/she was reminded that if everyone in the military adopted his/her unlawful attitude, anarchy would result.

B. The service member was taught that respect for law and order and the rights of others is the only way that the military can function and the mission can be accomplished.

C. The service member was reinforced as he/she admitted to his/her pattern of lawlessness and how this will result in anarchy rather than a functional military.

D. The service member denied any pattern of lawlessness to his/her behavior, despite facts to the contrary, and was confronted for this denial.

5. Solicit Commitment to Lawfulness (5)

A. The service member was asked to give his/her commitment to conforming to the laws of society.

B. The service member was asked to give a rationale for adopting a prosocial, law-abiding lifestyle.

C. The service member was asked to list 10 reasons why he/she would commit himself/herself to a law-abiding lifestyle.

D. The service member was assigned the homework exercise "Crooked Thinking Leads to Crooked Behavior" from the *Adult Psychotherapy Homework Planner*, 2nd ed. (Jongsma).

E. Positive feedback was given to the service member for his/her commitment to lawfulness.

F. The service member declined to commit to living in a lawful manner and was provided with additional feedback regarding the negative consequences for such refusal.

6. Inhibit Future Lawlessness (6)

A. The service member was firmly and consistently reminded of the negative legal consequences that would accrue to him/her if continued disregard for military rules, laws, and regulations was practiced.

B. The service member was asked to list six future negative consequences of continued antisocial behavior.

C. The service member's list of negative consequences of continued antisocial behavior was reviewed and processed.

D. The service member was assisted in identifying how to dishonorable discharge, confinement, reduction in rank and/or pay, or extra duty may be levied for continued failure to obey military rules, laws, and regulations.

E. The service member has not completed a list of negative consequences of antisocial behavior and was redirected to do so.

7. Review Broken Relationships (7)

A. The service member was asked to list any and all relationships that have been lost due to his/her pattern of antisocial behavior.

B. The service member was assigned the homework exercise "How I Have Hurt Others" from the *Adult Psychotherapy Homework Planner*, 2nd ed. (Jongsma).

C. As lost relationships were reviewed, the service member was confronted with his/her responsibility for the actions that resulted in the broken relationships.

D. As broken relationships were reviewed, the service member was asked to identify what behavior of his/her own led to the broken relationship.

E. The service member was provided with support as he/she seemed to openly describe his/her broken relationships.

8. Confront Responsibility for Broken Relationships (8)

A. The service member was firmly and consistently confronted with the reality of his/her own behavior that caused pain to others and resulted in their breaking off the relationship.

B. The service member was asked to identify how he/she was insensitive to the needs and feelings of others.

C. Role-reversal techniques were used to attempt to get the service member in touch with the pain he/she has caused others due to disrespect, disloyalty, aggression, or dishonesty.

D. The service member was provided with positive feedback as he/she took responsibility for broken relationships.

E. The service member has not taken responsibility for broken relationships and was confronted for this denial.

9. Confront Self-Centeredness (9)

A. The service member was taught, through role-playing and role reversal, the value of being empathetic to the needs, rights, and feelings of others.

B. It was reflected to the service member that he/she presents his/her attitude of "look out for number one" as the only way to live.

C. Active listening skills were used as the service member justified his/her self-focused attitude as the way that he/she learned to live because of the abuse and abandonment suffered as a child.

D. Attempts were made to get the service member to view his/her own behavior from another person's perspective.

E. The service member was provided with positive feedback and verbal reinforcement whenever he/she made comments that were less self-centered.

10. Discuss Inconsistency of Self-Centeredness with Military Values (10)

A. This discussion was held regarding how the me-first approach to life is inconsistent with military values and traditions.

B. The service member was able to identify how the me-first approach is contrary to military values and traditions.

C. The service member was supported as he/she processed feelings about the difference between his/her me-first approach and military tradition.

11. Teach the Value of Honesty (11)

A. The service member was asked to list the benefits of honesty and reliability for himself/herself and others.

B. The service member was taught the absolute necessity for honesty as the basis for trust in all human relationships; examples of the different forms of relationships that are based in trust and honesty were reviewed.

C. The service member was asked to list the positive effects for others when he/she is honest and reliable.

D. The service member was taught about how honesty and reliability results in approval from superiors and increased trust from comrades.

E. Positive feedback was provided as the service member identified the positive effects for others when he/she is honest and reliable.

F. It was reflected to the service member that he/she continues to be dishonest in relationships.

12. List Honesty/Dishonesty Consequences (12)

A. The service member was asked to list the positive effects for others when he/she is honest and reliable.

B. The service member was taught that pain and disappointment result when honesty and reliability are not given the highest priority in one's life.

C. The service member was provided with positive feedback for his/her understanding of the effects of honesty versus dishonesty.

D. The service member failed to identify the effects of honesty and dishonesty and was provided with tentative examples in this area.

13. Solicit a Commitment to Honesty (13)

A. The service member was asked to make a commitment to live a life based in honesty and reliability.

B. The service member was asked to sign a behavioral contract that focuses on keeping promises and being responsible to others.

C. The service member was asked to list five reasons why he/she should make a commitment to be honest and reliable.

D. Positive feedback was provided as the service member committed to living a life based in honesty and reliability.

14. Teach Empathy (14)

A. The service member was taught, through role-playing and role reversal, the value of being empathetic to the needs, rights, and feelings of others.

B. The service member was asked to commit himself/herself to acting more sensitively to the rights and feelings of others.

C. The service member was encouraged as he/she committed to acting more sensitively regarding the rights and feelings of others.

15. Confront Disrespect (15)

A. The service member was confronted consistently and firmly when he/she exhibited an attitude of disrespect and rudeness toward the rights and feelings of others.

B. It was emphasized to the service member firmly and consistently that others have a right to boundaries and privacy and respect for their feelings and property.

16. Solicit Kind Actions (16)

A. The service member was required, in an attempt to get him/her to focus on the needs and feelings of others, to list three actions that would be performed as acts of kindness toward someone else.

B. The service member and therapist signed a contract in which he/she committed to performing three acts of service toward the community or others that would not result in direct benefit to himself/herself.

C. Acts of kindness for the service member to perform were suggested, including volunteering for an extra shift or an undesirable task.

D. The service member's acts of kindness were reviewed, and the feelings associated with performing this assignment were processed.

E. The service member has not completed acts of kindness and was redirected to do so.

17. Solicit an Apology (17)

A. The service member was asked to make a list of those people who deserve an apology because they were injured by the service member's insensitive, impulsive, aggressive, or dishonest behavior.

B. The service member was confronted when he/she attempted to project the blame for his/her aggressive or dishonest actions onto others.

C. The service member was supported as he/she identified those people who deserve an apology because they were injured by his/her insensitive, impulsive, aggressive, or dishonest behavior.

D. Positive feedback was provided as the service member reported that he/she has given an apology to those who were injured by his/her insensitive, impulsive, aggressive, or dishonest behavior.

E. The service member has not made an apology to those identified as being injured by his/her insensitive, impulsive, aggressive, or dishonest behavior and was redirected to do so.

18. Teach Acceptance of Responsibility (18)

A. The value of taking full responsibility for one's own behavior and then apologizing for the pain caused to others because of that behavior was reviewed and emphasized.

B. Role-playing and modeling were used to teach how to apologize.

C. The service member was assigned the homework exercise "Letter of Apology" from the *Adult Psychotherapy Homework Planner*, 2nd ed. (Jongsma).

D. Positive feedback was provided to the service member for his/her understanding and use of apologies.

19. Review Elements of Apology (19)

A. The specific steps were laid out that would be necessary to begin to make amends to others who have been hurt by the service member's behavior.

B. The service member was asked to make a commitment to carry out those steps that would make restitution for the hurt caused to others.

C. Behavioral rehearsal was used to teach how to make amends or give an apology to those who have been hurt by the service member's behavior.

D. The service member's implementation of apologizing to others was reviewed, and the feelings associated with this action were processed.

E. The service member was strongly reinforced for taking responsibility for causing pain to others and apologizing for this behavior.

F. The service member has not taken responsibility for the pain he/she has caused others or apologized for this behavior and was redirected to do so.

20. Review Rules and Expectations (20)

A. The service member was asked to list the most important rules that should govern his/her behavior within the military work setting.

B. The service member was assisted in developing a specific list of rules and duties related to his/her military work behavior.

C. The service member reviewed the expectations regarding how he/she should respond to authority figures within the military work setting; his/her appropriate expectations were reinforced.

D. Role-playing was used to teach respectful responses to directives from authority figures.

21. Reinforce Employment Attendance (21)

A. The service member's attendance at work and his/her respect for authority were reviewed and reinforced.

B. The service member was asked to keep a journal of work attendance and instances of acceptance of directives from authority figures.

C. The service member's work records and journal material were reviewed, and successful prosocial behavior was reinforced.

D. The service member has not kept a record or journal of work attendance and acceptance of directives from authority figures.

22. Teach Prosocial Work Behavior (22)

A. The service member was asked to list those negative behaviors that have led to conflicts within the work setting with both coworkers and authority figures.

B. The service member was assisted in developing prosocial responses toward resolving conflicts with coworkers and acceptance of directives from authority figures.

C. The service member has implemented more prosocial responses at work, and the positive results of this attitude were reviewed.

23. Confront Projection (23)

A. The service member was consistently confronted whenever he/she failed to take responsibility for his/her own actions and instead placed blame for them onto others.

B. As the service member's pattern of projecting blame for his/her actions onto others began to weaken, he/she was reinforced for taking personal responsibility.

C. The importance of taking responsibility for one's own behavior and the positive implications of this for motivating change were reviewed.

24. Explore Reasons for Blaming (24)

A. The service member's history was explored with a focus on causes for the avoidance of acceptance of responsibility for behavior.

B. The service member's history of physical and emotional abuse was explored.

C. The service member's early history of lying was explored for causes and consequences.

D. Parental modeling of projection of responsibility for their behavior was examined.

E. The service member was provided with tentative examples of reasons why he/she tends to blame others for his/her actions (e.g., history of physically abusive punishment, parental modeling, fear of rejection, shame, low self-esteem, avoidance of facing consequences).

25. Reinforce Taking Personal Responsibility (25)

A. The service member was verbally reinforced in a strong and consistent manner when he/she took responsibility for his/her own behavior.

B. The service member was taught how others develop respect for someone who takes responsibility for his/her actions and admits to mistakes.

26. Explore Childhood Abuse and Neglect (26)

A. Active listening skills were used as the service member described instances from his/her own childhood of emotional, verbal, and physical abuse.

B. Support and empathy were provided as the service member described feelings of hurt, depression, abandonment, and fear related to parental abuse or neglect.

C. It was reflected to the service member that he/she was rather matter-of-fact in his/her description and showed little affect while describing a history of violence within the family during his/her childhood.

D. It was reflected to the service member that he/she has tended to minimize the negative impact of physical abuse that he/she suffered and, at times, even excused the behavior as something that he/she deserved.

E. The service member was shown the cycle of abuse.

27. Review Emotional Detachment (27)

A. The service member's pattern of emotional detachment from others was reviewed.

B. It was pointed out to the service member that his/her childhood history of abuse and neglect has led to a pattern of emotional detachment in current relationships.

C. The service member accepted that his/her emotional detachment is related to his/her childhood history of abuse and neglect and was supported for this insight.

D. The service member denied connection between any emotional detachment and any childhood abuse and was urged to consider this connection as he/she felt able to do so.

28. Teach Forgiveness (28)

A. The service member was taught the value of forgiveness as a means of overcoming pain and hurt rather than holding on to it and acting out the anger that results from it.

B. The service member was asked to list those parental figures from his/her childhood who have caused him/her pain and suffering.

C. The service member was assisted in developing a list of benefits of beginning a process of forgiveness toward those perpetrators of pain in his/her childhood.

29. Process Distrust (29)

A. The service member was asked to verbalize what he/she could be afraid of in placing trust in others.

B. The service member's fear of being taken advantage of, being disappointed, being abandoned, or being abused when trust is placed in another person was processed.

C. Positive feedback was provided to the service member as he/she displayed insight into his/her pattern of distrust.

30. Encourage Trust (30)

A. The service member was assisted in identifying some personal thoughts and feelings that he/she could disclose to another person as a means of beginning the process of showing trust in others.

B. The service member was assisted in identifying one or two other people within his/her life whom he/she could trust with personal information.

C. The service member was asked to commit to making a disclosure to a significant other that would demonstrate trust.

D. Positive feedback was provided as the service member identified that he/she has made trusting disclosures to others.

E. The service member did not make trusting disclosures to others, and the reasons behind this failure were processed.

31. Process Trust Exercise (31)

A. The service member's feelings of anxiety regarding trusting someone were explored.

B. The service member's experience with placing trust in another person was reviewed, and the success was reinforced.

C. The service member has not engaged in a trust exercise with a peer and was reminded to do so.

32. Identify Explore Intentions Regarding Military (32)

A. The service member's intentions regarding remaining in the military were exploited.

B. The service member was supported as he/she indicated that he/she intends to remain in the military.

C. The service member was supported as he/she indicates that he/she does not intend to remain in this military.

D. The service member is uncertain about his/her future in the military and was provided with additional support and direction in this area.

33. Explore Dishonorable Discharge Impact (33)

A. The impact of a dishonorable discharge on the service member's future was explored.

B. Examples of the effects of dishonorable discharge on the service member were reviewed (e.g., federal employment, prohibitions, student loan impact).

ANXIETY

VETERAN/SERVICE MEMBER PRESENTATION

1. Excessive Worry (1)[*]

A. The veteran/service member described symptoms of preoccupation with worry that something dire will happen.

B. The veteran/service member identified that his/her worry is military related.

C. The veteran/service member noted that his/her worry is not specifically related to military issues.

D. The veteran/service member showed some recognition that his/her excessive worry is beyond the scope of rationality, but he/she feels unable to control it.

E. The veteran/service member described that he/she worries about issues related to family, personal safety, health, and employment, among other things.

F. The veteran/service member reported that his/her worry about life circumstances has diminished and he/she is living with more of a sense of peace and confidence.

2. Motor Tension (2)

A. The veteran/service member described a history of restlessness, tiredness, muscle tension, and shaking.

B. The veteran/service member moved about in his/her chair frequently and sat stiffly.

C. The veteran/service member said that he/she is unable to relax and is always restless and stressed.

D. The veteran/service member reported that he/she has been successful at reducing levels of tension and increasing levels of relaxation.

3. Autonomic Hyperactivity (3)

A. The veteran/service member reported the presence of symptoms such as heart palpitations, dry mouth, tightness in the throat, and some shortness of breath.

B. The veteran/service member reported periods of nausea and some diarrhea when anxiety levels escalate.

C. The veteran/service member stated that occasional tension headaches are also occurring along with other anxiety-related symptoms.

D. Anxiety-related symptoms have diminished as the veteran/service member has learned new coping mechanisms.

4. Hypervigilance (4)

A. The veteran/service member related that he/she is constantly feeling on edge, that sleep is interrupted, and that concentration is difficult.

---

[*]The numbers in parentheses correlate to the number of the Behavioral Definition statement in the companion chapter with the same title in *The Veterans and Active Duty Military Psychotherapy Treatment Planner* (Moore and Jongsma) by John Wiley & Sons, 2009.

B. The veteran/service member reported being irritable and snappy in interaction with others as his/her patience is thin and he/she is worrying about everything.

C. The veteran's/service member's family members report that he/she is difficult to get along with as his/her irritability is high.

D. The veteran's/service member's level of tension has decreased, sleep has improved, and irritability has diminished as new anxiety-coping skills have been implemented.

INTERVENTIONS IMPLEMENTED

1. Assess Nature of Anxiety Symptoms (1)[*]

A. The veteran/service member was asked about the frequency, intensity, duration, and history of his/her anxiety symptoms, fear, and avoidance.

B. The *Anxiety Disorders Interview Schedule for DSM-IV* (DiNardo, Brown, and Barlow) was used to assess the veteran's/service member's anxiety symptoms.

C. The assessment of the veteran's/service member's anxiety symptoms indicated that his/her symptoms are extreme and severely interfere with his/her life.

D. The assessment of the veteran's/service member's anxiety symptoms indicates that these symptoms are moderate and occasionally interfere with his/her daily functioning.

E. The results of the assessment of the veteran's/service member's anxiety symptoms indicate that these symptoms are mild and rarely interfere with his/her daily functioning.

F. The results of the assessment of the veteran's/service member's anxiety symptoms were reviewed with the veteran/service member.

2. Administer Patient-Report Measure (2)

A. A patient-report measure was used to further assess the depth and breadth of the veteran's/service member's anxiety responses.

B. The Penn State Worry Questionnaire (Meyer, Miller, Metzger, and Borkevec) was used to assess the depth and breadth of the veteran's/service member's anxiety responses.

C. The *OQ-45.2* was used to assess the impact of the veteran's/service member's symptom's impact on his/her functioning.

D. The patient-report measure indicated that the veteran's/service member's anxiety is extreme and severely interferes with his/her life.

E. The patient-report measure indicated that the veteran's/service member's anxiety is moderate and occasionally interferes with his/her daily life.

F. The patient-report measure indicated that the veteran's/service member's anxiety is mild and rarely interferes with his/her daily life.

G. The veteran/service member declined to complete the patient-report measure, and the focus of treatment was changed to this resistance.

[*]The numbers in parentheses correlate to the number of the Therapeutic Intervention statement in the companion chapter with the same title in *The Veterans and Active Duty Military Psychotherapy Treatment Planner* (Moore and Jongsma) by John Wiley & Sons, 2009.

3. Refer for Medication Evaluation (3)

A. The veteran/service member was referred to a prescribing practitioner to evaluate him/her for psychotropic medication to reduce symptoms of anxiety.

B. The veteran/service member has completed an evaluation by the prescribing practitioner and has begun taking anti-anxiety medications.

C. The veteran/service member has resisted the referral to the prescribing practitioner physician and does not want to take any medication to reduce anxiety levels; his/her concerns were processed.

4. Monitor Medication Compliance (4)

A. The veteran's/service member's compliance with the prescription for psychotropic medication was monitored for the medication's effectiveness and side effects.

B. The veteran/service member reported that the medication has been beneficial to him/her in reducing his/her experience of anxiety symptoms; the benefits of this progress were reviewed.

C. The veteran/service member reported that the medication does not seem to be helpful in reducing anxiety experiences; this was reported to the prescribing clinician.

D. The therapist conferred with the physician to discuss the veteran's/service member's reaction to the psychotropic medication, and adjustments were made to the prescription by the prescribing practitioner.

5. Inform Chain of Command (5)

A. The service member's chain of command was informed about the service member's medication use.

B. The service member's medication was noted to have a change in her/his functioning, which is likely to put others at risk.

C. The service member's medication is not noted to have significant effects on his/her functioning, and this was related to the chain of command.

D. After a review of the medication being used by the service member, it was decided that there is no need to inform his/her chain of command.

6. Discuss Anxiety Cycle (6)

A. The veteran/service member was taught about how anxious fears are maintained by a cycle of unwarranted fear and avoidance that precludes positive, corrective experiences with the feared object or situation.

B. The veteran/service member was taught about how treatment breaks the anxiety cycle by encouraging positive, corrective experiences.

C. The veteran/service member was taught information from *Mastery of Your Anxiety and Worry—Therapist Guide* (Craske, Barlow, and O'Leary) regarding the anxiety pattern.

D. The veteran/service member was reinforced as he/she displayed a better understanding of the anxiety cycle of unwarranted fear and avoidance and how treatment breaks the cycle.

E. The veteran/service member displayed a poor understanding of the anxiety cycle and was provided with remedial feedback in this area.

7. Discuss Target of Treatment (7)

A. A discussion was held about how treatment targets worry, anxiety symptoms, and avoidance to help the veteran/service member manage worry effectively.

B. The reduction of overarousal and unnecessary avoidance were emphasized as treatment targets.

C. The veteran/service member displayed a clear understanding of the target of treatment and was provided with positive feedback in this area.

D. The veteran/service member struggled to understand the target of treatment and was provided with specific examples in this area.

8. Assign Reading on Anxiety (8)

A. The veteran/service member was assigned to read psychoeducational chapters of books or treatment manuals on anxiety.

B. The veteran/service member was assigned information from *Mastery of Your Anxiety and Worry—Client Manual* (Zinbarg, Craske, Barlow, and O'Leary).

C. The veteran/service member has read the assigned information on anxiety and key points were reviewed.

D. The veteran/service member has not read the assigned information on anxiety and was redirected to do so.

9. Teach Relaxation Skills (9)

A. The veteran/service member was taught relaxation skills.

B. The veteran/service member was taught progressive muscle relaxation, guided imagery, and slow diaphragmatic breathing.

C. The veteran/service member was taught how to discriminate better between relaxation and tension.

D. The veteran/service member was taught how to apply relaxation skills to his/her daily life.

E. The veteran/service member was taught relaxation skills as described in *Progressive Relaxation Training* (Bernstein and Borkovec).

F. The veteran/service member was taught relaxation skills as described in *Treating GAD* (Rygh and Sanderson).

G. The veteran/service member was provided with feedback about his/her use of relaxation skills.

10. Assign Relaxation Homework (10)

A. The veteran/service member was assigned to do homework exercises in which he/she practices relaxation on a daily basis.

B. The veteran/service member has regularly used relaxation exercises, and the helpful benefits of these exercises were reviewed.

C. The veteran/service member has not regularly used relaxation exercises and was provided with corrective feedback in this area.

D. The veteran/service member has used some relaxation exercises but does not find these to be helpful; he/she was assisted in brainstorming how to modify these exercises to be more helpful.

11. Assign Reading on Relaxation and Calming Strategies (11)

A. The veteran/service member was assigned to read about progressive muscle relaxation and other calming strategies in relevant books and treatment manuals.

B. The veteran/service member was directed to read about muscle relaxation and other calming strategies in *Progressive Relaxation Training* (Bernstein and Borkovec).

C. The veteran/service member was directed to read about muscle relaxation and other calming strategies in *Mastery of Your Anxiety and Worry—Client Guide* (Zinbarg, Craske, Barlow, and O'Leary).

D. The veteran/service member has read the assigned information on progressive muscle relaxation, and key points were reviewed.

E. The veteran/service member has not read the assigned information on progressive muscle relaxation and was redirected to do so.

12. Utilize Biofeedback (12)

A. Electromyograph (EMG) biofeedback techniques were used to facilitate the veteran/service member learning relaxation skills.

B. The veteran/service member reported that he/she has implemented his/her use of relaxation skills in daily life to reduce levels of muscle tension and the experience of anxiety; the benefits of this technique were reviewed.

C. The veteran/service member reported that his/her level of anxiety has decreased since relaxation techniques were implemented; he/she was encouraged to continue this technique.

D. The veteran/service member has not followed through on implementation of relaxation skills to reduce anxiety symptoms; he/she was redirected to do so.

13. Discuss Estimation Errors (13)

A. In today's session, examples were discussed about how unrealistic worry typically overestimates a probability of threats.

B. The veteran/service member was assigned "Past Successful Anxiety Coping" from the *Adult Psychotherapy Homework Planner,* 2nd ed. (Jongsma).

C. It was noted that unrealistic worry often underestimates the veteran's/service member's ability to manage realistic demands.

D. The veteran/service member was assisted in identifying specific examples of how his/her unrealistic worry involves estimation errors.

E. The veteran/service member was reinforced for his/her insightful identification of unrealistic worry and inappropriate estimation.

F. The veteran/service member has struggled to identify estimation errors in regard to his/her unrealistic worry and was provided with tentative examples in this area.

14. Analyze Fears Logically (14)

A. The veteran's/service member's fears were analyzed by examining the probability of his/her negative expectation becoming a reality, the consequences of the expectation if it occurred, his/her ability to control the outcome, the worst possible result if the expectation occurred, and his/her ability to cope if the expectation occurred.

B. The veteran/service member was assigned "Analyze the Probability of a Feared Event" from the *Adult Psychotherapy Homework Planner,* 2nd ed. (Jongsma).

C. The veteran's/service member's ability to control the outcome of circumstances was examined, and the effectiveness of his/her worry on that outcome was also examined.

D. Cognitive therapy techniques have been effective at helping the veteran/service member understand his/her beliefs and distorted messages that produce worry and anxiety.

E. As the veteran/service member has increased his/her understanding of distorted, anxiety-producing cognitions, his/her anxiety level has been noted to be decreasing.

F. Despite the veteran's/service member's increased understanding of distorted messages that produce worry and anxiety, his/her anxiety level has not diminished.

15. Develop Insight into Worry as Avoidance (15)

A. The veteran/service member was assisted in gaining insight into how worry is a form of avoidance of a feared problem and how it creates chronic tension.

B. The veteran/service member was reinforced for his/her insightful understanding about how his/her worry creates avoidance and tension.

C. The veteran/service member struggled to understand the nature of worry as a form of avoidance and was provided with remedial information in this area.

16. Identify Distorted Thoughts (16)

A. The veteran/service member was assisted in identifying the distorted schemas and related automatic thoughts that mediate anxiety responses.

B. The veteran/service member was taught the role of distorted thinking in precipitating emotional responses.

C. The veteran/service member was reinforced as he/she verbalized an understanding of the cognitive beliefs and messages that mediate his/her anxiety responses.

D. The veteran/service member was assisted in replacing distorted messages with positive, realistic cognitions.

E. The veteran/service member failed to identify his/her distorted thoughts and cognitions and was provided with tentative examples in this area.

17. Assign Exercises on Self-Talk (17)

A. The veteran/service member was assigned homework exercises in which he/she identifies fearful self-talk and creates reality-based alternatives.

B. The veteran's/service member's replacement of fearful self-talk with reality-based alternatives was critiqued.

C. The veteran/service member was reinforced for his/her successes at replacing fearful self-talk with reality-based alternatives.

D. The veteran/service member was provided with corrective feedback for his/her failures to replace fearful self-talk with reality-based alternatives.

E. The veteran/service member has not completed his/her assigned homework regarding fearful self-talk and was redirected to do so.

18. Teach Thought Stopping (18)

A. The veteran/service member was taught thought-stopping techniques that involve thinking of a stop sign and replacing negative thoughts with a pleasant scene.

B. The veteran/service member was assigned "Making Use of the Thought-Stopping Technique" from the *Adult Psychotherapy Homework Planner,* 2nd ed. (Jongsma).

C. The veteran's/service member's implementation of the thought-stopping technique was monitored, and his/her success with this technique was reinforced.

D. The veteran/service member reported that the thought-stopping technique has been beneficial in reducing his/her preoccupation with anxiety-producing cognitions; he/she was encouraged to continue this technique.

E. The veteran/service member has failed in his/her use the thought-stopping techniques; his/her attempts to use these techniques were reviewed and problem-solved.

19. Construct Anxiety Stimuli Hierarchy (19)

A. The veteran/service member was assisted in constructing a hierarchy of anxiety-producing situations associated with two or three spheres of worry.

B. It was difficult for the veteran/service member to develop a hierarchy of stimulus situations, as the causes of his/her anxiety remain quite vague; he/she was assisted in completing the hierarchy.

C. The veteran/service member was successful at creating a focused hierarchy of specific stimulus situations that provoke anxiety in a gradually increasing manner; this hierarchy was reviewed.

20. Select Initial Exposures (20)

A. Initial exposures were selected from the hierarchy of anxiety-producing situations, with a bias toward likelihood of being successful.

B. A plan was developed with the veteran/service member for managing the symptoms that may occur during the initial exposure.

C. The veteran/service member was assisted in rehearsing the plan for managing the exposure-related symptoms within his/her imagination.

D. Positive feedback was provided for the veteran's/service member's helpful use of symptom management techniques.

E. The veteran/service member was redirected in ways to improve his/her symptom management techniques.

21. Assign Imagination Exercises (21)

A. The veteran/service member was asked to vividly imagine worst-case consequences of worries, holding them in mind until the anxiety associated with them weakens.

B. The veteran/service member was asked to imagine consequences of his/her worries as described in *Mastery of Your Anxiety and Worry—Therapist Guide* (Craske, Barlow, and O'Leary).

C. The veteran/service member was supported as he/she has maintained a focus on the worst-case consequences of his/her worry until the anxiety weakened.

D. The veteran/service member was assisted in generating reality-based alternatives to the worst-case scenarios; these were processed within the session.

22. Assign Homework on Situational Exposures (22)

A. The veteran/service member was assigned homework exercises to perform worry exposures and record his/her experience.

B. The veteran/service member was assigned situational exposures homework from *Mastery of Your Anxiety and Worry—Client Guide* (Zinbarg, Craske, Barlow, and O'Leary)

C. The veteran/service member was assigned situational exposures homework from *Generalized Anxiety Disorder* (Brown, O'Leary, and Barlow).

D. The veteran's/service member's use of worry exposure techniques was reviewed and reinforced.

E. The veteran/service member has struggled in his/her implementation of worry exposure techniques and was provided with corrective feedback.

F. The veteran/service member has not attempted to use the worry exposure techniques and was redirected to do so.

23. Teach Problem-Solving Strategies (23)

A. The veteran/service member was taught the Military Problem-Solving Process strategy.

B. The veteran/service member was taught problem-solving strategies including recognizing and defining the problem, gathering facts and making assumptions, defining end states and establishing criteria, developing possible solutions, analyzing and comparing possible solutions, selecting and implementing solution, and analyzing solution for effectiveness.

C. The veteran/service member was provided feedback on his/her use of the problem-solving strategies.

24. Assign Problem-Solving Exercise (24)

A. The veteran/service member was assigned a homework exercise in which he/she problem-solves a current problem.

B. The veteran/service member was assigned to solve a problem as described in *Mastery of Your Anxiety and Worry—Client Guide* (Zinbarg, Craske, Barlow, and O'Leary).

C. The veteran/service member was assigned to solve a problem as described in *Generalized Anxiety Disorder* (Brown, O'Leary, and Barlow).

D. The veteran/service member was provided with feedback about his/her use of the problem-solving assignment.

25. Differentiate between Lapse and Relapse (25)

A. A discussion was held with the veteran/service member regarding the distinction between a lapse and a relapse.

B. A lapse was associated with an initial and reversible return of symptoms, fear, or urges to avoid.

C. A relapse was associated with the decision to return to fearful and avoidant patterns.

D. The veteran/service member was provided with support and encouragement as he/she displayed an understanding of the difference between a lapse and a relapse.

E. The veteran/service member struggled to understand the difference between a lapse and a relapse and was provided with remedial feedback in this area.

26. Discuss Management of Lapse Risk Situations (26)

A. The veteran/service member was assisted in identifying future situations or circumstances in which lapses could occur.

B. The session focused on rehearsing the management of future situations or circumstances in which lapses could occur.

C. The veteran/service member was reinforced for his/her appropriate use of lapse management skills.

D. The veteran/service member was redirected in regard to his/her poor use of lapse management skills.

27. Encourage Routine Use of Strategies (27)

A. The veteran/service member was instructed to routinely use the strategies that he/she has learned in therapy (e.g., cognitive restructuring, exposure).

B. The veteran/service member was urged to find ways to build his/her new strategies into his/her life as much as possible.

C. The veteran/service member was reinforced as he/she reported ways in which he/she has incorporated coping strategies into his/her life and routine.

D. The veteran/service member was redirected about ways to incorporate new strategies into his/her routine and life.

28. Develop a "Coping Card" (28)

A. The veteran/service member was provided with a "coping card" on which specific coping strategies were listed.

B. The veteran/service member was assisted in developing his/her "coping card" in order to list his/her helpful coping strategies.

C. The veteran/service member was encouraged to use his/her "coping card" when struggling with anxiety-producing situations.

29. Utilize Paradoxical Intervention (29)

A. A paradoxical intervention was developed with the veteran/service member in which he/she was encouraged to experience the anxiety at specific intervals each day for a defined length of time.

B. The veteran/service member has implemented the assigned paradoxical intervention and reported that it was difficult for him/her to maintain the anxiety as he/she was eager to get on with other activities.

C. The veteran/service member has experienced, in general, a reduction of his/her anxiety as he/she has developed an insight into his/her ability to control it; this insight was processed.

D. The veteran/service member has not used the paradoxical intervention and was redirected to do so.

30. Assign Cost-Benefit Analysis (30)

A. The veteran/service member was asked to complete a Cost-Benefit Analysis as found in *Ten Days to Self-Esteem!* (Burns) in which he/she was asked to list the advantages and disadvantages of maintaining the anxiety.

B. Completing the Cost-Benefit Analysis exercise has been noted to be beneficial to the veteran/service member as he/she developed more insight into the impact of anxiety on his/her daily life.

C. The veteran/service member has not followed through on completing the Cost-Benefit Analysis of his/her anxiety and was encouraged to do so.

31. Identify Unresolved Conflicts (31)

A. The veteran/service member was assisted in becoming aware of unresolved life conflicts that contribute to his/her persistent fears.

B. The veteran/service member was assisted in clarifying his/her feelings of anxiety as they relate to unresolved life conflicts.

C. The veteran/service member was assisted in identifying steps that could be taken to begin resolving issues in his/her life that contribute to persistent fear and worry.

D. As the veteran/service member has been helped to resolve life conflicts, his/her feelings of anxiety have diminished.

E. The veteran/service member did not display insight into unresolved conflicts and how they contribute to his/her persistent fears and was provided with tentative examples in this area.

32. Develop Insight into Past Traumas (32)

A. The veteran's/service member's past traumatic experiences that have become triggers for anxiety were examined.

B. The veteran/service member has been assisted in developing insight into how past traumatic experiences have led to anxiety in present unrelated circumstances.

C. The development of insight regarding past traumas has resulted in a reduction in the experience of anxiety.

33. List Life Conflicts (33)

A. The veteran/service member was asked to list his/her important past and present life conflicts that may contribute to his/her feelings of worry.

B. The veteran's/service member's list of life conflicts that trigger anxiety were processed.

C. The veteran/service member was assisted in clarifying the causes for his/her worry and to put them into better perspective.

D. The veteran/service member was unable to make a connection between life conflicts and his/her anxiety/worry and was provided with tentative examples in this area as well as ways to put them in better perspective.

34. Reinforce Responsibility Acceptance (34)

A. The veteran/service member was supported and reinforced for following through with work or military duties, family, and social responsibilities rather than using escape and avoidance to focus on anxiety symptoms.

B. The veteran/service member reported performing responsibilities more consistently and being less preoccupied with the worry symptoms or fear that worry symptoms might occur; his/her progress was highlighted.

35. Schedule a "Booster Session" (35)

A. The veteran/service member was scheduled for a "booster session" between one and three months after therapy ends.

B. The veteran/service member was advised to contact the therapist if he/she needs to be seen prior to the "booster session."

C. The veteran's/service member's "booster session" was held, and he/she was reinforced for his/her successful implementation of therapy techniques.

D. The veteran's/service member's "booster session" was held, and he/she was coordinated for further treatment, as his/her progress has not been sustained.

36. Identify Mental Health Resources (36)

A. The service member was assisted in identifying mental health resources at the location where he/she will be deployed.

B. The service member was provided with specific information for how to seek mental health services in the area where he/she will be deployed.

C. Contacts were made to assist in the transition for mental health services in the service member's new deployment.

ATTENTION AND CONCENTRATION DEFICITS

VETERAN/SERVICE MEMBER PRESENTATION

1. ADD Childhood History (1)[*]

A. The veteran/service member confirmed that his/her childhood history consisted of the following symptoms: behavioral problems at school, impulsivity, temper outbursts, and lack of concentration.

B. The veteran/service member had a diagnosed attention-deficit/hyperactivity disorder (AD/HD) condition in his/her childhood.

C. Although the veteran's/service member's symptoms were not diagnosed as AD/HD, it can be concluded from the childhood symptoms that the AD/HD condition was present at that time.

2. ADD in Adulthood (2)

A. The veteran/service member exhibits a persistent pattern of attention/concentration problems during adulthood.

B. The veteran/service member reports a lack of concentration, impulsivity, poor vigilance, and other symptoms associated with attention-deficit/hyperactivity disorder in his/her adulthood.

C. As treatment has progressed, the veteran's/service member's difficulties with attention and concentration have decreased.

3. Lack of Concentration (3)

A. The veteran/service member reported an inability to concentrate or pay attention to things of low interest, even though they may be important to his/her life.

B. The veteran's/service member's lack of ability to concentrate has resulted in his/her missing out on the comprehension of important details.

C. The veteran's/service member's ability to concentrate seems to be increasing as he/she reported increased attention skills.

4. Distractibility (4)

A. The veteran/service member reported that he/she is easily distracted and his/her attention is drawn away from the task at hand.

B. The veteran/service member gave evidence of distractibility within today's session.

C. The veteran's/service member's distractibility is diminishing and his/her focused concentration is increasing.

5. Disorganization (5)

A. The veteran/service member has a history of disorganization in many areas of his/her life.

B. The veteran's/service member's disorganization is evident in areas related to home and work, leading him/her to be less efficient and less effective than he/she could be.

[*]The numbers in parentheses correlate to the number of the Behavioral Definition statement in the companion chapter with the same title in *The Veterans and Active Duty Military Psychotherapy Treatment Planner* (Moore and Jongsma) by John Wiley & Sons, 2009.

C. The veteran/service member has made significant progress in increasing his/her organization and is using that organization to become more efficient.

D. The veteran/service member uses lists and reminders to increase his/her organizational ability.

6. Lack of Project Completion (6)

A. The veteran/service member reported that he/she has started many projects and has a history of rarely finishing them.

B. Family members reported frustration at the veteran's/service member's pattern of rarely finishing projects that he/she has begun.

C. The veteran/service member has shown progress in project completion and has moved to not begin a new project until the previous one is completed.

7. Superiors' Complaints (7)

A. The service member reported frequent complaints by superiors about lapses in concentration during meetings, training, and combat missions.

B. The service member acknowledges that he/she has missed information or been inattentive during important meetings, training, and combat missions.

C. As treatment has progressed, the service member reports better focus during meetings, training, and combat missions.

8. Reading Difficulties (8)

A. The veteran/service member reported difficulty staying focused when reading for extended periods of time.

B. The veteran/service member reports that he/she is often unable to recall what he/she read.

C. The veteran/service member reports that he/she may read for an extended period of time but finds that he/she is reading and rereading the same material.

D. As treatment has progressed, the veteran's/service member's concentration has improved, and his/her ability to read and recall information has improved.

9. Misplacing/Losing Personal Items (9)

A. The veteran/service member complains of often displacing and losing personal items.

B. The veteran/service member reports significant disorganization and that he/she often cannot locate important items.

C. As treatment has progressed, the veteran's/service member's organization has improved, and he/she has not misplaced many items recently.

10. Frequent Repetition (10)

A. The veteran/service member reports that he/she often asks others to repeat what was said during conversations.

B. The veteran's/service member's vigilance appears impaired, and he/she often needs to have others repeat information.

C. As the veteran's/service member's vigilance has improved, he/she is more attentive in conversations.

INTERVENTIONS IMPLEMENTED

1. Assess Symptoms (1)*

A. The history of the veteran's/service member's attention deficits was thoroughly assessed.

B. Information was developed regarding the course of progression of the veteran's/service member's attention deficits, including onset, frequency, and duration.

C. The level of impact that the veteran's/service member's attention deficits have had on his/her occupational, social, and academic functioning were assessed.

D. The veteran/service member was reinforced for full participation in assessing his/her history of attention deficits.

2. Evaluate Impact on Daily Functioning (2)

A. An evaluation was conducted in regard to the impact that the veteran's/service member's attention and concentration symptoms have had on his/her daily functioning.

B. Significant concerns were identified in regard to the impact of the veteran's/service member's attention/concentration deficits.

C. The veteran's/service member's attention/concentration deficits were noted to have only minimal impact on his/her daily functioning.

D. The etiological factors for the veteran's/service member's symptoms were noted.

E. The veteran's/service member's symptoms of attention and concentration problems appear to be worsening.

3. Conduct/Refer for Psychological Testing (3)

A. The veteran/service member was administered psychological testing in order to establish or rule out the presence of an AD/HD problem.

B. Psychological testing has established the presence of an AD/HD problem.

C. The psychological testing failed to confirm the presence of AD/HD.

D. The psychological testing results were processed with the veteran/service member to assist him/her in understanding his/her condition and to answer any questions that he/she might have.

E. The veteran/service member understood the explanation of the psychological testing and has accepted the presence of an AD/HD problem.

F. The veteran/service member has denied the presence of AD/HD and refused to accept the confirming results of the psychological testing; he/she was urged to be more open about this diagnosis.

4. Refer for Medical Evaluation (4)

A. The veteran/service member was referred for a medical evaluation to assess for deficits related to recent injuries.

B. The veteran/service member was assessed for traumatic brain injury concerns.

C. The veteran/service member assessed for possible exposure to toxins.

D. The veteran/service member was assessed for possible drug and alcohol effects.

E. The results of the medical evaluation were processed with the veteran/service member.

---

*The numbers in parentheses correlate to the number of the Therapeutic Intervention statement in the companion chapter with the same title in *The Veterans and Active Duty Military Psychotherapy Treatment Planner* (Moore and Jongsma) by John Wiley & Sons, 2009.

5. Refer for Medication Evaluation (5)

A. The veteran/service member was referred to a physician for an evaluation for psychotropic medication to help in controlling the AD/HD symptoms.

B. The veteran/service member complied with the medication evaluation and has attended the appointment.

C. The veteran/service member refused to attend an evaluation appointment with the physician for psychotropic medication; he/she was encouraged to proceed with the evaluation as he/she feels capable of doing so.

6. Process Psychiatric and Psychological Evaluation (6)

A. Results and recommendations of the psychiatric evaluation were processed with the veteran/service member, and all questions were answered.

B. Results and recommendations of the psychological evaluation were processed with the veteran/service member, and all questions were answered.

C. As a result of the physician's evaluation, the veteran/service member was prescribed medication to assist in the control of AD/HD symptomatology.

D. As a result of the psychological evaluation, the veteran/service member was provided with several different techniques to assist in the control of AD/HD symptomatology.

7. Hold a Conjoint Session to Give Evaluation Feedback (7)

A. A conjoint session was held with the veteran/service member and his/her significant others in order to present the results of the psychological and psychiatric evaluations.

B. All questions regarding the evaluation results were processed.

C. The veteran's/service member's family members were solicited for support regarding his/her compliance with treatment for his/her AD/HD symptoms.

D. The veteran's/service member's family was verbally reinforced as they gave strong support to the veteran/service member regarding medical and psychological treatment for his/her AD/HD symptoms.

8. Monitor Medication Compliance (8)

A. The veteran's/service member's compliance with the medication prescription was monitored, and the medication's effectiveness on his/her level of functioning was evaluated.

B. The veteran/service member has been taking the medication consistently as prescribed and reported that the medication was effective in helping to control the AD/HD symptoms; he/she was encouraged to continue taking the medication.

C. The veteran/service member has been taking the psychotropic medications as prescribed but reports that he/she has not noted any significant improvement in his/her AD/HD symptoms; this information was relayed to the prescribing clinician.

D. The veteran/service member has not been taking the psychotropic medication as prescribed by the physician and was redirected to do so.

9. Identify Difficult AD/HD Behaviors (9)

A. The veteran/service member was assisted in identifying the specific AD/HD behaviors that have caused him/her the most difficulty.

B. The veteran/service member was supported as he/she listed such things as distractibility, lack of concentration, impulsivity, restlessness, and disorganization as the most difficult for him/her.

C. The veteran/service member was resistive to identifying specific AD/HD behaviors that cause him/her the most difficulty; he/she was encouraged to do this as he/she feels capable.

D. The veteran/service member was assisted in ranking his/her list of work-related problems, ranking them from most to least troublesome.

10. Teach Military Problem-Solving Process (10)

A. The veteran/service member was taught the Military Problem-Solving Process.

B. The veteran/service member was taught problem-solving skills that involve recognizing and defining the problem, gathering facts and making assumptions, defining end states or goals and establishing criteria for success, developing possible solutions, analyzing and comparing possible solutions, selecting and implementing solution, and analyzing solution for effectiveness.

C. The veteran/service member was reinforced as he/she verbalized an understanding of the military problem-solving skill techniques.

D. Role-playing was used to help the veteran/service member apply problem-solving techniques to daily problems in his/her life.

E. The veteran/service member has not internalized the military problem-solving skills and was provided with remedial assistance in this area.

11. Utilize Structured Reminders/Organizers (11)

A. The veteran/service member was encouraged to use such techniques as lists, sticky notes, files, and maintenance of daily routines in order to reduce forgetfulness and increase organization of his/her life.

B. The veteran's/service member's implementation of structured reminders and organizers has been noted to be successful in reducing forgetfulness and helping him/her to complete necessary tasks.

C. The veteran/service member was encouraged to reward himself/herself for successful recall and follow-through using the structured reminders/organizers.

D. The veteran/service member has not used structured reminders/organizers and was redirected to do so.

12. Develop Classification and Management System (12)

A. The veteran/service member was assisted in developing a procedure for classifying and managing his/her mail.

B. The veteran/service member was assisted in developing a way to manage his/her expected scheduled appointments.

C. The veteran/service member was reinforced for his/her greater level of organization.

13. Assign and Monitor Behavioral Techniques for Improving Conversations (13)

A. The veteran/service member was assigned behavioral techniques to assist with improving conversations with others.

B. The veteran/service member was encouraged to keep conversations brief.

C. The veteran/service member was encouraged to bring up topics that are of interest to the veteran/service member.

D. The veteran/service member was encouraged to take notes after conversations and use the notes to initiate the discussion in a follow-up conversation.

E. The veteran/service member was encouraged to acknowledge and reward himself/herself for successful interactions.

14. Build Social and Communication Skills (14)

A. Instruction, modeling, and role-playing were used to build the veteran's/service member's general social and communication skills.

B. Techniques from *Social Effectiveness Therapy* (Turner, Beidel, and Cooley) were used to teach social and communication skills.

C. Positive feedback was provided to the veteran/service member for his/her use of increased use of social and communication skills.

D. Despite the instruction, modeling, and role-playing about social and communication skills, the veteran/service member continues to struggle with these techniques and was provided with additional feedback in this area.

15. Assign Information on Social and Communication Skills (15)

A. The veteran/service member was assigned to read about general social and/or communication skills in books or treatment manuals on building social skills.

B. The veteran/service member was assigned to read *Your Perfect Right* (Alberti and Emmons).

C. The veteran/service member was assigned to read *Conversationally Speaking* (Garner).

D. The veteran/service member has read the assigned information on social and communication skills and key points were reviewed.

E. The veteran/service member has not read the information on social and communication skills and was redirected to do so.

16. Review Intrusive Excessive, Comments (16)

A. Social situations in which the veteran/service member was intrusive or talked excessively without thoughtfulness were reviewed.

B. The veteran/service member was redirected for ways in which he/she could have more social success.

C. Modeling, role-playing, and instruction were used to help the veteran/service member identify better techniques for managing social conversations.

17. Teach Problem-Solving Skills (17)

A. The veteran/service member was taught problem-solving skills that involve identifying the problem, brainstorming solutions, evaluating options, implementing action, and evaluating results.

B. The veteran/service member was assigned "Applying Problem-Solving to Interpersonal Conflict" in the *Adult Psychotherapy Homework Planner,* 2nd ed. (Jongsma).

C. The veteran/service member was reinforced as he/she verbalized an understanding of the problem-solving skill techniques.

D. Role-playing was used to help the veteran/service member apply problem-solving techniques to daily problems in his/her life.

E. The veteran/service member has not internalized the problem-solving skills and was provided with remedial assistance in this area.

18. Assess Typical Attention Span (18)

A. The veteran's/service member's typical attention span was measured.

B. The veteran/service member was requested to do various tasks to the point that he/she indicates distraction.

C. The veteran/service member was noted to have a very short attention span.

D. The veteran/service member was noted to have an adequate attention span.

19. Break Tasks Down (19)

A. The veteran/service member was taught about breaking tasks down into meaningful units based on his/her demonstrated attention span.

B. The veteran/service member was reinforced for his/her ability to break tasks down into meaningful units.

C. The veteran/service member was provided with assistance in breaking tasks down into meaningful units based on his/her demonstrated attention span.

20. Teach about Timers and Cues (20)

A. The veteran/service member was taught about the use of timers and cues as a way to help him/her remember to stay on task.

B. The use of timers to remind the veteran/service member about being on task were discussed and practiced.

C. The veteran/service member was reinforced for his/her use of timers and other cues to help remind him/her to stay on task.

D. The veteran/service member has not used reminders and other cues to help him/her stay on task and was redirected to do so.

21. Assign Dysfunctional Thinking Journal (21)

A. The veteran/service member was requested to keep a daily journal that lists each situation associated with frustration feelings and the dysfunctional thinking that triggered the impulsivity.

B. The veteran/service member was directed to complete the "Negative Thoughts Trigger Negative Feelings" assignment from the *Adult Psychotherapy Homework Planner,* 2nd ed. (Jongsma).

C. The Socratic method was used to challenge the veteran's/service member's dysfunctional thoughts and to replace them with positive, reality-based thoughts.

D. The veteran/service member was reinforced for instances of successful replacement of negative thoughts with more realistic positive thinking.

E. The veteran/service member has not kept his/her record of automatic thoughts and was redirected to do so.

22. Assign Homework on Cognitive Restructuring (22)

A. The veteran/service member was assigned homework to implement cognitive restructuring skills on relevant tasks.

B. The veteran/service member has rarely used cognitive restructuring skills, and these were reviewed and emphasized.

C. The veteran/service member has not regularly used cognitive restructuring skills and was redirected to do so.

23. Assign Memory-Enhancement Activities (23)

A. The veteran/service member was encouraged to implement memory-enhancement activities, such as working crossword puzzles, playing card games, or watching TV game shows.

B. The veteran/service member was encouraged to use coping strategies, such as using lists, establishing routines, and labeling the environment, to adapt to his/her short-term memory loss.

C. The veteran/service member has implemented the memory-enhancing activities and reported some success at them; the benefits of this progress were reviewed.

D. The veteran/service member has implemented coping strategies for short-term memory loss, and this has been noted to be beneficial in enacting instrumental activities of daily living.

E. The veteran/service member has not used the assigned memory-enhancement activities and was redirected to do so.

24. Monitor Memory Compensatory Strategies (24)

A. The veteran/service member was assigned memory compensatory strategies (e.g., keeping a notebook on hand at all times, making to-do lists, utilizing mnemonics).

B. The veteran/service member was monitored in regard to his/her use of memory compensatory strategies.

C. The veteran/service member was reinforced for his/her regular use of memory compensatory strategies.

D. The veteran/service member has not regularly used memory compensatory strategies and was reminded to do so.

25. Encourage Acknowledgment of and Rewards for Successes (25)

A. The veteran/service member was encouraged to acknowledge himself/herself for successes.

B. The veteran/service member was consistently asked about situations in which he/she has been successful in managing his/her attention and concentration.

C. The veteran/service member was encouraged to reward himself/herself for successes.

26. Inform Chain of Command about Medications (26)

A. The service member was encouraged to disclose any symptoms or side effects that could interfere with his/her performance and put him/her or other unit members at risk.

B. The service member was encouraged to maintain contact with his/her chain of command about medications and potential side effects.

C. The service member was reinforced for being open and honest with his/her chain of command.

D. The service member has not been open and honest with his/her chain of command and was redirected to do so.

27. Accept Restrictions and Seek Responsibility (27)

A. The service member was instructed to comply with duty restrictions if imposed.

B. The service member was encouraged to seek out increased responsibility by having limitations removed once deficits are no longer impacting functioning.

C. The service member was instructed to gain greater responsibility by complying with duty restrictions and displaying increased ability.

D. The service member was reinforced for complying with duty restrictions and seeking out greater responsibility when applicable.

E. The service member struggles to comply with duty restrictions and was redirected in this area.

28. Update Chain of Command Regarding Progress (28)

A. The service member was encouraged to provide regular updates to his/her chain of command regarding his/her progress.

B. The service member was assisted in identifying what information is appropriate to provide to the chain of command.

C. As a release of information has been executed, updates to the service member's chain of command have been provided.

29. Schedule a "Booster Session" (29)

A. The veteran/service member was scheduled for a "booster session" between one and three months after therapy ends.

B. The veteran/service member was advised to contact the therapist if he/she needs to be seen prior to the "booster session."

C. The veteran's/service member's "booster session" was held, and he/she was reinforced for his/her successful implementation of therapy techniques.

D. The veteran's/service member's "booster session" was held, and he/she was coordinated for further treatment, as his/her progress has not been sustained.

BEREAVEMENT DUE TO THE LOSS OF A COMRADE

VETERAN/SERVICE MEMBER PRESENTATION

1. Emotional Reaction to Loss of Fellow Service Member (1)[*]

A. The veteran/service member reports feelings of sadness, despair, anger, and/ or confusion resulting from the loss of a fellow service member.

B. The veteran's/service member's thoughts have been dominated by the loss experienced, and he/she has not been able to maintain normal concentration on other tasks.

C. The veteran/service member reported waves of depression and grief that result in tearfulness on a frequent basis.

D. The veteran's/service member's pattern of sadness, despair, anger, and confusion resulting from the loss of a fellow service member has gradually decreased.

E. The veteran/service member has reported better control over his/her emotions.

2. Emotional Numbness (2)

A. The veteran/service member reports a pattern of emotional numbness and disconnection from others.

B. The veteran/service member displays a pattern of avoidance about talking about the loss except on a very superficial level.

C. The veteran/service member has reported a sense of disconnection from others and difficulty relating to those who are not so significantly affected by the loss.

D. The veteran/service member reports an increased connectedness to his/her emotions, even though this may be emotionally painful.

E. The veteran/service member reports that he/she feels more connected to others.

3. Physiological Complaints (3)

A. The veteran/service member reports physiological complaints, such as vague pain, weakness, dizziness, and fatigue.

B. The veteran/service member relates his/her physiological complaints to his/her loss of a comrade.

C. As treatment has progressed the veteran's/service member's pattern of physiological complaints has decreased.

4. Avoidance of Thinking or Talking about the Lost Comrade (4)

A. The veteran/service member has shown a pattern of avoidance of situations in which he/she might have to think about or talk about the fellow service member.

B. The veteran/service member reports that he/she often tries to avoid intrusive thoughts about the fallen service member by becoming busy with a variety of activities.

---

[*]The numbers in parentheses correlate to the number of the Behavioral Definition statement in the companion chapter with the same title in *The Veterans and Active Duty Military Psychotherapy Treatment Planner* (Moore and Jongsma) by John Wiley & Sons, 2009.

C. The veteran's/service member's feelings of grief are coming more to the surface as he/she faces the loss issue more directly.

D. The veteran/service member was able to talk about the loss directly without being overwhelmed by his/her feelings of grief.

5. Denies Negative Impact (5)

A. The veteran/service member denies any negative impact on his/her psychological well-being from the loss.

B. The veteran/service member has gradually become more open about identifying the psychological impacts of his/her loss.

C. The veteran/service member appears to be adequately in touch in regard to the negative impact of the loss on his/her psychological well-being.

6. Decreased Social and Occupational Functioning (6)

A. The veteran/service member reports decreased social involvement subsequent to the loss of a comrade.

B. The veteran/service member reports that his/her occupational functioning has decreased subsequent to the loss of a comrade.

C. The veteran/service member noted that he/she is less interested and motivated in regard to social and occupational needs since the loss of the comrade.

D. As treatment has progressed, the veteran/service member reports increased social and occupational functioning.

7. Guilt Feelings (7)

A. The veteran/service member reports that he/she feels responsible for the death of a comrade.

B. The veteran/service member reports significant guilt feelings about the death of his/her comrade.

C. The veteran/service member verbalized guilt over believing that he/she had not done enough for the lost comrade.

D. The veteran/service member verbalized an unreasonable belief of having contributed to the death of the comrade.

E. The veteran's/service member's feelings of guilt have diminished.

F. The veteran/service member reports that he/she no longer experiences guilt related to his/her loss.

8. Emotional Lability (8)

A. The veteran/service member reported unpredictable waves of sadness, tearfulness, confusion, and/or poor concentration.

B. The veteran/service member reports that his/her unpredictable emotional lability has occurred at unexpected and inopportune times.

C. The veteran's/service member's emotional reactions to the discussion of the loss are more controlled.

D. The veteran/service member is able to discuss and experience the emotions related to the loss without losing control of his/her emotions.

9. Rage (9)

A. The veteran/service member reports an unreasonable and unpredictable pattern of rage in regard to the loss of his/her comrade.

B. The veteran/service member has displayed rage toward those he/she sees as responsible for the loss of the comrade.

C. The veteran/service member displays rage in an unreasonable and unpredictable manner, even against those who had nothing to do with the loss.

D. As treatment has progressed, the veteran/service member reports that his/her anger has been more reasonable, predictable, and appropriately placed.

INTERVENTIONS IMPLEMENTED

1. Build Trust (1)*

A. Consistent eye contact, active listening, unconditional positive regard, and warm acceptance were used to help build trust with the veteran/service member.

B. The veteran/service member began to express feelings more freely as rapport and trust level increased.

C. The veteran/service member has continued to experience difficulty being open and direct in his/her expression of painful feelings and was encouraged to be as open as feelings of safety allow.

2. Encourage Telling Story of Loss (2)

A. The veteran/service member was treated with empathy and compassion as he/she was encouraged to tell the story of his/her recent loss in detail.

B. The veteran/service member was supported as he/she told the story of his/her recent loss.

C. The veteran/service member was reinforced for telling the entire story of the recent loss.

D. The veteran/service member has been guarded about telling the entire story of his/her recent loss and was encouraged to do this in a trusting environment.

3. Assess Grief Impact (3)

A. The type, intensity, and frequency of the veteran's/service member's symptoms were assessed.

B. The impact of the veteran's/service member's symptoms on social, occupational, and interpersonal functioning was assessed.

C. It was noted that the veteran's/service member's level of symptoms and impact were minimal in degree, and this was reported to the veteran/service member.

D. It was noted that the veteran's/service member's level of symptoms and impact were moderate in degree, and this was reported to the veteran/service member.

E. was noted that the veteran's/service member's level of symptoms and impact were severe in degree, and this was reported to the veteran/service member.

---

*The numbers in parentheses correlate to the number of the Therapeutic Intervention statement in the companion chapter with the same title in *The Veterans and Active Duty Military Psychotherapy Treatment Planner* (Moore and Jongsma) by John Wiley & Sons, 2009.

4. Discuss Impact of Loss of Comrade (4)

A. The veteran/service member was encouraged to discuss how the loss of his/her follow comrades has impacted him/her emotionally.

B. The veteran/service member was assisted in processing the relative content about how the loss of his/her fellow comrade has impacted him/her emotionally.

C. The veteran/service member reported very few emotional effects of the loss of a comrade, and he/she was assisted in processing these effects.

D. The veteran/service member reported significant emotional effects of the loss of a comrade, and he/she was assisted in processing these effects.

E. The veteran's/service member's pattern of functioning is not consistent with his/her description of the impact of the loss on his/her emotional well-being, and this was reflected to the veteran/service member.

5. Discuss Previous Feelings of Sadness or Guilt (5)

A. The veteran/service member was encouraged to identify prior times in his/her life when he/she felt such feelings of sadness or guilt.

B. The veteran/service member was assisted in listing situations in which he/she has felt feelings of sadness or guilt, regardless of whether they were loss related.

C. The veteran/service member has been able to identify situations in which he/she has experienced sadness or guilt, and these were processed.

D. The veteran/service member was unable to identify times when he/she has previously experienced sadness or guilt, and was assisted in identifying examples.

6. Review Past Coping Strategies (6)

A. The veteran/service member was assisted in reviewing past effective coping strategies that have helped him/her deal with negative emotions.

B. The veteran/service member has identified past effective coping strategies, and these were processed.

C. The veteran/service member was encouraged to use the past successful coping strategies to deal with current negative emotions.

D. The veteran/service member struggled to identify past effective coping strategies and was provided with remedial assistance in this area.

7. Refer for Medication Evaluation (7)

A. The veteran/service member was referred for a medication evaluation to help stabilize his/her moods and decrease the intensity of his/her feelings.

B. The veteran/service member was reinforced as he/she agreed to follow through with the medication evaluation.

C. The veteran/service member was strongly opposed to being placed on medication to help stabilize his/her moods and reduce emotional distress; his/her objections were processed.

8. Monitor Effects of Medication (8)

A. The veteran's/service member's response to the medication was discussed in today's therapy session.

B. The veteran/service member reported that the medication has helped to stabilize his/her moods and decrease the intensity of his/her feelings; he/she was directed to share this information with the prescribing clinician.

C. The veteran/service member reports little to no improvement in his/her moods or anger control since being placed on the medication; he/she was directed to share this information with the prescribing clinician.

D. The veteran/service member was reinforced for consistently taking the medication as prescribed.

E. The veteran/service member has failed to take the medication as prescribed; he/she was encouraged to take the medication as prescribed.

9. Assess Chemical Dependence (9)

A. The veteran/service member was asked to describe his/her use of alcohol and/or drugs as a means of escape from negative emotions.

B. The veteran/service member was supported as he/she acknowledged that he/she has abused alcohol and/or drugs as a means of coping with the negative consequences associated with the traumatic event.

C. The veteran/service member was quite defensive about giving information regarding his/her substance abuse history and minimized any such behavior; this was reflected to him/her, and he/she was urged to be more open.

D. The veteran/service member reported no pattern of substance abuse.

10. Refer to Chemical Dependence Treatment (10)

A. The veteran/service member was referred for chemical dependence treatment.

B. The veteran/service member consented to chemical dependence treatment referral, as he/she has acknowledged it as a significant problem.

C. The veteran/service member refused to accept a referral for chemical dependence treatment and continued to deny that substance abuse is a problem.

D. The veteran/service member was reinforced for following through on obtaining chemical dependence treatment.

E. The veteran's/service member's treatment focus was switched to his/her chemical dependence problem.

11. Explain Uncomplicated versus Complicated Bereavement (11)

A. The veteran/service member was educated on the difference between uncomplicated and complicated bereavement.

B. Uncomplicated bereavement was defined as when symptoms are present (e.g., sadness, crying, and grief) but are time limited and have minimal impact on social and occupational functioning.

C. Complicated grief was defined as when symptoms persist and seriously interrupt social and occupational activity.

D. The veteran/service member was able to display a clear understanding of the difference between complicated and uncomplicated bereavement, and was reinforced for this insight.

E. The veteran/service member has struggled to identify the difference between complicated and uncomplicated bereavement, and was provided with remedial information in this area.

12. Identify Complicated Bereavement Symptoms (12)

A. The veteran/service member was assisted in identifying symptoms that would lead him/her to believe that he/she was experiencing complicated bereavement.

B. The veteran/service member was able to identify several symptoms that indicate complicated bereavement, and he/she was assisted in processing these symptoms.

C. The veteran/service member does not identify significant symptoms that would indicate complicated bereavement, and he/she was assisted in processing this.

13. Educate about Stages of Grief (13)

A. The veteran/service member was educated regarding the stages of the grieving process.

B. The five stages of grief (denial, anger, bargaining, depression, and acceptance) were presented to the veteran/service member, with specific examples of how each occurs.

C. The veteran/service member was taught about how grief is not an all-or-none or stepwise progression.

D. The veteran/service member verbalized an increased understanding of the steps of the grieving process and was helped to identify the stages he/she has experienced personally.

E. The veteran/service member has struggled to understand the steps of the grieving process and was assisted in learning more about this as well as identifying his/her own current stage.

14. Identify Current Stage of Grief (14)

A. The veteran/service member was assisted in identifying the stages of grief that he/she has experienced and which stage he/she currently is working through.

B. Positive feedback was provided to the veteran/service member as he/she identified his/her current grief stage.

C. The veteran/service member struggled to identify the current grief stage and was provided with tentative feedback in this area.

15. Encourage Expression of Emotions to Support System (15)

A. The veteran/service member was encouraged to acknowledge and express his/her emotions to trustworthy friends and family.

B. The veteran/service member was encouraged to share his/her feelings of sadness and loss with trusted family members.

C. The veteran/service member has talked with family members about his/her feelings of sadness and loss, and his/her experience was processed within the session.

D. The veteran/service member has not utilized support from his/her friends and family and was redirected to do so.

16. Explore Anger Feelings (16)

A. The veteran's/service member's feelings of anger or guilt that surround the loss were explored as to their depth and causes.

B. The veteran/service member was supported as he/she verbalized feelings of anger and guilt focused on himself/herself that surround the grief experience of loss.

C. It was reflected to the veteran/service member that he/she has begun to resolve the feelings of anger and guilt, which will allow the grieving process to continue.

17. Assign Anger Management Material (17)

A. The veteran/service member was assigned to read material on anger management.

B. The veteran/service member was assigned to read *Anger: Handling a Powerful Emotion in a Healthy Way* (Chapman).

C. The veteran/service member was assigned to read *Of Course You're Angry* (Rossellini).

D. The veteran/service member was assigned to read *The Anger Control Workbook* (McKay).

E. The veteran/service member has read the assigned material on anger management, and key points were processed.

F. The veteran/service member has not read assigned material on anger management and was redirected to do so.

18. Encourage Acknowledgment of Guilt and Shame (18)

A. The veteran/service member was encouraged to acknowledge his/her feelings of guilt and shame.

B. The veteran/service member was asked to identify the unrealistic and unwarranted nature of the thoughts of guilt related to his/her loss.

C. The realistic sense of guilt related to the loss was reviewed and processed.

D. The veteran/service member was reinforced for his/her open acknowledgment of feelings of shame and guilt.

E. The veteran/service member has struggled to acknowledge any sense of shame or guilt and was encouraged to review these concepts.

19. Assign Journal of Automatic Thoughts (19)

A. The veteran/service member was assigned to keep a record of automatic thoughts associated with guilt feelings.

B. "Negative Thoughts Trigger Negative Feelings" from the *Adult Psychotherapy Homework Planner*, 2nd ed. (Jongsma) was assigned to the veteran/service member.

C. "Daily Record of Dysfunctional Thoughts" in *Cognitive Therapy of Depression* (Beck, Rush, Shaw, & Emery) was assigned to the veteran/service member.

D. The veteran/service member has kept a daily journal of dysfunctional thoughts, which was reviewed and processed, challenging guilty feelings to replace them with reality-based thoughts.

E. The veteran/service member has not kept a record of dysfunctional thoughts and was not directed to do so.

20. Conduct Behavioral Experiments (20)

A. The veteran/service member was encouraged to do "behavioral experiments" in which guilt-inducing automatic thoughts are treated as hypotheses/predictions and are tested against reality-based alternative hypotheses.

B. The veteran's/service member's automatic guilt-inducing thoughts were tested against his/her past, present, and/or future experiences.

C. The veteran/service member was assisted in processing the outcome of his/her behavioral experiences.

D. The veteran/service member was encouraged by his/her experience of the more reality-based hypotheses/predictions; this progress was reinforced.

E. The veteran/service member continues to focus on guilt-inducing automatic thoughts and was redirected toward the behavioral evidence of the more reality-based alternative hypotheses.

21. Reinforce Positive Self-Talk (21)

A. The veteran/service member was reinforced for any successful replacement of distorted negative thinking with positive, reality-based cognitive messages.

B. It was noted that the veteran/service member has been engaging in positive, reality-based thinking that has enhanced his/her self-confidence and increased adaptive action.

C. The veteran/service member was assigned to complete the "Positive Self-Talk" assignment from the *Adult Psychotherapy Homework Planner,* 2nd ed. (Jongsma).

D. The veteran/service member completed the homework assignment, and the content was processed within the session.

E. The veteran/service member has not completed the homework assignment and was reminded to do so.

22. Assign Reading Material on Shame (22)

A. The veteran/service member was assigned to read material on shame.

B. The veteran/service member was assigned to read *Shame and Grace* (Smedes).

C. The veteran/service member has read the assigned material on shame, and key points were discussed.

D. The veteran/service member has not read the assigned material on shame and was redirected to do so.

23. Normalize Grief Reactions (23)

A. The veteran's/service member's feelings and reaction to his/her loss were normalized.

B. The veteran/service member was educated about the common nature of symptoms developed during grief reactions.

C. The veteran/service member noted that his/her symptoms fit the pattern described as the normal and common pattern, and was reinforced for this insight.

D. The veteran/service member does not see his/her symptoms as being the typical pattern of grief reaction, and this was processed.

24. Emphasize Recovery and Growth (24)

A. A sense of recovery and growth was emphasized.

B. Use of "pathological" labels was minimized.

C. The veteran/service member was assisted in identifying how his/her focus is on recovery and growth rather than on pathology.

25. Educate about Differences within Culture (25)

A. The veteran/service member was taught how grief reactions differ between cultures.

B. The military was identified as a specific "culture" with its own expectations and patterns of grief reaction.

C. The veteran/service member was assisted in identifying how the military culture differs from civilian culture in grief reaction.

26. Conduct Empty-Chair Exercise (26)

A. An empty-chair exercise was conducted with the veteran/service member in which he/she focused on expressing to the fallen comrade what he/she never said while that comrade was present.

B. The veteran/service member was supported as he/she expressed many thoughts and feelings that had been suppressed while the comrade was present.

27. Write a Letter to Lost Comrade (27)

A. The veteran/service member was instructed to write a letter detailing those things he/she wishes he/she could have said to the fellow service member.

B. The veteran/service member was assigned "A Letter to a Lost Loved One" from the *Adult Psychotherapy Homework Planner*, 2nd ed. (Jongsma).

C. The veteran/service member completed the homework assignment, and the content was processed within the session.

D. The veteran/service member was assisted in processing his/her emotions related to the exercise in communicating to the lost comrade.

E. The veteran/service member has struggled to express his/her thoughts and emotions in regard to communication to a lost comrade and was redirected to do so.

28. Encourage Meeting with Coping Peer (28)

A. The veteran/service member was encouraged to meet with a current service member or veteran who has experienced the loss of a fellow comrade.

B. The veteran/service member was encouraged to inquire as to how the individual has dealt with his/her loss.

C. The veteran/service member has met with a service member or veteran who has experienced the loss of a fellow comrade, and his/her insights were reviewed.

D. The veteran/service member has not met with a current service member or veteran who has experienced the loss of a fellow comrade and was redirected to do so.

29. Reflect on Purpose in Life (29)

A. The veteran/service member was encouraged to use this opportunity to reflect on his/her purpose in life.

B. The veteran/service member was encouraged to identify what is important to him/her in life.

C. The veteran/service member was encouraged to honor his/her fallen comrade by making necessary changes in his/her life.

D. The veteran/service member has reflected on his/her life, purpose, and values, and this was processed within the session.

E. The veteran/service member has struggled to reflect on his/her life, purpose, and values, and was redirected to do so.

30. Utilize Spiritual Resources (30)

A. The veteran/service member was encouraged to meet with spiritual resources to assist in dealing with the loss.

B. The veteran/service member was encouraged to meet with a military chaplain or local clergy member to assist with dealing with the loss.

C. The veteran/service member has met with a clergy member, and his/her experience and progress were reviewed.

D. The veteran/service member has not met with the spiritual resources available and was redirected to do so.

31. Recommend Depression Self-Help Books (31)

A. Several self-help books on the topic of coping with depression were recommended to the veteran/service member.

B. The veteran/service member was directed to read *The Feeling Good Handbook* (Burns).

C. The veteran/service member was directed to read *Mind Over Mood* (Prentky & Padesky).

D. The veteran/service member has followed through with reading self-help books on depression and reported key ideas that were processed.

E. The veteran/service member reported that reading the assigned self-help books on depression has been beneficial and identified several coping techniques that he/she has implemented as a result of the reading.

F. The veteran/service member has not followed through with reading the self-help books that were recommended and was encouraged to do so.

32. Assign Reading Material on Grief and Loss (32)

A. The veteran/service member was assigned to read books on grief and loss.

B. The veteran/service member was assigned to read *When Will I Stop Hurting? Dealing With a Recent Death* (Kolf).

C. The veteran/service member was assigned to read *How Can It Be All Right When Everything Is All Wrong?* (Smedes).

D. The veteran/service member was assigned to read *Good Grief* (Westberg).

E. The veteran/service member was assigned to read *Getting Through the Night: Finding Your Way After Loss of a Loved One* (Price).

F. The veteran/service member has read the assigned material on grief and loss, and key points were processed.

G. The veteran/service member has not read the assigned material on grief and loss, and was redirected to do so.

33. Encourage Creation of a Memorial (33)

A. The veteran/service member was asked to collect and bring to a session various photos and other memorabilia related to the lost loved one.

B. The veteran/service member was asked to complete the "Creating a Memorial Collage" exercise from the *Adult Psychotherapy Homework Planner,* 2nd ed. (Jongsma) to facilitate expression and sharing of grief.

C. The veteran/service member was asked to create a memorial that honors the fallen comrade (i.e., plaque, drawing/painting, tattoo).

D. The veteran's/service member's memorial to the fallen comrade was reviewed, and important memories were identified and reinforced.

E. The veteran/service member has not worked on creating a memorial and was encouraged to give effort to this assignment soon.

BORDERLINE PERSONALITY

VETERAN/SERVICE MEMBER PRESENTATION

1. Emotional Reactivity (1)*

A. The veteran/service member described a history of extreme emotional reactivity when minor stresses occur in his/her life.

B. The veteran's/service member's emotional reactivity is usually quite short lived, as he/she returns to a calm state after demonstrating strong feelings of anger, anxiety, or depression.

C. The veteran's/service member's emotional lability has been reduced and he/she reported less frequent incidents of emotional reactivity.

2. Chaotic Interpersonal Relationships (2)

A. The veteran/service member has a pattern of intense, but chaotic, interpersonal relationships as he/she puts high expectations on others and is easily threatened that the relationship might be in jeopardy.

B. The veteran/service member has had many relationships that have ended because of the intense demands that he/she placed on the relationship.

C. The veteran/service member reported incidents that have occurred recently with friends, whereby he/she continued placing inappropriately intense demands on the relationship.

D. The veteran/service member has made progress in stabilizing his/her relationship with others by diminishing the degree of demands that he/she places on the relationship and reducing dependency on it.

3. Identity Disturbance (3)

A. The veteran/service member has a history of being confused as to who he/she is and what his/her goals are in life.

B. The veteran/service member has become very intense about questioning his/her identity.

C. The veteran/service member has become more assured about his/her identity and is less reactive to this issue.

D. The veteran/service member no longer questions his/her identity.

4. Impulsivity (4)

A. The veteran/service member described a history of engaging in impulsive behaviors that have the potential for producing harmful consequences for him/her.

B. The veteran/service member has engaged in impulsive behaviors that compromise his/her reputation with others.

C. The veteran/service member has established improved control over impulsivity and considers the consequences of his/her actions more deliberately before engaging in behavior.

---

*The numbers in parentheses correlate to the number of the Behavioral Definition statement in the companion chapter with the same title in *The Veterans and Active Duty Military Psychotherapy Treatment Planner* (Moore and Jongsma) by John Wiley & Sons, 2009.

5. Suicidal/Self-Mutilating Behavior (5)

A. The veteran/service member reported a history of suicidal gestures and/or threats.

B. The veteran/service member has engaged in self-mutilating behavior on several occasions.

C. The veteran/service member made a commitment to terminate suicidal gestures and threats.

D. The veteran/service member agreed to stop the pattern of self-mutilating behavior.

E. There have been no recent reports of occurrences of suicidal gestures, threats, or self-mutilating behavior.

6. Feelings of Emptiness (6)

A. The veteran/service member reported a chronic history of feeling empty and bored with life.

B. The veteran's/service member's frequent complaints of feeling bored and that life had no meaning had alienated him/her from others.

C. The veteran/service member has not complained recently about feeling empty or bored but appears to be more challenged and at peace with life.

7. Intense Anger Eruptions (7)

A. The veteran/service member frequently has eruptions of intense and inappropriate anger triggered by seemingly insignificant stressors.

B. The veteran/service member seems to live in a state of chronic anger and displeasure with others.

C. The veteran's/service member's eruptions of intense and inappropriate anger have diminished in their frequency and intensity.

D. The veteran/service member reported that there have been no incidents of recent eruptions of anger.

8. Feels Others Are Unfair (8)

A. The veteran/service member made frequent complaints about the unfair treatment he/she believes that others have given him/her.

B. The veteran/service member frequently verbalized distrust of others and questioned their motives.

C. The veteran/service member has demonstrated increased trust of others and has not complained about unfair treatment from them recently.

9. Black-or-White Thinking (9)

A. The veteran/service member demonstrated a pattern of analyzing issues in simple terms of right or wrong, black or white, trustworthy versus deceitful, without regard for extenuating circumstances and before considering the complexity of the situations.

B. The veteran's/service member's black-or-white thinking has caused him/her to be quite judgmental of others.

C. The veteran/service member finds it difficult to consider the complexity of situations but prefers to think in simple terms of right versus wrong.

D. The veteran/service member has shown some progress in allowing for the complexity of some situations and extenuating circumstances that might contribute to some other people's actions.

10. Abandonment Fears (10)

A. The veteran/service member described a history of becoming very anxious whenever there is any hint of abandonment present in an established relationship.

B. The veteran's/service member's hypersensitivity to abandonment has caused him/her to place excessive demands of loyalty and proof of commitment on relationships.

C. The veteran/service member has begun to acknowledge his/her fear of abandonment as being excessive and irrational.

D. Conflicts within a relationship have been reported by the veteran/service member, but he/she has not automatically assumed that abandonment will be the result.

11. Frequent Disciplinary Action (11)

A. The service member often receives disciplinary action for disruptive behavior.

B. The service member is at risk for demotion due to his/her disruptive behavior.

C. As treatment has progressed, the service member has become less disruptive in his/her behavior.

D. There have no incidents recently of disciplinary action against the service member.

12. Threats for Dishonorable Discharge (12)

A. The service member reports that he/she has been advised that he/she is at risk of being dishonorably discharged from the military.

B. The service member reports that his/her dishonorable discharge seems inevitable.

C. As treatment has progressed, the service member has become more stable in his/her behavior, and the threat of being dishonorably discharged has been decreased.

D. The service member is no longer under any threat of dishonorable discharge.

13. Personality Disorder Leading toward Military Separation (13)

A. The service member has had frequent visits to military behavioral professionals regarding personality disorder issues.

B. The service member has been identified as being at risk for being separated from the military due to his/her personality disorder concerns.

C. The service member is uncertain whether he/she can stay in the military due to personality disorder problems.

D. As treatment has progressed, the service member's behavior has stabilized, and his/her risk for being separated from the military has ended.

14. Failure to Function as a Team Member (14)

A. The service member indicated that his/her difficulties with interpersonal functioning have led to problems within his/her unit team.

B. The service member has been identified as not being a team player.

C. The service member's team members complained that he/she fails to function in a productive manner.

D. The service member has improved his/her functioning within the team.

INTERVENTIONS IMPLEMENTED

1. Assess Behavior, Affect, and Cognitions (1)*

A. The veteran's/service member's experience of distress and disability was assessed to identify targets of therapy.

B. The veteran's/service member's pattern of behaviors (e.g., parasuicidal acts, angry outbursts, overattachment) was assessed to help identify targets for therapy.

C. The veteran's/service member's affect was assessed, including emotional overreactions and painful emptiness, in regard to targets for therapy.

D. The veteran's/service member's cognitions were assessed, including biases such as dichotomous thinking, overgeneralization, and catastrophizing, to assist in identifying targets for therapy.

E. Specific target behaviors, affect, and thought patterns for therapy were identified.

2. Explore Childhood Abuse/Abandonment (2)

A. Experiences of childhood physical or emotional abuse, neglect, or abandonment were explored.

B. As the veteran/service member identified instances of abuse and neglect, the feelings surrounding these experiences were processed.

C. The veteran's/service member's experiences with perceived abandonment were highlighted and related to his/her current fears of this experience occurring in the present.

D. As the veteran's/service member's experience of abuse and abandonment in his/her childhood was processed, he/she denied any emotional impact of these experiences on himself/herself.

E. The veteran/service member denied any experience of abuse and abandonment in his/her childhood, and he/she was urged to talk about these types of concerns as he/she deems it necessary in the future.

3. Validate Distress and Difficulties (3)

A. The veteran's/service member's experience of distress and subsequent difficulties were validated as understandable, given his/her particular circumstances, thoughts, and feelings.

B. It was reflected to the veteran/service member that most people would experience the same distress and difficulties, given the same circumstances, thoughts, and feelings.

C. The veteran/service member was noted to accept the validation about his/her level of distress.

4. Orient to DBT (4)

A. The veteran/service member was oriented to the process of dialectical behavioral therapy (DBT).

B. The multiple facets of DBT were highlighted, including support, collaboration, challenge, problem solving, and skill building.

---

*The numbers in parentheses correlate to the number of the Therapeutic Intervention statement in the companion chapter with the same title in *The Veterans and Active Duty Military Psychotherapy Treatment Planner* (Moore and Jongsma) by John Wiley & Sons, 2009.

C. The biosocial view related to borderline personality disorder was emphasized, including the constitutional and social influences.

D. The concept of dialectics was reviewed with the veteran/service member.

E. Information from *Cognitive-Behavioral Treatment of Borderline Personality* (Linehan) was reviewed with the veteran/service member.

5. Assign Reading on Borderline Personality Disorder (5)

A. The veteran/service member was asked to read selected sections of books or manuals that reinforce therapeutic interventions.

B. Portions of *Skills Training Manual for Treating Borderline Personality Disorder* (Linehan) were assigned to the veteran/service member.

C. The veteran/service member has read assigned information from books or manuals and key concepts were reinforced.

D. The veteran/service member has not read assigned portions of books or manuals that reinforce therapeutic interventions and was redirected to do so.

6. Solicit Agreement for DBT (6)

A. An agreement was solicited from the veteran/service member to work collaboratively within the parameters of the DBT approach.

B. A written agreement was developed with the veteran/service member to work collaboratively within the parameters of the DBT approach.

C. The veteran/service member has agreed to work within the parameters of the DBT approach to overcome the behaviors, emotions, and cognitions that have been identified as causing problems in his/her life.

D. The veteran/service member was reinforced for his/her commitment to working within the DBT program.

E. The veteran/service member has not agreed to work within the DBT program.

7. Explore Self-Mutilating Behavior (7)

A. The veteran's/service member's history and nature of self-mutilating behavior were explored thoroughly.

B. The veteran/service member helped to recall a pattern of self-mutilating behavior that has dated back several years.

C. The veteran's/service member's self-mutilating behavior was identified as being associated with feelings of depression, fear, and anger as well as a lack of self-identity.

8. Assess Suicidal Behavior (8)

A. The veteran's/service member's history and current status regarding suicidal gestures were assessed.

B. The secondary gain associated with suicidal gestures was identified.

C. Triggers for suicidal thoughts were identified, and alternative responses to these trigger situations were proposed.

9. Arrange Hospitalization (9)

A. As the veteran/service member was judged to be harmful of self, arrangements were made for a voluntary psychiatric hospitalization.

B. As the veteran/service member refused a necessary psychiatric hospitalization, the proper steps were initiated to involuntarily hospitalize him/her.

C. The veteran/service member has been psychiatrically hospitalized.

D. Ongoing contact with the psychiatric hospital has been maintained in order to coordinate the most helpful treatment while in the hospital.

E. The "buddy watch" system was used to help manage the veteran's/service member's behavior.

10. Refer to Emergency Helpline (10)

A. The veteran/service member was provided with an emergency helpline telephone number that is available 24 hours a day.

B. A contact person within the veteran's/service member's support system was identified as being available 24 hours a day.

C. Positive feedback was provided as the veteran/service member promised to utilize the emergency contacts rather than engaging in any self-harm behaviors.

D. The veteran/service member has not used the emergency contacts in place of engaging in self-harm behaviors and was reminded about this useful resource.

11. Interpret Self-Mutilating Behavior (11)

A. The veteran's/service member's self-mutilation was interpreted as an expression of the rage and helplessness that could not be expressed as a child victim of emotional abandonment and abuse.

B. The veteran/service member accepted the interpretation of his/her self-mutilation and more directly expressed his/her feelings of hurt and anger associated with childhood abuse experiences.

C. The veteran/service member rejected the interpretation of self-mutilating behavior as an expression of rage associated with childhood abandonment or neglect experiences.

D. An expectation that the veteran/service member will be able to control his/her urge for self-mutilation was expressed.

12. Elicit No-Suicide Contract (12)

A. A promise was elicited from the veteran/service member that he/she will initiate contact with the therapist or an emergency helpline if the suicidal urge becomes strong and before any self-injurious behavior is enacted.

B. The veteran/service member was reinforced as he/she promised to terminate self-mutilation behavior and to contact emergency personnel if urges for such behavior arise.

C. The veteran/service member has followed through on the non–self-harm contract by contacting emergency service personnel rather than enacting any suicidal gestures or self-mutilating behavior; he/she was reinforced for this healthy use of support.

D. The veteran's/service member's potential for suicide was consistently assessed despite the suicide prevention contract.

13. Resolve Therapy-Interfering Behaviors (13)

A. The veteran's/service member's pattern of therapy-interfering behavior, such as missing appointments, noncompliance, and abruptly leaving therapy, was consistently monitored.

B. The veteran/service member was confronted for his/her therapy-interfering behaviors.

C. The clinician took appropriate responsibility for his/her own therapy-interfering behaviors.

D. Therapy-interfering behaviors were problem-solved.

14. Refer for Medication Evaluation (14)

A. The veteran/service member was assessed in regard to the need for psychotropic medication.

B. The veteran/service member was referred to a physician to be evaluated for psychotropic medications to stabilize his/her mood.

C. The veteran/service member has cooperated with a referral to a physician and has attended the evaluation for psychotropic medications.

D. The veteran/service member has refused to attend a physician evaluation for psychotropic medications and was redirected to do so.

15. Monitor Medication Compliance (15)

A. The veteran's/service member's compliance with prescribed medications was monitored, and effectiveness of the medication on his/her level of functioning was noted.

B. The veteran/service member reported that the medication has been beneficial in stabilizing his/her mood, and he/she was encouraged to continue its use.

C. The veteran/service member reported that the medication has not been beneficial in stabilizing his/her mood; this was reported to the prescribing clinician.

D. The veteran/service member reported side effects of the medication that he/she found intolerable; these side effects were reported to the physician.

16. Use Strategies to Manage Maladaptive Behaviors, Thoughts, and Feelings (16)

A. Validation, dialectical strategies, and problem-solving strategies were used to help the veteran/service member manage, reduce, or stabilize maladaptive behaviors, thoughts, and feelings.

B. Therapeutic techniques as described in *Cognitive-Behavioral Treatment of Borderline Personality* (Linehan) were used to help the veteran/service member manage his/her symptoms.

C. Validation was consistently used to help the veteran/service member manage, reduce, and stabilize maladaptive behaviors, thoughts, and feelings.

D. Dialectical strategies, such as metaphor or devil's advocacy, were used to help the veteran/service member manage, reduce, or stabilize maladaptive behaviors, thoughts, and feelings.

E. Problem-solving strategies, such as behavioral analysis, cognitive restructuring, skills training, and exposure, were used to help the veteran/service member manage, reduce, or stabilize his/her maladaptive behaviors, thoughts, and feelings.

F. It was noted that the veteran/service member has decreased maladaptive behaviors (e.g., angry outbursts, binge drinking, abusive relationships, high-risk sex, uncontrolled spending), maladaptive thought patterns (e.g., all-or-nothing thinking, catastrophizing, personalizing), and maladaptive feelings (e.g., rage, hopelessness, abandonment).

17. Conduct Skills Training (17)

A. Group skills training was used to teach the veteran/service member responses to identified problem behaviors.

B. Individual skills training was used to teach the veteran/service member responses to identified behavioral problem patterns.

C. The veteran/service member was taught assertiveness for use in abusive relationships.

D. The veteran/service member was taught cognitive strategies for identifying and controlling financial, sexual, and other impulsivity.

E. The veteran/service member has participated in skills training for specific behavioral problems, and the benefits of this treatment was reviewed.

F. The veteran/service member has not participated in group skills training and was redirected to do so.

18. Teach Skills for Regular Use (18)

A. Behavioral strategies were taught to the veteran/service member via instruction, modeling, and advising.

B. Role-playing and exposure exercises were used to strengthen the veteran's/service member's use of behavioral strategies.

C. The veteran/service member was provided with regular homework assignments to help incorporate the behavioral strategies into his/her everyday life.

D. The veteran/service member was reinforced for his/her regular use and understanding of behavioral strategies.

E. The veteran/service member has struggled to understand the behavioral strategies and was provided with remedial information in this area.

19. Conduct Trauma Work (19)

A. As the veteran's/service member's adaptive behavior patterns have been evident, work on remembering and accepting the facts of previous trauma was initiated.

B. The veteran/service member was assisted in using his/her new adaptive behavior patterns and emotional regulation skills to reduce denial and increase insight into the effects of previous trauma.

C. The veteran/service member was helped to reduce maladaptive emotional and/or behavioral responses to trauma-related stimuli through the regular use of adaptive behavioral patterns and emotional skills.

D. The veteran/service member was assisted in tolerating the distress of remembering and accepting the facts of previous trauma and in reducing self-blame.

E. The veteran/service member has been noted to be successful in using his/her adaptive behavioral patterns and emotional regulation skills in managing the effects of previous trauma.

F. The veteran/service member has become more emotionally disregulated due to the trauma work and was redirected to use behavioral and emotional regulation skills.

20. Explore Schema and Self-Talk (20)

A. The veteran/service member was assisted in exploring how his/her schema and self-talk mediate his/her trauma-related and other fears.

B. "Negative Thoughts Trigger Negative Feelings" from the *Adult Psychotherapy Homework Planner*, 2nd ed. (Jongsma), was assigned to the veteran/service member.

C. The veteran/service member completed the homework assignment, and the content was processed within the session.

D. The veteran's/service member's distorted schema and self-talk were reviewed.

E. The veteran/service member was reinforced for his/her insight into his/her self-talk and schema that support his/her trauma-related and other fears.

F. The veteran/service member struggled to develop insight into his/her own self-talk and schema and was provided with tentative examples of these concepts.

21. Assign Exercises on Self-Talk (21)

A. The veteran/service member was assigned homework exercises in which he/she identifies fearful self-talk and creates reality-based alternatives.

B. The veteran/service member was assigned the homework exercise "Journal and Replace Self-Defeating Thoughts" from the *Adult Psychotherapy Homework Planner*, 2nd ed. (Jongsma).

C. The veteran/service member was directed to complete the "Daily Record of Dysfunctional Thoughts" from *Cognitive-Behavioral Therapy of Depression* (Beck, Rush, Shaw, and Emery).

D. The veteran's/service member's replacement of fearful self-talk with reality-based alternatives was critiqued.

E. The veteran/service member was reinforced for his/her successes at replacing fearful self-talk with reality-based alternatives.

22. Reinforce Positive Self-Talk (22)

A. The veteran/service member was reinforced for implementing positive, realistic self-talk that enhances self-confidence and increases adaptive action.

B. The veteran/service member noted several instances from his/her daily life that reflected the implementation of positive self-talk, and these successful experiences were reinforced.

23. Develop Hierarchy of Triggers (23)

A. The veteran/service member was directed to develop a hierarchy of feared and avoided trauma-related stimuli.

B. The veteran/service member was helped to list many of the feared and avoided trauma-related stimuli.

C. The veteran/service member was assisted in developing a hierarchy of feared and avoided trauma-related stimuli.

D. The veteran's/service member's journaling was used to assist in developing a hierarchy of feared and avoided trauma-related stimuli.

24. Direct Imaginal Exposure (24)

A. Imaginal exposure was directed by having the veteran/service member describe a chosen traumatic experience at an increasing, but self-chosen, level of detail.

B. Cognitive restructuring techniques were integrated with the exposure and repeated until the associated anxiety regarding childhood trauma was reduced and stabilized.

C. The session was recorded and provided to the veteran/service member to listen to between sessions.

D. "Share the Painful Memory" from the *Adult Psychotherapy Homework Planner*, 2nd ed. (Jongsma), was assigned to help direct the veteran's/service member's imaginal exposure.

E. Techniques from *Posttraumatic Stress Disorder* (Resick and Calhoun) were used to direct the veteran's/service member's imaginal exposure.

F. The veteran's/service member's progress was reviewed, reinforced, and problem-solved.

25. Assign Homework on Exposure (25)

A. The veteran/service member was assigned homework exercises to perform exposure to feared stimuli and record his/her experience.

B. The veteran/service member was directed to listen to the taped exposure session to consolidate his/her skills for exposure to feared stimuli.

C. The veteran/service member was assigned situational exposures homework from *Posttraumatic Stress Disorder* (Resick and Calhoun).

D. The veteran's/service member's use of exposure techniques was reviewed and reinforced.

E. The veteran/service member has struggled in his/her implementations of exposure techniques and was provided with corrective feedback.

F. The veteran/service member has not attempted to use the exposure techniques and was redirected to do so.

26. Encourage Trust in Own Evaluations (26)

A. The veteran/service member was encouraged to value, believe, and trust in his/her evaluations of himself/herself, others, and situations.

B. The veteran/service member was encouraged to examine situations in a nondefensive manner, independent of other's opinions.

C. The veteran/service member was encouraged to build self-reliance through trusting his/her own evaluations.

D. The veteran/service member was reinforced for his/her value, belief, and trust in his/her own evaluations of himself/herself, others, and situations.

E. The veteran/service member was redirected when he/she tended to devalue, disbelieve, and distrust his/her own evaluations.

27. Encourage Positive Experiences (27)

A. The veteran/service member was encouraged to facilitate his/her personal growth by choosing experiences that strengthen self-awareness, personal values, and appreciation of life.

B. The veteran/service member was encouraged to use spiritual practices and other relative life experiences to help increase his/her positive experiences.

28. Teach Self-Control Strategies (28)

A. The veteran/service member was taught mediational and self-control strategies to delay gratification and reduce impulsivity.

B. The veteran/service member was instructed to use a "stop, think, react" technique as a way to decrease his/her impulsive acting out.

C. The veteran/service member demonstrated an understanding of the concepts related to self-control strategies that have been taught, and found this helpful to control impulses.

D. The veteran/service member has not adequately learned the concepts related to self-control strategies and was provided with additional examples.

29. Review Use of Thinking before Action (29)

A. The veteran's/service member's use of the "stop, listen, and think" plan was reviewed.

B. The veteran/service member was reinforced for his/her use of the "stop, listen, and think" plan.

C. The veteran's/service member's problems with utilizing the "stop, listen, and think" plan were reviewed.

D. The veteran/service member was assisted in identifying the positive consequences that come from using the "stop, listen, and think" plan.

30. Teach Problem-Solving Strategies (30)

A. The veteran/service member was taught problem-solving strategies involving several concrete steps.

B. The veteran/service member was taught to define a problem, generate options for addressing it, evaluate options, implement a plan, and reevaluate/refine the plan.

C. The veteran/service member was assigned "Plan before Acting" from the *Adult Psychotherapy Homework Planner*, 2nd ed. (Jongsma).

D. The veteran/service member completed the homework assignment and the content was processed within the session.

E. The veteran/service member was reinforced for his/her use of problem-solving strategies.

F. The veteran/service member has not used problem-solving strategies and was redirected to use these helpful techniques.

31. Explore Intent to Remain in the Military (31)

A. The service member was asked if it was his/her intent to remain in the military.

B. The service member was engaged in discussion about whether remaining in the military is appropriate for him/her.

C. The service member has decided to leave the military, and this decision was accepted.

D. The service member remains uncertain about whether he/she should stay in the military and was assisted in developing a greater understanding of this option.

E. The service member has decided to remain in the military, and this decision was accepted.

32. Discuss Implications of Discharge (32)

A. The implications of discharge from the military based on a personality disorder were discussed.

B. The service member was able to identify both positive and negative aspects of possible discharge from the military due to a personality disorder.

BRIEF REACTIVE PSYCHOTIC EPISODE

VETERAN/SERVICE MEMBER PRESENTATION

1. Rapid Onset of Sensory Hallucinations (1)[*]

A. The veteran/service member has experienced sensory hallucinations after a marked stressor.

B. The veteran/service member has experienced auditory, visual, olfactory, gustatory, or somatic hallucinations.

C. The veteran's/service member's onset of sensory hallucinations has been rapid, subsequent to his/her experiencing severe stressors.

D. The veteran's/service member's hallucinations have diminished in frequency and intensity.

E. The veteran/service member reported no longer experiencing sensory hallucinations.

2. Rapid Onset of Bizarre Thought Content (2)

A. The veteran/service member has displayed a rapid onset of bizarre thought content, or erotomania.

B. The veteran/service member has displayed delusions of persecution, control, infidelity, or jealousy.

C. The veteran/service member has displayed delusions of nihilism, grandiosity, or reference.

D. The veteran's/service member's delusional thoughts have diminished in frequency and intensity.

E. The veteran/service member no longer experiences delusional thoughts.

3. Illogical Thought/Speech (3)

A. The veteran's/service member's speech and thought patterns are incoherent and illogical.

B. The veteran/service member demonstrated loose association of ideas and vague speech.

C. The veteran's/service member's speech and thought patterns display derailment and flight of ideas.

D. The veteran's/service member's speech and thought patterns displayed neologisms and echolalia.

E. The veteran's/service member's illogical thought and speech have become less frequent.

F. The veteran/service member no longer displays evidence of illogical form of thought and speech.

4. Strange and Disorganized Behavior (4)

A. The veteran/service member displayed strange and disorganized behavior.

B. The veteran/service member displays a pattern of perseveration.

C. The veteran/service member displays inappropriate and odd dress.

---

[*]The numbers in parentheses correlate to the number of the Behavioral Definition statement in the companion chapter with the same title in *The Veterans and Active Duty Military Psychotherapy Treatment Planner* (Moore and Jongsma) by John Wiley & Sons, 2009.

D. The veteran/service member displays uncharacteristic disrespect to superiors.

E. The veteran/service member displays increased risky behavior.

F. As treatment has progressed, the veteran/service member displays decreased frequency and intensity of strange and disorganized behavior.

G. The veteran/service member no longer experiences strange and disorganized behavior.

5. Psychomotor Abnormalities (5)

A. The veteran/service member demonstrated a marked decrease in reactivity to his/her environment.

B. The veteran/service member demonstrated various catatonic patterns, such as stupor, rigidity, posturing, negativism, and excitement.

C. The veteran/service member displayed unusual mannerisms or grimacing.

D. The veteran's/service member's psychomotor abnormalities have diminished, and his/her pattern of relating has become more typical and less alienating.

6. Emotional Agitation (6)

A. The veteran/service member displays a high degree of irritability and unpredictability in his/her actions.

B. The veteran/service member displays agitation through anger outbursts and impulsive, physical acting out.

C. The veteran/service member is difficult to approach due to his/her extreme agitation.

D. As treatment has progressed, the veteran/service member has decreased his/her level of agitation and is less irritable, angry, unpredictable, and impulsive.

7. Social Withdrawal/Isolation (7)

A. The veteran/service member has been withdrawn from involvement with the external world and has been preoccupied with egocentric ideas and fantasies.

B. The veteran/service member has shown a slight improvement in his/her ability to demonstrate relationship skills.

C. The veteran/service member has shown an interest in relating to others in a more appropriate manner.

8. Diminished Volition (8)

A. The veteran/service member gave evidence of inadequate interest, drive, or ability to follow a course of action to its logical conclusion.

B. The veteran/service member has demonstrated pronounced ambivalence or cessation of goal-directed activity.

C. The veteran/service member has shown improvement in volitional behavior and has become more goal directed in his/her actions.

INTERVENTIONS IMPLEMENTED

1. Demonstrate Empathy and Understanding (1)[*]

A. The veteran/service member was shown empathy and understanding through a calm, nurturing manner, good eye contact, and active listening.

B. The veteran/service member responded to calm acceptance by beginning to describe his/her psychotic symptoms.

C. The veteran/service member remained agitated, tense, and preoccupied with his/her own internal stimuli, despite the use of warm acceptance.

2. Assess Thought Disorder Severity (2)

A. The severity of the veteran's/service member's thought disorder, history, and type of symptoms was assessed through clinical interview.

B. Psychological testing was used to assess the veteran's/service member's psychotic process.

C. The veteran/service member was assessed as displaying a significant and pervasive psychotic disorder.

D. The veteran's/service member's psychotic disorder was assessed as mild, and he/she demonstrated some capability to remain reality based and to relate appropriately.

3. Assess Psychosis History (3)

A. The history of the veteran's/service member's illness revealed that his/her symptom pattern is chronic with prodromal elements.

B. The veteran's/service member's psychosis is judged to be reactive and acute.

4. Determine Etiology of Marked Stressor (4)

A. The source of the marked stressor was investigated.

B. The source of the intense stressor was determined to be related to a combat situation.

C. The source of the marked stressor was determined to be interpersonal in nature.

D. The source of the stressor was determined to be environmental in nature.

E. Attempts were made to remove the stressor contributing to the psychosis.

5. Assess Substance Abuse Contribution to Psychosis (5)

A. The veteran's/service member's experience of substance use was assessed.

B. The veteran/service member was assessed in regard to his/her use of alcohol, amphetamines, caffeine, marijuana, ephedrine, and other substances.

C. The veteran's/service member's use of substances was determined to be significant related to his/her current psychotic episode.

D. The veteran's/service member's use of substances was deemed not to be an influence to his/her current psychotic episode.

6. Explore History of Psychotic Episodes (6)

A. The veteran's/service member's history of bizarre behavior was explored.

---

[*]The numbers in parentheses correlate to the number of the Therapeutic Intervention statement in the companion chapter with the same title in *The Veterans and Active Duty Military Psychotherapy Treatment Planner* (Moore and Jongsma) by John Wiley & Sons, 2009.

B. An attempt was made to determine if the veteran/service member has experienced prior psychotic episodes.

C. Ancillary information was requested regarding the veteran's/service member's past behavior.

D. The veteran/service member was determined to have had prior psychotic episodes.

E. The veteran/service member was determined not to have had any previous psychotic episodes.

7. Explain Nature of Psychotic Illness (7)

A. The nature of the veteran's/service member's psychotic illness was explained as a biological or genetic vulnerability interacting with the environment and life events.

B. The nature of the veteran's/service member's genetic vulnerability or predisposition to psychosis (diathesis) was investigated and reviewed.

C. The nature of the veteran's/service member's environment and life events (stressors) were reviewed.

D. The interaction of the diathesis and stressors were reviewed and explained.

8. Educate about Future Military Service Options (8)

A. The veteran/service member was educated regarding future military service options as they relate to his/her brief psychotic illness.

B. The veteran/service member was advised about how his/her brief psychotic illness may affect his/her future military service.

9. Arrange Medication Evaluation (9)

A. The veteran/service member was referred for an immediate evaluation for psychotropic medication.

B. Arrangements were made for the administration of appropriate psychotropic medications through a physician.

C. The veteran/service member has attended an appointment with a physician and has accepted the need for psychotropic medication.

D. Although the veteran/service member seems confused as to the need for medication, he/she is cooperative with taking it as directed.

E. The veteran/service member has not attended the evaluation regarding the need for psychotropic medication and was redirected to do so.

10. Educate about Psychotropic Medications (10)

A. The veteran/service member was taught about the indications for and the expected benefits of psychotropic medications.

B. As the veteran's/service member's psychotropic medications were reviewed, he/she displayed an understanding about the indications for and expected benefits of the medications.

C. The veteran/service member displayed a lack of understanding of the indications for and expected benefits of psychotropic medications and was provided with additional information and feedback regarding his/her medications.

11. Monitor Medication Compliance (11)

A. The veteran/service member is taking his/her antipsychotic medication consistently but only under supervision.

B. The veteran/service member has been taking his/her antipsychotic medication consistently without supervision.

C. The veteran/service member was reinforced for taking medication consistently, and the need to continue to do so was stressed.

D. The effectiveness and side effects of the veteran's/service member's medications were monitored.

E. The veteran/service member is not at all consistent about taking his/her psychotropic medications, and more supervision of this is necessary.

12. Reinforce Continued Medication Use (12)

A. The veteran/service member was monitored in regard to his/her continued psychotropic medication use.

B. The veteran/service member was encouraged to continue to use his/her psychotropic medications as prescribed.

C. The veteran/service member was reinforced for his/her appropriate use of psychotropic medication.

13. Confront Illogical Thoughts/Speech (13)

A. The veteran's/service member's illogical thinking and speech were gently confronted, and attempts were made to refocus the thinking toward a stronger reality basis.

B. The veteran/service member responded positively to the gentle confrontation of his/her illogical thoughts and speech and is speaking more logically and coherently.

C. As the veteran/service member has taken his/her antipsychotic medication more consistently, he/she is demonstrating more logical, coherent speech; this progress was encouraged.

14. Assist with Identification of Stimuli Source (14)

A. The veteran/service member was assisted in identifying the source of his/her stimuli.

B. The veteran/service member was assisted in identifying stimuli that are from internal sources.

C. The veteran/service member was assisted in identifying stimuli that are from external sources.

D. The veteran/service member was reinforced for his/her appropriate identification of the internal/external sources of stimuli.

E. The veteran/service member has struggled to identify and differentiate between internal and external sources of stimuli and was provided with additional feedback in this area.

15. Provide Social interactions (15)

A. The veteran/service member was provided with opportunities for rewarding and nonthreatening social interaction.

B. The veteran/service member has engaged in rewarding nonthreatening social interactions, and his/her experiences were reviewed and processed.

C. The veteran/service member has failed to utilize rewarding and nonthreatening social interactions and was reminded to do so.

16. Reward Social Interaction (16)

A. The veteran/service member was provided with consistent rewards and encouragement for positive social interactions.

B. The veteran/service member has increased his/her positive social interactions, and the benefits of this were noted.

C. The veteran/service member was encouraged to monitor and increase his/her positive social interactions.

17. Provide Reassurance for Failed Social Interactions (17)

A. The veteran/service member has experienced failed social interactions due to his/her psychosis symptoms; these interactions were processed.

B. The veteran/service member was provided with empathy in regard to his/her failed social interactions.

C. The veteran/service member was provided with reassurance about his/her failed social interactions.

18. Confront Illogical Thinking and Speech (18)

A. The veteran's/service member's illogical thinking and speech was slowly and gently confronted.

B. Redirection for the veteran's/service member's illogical thinking and speech was provided in a tentative manner.

C. The veteran/service member was reinforced for his/her logical and goal-directed thinking.

D. Role-playing and cognitive-behavioral techniques were used to reinforce logical and goal directed thinking.

19. Explore Feelings Regarding Stressors (19)

A. The veteran/service member was encouraged to share his/her feelings and needs associated with stressors present in his/her environment.

B. The veteran/service member was supported as he/she shared feelings of fear, helplessness, and confusion associated with external stressors.

C. The veteran/service member was reinforced as he/she identified his/her basic unmet needs that contribute to the irrational thoughts.

D. The veteran/service member was unable to articulate his/her feelings associated with the stressful environment; possible feelings were presented to him/her in a tentative manner.

20. Restructure Irrational Beliefs (20)

A. As the veteran/service member verbalized irrational beliefs, illogical thoughts, and perceptual disturbances, reality-based evidence was reviewed in an attempt to get the veteran/service member to restructure his/her irrational thoughts.

B. The veteran/service member was able to comprehend the reality-based evidence and modify his/her irrational beliefs; he/she was reinforced for this progress.

C. The veteran's/service member's psychotic process prohibited him/her from accepting the reality-based evidence that would modify his/her irrational beliefs.

21. **Educate Family Members (21)**

A. A family session was held to educate the family and significant others regarding the veteran's/service member's illness, treatment, and prognosis.

B. Support was provided as family members expressed their positive support of the veteran/service member and a more accurate understanding of his/her severe and persistent mental illness.

C. Family members were not understanding or willing to provide support to the veteran/service member in spite of his/her persistent mental illness; they were encouraged to provide this support.

22. **Assist Family in Managing Strong Expressed Emotions (22)**

A. The family members were assisted in identifying the strong expressed emotions that the veteran/service member displays.

B. The etiology of the veteran's/service member's strong expressed emotions was reviewed.

C. The family members were assisted in keeping strong expressed emotions from interfering with the veteran's/service member's progress.

23. **Teach Double-Bind Avoidance (23)**

A. Family members were taught the meaning of giving double-binding messages to the veteran/service member and that avoidance of this type of communication is important to reduce the veteran's/service member's feelings of stress and anxiety.

B. Family members were reinforced as they displayed openness to understanding the role of double-binding messages and committed themselves to more direct and honest communication.

C. Family members denied engaging in any double-binding messages and seemed defensive regarding any acknowledgment of this type of communication; they were urged to watch for this type of message.

24. **Explore Family Members' Feelings (24)**

A. Family members were encouraged to share their feelings of frustration, guilt, fear, or depression surrounding the veteran's/service member's mental illness and behavior problems.

B. Active listening was used as family members shared their feelings of helplessness, embarrassment, and frustration surrounding the veteran's/service member's behavior.

C. Although family members had been feeling frustrated and helpless at times, they also expressed feelings of empathy and support for the veteran/service member; their honesty was reinforced.

D. Family members were rather guarded about their emotions related to the veteran's/service member's mental illness and behavior problems; common emotions experienced by family members were presented to them.

25. **Assist Family in Finding Personal Outlets (25)**

A. Family members were assisted in finding personal outlets that prevent burnout.

B. Family members were referred to support groups to assist in preventing burnout.

C. Family members were directed to utilize hobbies to relieve stress.

D. Family members were encouraged to engage in advocacy tasks.

26. Initiate Review of Fitness for Duty (26)

A. The process of a medical review of the veteran's/service member's fitness for duty was reviewed.

B. The medical review of the veteran's/service member's fitness for duty was completed, and he/she will be maintained in the active military.

C. A review for the veteran's/service member's fitness for duty has been completed, and he/she will not remain in active military duty.

27. Assist in Acceptance of Review Board Determination (27)

A. The veteran/service member has been reviewed for military service, and the determination has been provided that he/she is not fit for military service due to his/her psychiatric condition.

B. The veteran/service member was assisted in processing his/her reactions to the review board's decision.

C. The veteran/service member was supported for his/her acceptance of the determination of the Medical Review Board.

D. The veteran/service member has had great difficulty accepting the determination of the Medical Review Board and was provided with additional support and direction in this area.

28. Explore Vocational and Living Options (28)

A. The veteran/service member was assisted in exploring vocational options as a civilian.

B. The veteran/service member was assisted in exploring living options as a civilian.

C. The veteran/service member was reinforced for his/her healthy approach to vocational living options.

D. The veteran/service member has struggled to identify any vocational or living options that may assist his/her functioning and was provided with remedial feedback in this area.

29. Refer for Vocational Rehabilitation Services (29)

A. The veteran/service member was referred for vocational rehabilitation services.

B. The veteran/service member has engaged in vocational rehabilitation services and his/her experience was processed.

C. The veteran/service member did not engage in vocational rehabilitation services and was urged to do so.

30. Assess Ability to Manage Activities of Daily Living (30)

A. The veteran/service member was assessed for his/her progress and overall ability in managing activities of daily living (ADLs).

B. The veteran/service member was assessed for tasks such as paying bills.

C. The veteran/service member was assessed in regard to his/her ability to complete household tasks, such as cooking and cleaning.

D. The veteran/service member was assessed in regard to his/her ability to complete basic hygiene needs.

E. The veteran/service member was noted to have functional abilities in regard to ADLs, and this was reflected to him/her.

F. The veteran/service member was noted to have significant deficiencies in his/her ADLs, and this was reflected to him/her.

31. Ensure Attendance at Scheduled Follow-up Appointments (31)

A. The veteran/service member was reminded about his/her scheduled follow-up appointments for psychiatric, case management, psychotherapy, and medical services.

B. The veteran/service member was directed to attend scheduled follow-up appointments.

C. The veteran/service member was assisted in attendance at scheduled follow-up appointments.

D. The veteran/service member was reinforced for his/her regular involvement in follow-up appointments.

E. The veteran/service member has not maintained his/her involvement in typical follow-up appointments and was redirected to do so.

CHRONIC PAIN AFTER INJURY

VETERAN/SERVICE MEMBER PRESENTATION

1. Injury-Related Pain (1)*

A. The veteran/service member has experienced chronic injury-related pain that is present most days of the week.

B. The veteran/service member has experienced a pain beyond that which would be expected through the normal healing process, and it has significantly limited his/her physical activities.

C. The veteran/service member has not discovered ways to manage or decrease his/her pain effectively.

D. The veteran/service member reported that the pain management strategies have helped to reduce his/her preoccupation with his/her injury-related pain.

E. The veteran/service member has increased involvement in physical activities as he/she has acquired pain management skills.

2. Pain Interrupts Concentration (2)

A. The veteran/service member reported pain intruding on his/her ability to concentrate.

B. Due to the injury-related pain, the veteran/service member has difficulty concentrating and paying attention to things of low interest, even though they may be important.

C. The veteran's/service member's lack of ability to concentrate has resulted in his/her not comprehending important details.

D. The veteran's/service member's ability to concentrate seems to have increased as he/she has reported better management of his/her pain.

3. Grimacing (3)

A. The veteran/service member displays grimacing expressions when attempting to move about.

B. The veteran/service member displays pain-related facial expressions when moving around.

C. As the veteran/service member has improved his/her management of the injury-related pain, his/her grimacing has decreased.

4. Unable to Fully Participate in Military Training (4)

A. The service member reports difficulty participating in military training.

B. The service member has difficulties with specific facets of military training (e.g., wearing body armor, riding in military vehicles for extended periods, performing physically strenuous routine) due to his/her pain.

C. The service member has significantly decreased or stopped his/her activities related to his/her military training and performance due to pain.

---

*The numbers in parentheses correlate to the number of the Behavioral Definition statement in the companion chapter with the same title in *The Veterans and Active Duty Military Psychotherapy Treatment Planner* (Moore and Jongsma) by John Wiley & Sons, 2009.

D. As the service member has learned to regulate pain more effectively, normal activities have been resumed.

E. The service member has returned to full participation in military training and exercises.

5. Lateness/Absence (5)

A. The service member has repeatedly reported late for accountability formations due to the severity of pain.

B. The veteran/service member reports missing work due to the severity of pain.

C. The veteran/service member has received official sanction due to his/her repeated lateness or absence.

D. As treatment has progressed, the veteran/service member has attended work on a more regular basis.

E. As treatment has progressed, the service member has been more regularly on time for accountability formations.

6. Pain Medication Use (6)

A. The veteran/service member reported that he/she has become heavily reliant on pain medication but that in spite of this dependence, he/she experiences little pain relief.

B. The veteran/service member has increased his/her pain medication use beyond the prescription level in an attempt to obtain relief.

C. The veteran/service member has become dependent on the use of medication and may be physiologically addicted.

D. The veteran/service member has acknowledged his/her overuse of medication and has begun to reduce this dependency and utilize other pain management techniques.

E. The veteran/service member has terminated the use of pain medication that was offering little benefit and has found more adaptive ways to regulate pain.

7. Dependent on Narcotic Pain Relievers (7)

A. The veteran/service member acknowledges that he/she has become addicted to narcotic pain relievers as a result of trying to cover the chronic pain.

B. In spite of the fact that the veteran/service member has been using narcotic pain relievers beyond the level prescribed, he/she is not experiencing significant relief from them.

C. The veteran/service member has begun to detoxify from his/her narcotic addiction under the supervision of medical personnel.

D. The veteran/service member describes withdrawal symptoms experienced as he/she is terminating the abuse of narcotic pain relievers.

E. The veteran/service member has successfully withdrawn from narcotic pain relievers and is coping with the pain with more constructive means.

8. Alcohol/Drug Use (8)

A. The veteran/service member reported that he/she has become heavily reliant on alcohol and/or drug use, but that in spite of this dependence, he/she experiences little pain relief.

B. The veteran/service member has increased his/her drug use beyond the prescription level in an attempt to obtain relief.

C. The veteran/service member has become dependent on the use of alcohol and illicit drugs and may be physiologically addicted.

D. The veteran/service member has acknowledged his/her overuse of alcohol and illicit drugs and has begun to reduce this dependency and utilize other pain management techniques.

E. The veteran/service member has terminated the use of alcohol and illicit drugs that were offering little benefit and has found more adaptive ways to regulate pain.

9. Pain Dominates Conversations (9)

A. The veteran/service member frequently talks about the pain and his/her inability to control it.

B. Friends, family, and work associates have indicated concern that the veteran/service member is overly preoccupied with his/her pain-related issues.

C. As treatment has progressed, the veteran/service member has begun talking about a variety of topics rather than just focusing on his/her pain.

10. Physical Limitation Profiles (10)

A. The service member reports being repeatedly placed on physical limitation profiles by military healthcare providers.

B. The service member is concerned about his/her military status due to being placed on physical limitation profiles by military healthcare providers.

C. As treatment has progressed, the service member has been able to manage his/her pain better, and physical limitation profiles are no longer necessary.

D. The service member has become more at ease with being on a physical limitation profile.

11. Potential Medical Separation (11)

A. The service member reports that he/she is at risk for a medical separation from the service.

B. The service member reports a desire to separate from the military.

C. The service member has specific plans to separate from the military.

D. The veteran indicated that he/she separated from the military because of his/her constant pain.

E. As treatment has progressed, the service member reports being more at ease with remaining in the military.

F. The service member has made a final decision as to his/her military status.

INTERVENTIONS IMPLEMENTED

1. Gather Pain History (1)*

A. A history of the veteran's/service member's experience of chronic pain and his/her associated medical conditions was gathered.

B. The duration and severity of the pain were assessed.

C. The limitations caused by the pain were assessed.

D. Active listening was provided as the veteran/service member described the nature of his/her pain and explained the causes for it.

---

*The numbers in parentheses correlate to the number of the Therapeutic Intervention statement in the companion chapter with the same title in *The Veterans and Active Duty Military Psychotherapy Treatment Planner* (Moore and Jongsma) by John Wiley & Sons, 2009.

E. It was noted that the veteran/service member does not have a clear understanding of the causes for his/her pain or effective ways to manage it.

2. Inquire about Injury (2)

A. Inquiries were made in regard to the veteran's/service member's precipitating injury.

B. Active listening was used as the veteran/service member described the precipitating injury for his/her pain symptoms.

C. The veteran/service member was assisted in processing negative emotional content from his/her description of the precipitating injury.

3. Refer to Physician (3)

A. The veteran/service member was referred to a physician to undergo a thorough examination to rule out any undiagnosed condition and to receive recommendations for further treatment options.

B. The veteran/service member has followed through on the physician evaluation referral, and new treatment options were reviewed.

C. The veteran/service member was encouraged by the prospect of new medical procedures that may offer hope in terms of pain relief; he/she was directed to pursue these options.

D. The veteran/service member was discouraged to discover that no new medical procedures could offer hope of pain relief; his/her emotions were processed.

E. The veteran/service member has not followed through on obtaining a new evaluation by a physician and was encouraged to do so.

4. Monitor Treatment Compliance (4)

A. The veteran's/service member's compliance with the pain management program was monitored.

B. The veteran/service member has made a commitment to participating in the pain management program, and his/her cooperation with the full regimen of pain management treatment was monitored.

C. The veteran/service member was supported as he/she has regularly complied with treatment recommendations.

D. The veteran/service member has not regularly complied with treatment recommendations and was provided with redirection in this area.

5. Administer Assessment for Treatment Adherence Problems (5)

A. The veteran/service member was administered psychological instruments designed to objectively assess the ability to adhere to medical treatment expectations and potential poor adherence problems.

B. The veteran/service member was administered the Millon Behavioral Medicine Diagnostic (MBMD) to identify potential treatment adherence problems.

C. The results of the assessment for potential treatment adherence problems were reviewed with the veteran/service member.

D. The veteran/service member was noted to have positive ratings regarding his/her ability to adhere to treatment, and this was reflected to him/her.

E. The veteran/service member was noted to have many potential treatment adherence problems on the assessment for such, and this was reflected to him/her.

6. Problem-Solve Treatment Compliance Problems (6)

A. Treatment compliance issues were identified and problem-solved with the veteran/service member.

B. The veteran/service member was assisted in identifying resources to help ensure his/her compliance with medical pain management recommendations.

C. The veteran/service member was reinforced for his/her compliance with treatment recommendations.

D. The veteran/service member has not been compliant with treatment recommendations and was provided with additional assistance in this area.

7. Administer Testing for Psychiatric Concerns (7)

A. The veteran/service member was assessed for psychiatric symptoms related to the pain.

B. The Millon Clinical Multiaxial Inventory-III (MCMI-III) was administered to the veteran/service member in order to assess for psychiatric symptoms related to the pain.

C. The Minnesota Multiphasic Personality Inventory, 2nd ed. (MMPI-2) was administered to the veteran/service member in order to assess for psychiatric symptoms related to the pain.

D. The veteran/service member has completed the assessment for psychiatric symptoms, but minimal concerns were identified; this was reflected to the veteran/service member.

E. The results of the assessment for psychiatric symptoms indicated significant concerns that would contribute to the veteran's/service member's difficulty managing pain, and these results were reflected to him/her.

F. The veteran/service member has not completed the assessment for psychiatric symptoms related to the pain and was redirected to do so.

8. Refer for Medication Review (8)

A. The veteran/service member was referred to a physician who specializes in chronic pain management to obtain a medication review.

B. The veteran/service member has followed through with attending an appointment with a physician who reviewed his/her medications; the results of this evaluation were discussed.

C. The veteran/service member has begun taking the new medications prescribed by the physician to regulate the pain, and his/her reaction to the medication was reviewed.

D. The veteran/service member has not followed through with a referral to a physician for a medication review and was redirected to do so.

E. Contact was made with the veteran's/service member's physician who evaluated pain control medications.

F. The physician was given a progress report regarding the veteran's/service member's chronic pain management.

G. The veteran's/service member's physician indicated that no further medication options were available to manage his/her chronic pain, and this has been reviewed with the veteran/service member.

9. Monitor Medication Compliance (9)

A. As the veteran/service member has taken the antidepressant medication prescribed by his/her physician, the effectiveness and side effects of the medication were monitored.

B. The veteran/service member reported that the antidepressant medication has been beneficial in reducing sleep interference and in stabilizing mood; the benefits of this progress were reviewed.

C. The veteran/service member reported that the antidepressant medication has not been beneficial; this was relayed to the prescribing clinician.

D. The veteran/service member was assessed for side effects from his/her medication.

E. The veteran/service member has not consistently taken the prescribed antidepressant medication and was redirected to do so.

10. Refer for Physical Therapy (10)

A. As the veteran's/service member's pain has been noted to be heterogeneous, he/she has been referred for physical therapy.

B. The veteran/service member has been involved in physical therapy, and his/her experience was reviewed.

C. The veteran/service member has not sought out involvement in physical therapy and was redirected to do so.

11. Reinforce Physical Therapy Gains (11)

A. The veteran/service member was assisted in identifying the gains made from physical therapy.

B. The veteran/service member was asked to identify his/her gains in regard to mobility, pain decrease, and overall physical functioning.

C. The veteran/service member was reinforced for his/her progress in physical therapy.

D. The veteran/service member has not made significant progress in physical therapy, and the barriers to this progress were reviewed.

12. Explain Evidence for Cognitive-Behavioral Therapy (12)

A. The evidence supporting the use of cognitive-behavioral therapy for the management of chronic pain was explained to the veteran/service member.

B. The veteran/service member displayed a clear understanding of the manner in which cognitive-behavioral therapy can help in the management of chronic pain, and this was reinforced.

C. The veteran/service member struggled to understand how cognitive-behavioral therapy can help in the management of chronic pain and was provided with remedial information in this area.

13. Provide Rationale for Treatment (13)

A. The veteran/service member was taught how treatment can help him/her understand how thoughts, feelings, and behavior can affect pain.

B. The veteran/service member was taught about how he/she can play a role in managing his/her own pain.

C. The veteran/service member was reinforced as he/she has embraced the rationale for treatment and the management of his/her own pain.

D. The veteran/service member has not accepted the rationale for treatment and the concept of managing his/her own pain and was provided with additional feedback in this area.

14. Identify Negative Connotations (14)

A. The veteran/service member was assisted in exploring his/her schema and self-talk that result in negative cognitions to influence pain levels.

B. The veteran's/service member's negative cognitions that influence pain levels were identified and challenged.

C. The veteran/service member was assisted in developing more adaptive cognitions that mitigate pain symptoms.

D. The veteran/service member was assisted in generating alternative thoughts that correct for his/her biased schema and negative self-talk/cognitions.

E. The veteran/service member was assisted in developing better coping skills and building confidence in managing pain.

F. The veteran/service member struggled to identify his/her schema, self-talk, or negative cognitions and was provided with tentative examples in this area.

15. Assign Pain Thoughts Journal (15)

A. The veteran/service member was asked to keep a journal of thoughts and activities that worsen and mitigate pain symptoms.

B. The veteran/service member has followed through on completing the pain/thought journal, and his/her journal was reviewed.

C. The material from veteran's/service member's pain journal was processed to assist him/her in developing insight into triggers and mediating factors for his/her pain.

D. Interventions were discussed that could help the veteran/service member alleviate the frequency, duration, and severity of his/her pain.

E. The veteran/service member reported that he/she has not kept a pain/thought journal and was redirected to do so.

16. Discuss Learned Helplessness (16)

A. The concept of learned helplessness was presented to the veteran/service member.

B. The veteran/service member was helped to identify how learned helplessness relates to exacerbation and continuation of chronic pain symptoms.

C. The veteran's/service member's experience of learned helplessness was reviewed and processed.

D. The veteran/service member denied any experience of learned helplessness and was reminded to be alert for these symptoms.

17. Identify Past Opportunities for Overcoming Obstacles (17)

A. The veteran/service member was asked to explore periods during his/her military career where he/she took control of a situation and overcame an obstacle.

B. The veteran/service member was helped to process and review experiences of overcoming obstacles.

C. The veteran/service member was assisted in applying this successful problem-solving approach to the current situation.

D. The veteran/service member struggled to identify situations in which he/she has successfully problem-solved and was assisted in identifying these and applying them to the current situation.

18. Assign Pain Journal (18)

A. The veteran/service member was taught to keep a daily log of emotions, behaviors, situations, and environmental factors that influence his/her pain experience.

B. The veteran/service member was asked to focus on the severity and duration of symptoms and what behaviors mitigate the pain experience.

C. The veteran/service member has kept a daily pain log, and his/her entries were processed within the session.

D. The veteran/service member has not regularly completed a daily pain log and was redirected to do so.

19. Arrange for Biofeedback Training (19)

A. The veteran/service member was referred for biofeedback training to help him/her develop more precise relaxation skills.

B. The veteran/service member was referred for electromyograph (EMG) for muscle tension–related pain.

C. The veteran/service member was referred for thermal biofeedback for migraine pain.

D. The veteran/service member was administered biofeedback training to teach him/her more in-depth relaxation skills.

E. The biofeedback training sessions have been helpful in training the veteran/service member to relax more deeply.

F. The veteran/service member has not used the skills learned in biofeedback training and was redirected to do so.

G. The veteran/service member has not attended biofeedback training and was redirected to do so.

20. Teach Relaxation Skills (20)

A. The veteran/service member was taught relaxation skills.

B. The veteran/service member was taught skills such as progressive muscle relaxation, guided imagery, and slow diaphragmatic breathing.

C. The veteran/service member was taught how to better discriminate between relaxation and tension.

D. The veteran/service member was taught how to apply relaxation skills in his/her daily life.

E. The veteran/service member has learned how to better discriminate between relaxation and tension and has learned relaxation skills; this progress was reinforced.

F. The veteran/service member has not learned relaxation skills or how to discriminate between relaxation and tension and was provided with remedial feedback in this area.

21. Assign Self-Care Practice (21)

A. The veteran/service member was assigned to practice self-care techniques at home on a daily basis.

B. The veteran/service member was prompted to continue the biofeedback techniques on a daily basis.

C. The veteran/service member was urged to continue the progressive muscle relaxation, diaphragmatic breathing, and imagery techniques on a daily basis.

D. The veteran/service member has continued his/her self-care techniques on a regular basis and was reinforced for this.

E. The veteran/service member has not continued the self-care techniques and was reminded to do so.

22. **Refer to Physical Rehabilitation Trainer (22)**

A. The veteran/service member was referred to a physical rehabilitation trainer for assistance in developing an individually tailored exercise program that is approved by the veteran's/service member's personal physician.

B. The veteran/service member accepted the referral for the development of a physical exercise program that will increase physical fitness while minimizing the pain of the injury, and has committed to regular participation.

C. The veteran/service member refused to participate in an exercise program and would not accept a referral to such a program.

D. The veteran/service member postponed participation in the development of an exercise program and was encouraged to follow-through on this when he/she is able to do so.

23. **Discuss Physical Training Alterations (23)**

A. The service member was encouraged to discuss alterations in his/her current unit physical training program based on his/her limitations.

B. The service member identified the physical training alterations he/she might need based on his/her limitations.

C. The service member was reluctant to request any physical training program alterations and was assisted in processing his/her beliefs in this area.

24. **Encourage Work Environment Accommodation Discussion (24)**

A. The service member was encouraged to discuss needed work accommodations with his/her chain of command.

B. The service member has discussed needed accommodations in the work environment with his/her chain of command, and his/her experience was processed.

C. The service member has not discussed needed accommodations in the work environment and was reminded to do so.

25. **Assess Social Support Network (25)**

A. The veteran's/service member's social support network was assessed.

B. The veteran/service member was encouraged to connect with people within his/her social support network who facilitate or support his/her positive change.

C. The veteran/service member has not regularly used his/her social support network and was redirected to do so.

26. **Refer to a Support Group (26)**

A. The veteran/service member was referred to a chronic pain support group.

B. The veteran/service member has attended the chronic pain support group, and his/her experience was processed.

C. The veteran/service member has not attended the chronic pain support group and was reminded to do so.

27. Encourage Medical Separation Appointments (27)

A. The service member was encouraged to attend all medical separation appointments.

B. The service member was reinforced for his/her attendance at all medical separation appointments.

C. The service member was redirected as he/she has not attended all medical separation appointments.

28. Explore Appeal Opportunities (28)

A. The service member does not agree with the medical separation finding and was provided with options for appeal.

B. The service member was urged to request a second opinion.

C. Consultation with judge advocate general or a civilian attorney was suggested to the service member.

29. Facilitate Veterans Affairs Representative Meeting (29)

A. A Veterans Affairs representative from the appropriate geographical region was contacted.

B. The veteran has been coordinated with the appropriate Veterans Affairs representative.

30. Provide Veterans Affairs Benefits Information (30)

A. The veteran was provided with the appropriate in regard to his/her Veterans Affairs benefits.

B. The veteran was referred to a Web site for Veterans Affairs: www.vba.va.gov/vba.

31. Emphasize Importance of Veterans Affairs Meetings (31)

A. The importance of attending all Veterans Affairs medical appointments was stressed to the veteran.

B. The importance of attending compensation evaluations was stressed to the veteran.

C. The importance of attending regular health care appointments was stressed to the veteran.

D. The veteran has attended all scheduled appointments and was provided with positive feedback in this area.

E. The veteran has not attended all scheduled appointments and was reminded to do so.

COMBAT AND OPERATIONAL STRESS REACTION

SERVICE MEMBER PRESENTATION

1. Intense Fear of Combat (1)*

A. The service member frequently verbalizes an intensive fear associated with going on combat missions.

B. The service member reports that he/she experiences intense fear, helplessness, and horror related to a previous combat mission.

C. The service member has not yet gone on any combat missions but indicates intense fear from what he/she anticipates this will be like.

D. The service member's severe emotional response of fear related to combat missions has somewhat diminished.

E. The service member can now focus on his/her upcoming combat missions without debilitating fear.

2. Immobility during Combat (2)

A. The service member reported a history of becoming immobile during combat operations.

B. The service member described how he/she "freezes under fire."

C. As treatment has progressed, the service member reports optimism that he/she will be able to function within a combat setting.

D. As treatment has progressed, the service member has displayed greater ability to function in a combat situation.

3. Hypervigilance (3)

A. The service member described a pattern of hypervigilance in noncombat situations.

B. The service member's hypervigilant pattern has diminished.

C. The service member reported no longer experiencing hypervigilance.

4. Irritability (4)

A. The service member described a pattern of irritability that was not present before the traumatic event occurred.

B. The service member reported incidents of becoming angry and losing his/her temper easily, resulting in explosive outbursts.

C. The service member's irritability has diminished somewhat and the intensity of the explosive outbursts has lessened.

D. The service member reported no recent incidents of explosive, angry outbursts.

---

*The numbers in parentheses correlate to the number of the Behavioral Definition statement in the companion chapter with the same title in *The Veterans and Active Duty Military Psychotherapy Treatment Planner* (Moore and Jongsma) by John Wiley & Sons, 2009.

5. Chronic Pain Preoccupation (5)

A. The service member presented with a history of preoccupation with pain that is beyond what is expected for his/her physical malady.

B. The service member is so pain focused that he/she is unable to carry on the responsibilities of day-to-day living.

C. The service member has learned management techniques and has become less preoccupied with the chronic pain problem.

6. Decreased Confidence in Combat Skills (6)

A. The service member demonstrates a loss of confidence in his/her combat skills.

B. The service member demonstrates a loss of capability in regard to combat skills.

C. As treatment has progressed, the service member has returned to his/her previous level of confidence and ability in regard to combat skills.

7. Lack of Concentration (7)

A. The service member described a pattern of lack of concentration that began with the exposure to the traumatic event.

B. The service member reports a decreased pattern of attention capabilities.

C. The service member reports recent problems with poor memory.

D. The service member reported that he/she is now able to focus more clearly on cognitive processing.

E. The service member's ability to concentrate has returned to normal levels.

8. Verbalizes Hopelessness (8)

A. The service member has experienced feelings of hopelessness and loss of faith in the mission and himself/herself.

B. The service member does not see much hope for his/her future.

C. The service member's feelings of hopelessness and worthlessness have diminished.

D. The service member reports experiencing feelings of hope for the future and affirmation of his/her own self-worth as well as the worth of the mission and the unit.

9. Sensory Disturbance (9)

A. The service member reports a loss of functioning of his/her senses.

B. The service member has experienced loss of vision or blindness in connection with his/her combat stress reaction.

C. The service member has lost the sense of touch in connection with his/her combat stress reaction.

D. The service member has lost the sense of hearing in connection with his/her combat stress reaction.

E. As treatment has progressed, the service member's complaints about sensory disturbances have diminished.

F. The service member does not experience any sensory disturbance.

10. Erratic and Uncharacteristic Behavior (10)

A. The service member was noted to be displaying erratic and uncharacteristic behavior.

B. The service member has had frequent emotional outbursts.

C. The service member has engaged in fighting and other illegal acts.

D. As treatment has progressed, the service member has decreased his/her erratic and uncharacteristic behavior.

11. Impaired Speech/ Muteness (11)

A. The service member presents as being unable to speak.

B. The service member is able to produce some speech, but his/her functioning is significantly impaired.

C. As treatment has progressed, the service member's functional speech has returned.

INTERVENTIONS IMPLEMENTED

1. Explore Symptoms of Combat/Operational Stress (1)[*]

A. Today's clinical contact focused on exploring the different signs and symptoms of combat/operational stress.

B. The service member was assessed for a variety of symptoms related to combat/operational stress, including fear, apathy, loss of confidence, irritability, and sensory disturbance.

C. It was noted that the service member experiences mild signs of combat/operational stress.

D. It was noted that the service member experiences moderate signs of combat/operational stress.

E. It was noted that the service member experiences severe signs of combat/operational stress.

2. Assess for Alternate Etiology (2)

A. The service member was assessed for other explanations for his/her reported symptoms.

B. The service member was assessed for psychiatric illness.

C. The service member was assessed for traumatic brain injury concerns.

D. The service member was assessed for substance abuse problems.

E. Alternative explanations for the service member's difficulties were identified, and treatment has been refocused to these concerns.

F. No other explanations for the service member's symptoms were uncovered.

3. Assess Severity of Symptoms (3)

A. The severity of the service members symptoms were assessed by utilizing brief self-reporting skills.

B. The service member was administered the PTSD Checklist—Military Version.

C. The Beck Depression Inventory-II was administered to the service member.

D. The Beck Anxiety Inventory was administered to the service member.

E. The results of the self-reporting scales were presented to the service member.

[*]The numbers in parentheses correlate to the number of the Therapeutic Intervention statement in the companion chapter with the same title in *The Veterans and Active Duty Military Psychotherapy Treatment Planner* (Moore and Jongsma) by John Wiley & Sons, 2009.

F. The service member declined to participate in the administrations of the self-report rating scales and was redirected to do so.

4. Collect Collateral Information (4)

A. The service member's family and friends were sought out to collect collateral information about changes in behavior, personality, or cognitive abilities subsequent to the combat/operational stress concerns.

B. The service member's chain of command was consulted regarding changes in behavior, personality, or cognitive abilities subsequent to the combat/operational stress concerns.

C. Sufficient information has been collected regarding the service member's changes in behavior, personality, or cognitive abilities subsequent to the combat/operational stress concerns, and treatment should be able to progress.

D. Insufficient information has been provided in regard to the changes in the service member's behavior, personality, or cognitive abilities subsequent to the combat/operational stress concerns, and additional sources were sought.

5. Observe in the Environment (5)

A. The service member was observed in his/her regular environment in order to gather information regarding the impact of stress symptoms.

B. The service member was assessed during training.

C. The service member was assessed while performing routine job duties.

D. Stress symptoms were noted to be present during the environmental observations of the service member, and this was reflected to him/her.

E. No stress symptoms were noted to be present during the environmental observations of the service member, and this was reflected to him/her.

6. Place in Restoration Program (6)

A. The service member was removed from his/her unit and placed in a restoration program for three to five days.

B. The placement in the restoration program has assisted the service member in alleviating stress symptoms severity, and he/she can be returned to his/her unit.

C. The placement in the restoration program has not significantly alleviated the service members stress symptoms severity, and he/she has not returned to his/her unit.

7. Educate about Stress Symptoms (7)

A. The service member was educated about how some symptoms of combat and operational stress are normal and expected.

B. The service member was taught about how some symptoms of combat/operational stress may be adaptive (e.g., hyperarousal, hypervigilance).

C. Active listening was provided to the service member as he/she was able to identify how his/her symptoms have been adaptive.

D. Active listening was provided to the service member as he/she was able to identify some symptoms that have not been adaptive.

8. Review Prior Episodes (8)

A. The service member was assisted in identifying prior episodes of combat/operational stress reactions.

B. The service member was asked to emphasize how he/she recovered from his/her episodes of combat/operational stress.

C. Active listening was provided as the service member identified his/her previous episodes of combat/operational stress reaction.

D. The service member denied any previous episodes of combat/stress reaction, and this was accepted.

9. Differentiate from Severe Psychiatric Disorders (9)

A. The service member was educated about the difference between severe psychiatric disorders (e.g., psychosis) and combat/operation stress reactions.

B. The long-standing nature of severe psychiatric disorders was emphasized as opposed to the brief reactive nature of combat/operational stress.

C. The service member was reinforced for his/her understanding of the differences between severe psychiatric disorders and combat/operational stress reactions.

D. The service member appeared to have a difficult time understanding the differences between more severe psychiatric disorders and acute stress reactions, and was provided with remedial information in this area.

10. Provide Nonthreatening Environment (10)

A. The service member was provided with a quiet and nonthreatening environment in which to relax.

B. The service member was encouraged to meet his/her basic physiological needs of rest and sleep by coordinating a quiet and nonthreatening environment in which to relax.

C. The service member has been able to relax through the use of quiet and nonthreatening environments, and the benefits of this relaxation were emphasized.

D. The service member continues to be quite agitated despite attempting a quiet, nonthreatening environment, and was provided with additional assistance in this area.

11. Coordinate Sleep Medication (11)

A. As the service member has continued to struggle with obtaining sleep, despite significant assistance in this area, he/she was coordinated for a provision of medication for the purposes of initiating and maintaining sleep.

B. The service member has utilized medication to help him/her sleep, and the benefits of this were reviewed.

C. The service member has not been able to use medication to help obtain sleep and was provided with additional assistance in this area.

12. Monitor Healthy Diet (12)

A. The service member was encouraged to maintain the opportunity to eat nutritious foods and hydrate properly.

B. The service member was provided with nutritious foods and appropriate resources for hydration.

C. The service member has maintained a pattern of a healthy diet, and his/her benefits were reviewed.

D. The service member has not been maintaining a healthy diet and was redirected in this area.

13. Identify Distorted thoughts (13)

A. The service member was assisted in identifying the distorted schemas and related automatic thoughts that mediate fear or loss of competence schema.

B. The service member was taught the role of distorted thinking in precipitating emotional responses.

C. The service member was reinforced as he/she verbalized an understanding of the cognitive beliefs and messages that mediate his/her fear of loss of competence.

D. The service member was assisted in replacing distorted messages with positive, realistic cognitions.

E. The service member failed to identify his/her distorted thoughts and cognitions and was provided with tentative examples in this area.

14. Assign Self-Talk Homework (14)

A. The service member was assigned homework exercises in which he/she identifies fearful self-talk and creates reality-based alternatives.

B. The "Negative Thoughts Trigger Negative Feelings" exercise from the *Adult Psychotherapy Homework Planner,* 2nd ed. (Jongsma) was used to help the service member develop health self-talk.

C. The service member has completed his/her homework related to self-talk and creating reality-based alternatives; he/she was provided with positive reinforcement for his/her success in this area.

D. The service member has completed his/her homework related to self-talk and creating reality-based alternatives; he/she was provided with corrective feedback for his/her failure to identify and replace self-talk with reality-based alternatives.

E. The service member has not attempted his/her homework related to fearful self-talk and reality-based alternatives and was redirected to do so.

15. Conduct Behavioral Experiments (15)

A. The service member was encouraged to do "behavioral experiments" in which depressive automatic thoughts are treated as hypotheses/predictions and are tested against reality-based alternative hypothesis.

B. The service member's automatic depressive thoughts were tested against his/her past, present, and/or future experiences.

C. The service member was assisted in processing the outcome of his/her behavioral experiences.

D. The service member was encouraged by his/her experience of the more reality-based hypotheses/predictions; this progress was reinforced.

E. The service member continues to focus on depressive automatic thoughts and was redirected toward the behavioral evidence of the more reality-based alternative hypotheses.

16. Reinforce Positive Self-Talk (16)

A. The service member was reinforced for any successful replacement of distorted negative thinking with positive, reality-based cognitive messages.

B. It was noted that the service member has been engaging in positive, reality-based thinking that has enhanced his/her self-confidence and increased adaptive action.

C. The service member was assigned to complete the "Positive Self-Talk" assignment from the *Adult Psychotherapy Homework Planner,* 2nd ed. (Jongsma).

17. Teach Thought Stopping (17)

A. The service member was taught a thought-stopping technique.

B. The service member was taught to internally voice the word STOP immediately upon noticing unwanted traumatic or otherwise negative unwanted thoughts.

C. The service member was taught to imagine something representing the concept of stopping (e.g., a stop sign or stoplight) immediately upon noticing unwanted trauma or otherwise negative unwanted thoughts.

D. The service member was assigned "Making Use of the Thought-Stopping Technique" in the *Adult Psychotherapy Homework Planner,* 2nd ed. (Jongsma).

E. The service member was assisted in reviewing his/her use of thought-stopping techniques and was provided with positive feedback for his/her appropriate use of this technique.

F. Redirection was provided, as the service member has not learned to use the thought-stopping technique.

18. Teach Relaxation Skills (18)

A. The service member was taught relaxation skills.

B. The service member was taught progressive muscle relaxation, guided imagery, and slow diaphragmatic breathing.

C. The service member was taught how to discriminate better between relaxation and tension.

D. The service member was taught how to apply relaxation skills to his/her daily life.

E. The service member was provided with feedback about his/her use of relaxation skills.

19. Assign Relaxation Exercises (19)

A. The service member was taught relaxation techniques (e.g., progressive relaxation, self-hypnosis, biofeedback) in order to help him/her relax completely.

B. The service member was assigned "Learning to Self-Soothe" from the *Addiction Treatment Homework Planner,* 4th ed. (Finley and Lenz).

C. The service member was encouraged to use relaxation skills when feeling tense or anxious.

D. The service member has implemented the relaxation techniques and reported a decreased reactivity to anxious feelings; this progress was highlighted.

E. The service member has not implemented the relaxation techniques and continues to feel quite stressed and anxious in anxiety-producing situations, and was redirected to implement the techniques.

F. The service member did not complete the assignment related to self-soothing and was redirected to do so.

20. Teach Progressive Muscle Relaxation and Calming Strategies (20)

A. The service member was taught progressive muscle relaxation skills.

B. The service member was taught diaphragmatic breathing skills.

C. The service member was assigned to engage in calming strategies twice per day for 15 minutes each time.

D. The service member was encouraged to implement the calming strategies when anxiety or stress arises.

E. The service member was taught how to apply progressive muscle relaxation skills to his/her daily life.

F. The service member was provided with feedback about his/her use of progressive muscle relaxation skills.

21. Utilize Biofeedback (21)

A. Electromyograph (EMG) biofeedback techniques were used to facilitate the service member learning relaxation skills.

B. The service member reported that he/she has implemented his/her use of relaxation skills in daily life to reduce levels of muscle tension and the experience of anxiety; the benefits of this technique were reviewed.

C. The service member reported that his/her level of anxiety has decreased since relaxation techniques were implemented; he/she was encouraged to continue this technique.

D. The service member has not followed through on implementation of relaxation skills to reduce anxiety symptoms; he/she was redirected to do so.

22. Construct Anxiety Stimuli Hierarchy (22)

A. The service member was assisted in constructing a hierarchy of anxiety-producing situations associated with two or three spheres of worry.

B. It was difficult for the service member to develop a hierarchy of stimulus situations, as the causes of his/her anxiety remain quite vague; he/she was assisted in completing the hierarchy.

C. The service member was successful at creating a focused hierarchy of specific stimulus situations that provoke anxiety in a gradually increasing manner; this hierarchy was reviewed.

23. Select Initial Exposures (23)

A. Initial exposures were selected from the hierarchy of anxiety-producing situations, with a bias toward likelihood of being successful.

B. A plan was developed with the service member for managing the symptoms that may occur during the initial exposure.

C. The service member was assisted in rehearsing the plan for managing the exposure-related symptoms within his/her imagination.

D. Positive feedback was provided for the service member's helpful use of symptom management techniques.

E. The service member was redirected for ways to improve his/her symptom management techniques.

24. Assign Imagination Exercises (24)

A. The service member was asked to vividly imagine worst-case consequences of worries, holding them in mind until the anxiety associated with them weakens.

B. The service member was asked to imagine consequences of his/her worries as described in *Mastery of Your Anxiety and Worry—Therapist Guide* (Craske, Barlow, and O'Leary).

C. The service member was supported as he/she has maintained a focus on the worst-case consequences of his/her worry until the anxiety weakened.

D. The service member was assisted in generating reality-based alternatives to the worst-case scenarios, and these were processed within the session.

25. Assign Homework on Situational Exposures (25)

A. The service member was assigned homework exercises to perform worry exposures and record his/her experience.

B. The service member was assigned situational exposures homework from *Mastery of Your Anxiety and Worry—Service Member Guide* (Zinbarg, Craske, Barlow, and O'Leary)

C. The service member was assigned situational exposures homework from *Generalized Anxiety Disorder* (Brown, O'Leary, and Barlow).

D. The service member's use of worry exposure techniques was reviewed and reinforced.

E. The service member has struggled in his/her implementation of worry exposure techniques and was provided with corrective feedback.

F. The service member has not attempted to use the worry exposure techniques and was redirected to do so.

26. Refer to Stress Management Group (26)

A. The service member was referred to a stress management group designed to teach individuals how to recognize and manage stress symptoms before the symptoms impact functioning.

B. The service member has attended a stress management group, and the benefits of this treatment were reviewed.

C. The service member has not attended the stress management group and was redirected to do so.

27. Implement Regular Physical Exercise (27)

A. The service member was assisted in developing a regular physical exercise program.

B. The service member was assisted in implementing a regular physical exercise program.

C. The service member was reinforced for implementation of a regular physical exercise program.

D. The benefits of a regular physical exercise program were reviewed with the service member.

E. The service member has not implemented a regular physical exercise program and was redirected to do so.

28. Return to Job Duties (28)

A. The service member was assisted in identifying job duties that are at a moderate level of stress.

B. The service member was directed to begin working again at the moderate level of stress job duties.

C. The service member was encouraged and supported as he/she returned to some job duties.

D. The service member has not returned to any job duties and was redirected to do so.

29. Reinforce Completion of Job Responsibilities (29)

A. The service member was noted to have successfully completed his/her job responsibilities.

B. The service member was reinforced for his/her completion of job duties.

C. The service member's success at completing his/her job duties was celebrated.

D. The service member has not completed his/her job duties and was provided with additional support in this area.

CONFLICT WITH COMRADES

SERVICE MEMBER PRESENTATION

1. Frequent Arguments (1)[*]

A. The service member reported frequent or continual arguing with his/her fellow service members.

B. The service member reported implementation of conflict resolution skills.

C. The frequency of conflict with fellow service members has diminished.

D. The service member reported that his/her relationship with other service members has improved significantly and arguing has become very infrequent.

2. Confrontation with Superiors (2)

A. The service member described a pattern of rebellion against and conflict with his/her immediate superiors.

B. The service member's rebellion against authority has resulted in confrontation and discipline by superiors.

C. The service member's authority conflicts with his/her superiors have resulted in failure to achieve promotions.

D. The service member has developed a more accepting attitude toward authority and is willing to take direction from his/her superiors.

3. Unable to Make Friends (3)

A. The service member reports no close friends or confidants outside of first-degree relatives.

B. The service member reports that conflict with comrades has prevented him/her from building and maintaining a social network of friends and acquaintances within the military.

C. The service member has begun to reach out socially and to respond favorably to the overtures of others.

D. The service member reported enjoying contact with friends and sharing personal information with them.

4. Interpersonal and Problem-Solving Skill Deficits (4)

A. The service member displays deficiencies in regard to interpersonal skills during confrontation.

B. The service member has difficulty determining how to solve problems with his/her peers.

C. As treatment has progressed, the service member has displayed increased problem-solving and interpersonal abilities.

D. The service member has greatly decreased confrontation and conflict due to increased interpersonal skills.

---

[*]The numbers in parentheses correlate to the number of the Behavioral Definition statement in the companion chapter with the same title in *The Veterans and Active Duty Military Psychotherapy Treatment Planner* (Moore and Jongsma) by John Wiley & Sons, 2009.

5. Physical Confrontation (5)

A. The service member described a history of loss of temper in which he/she has physically confronted peers or superiors.

B. The service member described a history of physical confrontation dating back to childhood, involving verbal outbursts and property destruction.

C. As therapy has progressed, the service member has reported increased control over his/her temper and a significant reduction in incidents of poor anger management.

D. The service member has had no recent incidents of explosive outbursts that have resulted in destruction of property or intimidating verbal or physical assaults.

6. Repeated Discipline (6)

A. The service member reported that he/she has received repeated disciplinary actions due to conflicts with peers and/or superiors.

B. The service member reported that he/she has not received promotions due to conflict with peers and/or superiors.

C. The service member reported that he/she has been demoted due to conflicts with peers or superiors.

D. As treatment has progressed, the service member has improved his/her relationships with peers and superiors, and no disciplinary actions have been taken recently.

7. Contempt and Disdain for the Military (7)

A. The service member described a pervasive contempt and disdain for the military.

B. The service member has allowed his/her pattern of contempt and disdain for the military to affect his/her relationships with comrades.

C. As treatment has progressed, the service member has been able to better manage his/her relationships with comrades, despite pervasive contempt and disdain for the military.

D. As treatment has continued, the service member has become more accepting of military expectations and traditions.

8. Outcast/Misfit Identity (8)

A. The service member reports feelings of being an outcast or misfit within his/her unit.

B. The service member reports experiences that he/she interprets as evidence of his/her being an outcast or a misfit in his/her unit.

C. The service member fears rejection from his/her unit comrades.

D. The services member reports that he/she has become more at ease within his/her unit and feels more accepted.

INTERVENTIONS IMPLEMENTED

1. Assess Conflict (1)[*]

A. The frequency and severity of conflicts experienced by the service member were assessed.

---

[*]The numbers in parentheses correlate to the number of the Therapeutic Intervention statement in the companion chapter with the same title in *The Veterans and Active Duty Military Psychotherapy Treatment Planner* (Moore and Jongsma) by John Wiley & Sons, 2009.

B. The service member was assessed in regards to the type of conflict situations in which he/she is typically involved.

C. Active listening was provided as the service member described verbal conflicts in which he/she typically is involved.

D. Active listening was provided as the service member described physical conflicts in which he/she typically is involved.

2. Assess Precipitating Events (2)

A. The service member was asked to identify the precipitating events that seem to precede the conflicts.

B. The service member identified that most of his/her conflicts are precipitated when he/she is given direction by others.

C. The service member described that most of his/her conflicts are precipitated by teasing.

D. Support and encouragement were provided as the service member described the precipitating events for the conflicts.

E. The service member was unable to identify specific precipitating events for his/her conflicts and was encouraged to pay close attention to this in the near future.

3. Explore Earlier Oppositional and Disruptive Behavior (3)

A. The service member's childhood and adolescent history were explored for evidence of oppositional and disruptive behaviors.

B. Active listening was used as the service member described the nature and extent of oppositional and destructive behavior from his/her childhood/adolescent years.

C. The service member denied any pattern of oppositional or disruptive behavior in his/her childhood/adolescence; this was accepted at face value.

4. Inquire about Mental Health Services (4)

A. The service member was asked about his/her previous experience with mental health services for behavioral problems.

B. The service member was asked to compare and contrast his/her past behavioral problems and current concerns.

C. The service member was assisted in identifying patterns in his/her earlier and current behavior.

D. The service member denied any connection between his/her youthful behavior and current concerns; he/she was asked to give further thought in this area.

5. Assess Mood Impact (5)

A. The service member was assessed for the negative impact that conflict with peers and/or supervisors has on his/her mood.

B. The service member was assessed for depression symptoms.

C. The service member was assessed for worrying and anxiety symptoms.

D. The service member was assessed for agitated mood due to his/her conflict with others.

E. The service member's description of his/her mood was accepted and processed.

6. Assess Impact on Job Performance (6)

A. The negative impact of the service member's conflict was assessed, with focus on the service member's job performance.

B. The service member was reviewed for how conflict may have caused him/her to be passed over for a promotion.

C. The service member's history of disciplinary actions was reviewed as it relates to his/her history of conflict.

D. Use of Article 15 actions was reviewed.

E. The service member was assisted in processing the concerns related to the negative impact that his/her conflict has had on his/her job performance.

7. Assess Homicidal Ideation (7)

A. The presence of homicidal ideation was assessed in regard to the service member's conflict with comrades.

B. It was reflected to the service member that homicidal ideation did not appear to be a concern in his/her conflict with comrades.

C. Significant concern was raised in regard to homicidal ideation in the service member's conflicts with comrades.

8. Inform of Viable Threats (8)

A. As a viable threat was identified, appropriate parties were informed.

B. Military police were contacted in regard to the viable threat that has been identified.

C. The potential victim has been informed of the viable threat that has been identified.

D. Chain of command has been informed as a viable threat has been identified.

E. No viable treat has been identified, and therefore no duty to inform was indicated.

9. Coordinate Substance Abuse Assessment (9)

A. The service member was assessed for substance abuse problems that may contribute to his/her legal concerns.

B. The service member was identified as having a concomitant substance abuse problem.

C. Upon review, the service member does not display evidence of a substance abuse problem.

D. The service member's mental health and substance abuse treatment services were coordinated in an integrated fashion.

E. The service member's substance abuse treatment providers have been furnished with increased information about his/her mental health diagnosis and treatment.

F. The service member's mental health treatment providers have been provided with increased information about his/her substance abuse diagnosis and treatment.

10. Refer for Substance Abuse/Dependence Treatment (10)

A. The service member was evaluated regarding his/her use of substances, the severity of his/her substance abuse, and treatment needs/options.

B. The service member was referred to a substance abuse program knowledgeable in the treatment of both substance abuse and severe and persistent mental illness.

C. The service member was compliant with the substance abuse evaluation, and the results of the evaluation were discussed with him/her, resulting in admission to a substance abuse program.

D. The service member declined to participate in the substance abuse evaluation or treatment and was encouraged to do so.

11. Arrange for Psychiatric Evaluation (11)

A. The service member was referred for a medication evaluation to determine if antidepressant, anxiolitic, or hypnotic medication is needed to relieve more significant mood or anger symptoms and/or impulsivity.

B. The service member was reinforced as he/she agreed to follow through with the medication evaluation.

C. The service member strongly opposed being placed on medication to help stabilize his/her mood and anger symptoms; his/her objections were processed.

D. The service member was assessed for psychiatric medication, and a prescription was provided by the prescribing clinician.

E. The service member was assessed for possible medication to assist in controlling his/her more significant mood, anxiety, and sleep disturbance systems, but no medication was prescribed.

12. Monitor Effects of Medication (12)

A. The service member's response to the medication was discussed in today's therapy session.

B. The service member reported that the medication has helped to stabilize his/her moods and decrease the intensity of his/her feelings; he/she was directed to share this information with the prescribing clinician.

C. The service member reports little to no improvement in his/her moods or anger control since being placed on the medication; he/she was directed to share this information with the prescribing clinician.

D. The service member was reinforced for consistently taking the medication as prescribed.

E. The service member has failed to comply with taking the medication as prescribed; he/she was encouraged to take the medication as prescribed.

F. Consistent contact was kept with the service member's prescribing professional in regard to the service member's medication compliance, side effects, and efficacy.

13. Identify Anger Expression Models (13)

A. The service member was assisted in identifying key figures in his/her life who have provided examples to him/her of how to positively or negatively express anger.

B. The service member was reinforced as he/she identified several key figures who have been negative role models in expressing anger explosively and destructively.

C. The service member was supported and reinforced as he/she acknowledged that he/she manages anger in the same way that an explosive parent figure had done when he/she was growing up.

D. The service member was encouraged to identify positive role models throughout his/her life whom he/she could respect for their management of angry feelings.

E. The service member was supported as he/she acknowledged that others have been influential in teaching him/her destructive patterns of anger management.

F. The service member failed to identify key figures in his/her life who have provided examples as to how to positively express anger and was questioned more specifically in this area.

14. Assign Lessons Learned List (14)

A. The service member was assigned to develop a "Lesson's Learned List," which includes any negative means of handing conflict that he/she remembers his/her parents/caretakers engaging in.

B. The service member has developed a list of lessons learned about how to manage conflict, and this was processed.

C. It was reflected that the service member has identified mostly positive means that his/her parents/caretakers used to manage conflict.

D. It was reflected that the service member has identified negative means that his/her parents/caretakers used to manager conflict.

15. Visual Changes (15)

A. The service member was asked to visual himself/herself in the future as a parent, and how he/she would do things differently from his/her parents/caretakers.

B. Active listening was used as the service member identified how he/she would change his/her parents' responses.

C. The service member struggled to identify how he/she would change his/her parents'/caretakers' handling of angry situations and was provided with remedial feedback in this area.

16. Identify Resolvable Conflicts (16)

A. The service member was assisted in identifying conflicts that can be handled through the use of open and honest verbal communication.

B. The service member was assisted in identifying conflicts that can be handled through the use of appropriate nonverbal signals.

C. The service member was assisted in identifying conflicts that can be resolved through the use of compromise.

D. The service member was assisted in identifying conflicts that can be resolved through the use of "swallowing" his/her pride.

17. Use the Empty-Chair Technique (17)

A. The empty-chair technique was used to assist the service member in practicing conflict resolution.

B. The empty-chair technique was used in regard to the typical conflict with military peers and superiors.

C. Rehearsal of the empty-chair technique was used until the service member feels comfortable with the confrontation.

18. Help Resolve Interpersonal Problems (18)

A. The service member was assisted in resolving interpersonal problems through the use of reassurance and support.

B. The "Applying Problem-Solving to Interpersonal Conflict" assignment from the *Adult Psychotherapy Homework Planner*, 2nd ed. (Jongsma) was used to help resolve interpersonal problems.

C. The service member was helped to clarify cognitive and affective triggers that ignite conflicts.

D. The service member was taught active problem-solving techniques to help him/her resolve interpersonal problems.

E. It was reflected to the service member that he/she has significantly reduced his/her interpersonal problems.

F. The service member continues to have significant interpersonal problems, and he/she was provided with remedial assistance in this area.

19. Assign Anger Journal (19)

A. The service member was assigned to keep a daily journal in which he/she will document persons or situations that cause anger, irritation, or disappointment.

B. The service member was assigned "Anger Journal" in the *Adult Psychotherapy Homework Planner*, 2nd ed. (Jongsma).

C. The service member has kept a journal of anger-producing situations, and this material was processed within the session.

D. The service member has become more aware of the causes for and targets of his/her anger as a result of journaling these experiences on a daily basis; the benefits of this insight were reflected to him/her.

E. The service member has not kept an anger journal and was redirected to do so.

20. Identify Physical and Behavioral Cues (20)

A. The service member was taught on how to recognize physical cues for when he/she gets angry (i.e., clenching fists, tensing muscles).

B. The service member was taught how to recognize behavioral cues for when he/she gets angry (i.e., raising voice, threatening nonverbal behaviors).

C. The service member acknowledged his/her physical and behavioral cues for anger.

D. The service member was unable to identify physical and verbal cues for anger and was provided remedial examples in this area.

21. Consolidate Anger Management Skills (21)

A. Techniques were used to help the service member consolidate his/her new anger management skills.

B. Techniques such as relaxation, imagery, behavioral rehearsal, modeling, role-playing, or in vivo exposure/behavioral experiences were used to help the service member consolidate the use of his/her new anger management skills.

C. The service member was assigned "Alternatives to Destructive Anger" in the *Adult Psychotherapy Homework Planner*, 2nd ed. (Jongsma).

D. The service member's use of techniques to consolidate his/her anger management skills was reviewed and reinforced.

22. **Explore Self-Thought (22)**

  A. The service member was assisted in exploring his/her self-thoughts that create and maintain anger.

  B. The service member was provided with examples of self-thoughts that tend to create and maintain anger.

  C. The service member was assisted in developing replacement thoughts for his/her maladaptive thoughts.

  D. This service member was encouraged to use alternate thoughts that help him/her to seek understanding and a healthier reaction to the situation.

  E. The service member was reinforced for replacing angry thoughts with greater understanding and options for reaction.

  F. The service member continues to focus on thoughts that create and maintain anger and was provided with remedial feedback in this area.

23. **Teach Thought Stopping (23)**

  A. The service member was taught how to utilize "thoughts stopping" as a means to interrupt thoughts that promote anger.

  B. The service member was assigned "Making Use of the Thought-Stopping Technique" from the *Adult Psychotherapy Homework Planner*, 2nd ed. (Jongsma).

  C. The service member was reinforced for his/her use of thought-stopping techniques.

  D. The service member has not developed thought-stopping techniques and was reminded to do so.

24. **Visualize Empathy for Conflict Reactions (24)**

  A. The service member was encouraged to visualize how he/she would feel if someone acted the way he/she did to someone he/she was close to.

  B. The service member was assisted in developing visual imagery about how it would feel to be treated the way he/she treats others.

  C. The service member was encouraged to compare and contrast his/her emotional reactions to being the aggressor versus being victimized.

25. **Reinforce Positive Use of Cognitive Techniques (25)**

  A. The service member was reinforced each time he/she identified success at using the cognitive techniques.

  B. Although the service member has not utilized the cognitive techniques, he/she was reinforced for simply knowing how they should have been used.

  C. The service member's behavior was gradually shaped toward more complete success.

26. **Encourage Relaxing Activities (26)**

  A. The service member was encouraged to increase time spent in activities he/she finds relaxing or that decrease perceived levels of tension and stress.

  B. The service member was encouraged to exercise, hit a punching bag, play cards with friends, etc.

  C. The service member was reinforced for his/her use of relaxing and stress-decreasing activities.

D. The service member has not engaged in relaxing or stress-decreasing activities.

E. The service member has not engaged in relaxing or stress-decreasing activities and was redirected to do so.

27. Explore Views about Hierarchical Structure (27)

A. The service member's views about the hierarchical structure (i.e., chain of command) were reviewed.

B. The service member was encouraged to identify the perceived the value of this type of organization.

C. The service member was reinforced as he/she identified the positive aspects of a hierarchical structure.

D. The service member was unable to identify the positive aspects of a hierarchical structure such as in the military and was requested to look for these positives.

28. List and Problem-Solve Anger Triggers (28)

A. The service member was requested to make a list of rules and regulations that create hostility (e.g., having to say "Yes, sir" to someone he/she does not respect).

B. The service member has developed a list of anger triggers, and these were processed.

C. The service member was assisted in developing a list of anger triggers.

D. The service member was assisted to identify responses to anger triggers (i.e., focusing on the rank rather than the person when required to be respectful).

E. The service member was able to identify responses to anger triggers and was urged to implement them.

F. The service member was assisted in developing responses to anger triggers.

29. Identify Other Conflicts (29)

A. The service member was asked to identify other aspects of his/her life that have conflict.

B. Parallels were drawn between the service member's work conflict and personal life conflicts.

C. The service member was prompted to identify how his/her pattern of conflict is not limited to military concerns.

D. The service member was reinforced for identifying the conflict pattern he/she experiences.

E. The service member has not identified the conflict patterns that he/she experiences and was redirected to identify such.

30. Encourage Acceptance of Consequences (30)

A. The service member was encouraged to accept the consequences of his/her behavior without getting into verbal confrontation with superiors.

B. The service member was reminded that confrontation with superiors about consequences could simply lead to more consequences.

C. The service member was taught to ask himself/herself questions while contemplating a response to a consequence, such as "Would you rather do 50 pushups for making a mistake or 100?"

D. The service member was reinforced for accepting consequences of his/her behavior without getting into verbal confrontations.

E. The service member continues to fight against the consequences for his/her behavior, enduring additional consequences; he/she was urged to practice the opportunity to accept consequences.

31. Make Amends (31)

A. The service member was assisted in creating a list of people he/she has offended, disrespected, or assaulted.

B. The service member was encouraged to offer an apology to those harmed by his/her past behavior.

C. The service member was reinforced for making amends with others.

D. The service member has not made amends with others and was redirected to do so.

32. Explore Motivation and Intent (32)

A. The service member was asked to explore whether he/she wants to remain in the military.

B. The service member was asked to review whether his/her episodes of confrontation with comrades are a means to be separated/discharged from the service.

C. The service member has identified that his/her confrontation with comrades is a means to be separated/discharged from the service and was assisted in exploring other options for leaving the military (e.g., hardship discharge, failure to adapt).

D. The service member denies that his/her confrontation with comrades is a means to be separated/discharged from the service and was asked to look at other intensions for such behavior.

DEPRESSION

VETERAN/SERVICE MEMBER PRESENTATION

1. Depressed Affect (1)[*]

A. The veteran/service member reported that he/she feels deeply sad and has periods of tearfulness on an almost daily basis.

B. The veteran's/service member's depressed affect was clearly evident within the session as tears were shed on more than one occasion.

C. The veteran/service member reported that he/she has begun to feel less sad and can experience periods of joy.

D. The veteran/service member appeared to be happier within the session, and there is no evidence of tearfulness.

2. Loss of Appetite (2)

A. The veteran/service member reported that he/she has not had a normal and consistent appetite.

B. The veteran's/service member's loss of appetite has resulted in a significant weight loss associated with the depression.

C. The veteran's/service member's loss of appetite has resulted in a significant weight gain associated with the depression.

D. As the depression has begun to lift, the veteran's/service member's appetite has stabilized.

E. The veteran/service member reported that his/her appetite is at normal levels.

3. Lack of Activity Enjoyment (3)

A. The veteran/service member reported a diminished interest in or enjoyment of activities that were previously found pleasurable.

B. The veteran/service member has begun to involve himself/herself with activities that he/she previously found pleasurable.

C. The veteran/service member has returned to an active interest in and enjoyment of activities.

4. Psychomotor Agitation (4)

A. The veteran/service member demonstrated psychomotor agitation within the session.

B. The veteran/service member reported that with the onset of the depression, he/she has felt unable to relax or sit quietly.

C. The veteran/service member reported a significant decrease in psychomotor agitation and the ability to sit more quietly.

D. It was evident within the session that the veteran/service member has become more relaxed and less agitated.

---

[*]The numbers in parentheses correlate to the number of the Behavioral Definition statement in the companion chapter with the same title in T*he Veterans and Active Duty Military Psychotherapy Treatment Planner* (Moore and Jongsma) by John Wiley & Sons, 2009.

5. Psychomotor Retardation (4)

A. The veteran/service member demonstrated evidence of psychomotor retardation within the session.

B. The veteran/service member moved and responded very slowly, showing a lack of energy and motivation.

C. As the depression has lifted, the veteran/service member has responded more quickly and psychomotor retardation has diminished.

6. Sleeplessness/Hypersomnia (5)

A. The veteran/service member reported periods of inability to sleep and other periods of sleeping for many hours without the desire to get out of bed.

B. The veteran's/service member's problem with sleep interference has diminished as the depression has lifted.

C. Medication has improved the veteran's/service member's problems with sleep disturbance.

7. Lack of Energy (6)

A. The veteran/service member reported that he/she feels a very low level of energy compared to normal times in his/her life.

B. It was evident within the session that the veteran/service member has low levels of energy, as demonstrated by slow walking, minimal movement, lack of animation, and slow responses.

C. The veteran's/service member's energy level has increased as the depression has lifted.

D. It was evident within the session that the veteran/service member is demonstrating normal levels of energy.

8. Lack of Concentration (7)

A. The veteran/service member reported that he/she is unable to maintain concentration and is easily distracted.

B. The veteran/service member reported that he/she is unable to read material with good comprehension because of being easily distracted.

C. The veteran/service member reported increased ability to concentrate as his/her depression has lifted.

9. Indecisiveness (7)

A. The veteran/service member reported a decrease in his/her ability to make decisions based on lack of confidence, low self-esteem, and low energy.

B. It was evident within the session that the veteran/service member does not have normal decision-making capabilities.

C. The veteran/service member reported an increased ability to make decisions as the depression is lifting.

10. Social Withdrawal (8)

A. The veteran/service member has withdrawn from social relationships that were important to him/her.

B. As the veteran's/service member's depression has deepened, he/she has increasingly isolated himself/herself.

C. The veteran/service member has begun to reach out to social contacts as the depression has begun to lift.

D. The veteran/service member has resumed normal social interactions.

11. Suicidal Thoughts/Gestures (9)

A. The veteran/service member expressed that he/she is experiencing suicidal thoughts but has not taken any action on these thoughts.

B. The veteran/service member reported suicidal thoughts that have resulted in suicidal gestures.

C. Suicidal urges have been reported as diminished as the depression has lifted.

D. The veteran/service member denied any suicidal thoughts or gestures and is more hopeful about the future.

12. Feelings of Hopelessness/Worthlessness (10)

A. The veteran/service member has experienced feelings of hopelessness and worthlessness that began as the depression deepened.

B. The veteran's/service member's feelings of hopelessness and worthlessness have diminished as the depression is beginning to lift.

C. The veteran/service member expressed feelings of hope for the future and affirmation of his/her own self-worth.

13. Inappropriate Guilt (10)

A. The veteran/service member described feelings of pervasive, irrational guilt.

B. Although the veteran/service member verbalized an understanding that his/her guilt was irrational, it continues to plague him/her.

C. The depth of irrational guilt has lifted as the depression has subsided.

D. The veteran/service member no longer expresses feelings of irrational guilt.

14. Low Self-Esteem (11)

A. The veteran/service member stated that he/she has a very negative perception of himself/herself.

B. The veteran's/service member's low self-esteem was evident within the session as he/she made many self-disparaging remarks and maintained very little eye contact.

C. The veteran's/service member's self-esteem has increased as he/she is beginning to affirm his/her self-worth.

D. The veteran/service member verbalized positive feelings toward himself/herself.

15. Unresolved Grief (12)

A. The veteran/service member has experienced losses about which he/she has been unable to resolve feelings of grief.

B. The veteran's/service member's feelings of grief have turned to major depression as energy has diminished and sadness/hopelessness dominate his/her life.

C. The veteran/service member has begun to resolve the feelings of grief associated with the loss in his/her life.

D. The veteran/service member has verbalized feelings of hopefulness regarding the future and acceptance of the loss of the past.

16. Hallucinations/Delusions (13)

A. The veteran/service member has experienced mood-related hallucinations or delusions indicating that the depression has a psychotic component.

B. The veteran's/service member's thought disorder has begun to diminish as the depression has been treated.

C. The veteran/service member reported no longer experiencing any thought disorder symptoms.

17. Physical Aches and Pains (14)

A. The veteran/service member reported the development of general physical aches and pains.

B. The veteran/service member reported the exacerbation of general physical aches and pains.

C. As treatment has progressed, the veteran/service member reports a decrease in his/her physical aches and pains.

18. Recurrent Depression Pattern (15)

A. The veteran/service member reported a recurrent pattern of depressive episodes that have been treated with a variety of approaches.

B. The veteran/service member has a history of depression within the family that parallels his/her own experience of depression.

INTERVENTIONS IMPLEMENTED

1. Assess Mood Episodes (1)[*]

A. An assessment was conducted of the veteran's/service member's current and past mood episodes, including the features, frequency, intensity, and duration of the mood episodes.

B. The Inventory to Diagnose Depression (Zimmerman, Coryell, Corenthal, and Wilson) was used to assess the veteran's/service member's current and past mood episodes.

C. The results of the mood episode assessment reflected severe mood concerns, and this was presented to the veteran/service member.

D. The results of the mood episode assessment reflected moderate mood concerns, and this was presented to the veteran/service member.

E. The results of the mood episode assessment reflected mild mood concerns, and this was presented to the veteran/service member.

2. Identify Depression Causes (2)

A. The veteran/service member was asked to verbally identify the source of his/her depressed mood.

---

[*]The numbers in parentheses correlate to the number of the Therapeutic Intervention statement in the companion chapter with the same title in *The Veterans and Active Duty Military Psychotherapy Treatment Planner* (Moore and Jongsma) by John Wiley & Sons, 2009.

B. Active listening skills were used as the veteran/service member listed several factors that he/she believes contribute to his/her feelings of hopelessness and sadness.

C. The veteran/service member struggled to identify significant causes for his/her depression and was provided with tentative examples in this area.

3. Clarify Depressed Feelings (3)

A. The veteran/service member was encouraged to share his/her feelings of depression in order to clarify them and gain insight into their causes.

B. The veteran/service member was supported as he/she continued to share his/her feelings of depression and has identified causes for them.

C. Distorted cognitive messages were noted to contribute to the veteran's/service member's feelings of depression.

D. It was noted that the veteran/service member demonstrated sad affect and tearfulness when describing his/her feelings.

4. Administer Psychological Tests for Depression (4)

A. Psychological testing was arranged to objectively assess the veteran's/service member's depression and suicide risk.

B. The Beck Depression Inventory-II was used to assess the veteran's/service member's depression and suicide risk.

C. The Beck Hopelessness Scale was used to assess the veteran's/service member's depression and suicide risk.

D. The results of the testing indicated severe concerns related to the veteran's/service member's depression and suicide risk, and this was reflected to the veteran/service member.

E. The results of the testing indicated moderate concerns related to the veteran's/service member's depression and suicide risk, and this was reflected to the veteran/service member.

F. The results of the testing indicated mild concerns related to the veteran's/service member's depression and suicide risk, and this was reflected to the veteran/service member.

5. Explore Suicide Potential (5)

A. The veteran's/service member's experience of suicidal urges and his/her history of suicidal behavior were explored.

B. It was noted that the veteran/service member has stated that he/she does experience suicidal urges but feels that they are clearly under his/her control and that there is no risk of engagement in suicidal behavior.

C. The veteran/service member identified suicidal urges as being present but contracted to contact others if the urges became strong.

D. Because the veteran's/service member's suicidal urges were assessed to be very serious, immediate referral to a more intensive supervised level of care was made.

E. Due to the veteran's/service member's suicidal urges and his/her unwillingness to voluntarily admit himself/herself to a more intensive, supervised level of care, involuntary commitment procedures were begun.

6. Monitor Ongoing Suicide Potential (6)

A. The veteran/service member was asked to report any suicidal urges or increase in the strength of these urges.

B. The veteran/service member stated that suicidal urges are diminishing and that they are under his/her control; he/she was praised for this progress.

C. The veteran/service member stated that he/she has no longer experienced thoughts of self-harm; he/she will continue to be monitored.

D. The veteran/service member stated that his/her suicide urges are strong and present a threat; a transfer to a more supervised setting was coordinated.

7. Refer for Hospitalization (7)

A. Because the veteran/service member was judged to be harmful to himself/herself, a referral was made for immediate hospitalization.

B. The veteran/service member was resistive to hospitalization for treatment of his/her suicide potential, so a commitment procedure was utilized.

C. The veteran/service member cooperated with hospitalization to treat the serious suicidal urges.

8. Implement Buddy Watch System (8)

A. The Buddy Watch System was implemented to monitor the service member's actions regarding self-harm and suicide.

B. The service member's chain of command was advised about the need for a Buddy Watch System.

C. The service member's peers were coordinated to spend time with and monitor the service member.

D. Due to the use of the Buddy Watch System, the service member remained safe.

E. Despite the use of the Buddy Watch System, severe suicide concerns remain, so psychiatric hospitalization was pursued.

9. Refer to Physician (9)

A. The veteran/service member was referred to a physician for a physical examination to rule out organic causes for depression.

B. A referral to a physician was made for the purpose of evaluating the veteran/service member for a prescription for psychotropic medication.

C. The veteran/service member has followed through on a referral to a physician and has been assessed for a prescription of psychotropic medication.

D. The veteran/service member has been prescribed antidepressant medication.

E. The veteran/service member has refused the prescription of psychotropic medication prescribed by the physician.

10. Monitor Medication Compliance (10)

A. As the veteran/service member has taken the antidepressant medication prescribed by his/her physician, the effectiveness and side effects of the medication were monitored.

B. The veteran/service member reported that the antidepressant medication has been beneficial in reducing sleep interference and in stabilizing mood; the benefits of this progress were reviewed.

C. The veteran/service member reported that the antidepressant medication has not been beneficial; this was relayed to the prescribing clinician.

D. The veteran/service member was assessed for side effects from his/her medication.

E. The veteran/service member has not consistently taken the prescribed antidepressant medication and was redirected to do so.

11. Identify Depressogenic Schemata (11)

A. The veteran/service member was assisted in developing an awareness of his/her automatic thoughts that reflect depressogenic schemata.

B. The veteran/service member was assisted in developing an awareness of his/her distorted cognitive messages that reinforce hopelessness and helplessness.

C. The veteran/service member was helped to identify several cognitive messages that occur on a regular basis and feed feelings of depression.

D. The veteran/service member recalled several instances of engaging in negative self-talk that precipitated feelings of helplessness, hopelessness, and depression; these were processed.

12. Assign Dysfunctional Thinking Journal (12)

A. The veteran/service member was requested to keep a daily journal that lists each situation associated with depressed feelings and the dysfunctional thinking that triggered the depression.

B. The veteran/service member was assigned to use the "Daily Record of Dysfunctional Thoughts," as described in *Cognitive Therapy of Depression* (Beck, Rush, Shaw, and Emery).

C. The veteran/service member was directed to complete the "Negative Thoughts Trigger Negative Feelings" assignment from the *Adult Psychotherapy Homework Planner,* 2nd ed. (Jongsma).

D. The veteran/service member has completed the homework assignment, and the content was processed.

E. The Socratic method was used to challenge the veteran's/service member's dysfunctional thoughts and to replace them with positive, reality-based thoughts.

F. The veteran/service member was reinforced for instances of successful replacement of negative thoughts with more realistic positive thinking.

G. The veteran/service member has not kept his/her record of automatic thoughts and was redirected to do so.

13. Conduct Behavioral Experiments (13)

A. The veteran/service member was encouraged to do "behavioral experiments" in which depressive automatic thoughts are treated as hypotheses/predictions and are tested against reality-based alternative hypotheses.

B. The veteran's/service member's automatic depressive thoughts were tested against his/her past, present, and/or future experiences.

C. The veteran/service member was assisted in processing the outcome of his/her behavioral experiences.

D. The veteran/service member was encouraged by his/her experience of the more reality-based hypotheses/predictions; this progress was reinforced.

E. The veteran/service member continues to focus on depressive automatic thoughts and was redirected toward the behavioral evidence of the more reality-based alternative hypotheses.

14. Reinforce Positive Self-Talk (14)

A. The veteran/service member was reinforced for any successful replacement of distorted negative thinking with positive, reality-based cognitive messages.

B. It was noted that the veteran/service member has been engaging in positive, reality-based thinking that has enhanced his/her self-confidence and increased adaptive action.

C. The veteran/service member was assigned to complete the "Positive Self-Talk" assignment from the *Adult Psychotherapy Homework Planner,* 2nd ed. (Jongsma).

D. The veteran/service member has completed the homework assignment, and the content was processed.

15. Teach Behavioral Coping Strategies (15)

A. The veteran/service member was taught behavioral coping strategies such as physical exercise, increased social involvement, sharing of feelings, and increased assertiveness as ways to reduce feelings of depression.

B. The veteran/service member has implemented behavioral coping strategies to reduce feelings of depression and was reinforced for doing so.

C. The veteran/service member reported that the utilization of behavioral coping strategies has been successful at reducing feelings of depression; the benefits of this progress were reviewed.

D. The veteran/service member was assisted in identifying several instances in which behavioral coping strategies were helpful in reducing depressive feelings.

E. The veteran/service member has not used behavioral coping strategies and was redirected to use this important resource.

16. Engage in Behavioral Activation (16)

A. The veteran/service member was engaged in "behavioral activation" by scheduling activities that have a high likelihood for pleasure and mastery.

B. The veteran/service member was directed to complete tasks from the "Identify and Schedule Pleasant Events" assignment from the *Adult Psychotherapy Homework Planner,* 2nd ed. (Jongsma).

C. The veteran/service member has completed the homework assignment and the content was processed.

D. Rehearsal, role-playing, role reversal, and other techniques were used to engage the veteran/service member in behavioral activation.

E. The veteran/service member was reinforced for his/her successes in scheduling activities that have a high likelihood for pleasure and mastery.

F. The veteran/service member has not engaged in pleasurable activities and was redirected to do so.

17. Employ Self-Reliance Training (17)

A. Self-reliance training was used to help the veteran/service member assume increased responsibility for routine activities (e.g., cleaning, cooking, shopping).

B. The veteran/service member was urged to take responsibility for routine activities in order to overcome depression symptoms.

C. The veteran/service member was reinforced for his/her increased self-reliance.

D. The veteran/service member has not assumed increased responsibility for routine activities, and his/her struggles in this area were redirected.

18. Assess the Interpersonal Inventory (18)

A. The veteran/service member was asked to develop an "interpersonal inventory" of important past and present relationships.

B. The veteran's/service member's interpersonal inventory was assessed for potentially depressive themes (e.g., grief, interpersonal disputes, role transitions, interpersonal deficits).

C. The veteran's/service member's interpersonal inventory was found to have significant depressive themes, and this was reflected to him/her.

D. The veteran's/service member's interpersonal inventory was found to have minimal depressive themes, and this was reflected to him/her.

19. Explore Unresolved Grief (19)

A. The veteran's/service member's history of losses that have triggered feelings of grief were explored.

B. The veteran/service member was assisted in identifying losses that have contributed to feelings of grief that have not been resolved.

C. The veteran's/service member's unresolved feelings of grief are noted to be contributing to current feelings of depression and were provided a special focus.

20. Teach Conflict Resolution Skills (20)

A. The veteran/service member was taught conflict resolution skills such as practicing empathy, active listening, respectful communication, assertiveness, and compromise.

B. Using role-playing, modeling, and behavioral rehearsal, the veteran/service member was taught how to implement conflict resolution skills.

C. The veteran/service member reported implementation of conflict resolution skills in his/her daily life and was reinforced for this utilization.

D. The veteran/service member reported that resolving interpersonal conflicts has contributed to a lifting of his/her depression; the benefits of this progress were emphasized.

E. The veteran/service member has not used the conflict resolution skills that the/she has been taught and was provided with specific examples of when to use these skills.

21. Help Resolve Interpersonal Problems (21)

A. The veteran/service member was assisted in resolving interpersonal problems through the use of reassurance and support.

B. The "Applying Problem-Solving to Interpersonal Conflict" homework from the *Adult Psychotherapy Homework Planner,* 2nd ed. (Jongsma) was assigned to help resolve interpersonal problems.

C. The veteran/service member has completed the homework assignment, and the content was processed.

D. The veteran/service member was helped to clarify cognitive and affective triggers that ignite conflicts.

E. The veteran/service member was taught active problem-solving techniques to help him/her resolve interpersonal problems.

F. It was reflected to the veteran/service member that he/she has significantly reduced his/her interpersonal problems.

G. The veteran/service member continues to have significant interpersonal problems, and he/she was provided with remedial assistance in this area.

22. Address Interpersonal Conflict through Conjoint Sessions (22)

A. A conjoint session was held to assist the veteran/service member in resolving interpersonal conflicts with his/her partner.

B. The veteran/service member reported that the conjoint sessions have been helpful in resolving interpersonal conflicts with his/her partner, and this has contributed to a lifting of his/her depression.

C. It was reflected that ongoing conflicts with a partner have fostered feelings of depression and hopelessness.

23. Reinforce Physical Exercise (23)

A. A plan for routine physical exercise was developed with the veteran/service member and a rationale for including this in his/her daily routine was made.

B. The veteran/service member and therapist agreed to make a commitment toward implementing daily exercise as a depression reduction technique.

C. The veteran/service member has performed routine daily exercise, and he/she reports that it has been beneficial; these benefits were reinforced.

D. The veteran/service member has not followed through on maintaining a routine of physical exercise and was redirected to do so.

24. Recommend Meeting with Post/Base Physical Instructor (24)

A. The veteran/service member was encouraged to meet a certified physical trainer to introduce him/her to the concept of combating stress, depression, and anxiety with exercise.

B. The veteran/service member has followed through with the recommended meeting with a physical trainer and reported that it was beneficial; key points were reviewed.

C. The veteran/service member has implemented a regular exercise regimen as a depression reduction technique and reported successful results; he/she was verbally reinforced for this progress.

D. The veteran/service member has not followed through with the recommended meeting with a physical trainer and was encouraged to do so.

25. Build Relapse Prevention Skills (25)

A. The veteran/service member was assisted in building relapse prevention skills through the identification of early warning signs of relapse.

B. The veteran/service member was directed to consistently review skills learned during therapy.

C. The veteran/service member was assisted in developing an ongoing plan for managing his/her routine challenges.

26. Teach Assertiveness (26)

A. Role-playing, modeling, and behavioral rehearsal were used to train the veteran/service member in assertiveness.

B. The veteran/service member was referred to an assertiveness training group for intense education about acquiring assertiveness skills.

C. The veteran/service member reported that as a result of the training, he/she has become more assertive in expressing his/her needs, desires, and expectations.

D. The veteran/service member continues to have difficulties in being assertive, as lack of confidence, low self-esteem, and social withdrawal inhibit him/her; remedial education was provided in this area.

27. Recommend Depression Self-Help Books (27)

A. Several self-help books on the topic of coping with depression were recommended to the veteran/service member.

B. The veteran/service member was directed to read *The Feeling Good Handbook* (Burns).

C. The veteran/service member has followed through with reading self-help books on depression and reported key ideas that were processed.

D. The veteran/service member reported that reading the assigned self-help books on depression has been beneficial and identified several coping techniques that he/she has implemented as a result of the reading.

E. The veteran/service member has not followed through with reading the self-help books that were recommended and was encouraged to do so.

28. Monitor Grooming/Hygiene (28)

A. The veteran/service member was encouraged to practice consistent grooming and hygiene.

B. It was reflected to the veteran/service member that he/she has taken more pride in his/her personal appearance as evidenced by improved grooming and hygiene practices.

C. The veteran/service member was reinforced for practicing improved grooming and hygiene behavior.

D. The veteran/service member has displayed poor grooming and hygiene and was provided with specific redirection in this area.

29. Assign Positive Affirmations (29)

A. The veteran/service member was assigned to write at least one positive affirmation statement on a daily basis regarding himself/herself and the future.

B. The veteran/service member has followed through on the assignment of writing positive affirmation statements and reported that he/she is feeling more positive about the future.

C. The veteran/service member was reinforced for making positive statements regarding himself/herself and his/her ability to cope with the stresses of life.

D. The veteran/service member has not followed through on the assignment of writing positive affirmation statements and was encouraged to do so.

30. Teach Normalization of Sadness (30)

A. The veteran/service member was taught about the variation in mood that is within the normal sphere.

B. The veteran/service member reported that he/she is developing an increased tolerance to mood swings and is not attributing them to significant depression; this progress was reinforced.

C. The veteran/service member is verbalizing more hopeful and positive statements regarding the future and accepting some sadness as a normal variation and feeling; the benefits of this progress were highlighted.

31. Explore Childhood Pain (31)

A. Experiences from the veteran's/service member's childhood that contribute to his/her current depressed state were explored.

B. The veteran/service member identified painful childhood experiences that were interpreted as having continued to foster feelings of low self-esteem, sadness, and sleep disturbance.

C. As the veteran/service member has described his/her childhood experiences within an understanding atmosphere, sad feelings surrounding those experiences have diminished.

D. The veteran/service member has been guarded about discussing his/her experience of childhood pain and was redirected in this area.

32. Explore Suppressed Anger (32)

A. The veteran/service member was encouraged to share his/her feelings of anger regarding painful childhood experiences that contributed to his/her current depressed state.

B. As the veteran/service member described painful experiences from the past, he/she was helped to express feelings of anger, sadness, and suppressed rage.

C. The veteran/service member reported that he/she has begun to feel less depressed as suppressed feelings of anger and hurt have been expressed and processed.

D. The veteran/service member has not expressed his/her suppressed anger and was urged to do this as he/she feels able to do so.

33. Connect Anger with Depression (33)

A. The veteran/service member was taught the possible connection between previously unexpressed feelings of anger and helplessness and his/her current state of depression.

B. It was reflected to the veteran/service member that as he/she has gained insight into suppressed feelings from the past, his/her current feelings of depression have diminished.

C. The veteran/service member was reinforced as he/she verbalized an understanding of the relationship between his/her current depressed mood and the repression of anger, hurt, and sadness.

D. The veteran/service member has not displayed an understanding of the relationship between his/her current depressed mood and repression of anger, hurt, and sadness and was provided with remedial feedback in this area.

34. Schedule a "Booster Session" (34)

A. The veteran/service member was scheduled for a "booster session" between 1 and 3 months after therapy ends.

B. The veteran/service member was advised to contact the therapist if he/she needs to be seen prior to the "booster session."

C. The veteran's/service member's "booster session" was held, and he/she was reinforced for his/her successful implementation of therapy techniques.

D. The veteran's/service member's "booster session" was held, and he/she was coordinated for further treatment, as his/her progress has not been sustained.

35. Identify Mental Health Resources (35)

A. The service member was assisted in identifying mental health resources at the location where he/she will be deployed.

B. The service member was provided with specific information for how to seek mental health services in the area where he/she will be deployed.

C. Contacts were made to assist in the transition for mental health services in the service member's new deployment.

DIVERSITY ACCEPTANCE

VETERAN/SERVICE MEMBER PRESENTATION

1. Difficulty Accepting Different Groups (1)[*]

A. The veteran/service member reports difficulty adjusting to and accepting people from different cultural backgrounds.

B. The veteran/service member reports difficulty adjusting to and accepting people from different racial backgrounds.

C. The veteran/service member reports difficulty adjusting to and accepting people from different ethnic backgrounds.

D. The veteran/service member reports difficulty adjusting to and accepting people from different religious backgrounds.

E. As treatment has progressed, the veteran/service member reports greater acceptance of those from different backgrounds.

2. Pervasive Distrust (2)

A. The veteran/service member describes a pervasive mistrust of those from different cultural, racial, ethnic, and religious backgrounds.

B. The veteran/service member reports significant reluctance to rely on those from different backgrounds.

C. The veteran/service member cites specific situations that he/she believes supports distrust of people from different backgrounds than his/her own.

D. The veteran/service member has become more accepting of people from different backgrounds.

E. The veteran/service member reports that he/she has been able to rely on people from various backgrounds in important situations.

3. Feels Unsafe (3)

A. The veteran/service member described a sense of uncertainty and lack of safe feelings when around dissimilar people.

B. The veteran/service member identified experiences in which he/she felt unsafe, blaming another person's dissimilarity for this insecurity.

C. As treatment has progressed, the veteran/service member has become more at ease with people who are dissimilar from him/her in some manner.

4. Hostile, Critical Comments (4)

A. The veteran/service member openly makes hostile, critical comments about others from different backgrounds.

---

[*]The numbers in parentheses correlate to the number of the Behavioral Definition statement in the companion chapter with the same title in *The Veterans and Active Duty Military Psychotherapy Treatment Planner* (Moore and Jongsma) by John Wiley & Sons, 2009.

B. Directly hostile, critical comments have been made to others from different backgrounds.

C. Complaints have been levied about the veteran's/service member's hostile, critical comments about others' backgrounds.

D. As treatment has progressed, the veteran/service member has discontinued his/her hostile, critical comments toward others.

5. Intentional Desire to Alienate and Harm Others (5)

A. The veteran/service member identifies an intentional desire and expectation to alienate people with different backgrounds.

B. The veteran/service member has made threats to harm people from other backgrounds.

C. The veteran/service member reports an intentional desire to alienate or harm others from different backgrounds but has not followed through on these urges.

D. As treatment has progressed, the veteran/service member reports no further desire to alienate and harm others.

6. Altercations with Dissimilar People (6)

A. The veteran/service member has engaged in verbal altercations with dissimilar people.

B. The veteran/service member has engaged in physical altercations with dissimilar people.

C. The veteran/service member blames the other person's dissimilarity from him/her as the reason for his/her altercations.

D. The veteran/service member has greatly reduced his/her physical and verbal altercations with dissimilar people.

E. The veteran/service member has discontinued any physical and verbal altercations with dissimilar people.

F. The veteran/service member reports improving relationships with dissimilar people.

7. Avoids Contact with Dissimilar Comrades (7)

A. The veteran/service member avoids social contact with fellow service members who come from a different cultural, racial, religious, or ethnic background.

B. The veteran/service member is very direct about not wishing to be in social contact with fellow service members from dissimilar backgrounds.

C. The veteran/service member has indicated that although he/she will work with others from a dissimilar background, he/she refuses to socialize with them.

D. As treatment has progressed, the veteran/service member has developed social contacts and friendships with comrades from dissimilar backgrounds.

8. Refusal to Work as a Team (8)

A. The service member refuses to communicate with or trust people from different backgrounds, despite the expectation that they work together as a close-knit team.

B. The service member has refused to work with people from different backgrounds, despite the expectation that they should protect each other on a military assignment.

C. Concerns about the unit's safety have been raised because of the service member's failure to work together as a protection-oriented, close-knit team.

D. As treatment has progressed, the service member reports a greater ability to communicate and trust others from diverse backgrounds.

INTERVENTIONS IMPLEMENTED

1. Explore Extent of Animosity (1)[*]

A. The veteran/service member was asked to describe the extent and pervasiveness of his/her feelings of discomfort and animosity toward others from different backgrounds.

B. Clear limits were set and enforced on what type of disrespectful language will be tolerated within the session.

C. The veteran/service member was provided with reflective listening as he/she described his/her feelings of discomfort and animosity toward others from different backgrounds.

D. A clear focus was provided to the veteran/service member as he/she described his/her feelings of discomfort and animosity, accepting these as his/her thoughts and feelings, without necessarily agreeing.

2. Assess Effect on Job Performance (2)

A. The extent of the effect of the service member's views and beliefs about others has had on his/her job performance was assessed.

B. The specific effects of the service member's negative beliefs about others were assessed, including how individuals of other backgrounds may not want to work with him/her.

C. The service member's lack of promotion was identified as being connected to his/her hateful and disrespectful comments.

D. The service member's demotion was connected to his/her hateful and disrespectful comments toward people of a different background.

3. Assess Dangerousness (3)

A. An assessment was developed in regard to whether the service member's beliefs and actions have endangered the lives of other members of different cultural, racial, ethnic, and religious background.

B. Situations in which the service member has purposely put others at risk were reviewed.

C. Situations in which the service member failed to provide appropriate support to other service members because of their different backgrounds were reviewed.

D. Situations in which the service member has purposely attacked other service members of different backgrounds were reviewed.

E. Despite the service member's many comments and beliefs in regard to people of different backgrounds, it was noted that there is no evidence that he/she has endangered or threatened the lives of other service members.

F. It was noted that the service member has put others in danger because of his/her beliefs about cultural, racial, ethnic, and religious backgrounds.

[*]The numbers in parentheses correlate to the number of the Therapeutic Intervention statement in the companion chapter with the same title in *The Veterans and Active Duty Military Psychotherapy Treatment Planner* (Moore and Jongsma) by John Wiley & Sons, 2009.

4. Dialogue about Beliefs (4)

A. A respectful and nonjudgmental dialogue was held with the veteran/service member regarding his/her long-held beliefs about people from diverse backgrounds.

B. Open-ended questions were used to elicit information about the veteran's/service member's beliefs about people from diverse backgrounds.

C. Cognitive reframes were utilized when possible in order to help start changing the veteran's/service member's beliefs about people from other backgrounds.

D. The veteran/service member was open to discussion about his/her beliefs about people from diverse backgrounds and was reinforced for this open-mindedness.

E. The veteran/service member was not willing to dialogue significantly about his/her long-held beliefs about people from diverse backgrounds and was urged to do so as he/she feels capable.

5. Assess Etiology of Beliefs (5)

A. The etiology of the veteran's/service member's beliefs was reviewed.

B. The veteran/service member was noted to have developed his/her beliefs as a product of his/her own thoughts, experiences, and reflections.

C. The veteran/service member was noted to have developed his/her views as a product of adopting the beliefs of others.

D. The veteran/service member reports that his/her beliefs about other cultures, races, ethnicities, and religions come from his/her parents' beliefs.

E. The reality of the veteran's/service member's beliefs was challenged, and stereotypes were identified.

6. Identify Specific Fears (6)

A. Assistance was provided to the veteran/service member in regard to identifying his/her specific fears about being around people from diverse backgrounds.

B. The veteran/service member was supported and encouraged as he/she identified fears about being around people from diverse backgrounds.

7. Identify Irrational and Illogical Views (7)

A. The veteran/service member was assisted in identifying irrational and illogical views related to his/her fears about being around others from different backgrounds.

B. The veteran/service member was supported for those fears that he/she was able to identify as irrational and illogical.

C. Cognitive restructuring techniques were used to assist with replacing the veteran's/service member's dysfunctional views.

D. The veteran/service member was reinforced for his/her identification and replacement of dysfunctional views.

E. The veteran/service member has not made significant changes in his/her dysfunctional views and was encouraged to do so.

8. List Positive Experiences (8)

A. The veteran/service member was instructed to make a list of positive experiences with individuals from diverse backgrounds.

B. The veteran/service member was supported as he/she identified some positive experiences with individuals from diverse backgrounds.

C. The veteran/service member denied any positive experiences with any individual from a diverse background and was urged to continue to review his/her history.

9. Confront Logic of Stereotypes (9)

A. The veteran/service member was confronted on how his/her positive experiences with a person from a different background negates and makes broad judgments illogical.

B. The veteran/service member was reinforced as he/she agreed that his/her broad generalizations and judgments were not logical.

C. The veteran/service member was taught about the mistakes that can be made with sampling errors.

D. Despite evidence to the contrary, the veteran/service member maintains his/her broad generalizations and judgments.

10. Assign Introduction (10)

A. The veteran/service member was assigned to introduce himself/herself to at least one person from a different cultural, racial, ethnic, or religious background each day.

B. The veteran/service member was assisted in processing his/her experiences of introducing himself/herself to people from diverse backgrounds.

C. The veteran/service member was reinforced for his/her adaptive responses to people from different backgrounds.

D. The veteran/service member has failed to introduce himself/herself to people of different backgrounds and was reminded to do so.

11. Assign Questions about Others' Background (11)

A. The veteran/service member was assigned to construct a list of three questions that could focus on learning about culture, race, ethnicity, or religion.

B. The veteran/service member was assigned to ask one individual from a different background questions that focus on learning about his/her culture, race, ethnicity, or religion.

C. The veteran/service member has completed his/her assignments about learning about others backgrounds, and key points were processed.

D. The veteran/service member has not completed his/her assignments about learning about others backgrounds and was redirected to do so.

12. Explain about Stereotypes (12)

A. The concept of stereotypes was explained.

B. Examples were provided about how stereotypes injure both individuals and entire groups.

C. Stereotypes about the veteran's/service member's own culture, race, ethnicity, or religious group were identified in order to help make the point of how stereotypes injure others.

D. The veteran/service member was reinforced for his/her understanding of how stereotypes affect others.

E. The veteran/service member did not embrace concerns about how stereotypes affect others and was reminded about these concerns.

13. Identify Bigoted Schema (13)

A. The veteran/service member was assisted in identifying the distorted schemas and related automatic thoughts that mediated negative biases about individuals from different cultural, racial, ethnic, and religious backgrounds.

B. The veteran/service member was taught the role of distorted thinking and precipitating emotional responses.

C. The veteran/service member was reinforced as he/she verbalized an understanding of the cognitive beliefs and messages that mediate his/her bias responses.

D. The veteran/service member was assisted in replacing distorted messages with thoughts of realistic cognitions.

E. The veteran/service member failed to identify his/her distorted thoughts and cognitions and was provided with tentative examples in this area.

14. Assign Daily Log of Automatic Thoughts (14)

A. The veteran/service member was assigned homework exercises in which he/she identifies automatic thoughts associated with seeing others of different backgrounds as inferior or dangerous.

B. The veteran/service member was assigned "Journal and Replace Self-Defeating Thoughts" from the *Adult Psychotherapy Homework Planner*, 2nd ed. (Jongsma).

C. The veteran/service member completed the homework assignment, and the content was processed within the session.

D. The veteran/service member was assisted in challenging distorted thinking patterns with reality-based thoughts.

E. The veteran/service member was reinforced for his/her success at replacing biased, bigoted self-talk with reality-based alternatives.

F. The veteran/service member was provided with corrective feedback for his/her failures to replace bigoted self-talk with reality-based alternatives.

G. The veteran/service member has not completed his/her assigned homework regarding fearful self-talk and was redirected to do so.

15. Reinforce Positive Cognitions (15)

A. The veteran/service member was reinforced for positive cognitions that foster openness and acceptance of people from diverse backgrounds.

B. The veteran/service member was reinforced for identifying and challenging the cognitions that inhibit openness and acceptance of people from diverse backgrounds.

C. It was noted that as the veteran's/service member's positive cognitions are reinforced, he/she is becoming more accepting of people form diverse backgrounds.

16. Request Training with Comrade from a Different Background (16)

A. The service member was encouraged to request from superiors that he/she be paired with someone from a different background for a training mission.

B. Emphasis was made to the service member that purposely pairing himself/herself with a person from a different background will help to develop trust and foster a reliance on others.

C. The service member was reinforced as he/she has sought out training with an individual from a different background.

D. The service member has not sought out training with a person from a different background and was redirected to do so.

17. Reinforce Positive Interaction Experiences (17)

A. The veteran/service member was asked to identify positive interaction experiences with people from different backgrounds from him/her.

B. The veteran/service member was reinforced for his/her description of positive interactions with people from a different background.

C. The veteran/service member was assisted in processing his/her experiences with people from a different background in order to break down distorted beliefs about "them."

D. The veteran/service member was reinforced for his/her changes in beliefs about people from other backgrounds.

E. The veteran/service member did not identify any positive interactions from people with different backgrounds and was urged to monitor his/her experiences for such.

18. Encourage Friendship (18)

A. The veteran/service member was encouraged to develop a friendship with an individual from a different background.

B. The veteran/service member has developed a friendship with an individual from a different background, and he/she was reinforced for this.

C. The veteran/service member was assisted in processing his/her change in thoughts as he/she develops a friendship with someone from a different background.

D. The veteran/service member has not developed a friendship with anyone from a different background and was reminded to do so.

19. Encourage Mentoring Comrade of a Different Background (19)

A. The service member was encouraged to ask his/her superiors to allow him/her to mentor a fellow comrade who is of a different culture, race, ethnicity, or religion.

B. The service member has begun mentoring a fellow comrade who is of a different culture, race, ethnicity, or religion, and his/her experiences were processed.

C. The service member refuses to try to mentor a fellow comrade who is of a different culture, race ethnicity, or religion and was reminded about the usefulness of this change.

FINANCIAL DIFFICULTIES

VETERAN/SERVICE MEMBER PRESENTATION

1. Indebtedness (1)[*]

A. The veteran/service member described severe indebtedness and overdue bills that exceed his/her ability to meet the monthly payments.

B. The veteran/service member has developed a plan to reduce his/her indebtedness through increasing income and making systematic payments.

C. The veteran/service member has begun to reduce the level of indebtedness and is making systematic payments.

2. Decrease in Income (2)

A. The service member's monthly income has decreased subsequent to returning from deployment.

B. The service member has lost hazard duty pay.

C. The service member has lost tax-free status.

D. The service member has adjusted his/her budget or living expenses to accommodate the reduction in income.

3. Asset Depletion during Deployment (3)

A. While the veteran/service member was deployed, his/her assets were depleted and debt increased.

B. A family member, friend, or other party responsible for managing the veteran's/service member's finances has mismanaged the finances, causing asset depletion and debt increase.

C. As treatment has progressed, the veteran/service member has reasserted control over his/her finances and is managing them in a more responsible manner.

4. Hopelessness (4)

A. The veteran/service member described a feeling of hopelessness and low self-esteem associated with the lack of sufficient income to cover the cost of living.

B. As financial arrangements have been adjusted, the veteran's/service member's mood has improved.

C. The veteran/service member has developed a sense of hope for the future as financial assistance has been attained and the cost of living is covered.

5. Concern over Financial Issues (5)

A. The veteran/service member described a pattern of conflict with his/her spouse over money management and the definition of necessary expenditures and savings goals.

---

[*]The numbers in parentheses correlate to the number of the Behavioral Definition statement in the companion chapter with the same title in *The Veterans and Active Duty Military Psychotherapy Treatment Planner* (Moore and Jongsma) by John Wiley & Sons, 2009.

B. The veteran/service member described a pattern of conflict with his/her family members over money management and the definition of necessary expenditures and savings goals.

C. Work and social conflicts have been noted due to the veteran's/service member's sense of stress from overdue debts.

D. The veteran/service member has started communicating more within his/her important relationships in order to decrease the stress from overdue debts.

E. Agreement has been reached with the veteran's/service member's significant other/family members in order to develop realistic investing and savings goals.

6. Impulsive Spending (6)

A. The veteran/service member described a pattern of impulsive spending that does not consider the eventual financial consequences of such action.

B. The veteran/service member was in defensive denial regarding his/her pattern of impulsive spending.

C. The veteran/service member acknowledged his/her impulsive spending and has begun to develop a plan to help cope with this problem.

D. The veteran/service member has established a pattern of delay of any purchase until the financial consequences of the purchase can be planned for and met.

7. Reprimanded by Superiors (7)

A. The service member has been reprimanded by his/her superiors due to not fulfilling financial obligations.

B. The service member's superiors have expressed concern about the service member not fulfilling spousal and child support expectations.

C. The service member's superiors have expressed concern about the service member not fulfilling bill payment.

D. As the service member has become more responsible about his/her financial obligation, pressure from his/her superiors has decreased.

8. Poor Money Management Skills (8)

A. The veteran/service member has a long-term lack of discipline in money management that has led to excessive indebtedness.

B. The veteran/service member has filed for bankruptcy to protect himself/herself from creditors.

C. The client veteran/service member never established a budget with spending guidelines and savings goals that would allow for prompt payment of bills.

9. Concern about Loss of Rank/Separation (9)

A. The service member is concerned that he/she will lose rank.

B. The service member is concerned that he/she will be involuntarily separated from military service.

C. The service member is concerned about his/her change in income due to loss of rank or involuntary separation from military service.

D. As treatment has progressed, the service member has become more at ease regarding his/her military service status.

10. Damaged Credit Rating (10)

A. Overdue debts are being reported by creditors to credit boroughs, severely damaging the veteran's/service member's credit rating.

B. The veteran/service member has had credit denied due to his/her low credit rating.

C. The veteran/service member has been required to pay a higher interest rate due to his/her poor credit rating.

D. The veteran/service member has begun to manage his/her finances more responsibly, which has caused an increase in his/her credit rating.

11. Fear of Foreclosure (11)

A. The veteran/service member is concerned that that he/she will lose his/her home because of an inability to meet monthly mortgage payments.

B. Foreclosure papers have been served on the veteran/service member.

C. As the veteran/service member has emerged from his/her financial difficulties, his/her concern about loss of home ownership has been greatly decreased.

D. The veteran/service member is no longer at risk for foreclosure.

INTERVENTIONS IMPLEMENTED

1. Assist in Open Discussion of Financial Difficulties (1)[*]

A. Regular eye contact, active listening, unconditional positive regard, and warm acceptance were used to help build trust with the veteran/service member.

B. The veteran's/service member's emotional status was monitored as he/she was encouraged to discuss his/her financial difficulties, with a focus on acknowledgment of the shame, embarrassment, and guilt that may go along with discussing such issues.

C. The veteran/service member began to express feelings more freely as report and trust levels have increased.

D. The veteran/service member has continued to experience difficulty being open and direct in his/her expression of painful feelings; he/she was encouraged to become more open as he/she feels capable of doing so.

2. Explore the Financial Situation (2)

A. The veteran's/service member's current financial situation was explored in detail.

B. The veteran/service member was assisted in describing the details of his/her financial crisis, including his/her level of indebtedness and other monthly obligations.

C. The veteran/service member was supported as he/she described the past-due bills that have mounted and created a financial crisis.

D. Active listening was provided as the veteran/service member described his/her change of employment status that has reduced his/her level of income.

---

[*]The numbers in parentheses correlate to the number of the Therapeutic Intervention statement in the companion chapter with the same title in *The Veterans and Active Duty Military Psychotherapy Treatment Planner* (Moore and Jongsma) by John Wiley & Sons, 2009.

3. List Financial Obligations (3)

A. The veteran/service member was assisted in compiling a complete list of his/her financial obligations.

B. The veteran/service member was noted to have a pattern of minimization and denial in the area of acknowledging financial obligations.

C. The veteran's/service member's list of financial obligations was reviewed and checked for possible omissions.

4. Assess for Depression/Anxiety (4)

A. The veteran/service member was assessed for the presence of clinically significant depression symptoms.

B. The veteran/service member was assessed for the presence of clinically significant anxiety symptoms.

C. The veteran's/service member's level of depression and anxiety was reflected to him/her.

D. Clinically significant depression symptoms were identified, and the focus of treatment was turned toward these symptoms.

E. Clinically significant anxiety symptoms were identified, and the focus of treatment was turned toward these symptoms.

F. The veteran/service member was assessed for depression and anxiety symptoms, but none was noted.

5. Explore Severity of Clinical Symptoms (5)

A. The severity of the veteran's/service member's clinical symptoms was explored.

B. An assessment was made of the need for treatment targeted at the veteran's/service member's clinical symptoms.

C. The veteran/service member was referred for treatment for his/her clinical symptoms.

D. The veteran/service member was treated for his/her clinical symptoms.

E. The veteran/service member was assessed for depression and anxiety symptoms, but no severe symptoms were noted, and no treatment needs were identified.

6. Assess Suicide Potential (6)

A. The veteran/service member was directly assessed for any suicidal urges that have been experienced.

B. The veteran/service member denied any suicidal urges; he/she was encouraged to make contact if these urges increase.

C. Because the veteran/service member described serious suicidal urges, steps were taken to ensure his/her safety.

7. Develop Spending Priorities (7)

A. The veteran/service member was asked to compare net income while deployed versus current net income.

B. The veteran/service member was assigned the task of listing the priorities that he/she believes should give direction to how money is spent.

C. The veteran/service member was asked to identify expenses that will have to be cut to balance expenses with current income.

D. The veteran's/service member's list of priorities regarding how money is spent was processed and clarified.

E. The veteran/service member was reinforced as he/she agreed that an established set of priorities should govern his/her spending and has committed himself/herself to implementing that control.

F. It was reflected to the veteran/service member that he/she has demonstrated that his/her priorities have control over spending.

8. List Expense Changes Post-Deployment (8)

A. The veteran/service member was requested to list expenses that he/she now has that he/she did not have when deployed.

B. The veteran/service member was provided with examples of expenses that did not occur while deployed, including food, clothing, entertainment, and rent.

C. The veteran/service member was assisted in planning as to how his/her expenses will be paid.

D. The veteran/service member was reinforced for developing a more realistic understanding of his/her changes in finances.

E. The veteran/service member has struggled to understand the changes in his/her financial concerns since deployment ended and was provided with remedial feedback in this area.

9. Revisit Current Power of Attorney (9)

A. The veteran/service member was encouraged to revisit his/her current power of attorney put in place prior to deployment.

B. The veteran/service member was supported as he/she has decided to take legal control of his/her own finances.

C. The veteran/service member was assisted in taking legal control of his/her own finances.

D. The veteran/service member was supported as he/she has decided to allow the current power of attorney to remain in place.

10. Explore Revocation of Power of Attorney (10)

A. An exploration of the option of revoking the veteran's/service member's power of attorney was conducted.

B. As the individual responsible for managing the veteran's/service member's finances does not have wise financial judgment or has stolen assets from the veteran/service member, the power of attorney is being revoked.

C. The veteran/service member was reinforced for revoking his/her power of attorney.

D. Additional steps are being investigated in regard recouping money wasted or stolen from the individual responsible for the veteran's/service member's finances.

11. Encourage Communication to Unit Leadership (11)

A. The service member was encouraged to inform his/her unit leadership of financial difficulties as those difficulties appear to be affecting his/her military duties.

B. The service member does not believe his/her financial difficulties are affecting his/her military duties and has decided against informing his/her unit leadership.

C. The service member was supported as he/she has communicated with his/her unit leadership about the financial difficulties.

D. Although it would be helpful for the service member to inform his/her unit leadership about his/her financial difficulties, he/she has declined to do so and was encouraged to access this option.

12. Refer for Financial Assistance (12)

A. The veteran/service member was referred for financial assistance programs at his/her local base/post.

B. The veteran/service member was referred for a loan for financial assistance.

C. The veteran/service member was referred for programs that will assist in paying for or providing food, clothing, or household needs.

D. The veteran/service member has utilized financial assistance, and his/her reaction to this experience was processed.

E. The veteran/service member has declined to utilize the financial assistance programs and was reminded about this helpful resource.

13. Explore Natural Supports for Financial Help (13)

A. The veteran/service member was engaged in the discussion about how family, friends, or religious organizations could supply temporary financial support.

B. The veteran/service member has sought out help from family, friends, or religious organizations for temporary financial support and has experienced significant assistance.

C. The veteran/service member has sought out help from family, friends, or religious organizations but was noted to have had minimal positive results.

D. The veteran/service member has not sought out assistance from family, friends, or religious organizations, and his/her reasoning for this was assessed.

14. Refer to Financial Counselor (14)

A. The veteran/service member was referred to a financial counselor at his/her local base/post in order to review expenses versus income and create a budget.

B. The veteran/service member was reinforced for his/her use of a financial counselor at his/her local base/post.

C. The veteran/service member has developed a budget that matches expenses and income.

D. The veteran/service member has not utilized the financial counselor and was redirected to do so.

15. Create a Sound Budget (15)

A. The veteran/service member was directed to write a budget and long-range savings and investment plan.

B. The veteran/service member was referred to a professional financial planner.

C. The veteran/service member was assigned "Plan a Budget" from the *Adult Psychotherapy Homework Planner,* 2nd ed. (Jongsma).

D. The veteran/service member completed the homework assignment, and the content was processed within the session.

E. The veteran/service member has not developed a financial plan and was redirected to do so.

16. Encourage Adherence to Budget (16)

A. The veteran's/service member's budget was reviewed for completeness and reasonableness.

B. The veteran/service member was encouraged to adhere to his/her budget by making it a part of his/her daily routine.

C. The veteran/service member was reinforced for implementing the budget and allowing his/her spending to be strictly controlled by it.

D. Although the veteran/service member has created a comprehensive budget that balances income with expenses, it was noted that he/she has not been strictly controlled by it.

17. Encourage Accountability by Sharing Budget (17)

A. The veteran/service member was encouraged to give a copy of his/her budget to a superior in his/her unit whom he/she trusts.

B. The veteran/service member was encouraged to remain accountable to the trusted superior in regard to his/her budget.

C. Positive verbal reinforcement was provided to the veteran/service member as he/she has become accountable to his/her trusted superior by providing a copy of his/her budget.

D. The veteran/service member has declined to provide any additional information to his/her superiors and was encouraged to utilize this helpful opportunity as he/she feels more at ease doing so.

18. Review Elimination of Extra Expenses (18)

A. The veteran/service member was encouraged to review his/her current bills and determine if there are any "extras" that could be eliminated.

B. The veteran/service member was provided with examples of extras that could be eliminated, including cable television, cell phone, or magazine subscriptions.

C. The veteran/service member was reinforced for his/her reasonableness in determining his/her "extras" that can be eliminated from his/her current bills and expenses.

D. The veteran/service member has reviewed his/her current bills and expenses but is reluctant to eliminate "extras" and was encouraged to begin to do so.

19. Reinforce Conjoint Financial Planning (19)

A. A conjoint session was held to develop a mutually agreed on financial plan.

B. Both partners have committed themselves to a financial plan and have reinforced each other for implementing it consistently.

C. Although the partners have committed themselves to a financial plan, it was noted that they have not implemented it consistently; they were redirected to do so.

20. Reinforce Cooperative Financial Management (20)

A. The veteran/service member was reinforced for making changes in financial management that reflect compromise, reasonable planning, and respectful cooperation with his/her partner.

B. The veteran/service member has set financial goals and made budgetary decisions with his/her partner that allow for equal input and balanced control over financial matters; this change was reinforced.

C. The veteran/service member has not maintained a cooperative financial management pattern and was reminded to return to this helpful pattern.

21. Assign Financial Record Keeping (21)

A. The veteran/service member was assisted in developing a plan of weekly and monthly record keeping that reflects income and payments made.

B. The veteran/service member has consistently kept weekly and monthly records of financial income and expenses and was reinforced for doing so.

C. The veteran/service member has not consistently kept weekly and monthly records of financial income and expenses and was redirected to do so.

22. Explore the Emotional Vulnerability to Spending (22)

A. The veteran/service member was assessed as to feelings of low self-esteem, need to impress others, loneliness, or depression that may accelerate unnecessary and unwanted spending.

B. The veteran/service member identified negative emotional states that he/she attempts to cope with through unnecessary spending; he/she was supported as these were processed.

C. The veteran/service member was rather guarded regarding the emotional vulnerability that he/she experiences and was provided with tentative examples of how these emotions lead to unwanted and unnecessary spending.

23. Assess Mood Swings (23)

A. The veteran/service member was assessed for characteristics of bipolar disorder that could contribute to careless spending due to impaired mania-related judgment.

B. The veteran/service member was helped to identify impulsive spending as a part of a general pattern of impulsivity that is based on mood swings.

C. The veteran/service member was referred for a psychiatric evaluation to consider the possibility of medication to control mood swings.

D. The veteran/service member was assessed for the presence of mood swings that could contribute to careless spending, but no such pattern of bipolar disorder was identified.

24. Explore the Family-of-Origin Financial Patterns (24)

A. The veteran's/service member's family-of-origin patterns of earning, saving, and spending money were identified.

B. The veteran/service member was supported as he/she acknowledged that the financial patterns that he/she learned from his/her family of origin have influenced his/her own money management decisions.

C. It was reflected to the veteran/service member that he/she has allowed reasonable priorities to control financial decision making rather than following mismanagement patterns learned from his/her family of origin.

25. Explore Values and Beliefs from Family and Origin (25)

A. The veteran/service member was encouraged to explore the values and beliefs from his/her family of origin.

B. The veteran/service member was assisted in identifying the values and beliefs from his/her family or origin in regard to financial concerns.

C. The veteran/service member was assisted in identifying how his/her family-of-origin values contributed to the problem with his/her current financial needs.

D. The veteran/service member was assisted in identifying how his/her values and beliefs about money need to be reformulated.

26. Teach Purchase Delay (26)

A. The veteran/service member was taught the importance of delaying an impulse to make a purchase to allow time for reflection regarding the affordability and consequences of the expense.

B. The veteran/service member was encouraged to commit to delay any new purchases over a predetermined amount for at least 48 hours.

C. The veteran/service member has successfully implemented the delay of impulses to spend, and this delay has resulted in a reduction of unnecessary purchases; he/she was reinforced for this success.

D. The veteran/service member has failed to implement the delay of impulses to spend and was assisted in reviewing how to utilize this helpful technique.

27. Teach about Awareness and Challenging of Maladaptive Cognitions (27)

A. The veteran/service member was taught about becoming more aware of his/her thoughts and emotions when he/she has a desire to make a new purchase.

B. The veteran/service member was assisted in challenging maladaptive cognitions.

C. The veteran/service member was provided with examples of changes in maladaptive cognitions (i.e., changing "I need this item and can add it to my credit card" to "I want this item, but my credit card balance is to high for me to add this cost now").

D. The veteran/service member was assisted in using techniques to challenge his/her cognitions.

28. Teach about Pro and Con List (28)

A. The veteran/service member was taught how to create a pro and con list before any new purchase.

B. The veteran/service member was assisted in practicing the use of a pro and con list before a new purchase.

C. The veteran/service member has regularly used a pro and con list before a new purchase, and his/her experience was processed.

D. The veteran/service member has not regularly used a pro and con list prior to a new purchase and was reminded about this helpful technique.

29. Role-Play Resistance to External Pressure (29)

A. Role-playing and behavior rehearsal were used to help the veteran/service member develop coping mechanisms for external pressure to spend beyond what he/she can afford.

B. The veteran/service member identified pressure from family members and friends to spend beyond what he/she can afford; he/she was reminded to use his/her coping mechanisms.

C. Role-playing and behavioral rehearsal were used to help the veteran/service member develop coping mechanisms for internal pressure to spend beyond what he/she can afford.

D. The veteran/service member has not used his/her learned coping mechanisms for refusing pressure to spend money and was reminded about this helpful technique.

30. Review Options for Part-Time Work (30)

A. The service member was assisted in exploring the potential benefits of acquiring a part-time job after duty hours to increase income.

B. The service member was assisted in developing plausible options for part-time work after duty hours in order to increase income.

C. The service member was reinforced for his/her decision in regard to potential part-time work after duty hours.

31. Encourage Bimonthly Updates to Unit Leadership (31)

A. The service member was encouraged to provide bimonthly updates on his/her financial progress to his/her unit leadership.

B. The service member has provided bimonthly updates to his/her unit leadership and was reinforced for doing so.

C. The service member has not provided bimonthly updates on financial progress to his/her unit leadership and was redirected to do so.

32. Improve Credit Score (32)

A. The veteran/service member was referred to a financial counselor at his/her local base/post in order to gain knowledge on how to improve his/her credit score.

B. The veteran/service member has met with the financial counselor at his/her local base/post, and the results of this meeting were reviewed.

C. The veteran/service member has not met with his/her financial counselor at the local base/post and was reminded of this helpful resource.

D. The veteran/service member has utilized information gained from the financial counselor in order to start improving his/her credit score, and this progress was strongly reinforced.

33. Reinforce Positive Financial Decision Making (33)

A. The veteran/service member provided examples of the positive outcomes of his/her decision-making process for financial concerns, and this was strongly reinforced.

B. The veteran/service member was assisted in identifying the benefits of his/her healthy financial decision making.

C. The veteran/service member was unable to identify any positive financial decisions and was provided with remedial feedback in this area.

34. Refer to Attorney (34)

A. The service member was referred to a military attorney to explore the feasibility and impact of filing for bankruptcy.

B. The service member was referred to the judge advocate general in regard to the feasibility and impact of filing for bankruptcy.

C. The veteran/service member was referred to a private attorney in regard to the feasibility and impact of filing for bankruptcy.

D. The veteran/service member has decided to file for bankruptcy and was supported for taking steps to resolve his/her financial crisis.

E. The veteran/service member has declined to file for bankruptcy and was supported for this decision.

HOMESICKNESS/LONELINESS

SERVICE MEMBER PRESENTATION

1. Thoughts Dominated by Homesickness (1)[*]

A. The service member reported complaints of his/her thoughts being dominated by missing family, friends, and/or previous home environment.

B. The service member reported a sense of compulsion to think about his/her missed family, friends, and home environment.

C. As treatment has progressed, the service member reports a decreased sense of being overwhelmed by his/her thoughts of missing family, friends, and home environment.

D. The service member reports that he/she has adjusted to military life and his/her thoughts are no longer dominated by missing family, friends, or his/her previous home environment.

2. Mild Loneliness/Emptiness (2)

A. The service member reports a mild level of loneliness.

B. The service member reports a general sense of emptiness.

C. As treatment has progressed, the service member has reported fewer lonely feelings and greater acceptance of being apart from loved ones.

D. The service member reports feeling more fulfilled.

3. Focus on Leaving the Military (3)

A. The service member reports a constant focus on his/her desire to leave the military and return home to family.

B. The service member reports that he/she is overwhelmed with the desire to return to his/her family, even at the cost of leaving the military.

C. As treatment has progressed, the service member has become more accepting of the military and does no long so much to return to his/her family.

D. The service member reports that he/she has resolved concerns about leaving the military in order to return to family and feels well adjusted in this area.

4. Emotional Reaction to Living Independently (4)

A. The service member reports a sense of helplessness, dread, and uncertainty related to living independently.

B. The service member reports that he/she has never lived at this level of independence and is emotionally unprepared.

C. As treatment has progressed, the service member has reported that he/she is more at ease with living independently and has decreased his/her emotional reactivity.

[*]The numbers in parentheses correlate to the number of the Behavioral Definition statement in the companion chapter with the same title in *The Veterans and Active Duty Military Psychotherapy Treatment Planner* (Moore and Jongsma) by John Wiley & Sons, 2009.

5. Anxiety/Depression (5)

A. The service member reports a clinically significant level of anxiety related to being separated from his/her previous home environment.

B. The service member reports a clinically significant level of depression related to being separated from his/her previous home environment.

C. As treatment has progressed, the service member's anxiety and depression at being separated from his/her previous home environment have decreased.

D. The service member has resolved his/her emotional reaction from being separated from his/her previous home environment.

6. Too-Frequent Contact with Family Members (6)

A. The service member makes contact with family members whenever possible.

B. The service member has neglected other aspects of his/her duties and social opportunities in order to make contact with family members.

C. The service member has decreased his/her contact with family members and is becoming more independent.

D. The service member reports being more at ease with his/her occasional contact with family members.

7. Avoids Emotional Reaction to Contact with Family Members (7)

A. Due to a fear of overwhelming homesickness, the service member almost never makes contact with family members.

B. The service member reports that he/she is worried about how he/she will cope with the emotions that are brought up when contacting family members.

C. As treatment has progressed, the service member is more open to making contact with family members, as he/she does not experience overwhelming homesickness.

8. Social Struggles (8)

A. The service member displays an inability to make new friends within his/her new surroundings.

B. The service member reports that he/she does not feel very accepted in his/her new environment.

C. The service member rarely makes attempts to socialize with others.

D. As treatment has progressed, the service member feels more accepted and is friendlier with others within his/her new environment.

E. The service member describes feeling more at ease and accepted in the new environment.

9. Negative Emotions toward Loved Ones (9)

A. The service member reports feeling distant, angry, or resentful toward loved ones.

B. The service member is reluctant to share his/her negative emotions with loved ones.

C. As treatment has progressed, the service member has become more open about his/her distant, angry, and resentful feelings toward loved ones.

D. The service member reports a more positive emotional sense toward his/her loved ones.

10. Picked on by Comrades (10)

A. The service member has displayed his/her homesickness/loneliness to his/her comrades and is regularly picked on for these feelings.

B. The service member has discontinued sharing his/her feelings with comrades for fear of being teased.

C. As treatment has progressed, the service member has resolved his/her homesickness and loneliness and is no longer teased by his comrades.

INTERVENTIONS IMPLEMENTED

1. Develop Trust (1)*

A. Today's clinical contact focused on building a level of trust within the therapeutic relationship through consistent eye contact, active listening, unconditional positive regard, and warm acceptance.

B. Empathy and support were provided for the service member's expression of thoughts and feelings during today's clinical contact.

C. The service member was provided with support and feedback as he/she described his/her pattern of homesickness and loneliness.

D. As the service member has remained mistrustful and reluctant to share his/her underlying thoughts and feelings, he/she was provided with additional reassurance.

E. The service member verbally acknowledged that he/she has difficulty establishing trust, and this was accepted by the therapist.

2. Assess Level of Homesickness/Loneliness (2)

A. The service member's type, intensity, and frequency of homesickness and loneliness concerns were assessed.

B. The impact of the service member's homesickness and loneliness concerns on his/her social, occupational, and interpersonal functioning was assessed.

C. The impact of the service member's homesickness and loneliness concerns was rated as mild.

D. The impact of the service member's homesickness and loneliness concerns was rated as moderate.

E. The impact of the service member's homesickness and loneliness concerns was rated as severe.

3. Talk with Supervisor (3)

A. A discussion was held with the service member's first-line supervisor to assess the degree the homesickness and loneliness symptoms have impacted the service member's job performance.

B. The service member's squad leader, platoon sergeant, or first sergeant was consulted in regard to the impact of the homesickness and loneliness symptoms on the service member's job performance.

C. The service member's first-line supervisor indicated mild concerns in regard to the service member's job performance.

---

*The numbers in parentheses correlate to the number of the Therapeutic Intervention statement in the companion chapter with the same title in *The Veterans and Active Duty Military Psychotherapy Treatment Planner* (Moore and Jongsma) by John Wiley & Sons, 2009.

D. The service member's first-line supervisor indicated moderate concerns in regard to the service member's job performance.

E. The service member's first-line supervisor indicated serious concerns in regard to the service member's job performance.

4. Refer/Conduct Psychological Testing (4)

A. Psychological testing was administered to assess the presence and strength of anxiety and depressive symptoms related to homesickness and loneliness.

B. The Beck Depression Inventory-II was administered to the service member.

C. The Beck Anxiety Inventory was administered to the service member.

D. Psychological testing confirmed the presence of significant anxiety and depressive symptoms related to homesickness/loneliness.

E. Psychological testing confirmed mild anxiety and depressive symptoms related to homesickness/loneliness.

F. Psychological testing revealed that there are no significant depressive or anxiety symptoms related to homesickness/loneliness.

G. The results of the psychological testing were presented to the service member.

5. Refer for Medication Evaluation (5)

A. The service member was referred for a medication evaluation to help stabilize his/her moods and decrease the intensity of his/her feelings.

B. The service member was reinforced as he/she agreed to follow through with the medication evaluation.

C. The service member strongly opposed being placed on medication to help stabilize his/her moods and reduce emotional distress; his/her objections were processed.

6. Monitor Effects of Medication (6)

A. The service member's response to the medication was discussed in today's therapy session.

B. The service member reported that the medication has helped to stabilize his/her moods and decrease the intensity of his/her feelings; he/she was directed to share this information with the prescribing clinician.

C. The service member reports little to no improvement in his/her moods or anger control since being placed on the medication; he/she was directed to share this information with the prescribing clinician.

D. The service member was reinforced for consistently taking the medication as prescribed.

E. The service member has failed to comply with taking the medication as prescribed; he/she was encouraged to take the medication as prescribed.

7. Provide Update to Leadership (7)

A. An update was provided to the service member's unit leadership on his/her condition, potential negative impacts on safety, and any occupational limitations while taking medication.

B. The service member's unit leadership was advised about the service member's use of medication.

C. Periodic updates were provided to the service member's unit leadership about his/her medication treatment and progress.

8. Explore Feelings about New Environment and Military (8)

A. The service member was gently encouraged to tell about his/her feelings about being in such an unfamiliar environment.

B. The service member was encouraged to talk about how he/she feels about the military in general.

C. The service member was encouraged to process his/her emotions regarding his/her new environment and the military.

9. Develop Pro and Con List (9)

A. The service member was directed to create a pro and con list related to his/her new environment and newfound independence.

B. The service member was assisted in creating a pro and con list regarding his/her new environment and newfound independence.

C. The pro and con list developed by the service member in regard to his/her new environment and newfound independence was processed.

D. The service member has not created a pro and con list related to his/her newfound independence and was redirected to do so.

10. Normalize Emotions (10)

A. The service member was educated about how this initial separation from friends and family can be difficult for anyone.

B. The service member was educated about how separation is a normal part of the developmental process between adolescence and adulthood.

C. The service member was provided with examples of how other service members have experienced similar emotions.

D. The service member was supported and reinforced as he/she has indicated acceptance of the normal nature of his/her emotions.

E. The service member has not accepted the natural experience of his/her emotions and was provided with additional feedback in this area.

11. Role-Playing Normalizing of Emotions (11)

A. The service member was asked to role-play a situation in which he/she asked to convince the therapist that the personal effects of separation are normal.

B. The service member embraced the role-playing situation and learned about his/her own normal feelings.

C. The service member did not accept the role-play technique very well and continues to see his/her feelings as abnormal.

12. Share Personal Experiences of Homesickness/Loneliness (12)

A. As appropriate within the current therapeutic relation, the therapist shared personal experiences with the service member regarding periods of homesickness/loneliness with and how these feelings were overcome.

B. The therapist reviewed with the service member how homesickness and loneliness feelings were coped with and overcome.

C. The service member displayed understanding of how the therapist has been able to overcome homesickness and loneliness.

13. Assign Talk with Superiors (13)

A. The service member was assigned to select a superior whom he/she respects to talk to regarding his/her feelings of homesickness and loneliness.

B. The service member was encouraged to ask how the respected superior experienced homesickness and loneliness after leaving home for the first time.

C. The service member has had a discussion with a superior about homesickness/ loneliness, and key points were reviewed and processed.

D. The service member has not engaged in a discussion with his/her superior about homesickness/loneliness and was redirected to do so.

14. Encourage Discussion with Other Service Members (14)

A. The service member was encouraged to talk with fellow service members whom he/she trusts about their emancipation experiences.

B. The service member has talked with fellow service members, and key points were processed.

C. The service member has not talked with fellow service members about their emancipation experiences and was redirected to do so.

15. Develop Awareness of Automatic Thoughts (15)

A. The service member was assisting in developing an awareness of his/her automatic thoughts that are consistent with a homesickness/loneliness schema.

B. The service member was taught about how dysfunctional thoughts generate negative feelings.

C. The service member was assigned "Negative Thoughts Trigger Negative Feelings" from the *Adult Psychotherapy Homework Planner*, 2nd ed. (Jongsma).

D. The service member has completed assignments on negative thoughts and negative feelings, and key points were processed.

E. The service member displayed a clear awareness of his/her automatic thoughts that are consistent with homesickness/loneliness and was supported for this progress.

F. The service member has struggled to identify automatic thoughts that are consistent with a homesickness/loneliness schema and was provided with specific examples in this area.

16. Assign Dysfunctional Thinking Journal (16)

A. The service member was requested to keep a daily journal that lists each situation associated with depressed feelings and the dysfunctional thinking that triggered the depression.

B. The service member was directed to complete the "Journal and Replace Self-Defeating Thoughts" assignment from the *Adult Psychotherapy Homework Planner*, 2nd ed. (Jongsma).

C. The service member completed the homework assignment, and the content was processed within the session.

D. The Socratic method was used to challenge the service member's dysfunctional thoughts and to replace them with positive, reality-based thoughts.

E. The service member was reinforced for instances of successful replacement of negative thoughts with more realistic positive thinking.

F. The service member has not kept a record of his/her automatic thoughts and was redirected to do so.

17. Reinforce Positive Self-Talk (17)

A. The service member was reinforced for any successful replacement of distorted negative thinking with positive, reality-based cognitive messages.

B. It was noted that the service member has been engaging in positive, reality-based thinking that has enhanced his/her self-confidence and increased adaptive action.

C. The service member was assigned to complete the "Positive Self-Talk" assignment from the *Adult Psychotherapy Homework Planner*, 2nd ed. (Jongsma).

D. The service member completed the homework assignment, and the content was processed within the session.

18. Teach Thought-Stopping Technique (18)

A. The service member was taught to implement a thought-stopping technique for negative thoughts that have been addressed but persist.

B. The service member was taught a specific thought-stopping technique, focusing on a stop sign and then a pleasant scene.

C. The service member was assigned "Making Use of the Thought-Stopping Technique" from the *Adult Psychotherapy Homework Planner*, 2nd ed. (Jongsma).

D. The service member completed the homework assignment, and the content was processed within the session.

E. The service member was monitored and encouraged in his/her use of the thought-stopping technique between sessions.

19. Explore Prior Expectations (19)

A. The service member's expectations about the military prior to enlisting were explored.

B. The service member identified the specific expectations that he/she had about the military prior to enlisting, and these were processed.

C. The service member was asked to identify his/her expectations about the military, including those related to friendships and how leaving home would be.

D. The service member was assisted in processing his/her expectations about the military.

20. Compare Prior Expectations to Reality (20)

A. The service member was asked to compare prior expectations with current reality.

B. The service member was encouraged to focus on being flexible and adaptable.

C. The military mentality of "adapt and overcome" was emphasized as a way to change expectations to reality.

D. The service member's future expectations were reviewed.

21. Reinforce Correction of Negative Thoughts (21)

A. The service member was supported for his/her successes in recognizing negative thoughts.

B. The service member was reinforced for ways in which he/she has corrected negative thoughts.

C. Periodic booster sessions were used to focus on the impact of the service member's cognitions on his/her emotions.

D. The service member has struggled to recognize and correct negative thoughts and was provided with additional assistance in this area.

22. Maintain Consistent, Limited Contact (22)

A. The service member was encouraged to maintain consistent contact with family and friends from home while setting limits.

B. The service member was encouraged to call family and friends but not on a daily basis.

C. The service member was encouraged to keep some conversations brief, just checking in with family and friends.

D. The service member's limits on his/her contact with family and friends were processed.

23. Assist in Setting Limits (23)

A. The service member was assisted in setting limits on his/her friends and family from home.

B. The service member was assisted in creating a call schedule.

C. The service member was reinforced for setting limits on his/her contact with home.

D. The service member has not adhered to any limits on contact with home and was reminded to do so.

24. Review Information to Share (24)

A. The service member was assisted in sifting through the type and amount of information that would be helpful to share with family and friends.

B. The service member was asked to focus on maintaining communication with family and friends as a way of keeping connected with them, but with limits to the information provided.

C. The service member has limited the type and amount of information provided to family and friends at home, and his/her experience was processed.

25. Explore Difficulties in Establishing Relationships (25)

A. Reasons behind the service member's difficulties establishing new relationships and maintaining existing relationships were explored and processed.

B. The service member was assisted in exploring automatic thoughts that may trigger social anxiety.

C. The service member was assigned "Restoring Socialization Comfort" from the *Adult Psychotherapy Homework Planner*, 2nd ed. (Jongsma).

D. The service member has completed assignments to identify automatic thoughts that trigger social anxiety, and his/her progress was processed.

E. The service member has not completed assignments to identify automatic thoughts that trigger social anxiety and was reminded to do so.

26. Assign Introduction to Three New People (26)

A. The service member was assigned to introduce himself/herself to three new people between sessions.

B. The service member was reinforced for his/her success in introducing himself/herself to three new people.

C. The service member has not introduced himself/herself to three new people and was assisted in processing why he/she failed in this task.

27. Assign Attendance at Social Functions (27)

A. The service member was assigned to attend social functions that tend to make him/her feel uncomfortable.

B. The service member has attended social functions that have tended to make him/her feel uncomfortable, and his/her experience was processed.

C. The service member has not attended social functions that tend to make him/her feel uncomfortable and was redirected to do so.

28. Teach Relaxation Techniques (28)

A. The service member was taught relaxation techniques such as imagery or progressive muscle relaxation.

B. The service member was assigned to use the relaxation techniques to relax twice a day for 10 to 20 minutes.

C. The service member was directed to use the relaxation techniques prior to and during social interactions.

D. The service member reported that regular use of the relaxation techniques has led to decreased anxiety in social situations; he/she was encouraged to continue these techniques.

E. The service member has not implemented the relaxation techniques in social situations and continues to feel quite distressed; he/she was redirected to do so.

29. Conduct Systematic Desensitization Sessions (29)

A. The systematic desensitization technique was used to help reduce anxiety in social situations.

B. The service member was assisted in decreasing anxiety in social situations by gradually moving through a hierarchy of anxiety-producing social situations.

30. Encourage Exercise (30)

A. The service member was encouraged to exercise at least 30 to 45 minutes a day for five days a week as a means to improve mood and energy level.

B. The service member was reinforced for his/her regular exercise.

C. The service member reports an increases mood and energy level, and this was reinforced.

D. The service member has not used exercise as a way to improve his/her mood and energy level and was reminded to do so.

31. Assign Travel Schedule (31)

A. The service member was assigned to create a travel schedule, including dates to visit home, length of stay, whom to spend time with, and how to handle feelings upon departure.

B. The service member has created a travel schedule and was reinforced for his/her preparedness and feelings upon departure.

C. The service member has not created a travel schedule and was reminded to do so.

INSOMNIA

VETERAN/SERVICE MEMBER PRESENTATION

1. Sleep Initiation Problems (1)[*]

A. The veteran/service member reported that he/she finds it very difficult to fall asleep within a reasonable period of time.

B. The veteran/service member reported that his/her sleep disturbance has diminished and that he/she is beginning to return to a normal sleep cycle.

C. The veteran/service member reported longer experiences without sleep disturbance symptoms and is sleeping fairly consistently.

2. Sleep Maintenance Problems (2)

A. The veteran/service member reported that he/she can fall asleep within a reasonable period of time but often awakens and is unable to return to sleep easily.

B. The veteran/service member reported that he/she awakens at a very early hour and is unable to return to sleep.

C. The veteran/service member reported that his/her sleep disturbance has decreased, and he/she is beginning to return to the normal sleep cycle.

D. The veteran/service member reported longer experiences without sleep disturbance symptoms and is sleeping fairly consistently.

3. Not Feeling Rested (3)

A. Although the veteran/service member reports getting an average amount of sleep per night, he/she is not feeling refreshed or rested upon awakening.

B. Despite sleeping more than seven to eight hours per night, the veteran/service member feels a need to take a nap during the day as he/she does not feel rested with a normal amount of sleep.

C. The veteran/service member reported that he/she is feeling more rested and refreshed upon awakening.

4. Frightening Dreams Recalled (4)

A. The veteran/service member reported significant distress resulting from repeated awakening at night with detailed recall of extremely frightening dreams involving threats to himself/herself.

B. As the veteran's/service member's daily life external stressors have increased, he/she has experienced repeated awakening and detailed recall of extremely frightening dreams involving threats to himself/herself.

C. As the veteran/service member has resolved external stressors, incidences of experiencing nightmares have diminished significantly.

---

[*]The numbers in parentheses correlate to the number of the Behavioral Definition statement in the companion chapter with the same title in *The Veterans and Active Duty Military Psychotherapy Treatment Planner* (Moore and Jongsma) by John Wiley & Sons, 2009.

D. The veteran/service member reported that he/she no longer experiences extremely frightening dreams that awaken him/her in the night.

5. Daytime Sleepiness (5)

A. The veteran/service member reported that he/she feels very sleepy during the day and easily falls asleep, even while sitting in a chair.

B. The veteran/service member reported that he/she has fallen asleep in a chair in the presence of others in a social situation on many occasions.

C. The veteran/service member reported that he/she is beginning to feel more rested and alert during the day as his/her sleep pattern is returning to normal.

D. The veteran/service member reported no recent incidents of falling asleep too easily during the day.

6. Physical Effects of Sleep Deprivation (6)

A. The veteran/service member displays physical effects of sleep deprivation.

B. The veteran/service member displays psychomotor retardation.

C. The veteran/service member displays muscle weakness.

D. As treatment has progressed, the veteran's/service member's sleep has improved, and the physical effects of his/her sleep deprivation have been significantly decreased.

7. Mental/Emotional Effects of Sleep Deprivation (7)

A. The veteran/service member displays the mental/emotional effects of sleep deprivation.

B. The veteran/service member displays decreased concentration due to sleep deprivation.

C. The veteran/service member displays a general pattern of apathy.

D. The veteran/service member displays emotional lability.

E. As treatment has progressed, the mental/emotional effects of sleep deprivation have been decreased for the veteran/service member.

8. Inappropriate Dozing (8)

A. The veteran/service member reports dozing off at inappropriate times.

B. The veteran/service member has fallen asleep while driving.

C. The veteran/service member has fallen asleep during meetings.

D. The service member has fallen asleep while on military assignments.

E. As treatment has progressed, the veteran's/service member's insomnia has been significantly resolved, and he/she reports a cessation of dozing off at inappropriate times.

9. Rumination (9)

A. The veteran/service member reports excessive rumination prior to bedtime.

B. The veteran/service member has difficulty falling asleep because of his/her ruminating thoughts.

C. The veteran/service member reports a decrease in his/her ruminations and a better ability to induce sleep.

INTERVENTIONS IMPLEMENTED

1. Assess Sleep Disturbance (1)[*]

A. The exact nature of the veteran's/service member's sleep disturbance was assessed, including his/her bedtime routine, activity level while awake, nutritional habits, napping practice, actual sleep time, rhythm of time for being awake versus sleeping, and so on.

B. The assessment of the veteran's/service member's sleep disturbance found a chronic history of this problem, which becomes exacerbated at times of high stress.

C. The assessment of the veteran's/service member's sleep disturbance found that the veteran/service member does not practice behavioral habits that are conducive to a good sleep-wake routine.

2. Assess Sleep Hygiene Practices (2)

A. The veteran/service member was assessed in regard to appropriate sleep hygiene practices.

B. The veteran/service member was assessed about his/her food and drink intake pattern.

C. The veteran/service member was assessed in regard to activities directly before bedtime.

D. The veteran/service member was advised about the results of the assessment of his/her sleep hygiene techniques.

E. The veteran/service member was assessed in regard to his/her sleep hygiene techniques, but no changes were indicated.

3. Assess Views about Sleep (3)

A. The veteran's/service member's views about sleep were assessed.

B. Important concepts were reviewed with the veteran/service member, including how quantity is more important than quality of sleep.

C. The veteran/service member was interviewed about how much sleep he/she seems to need.

4. Administer Assessment of Sleep Problems (4)

A. The veteran's/service member's current level of sleep problems were assessed with objective means.

B. The veteran/service member was administered the Insomnia Severity Index (ISI).

C. The veteran/service member was administered the Sleep Impairment Index (SII).

D. Feedback from the objective measures of the veteran's/service member's insomnia problems in regard to sleep latency, maintenance, and quality was provided to the veteran/service member.

E. The veteran/service member declined to take the objective measures of sleep impairment, and his/her resistance in this area was processed.

5. Explain Connection Between Bad Sleep Habits and Insomnia (5)

A. The connection between the veteran's/service member's bad sleep habits and insomnia was the focus of today's session.

---

[*]The numbers in parentheses correlate to the number of the Therapeutic Intervention statement in the companion chapter with the same title in *The Veterans and Active Duty Military Psychotherapy Treatment Planner* (Moore and Jongsma) by John Wiley & Sons, 2009.

B. The veteran/service member was provided with examples of how bad sleep habits maintain insomnia (e.g., watching television in bed leading to an offset sleep pattern, causing poor sleep the next night).

C. The veteran/service member was able to identify how his/her bad sleep habits have created and maintained insomnia; this insight was supported.

D. The veteran/service member has struggled to identify how bad sleep habits have created and maintained his/her insomnia and was provided with additional feedback in this area.

6. List Bad Sleep Habits (6)

A. The veteran/service member was directed to create a list of bad sleep habits that he/she has developed.

B. The veteran/service member was assisted in identifying his/her bad sleep habits.

C. The veteran's/service member's list of poor sleep habits was reviewed and processed.

D. The veteran/service member has not completed a list of bad sleep habits and was redirected to do so.

7. Instruct on Behavioral Practices (7)

A. The veteran/service member was instructed on appropriate behavioral practices conducive to good sleep.

B. The veteran/service member was advised about restricting caffeine four hours prior to bedtime.

C. The veteran/service member was encouraged to exercise regularly but not in the evening.

D. The veteran/service member was advised to restrict spicy late-night snacks and heavy evening meals.

E. The veteran/service member was instructed to remove cues to time that may promote "clock watching" while in bed.

8. Assign Sleep Record (8)

A. The veteran/service member was assigned to keep a record of his/her sleep pattern.

B. The veteran/service member was assigned the "Sleep Pattern Record" exercise from the *Adult Psychotherapy Homework Planner,* 2nd ed. (Jongsma).

C. The veteran's/service member's record of his/her sleep pattern was reviewed and processed.

D. The veteran/service member has not completed the sleep pattern record and was redirected to do so.

9. Teach about Stimulus Control (9)

A. The veteran/service member was taught about the use of stimulus control.

B. Concepts from *Insomnia: A Clinician's Guide to Assessment and Treatment* (Moria & Espic) were taught to the veteran/service member.

C. The veteran/service member was taught how managing stimuli prior to sleep periods helps to make sleep more attainable.

D. The veteran/service member displayed a clear understanding about the use of stimulus control, and this insight was reinforced.

E. The veteran/service member struggled to understand the concept of stimulus control and was provided with additional information in this area.

10. Identify Stimulus-Conditioning Problems (10)

A. The veteran/service member was assigned to identify examples of stimulus conditioning that create and maintain insomnia.

B. The veteran/service member identified examples of his/her stimulus conditioning that create and maintain insomnia, and these were processed within session.

C. The veteran/service member was unable to identify any specific examples of stimulus conditioning that helped to create and maintain his/her insomnia and was provided with specific examples.

11. Teach Stimulus-Control Techniques (11)

A. The veteran/service member was taught specific stimulus-control techniques to assist in improving his/her sleep hygiene.

B. The veteran/service member was taught about restricting time in bed, including getting out of bed if unable to fall asleep after 15 minutes.

C. The veteran/service member was assisted in establishing a consistent sleep and wake time.

D. The veteran/service member was advised to go to bed only when sleepy and to avoid daytime naps.

E. The veteran/service member was taught about using the bed only for sleep and sex.

F. The veteran/service member displayed clear understanding of the stimulus-control techniques, and these were reinforced.

G. The veteran/service member struggled to understand the use of stimulus-control techniques, and remedial information was provided.

12. Monitor Stimulus-Control Compliance (12)

A. The veteran's/service member's sleep pattern was monitored.

B. Military lifestyle obstacles, such as decreased time for sleep and crowded barracks/home, were identified as barriers to the stimulus-control technique.

C. The veteran/service member was monitored for compliance with stimulus-control instructions.

D. Problem-solving techniques were used to help resolve obstacles to stimulus-control compliance.

E. The veteran/service member was reinforced for successful, consistent implementation of stimulus-control techniques.

13. Connect Psychiatric Disorders with High Arousal (13)

A. The veteran/service member was taught about how high levels of arousal interfere with sleep.

B. The veteran/service member was taught about how some psychiatric disorders (e.g., posttraumatic stress disorder) can contribute to elevated arousal patterns.

C. The veteran/service member identified how his/her psychiatric concerns may contribute to his/her sleep problems.

D. The veteran/service member denied any psychiatric concerns that would contribute to his/her elevated arousal.

14. Decreased Heightened Arousal Activities (14)

A. The veteran/service member was encouraged to decrease activities that create heightened arousal prior to bedtime.

B. The veteran/service member was urged to discontinue exercise just prior to bedtime.

C. The veteran/service member was directed to decrease emotionally upsetting events, such as relationship problems or thinking about past upsetting events, just prior to bedtime.

D. As the veteran/service member has implemented changes in his/her bedtime routine, he/she has experienced improved sleep.

E. The veteran's/service member's sleep has not improved despite attempts at changing his/her bedtime pattern, and he/she was provided with additional feedback in this area.

15. Implement Arousal-Decreasing Strategies (15)

A. The veteran/service member was assisted in implementing strategies to counter high levels of arousal before bedtime.

B. The veteran/service member was encouraged to use journaling and reading to decrease his/her high level of arousal prior to bedtime.

C. The veteran/service member was encouraged to listen to calming music and practice deep breathing techniques just prior to bedtime.

D. The veteran/service member was taught about using thought-stopping techniques to decrease his/her arousal prior to bedtime.

E. The veteran/service member has regularly used techniques to decrease his/her arousal, and his/her progress in this area was reinforced.

F. The veteran/service member has not regularly used techniques to decrease his/her pattern of arousal and was redirected to do so.

16. Explain Effects of Rumination on Sleep (16)

A. The veteran/service member was taught about the negative impact that ruminations and negative thinking can have on sleep.

B. The veteran/service member displayed a clear understanding of how his/her ruminations have affected his/her sleep pattern.

C. The veteran/service member struggled to identify how ruminations and negative thinking have affected his/her sleep and was provided with remedial information in this area.

17. Assign Self-Talk Homework (17)

A. The veteran/service member was assigned a homework exercise in which he/she identifies targeted self-talk and created reality-based alternatives.

B. The veteran/service member was assigned "Negative Thoughts Trigger Negative Feelings" in the *Adult Psychotherapy Homework Planner,* 2nd ed. (Jongsma).

C. The veteran's/service member's use of self-talk techniques was reviewed and reinforced for successes.

D. The veteran/service member was provided with corrective feedback toward improvement of his/her use of positive self-talk techniques.

18. Assign Thought-Stopping Techniques (18)

A. The veteran/service member was assigned to implement thought-stopping techniques on a daily basis in between sessions.

B. The veteran/service member was assigned "Making Use of the Thought-Stopping Technique" in the *Adult Psychotherapy Homework Planner,* 2nd ed. (Jongsma).

C. Role-plays were used to help the veteran/service member to practice the thought-stopping technique.

D. The veteran's/service member's use of thought-stopping techniques was reviewed, and his/her failures in this area were redirected.

19. Refer for Physician Evaluation (19)

A. The veteran/service member was referred to his/her physician to rule out any physical and/or pharmacological causes for his/her sleep disturbance.

B. The veteran/service member was referred to his/her physician to evaluate whether psychotropic medications might be helpful to induce sleep.

C. The veteran/service member was referred for sleep lab studies.

D. The physician has indicated that physical organic causes for the veteran's/service member's sleep disturbance have been found and a regimen of treatment for these problems has been initiated.

E. The physician ruled out any physical/organic or medication side effect as the cause for the veteran's/service member's sleep disturbance.

F. The physician has ordered psychotropic medications to help the veteran/service member return to a normal sleep pattern.

G. The veteran/service member has not followed through on the referral to his/her physician and was redirected to complete this task.

20. Monitor Medication Compliance (20)

A. The veteran/service member was noted to be consistently taking the psychotropic medication and stated that it was effective at increasing normal sleep routines.

B. The veteran/service member reported taking the psychotropic medication on a consistent basis but has not noted any positive effect on his/her sleep; he/she was directed to review this with the prescribing clinician.

C. The veteran/service member reported not consistently taking his/her psychotropic prescription and was encouraged to do so.

21. Utilize Imagery Rehearsal Therapy (21)

A. Imagery rehearsal therapy was utilized with the veteran/service member to decrease the intensity and frequency of nightmares.

B. Imagery rehearsal therapy has been helpful in decreasing the veteran's/service member's frequency and intensity of nightmares.

C. Despite the use of imagery rehearsal therapy, the veteran/service member continues to struggle with nightmares.

22. Refer for Sleep Study (22)

A. The veteran/service member was referred to a sleep medicine specialist for a sleep study to assess sleep-distorted breathing.

B. The veteran/service member was identified as having sleep apnea.

C. The veteran/service member was assessed to have a sleep disorder due to breathing problems.

D. The veteran/service member was assessed for sleep-disordered breathing but no concerns were identified.

E. The veteran/service member has not participated in the referral for a sleep medicine specialist and was reminded to do so.

23. Monitor CPAP Use (23)

A. The veteran's/service member's compliance with continuous positive airway pressure therapy (CPAP) was monitored.

B. The benefits and struggles of the veteran's/service member's use of the CPAP device were reviewed.

C. It was reflected to the veteran/service member that his/her use of CPAP therapy has greatly improved his/her sleep pattern.

D. Despite the use of CPAP therapy, the veteran/service member reports continuing sleep problems.

24. Discuss Risks Due to Sleep Problems (24)

A. The veteran/service member was encouraged to discuss potential risks to self and others due to sleep problems.

B. Problems like falling asleep on the shooting range or while driving a military vehicle were identified as potential risks due to the service member's sleep problems.

C. The veteran/service member identified problems that may occur due to his/her sleep problems, and these were reviewed with him/her.

D. The veteran/service member was unable to identify any risks to self or others that might occur because of sleep problems and was provided with additional specific examples.

25. Develop Strategies for Staying Awake (25)

A. The veteran/service member was assisted in developing strategies to keep from falling asleep during work activities (e.g., meetings, guard duty)

B. The veteran/service member identified several helpful techniques for making certain he/she stays awake during important work activities, and these were reviewed with him/her.

C. The veteran/service member struggled to identify any techniques that might help to keep him/her awake during important work activities and was provided with specific examples (e.g., standing up when he/she finds himself/herself nodding off, moderate caffeine usage).

D. The veteran/service member reports that he/she has used strategies to keep from falling asleep during work activities, and the benefit of these were reviewed.

26. Encourage Attendance at All Medical Separation Appointments (26)

A. The service member was encouraged to attend all medical separation appointments.

B. The service member has been attending medical separation appointments due to his/her sleep disorder breathing/sleep apnea and was reinforced for this.

C. The service member has not attended all medical separation appointments and was reminded to do so.

27. Explore Appeal Opportunities (27)

A. The service member does not agree with the medical separation finding and was assisted in exploring opportunities for appeal.

B. The service member was told about the right to request a second opinion.

C. The service member was assisted with consulting with a judge advocate general or civilian attorney.

D. Despite the service member's disagreement with the medical separation finding, he/she has decided not to pursue appeal.

28. Connect with Veterans Affairs (28)

A. The appropriate geographical region for the veteran/service member was identified.

B. Contact was facilitated with the Veterans Affairs representative from the veteran's/service member's region.

C. The veteran has connected with the Veterans Affairs representative.

D. The veteran has not connected with his/her Veterans Affairs representative and was reminded about this opportunity.

29. Provide Veterans Affairs Benefit Information (29)

A. The veteran was provided with information regarding Veterans Affairs benefits.

B. The veteran was directed to pursue veteran benefit information from the Web site at www.vba.va.gov/BBA.

30. Stress importance of Veterans Affairs medical appointments (30)

A. The importance of attending all scheduled medical appointment at the veteran's local Veterans Affairs facility was stressed.

B. The veteran has acknowledged the need to attend all scheduled medical appointments at his/her local Veterans Affairs facility.

MILD TRAUMATIC BRAIN INJURY

VETERAN/SERVICE MEMBER PRESENTATION

1. Head Injury (1)*

A. The veteran/service member reports that he/she experienced a blunt force trauma injury to the head.

B. The veteran/service member identified that he/she has experienced an acceleration injury to the head.

C. The veteran/service member identified that he/she has experienced a deceleration injury to the head.

D. The veteran/service member experienced no loss of consciousness related to his/her head injury.

E. The veteran/service member identified that he/she experienced less than 30 minutes loss of consciousness related to the head injury.

2. Neuropsychological Changes (1)

A. The veteran/service member has had neuropsychological changes secondary to a head injury.

B. The veteran/service member identified that he/she has experienced cognitive changes subsequent to his/her experience of a head injury.

C. As the veteran/service member has progressed through treatment, he/she has reported coping better with the neuropsychological effect of his/her head trauma.

D. The neuropsychological effects of the veteran's/service member's head trauma have ameliorated.

3. Cognitive Symptoms (2)

A. The veteran/service member complains of cognitive symptoms subsequent to his/her head injury.

B. The veteran/service member complains of difficulty paying attention.

C. The veteran/service member described problems with concentration.

D. The veteran/service member has experienced memory deficiencies.

E. As treatment has progressed, the veteran/service member has reported decreased cognitive symptoms.

4. Physical Symptoms (3)

A. The veteran/service member has identified physical symptoms that can be attributed to his/her head injury.

B. The veteran/service member has experienced headaches and blurred vision.

---

*The numbers in parentheses correlate to the number of the Behavioral Definition statement in the companion chapter with the same title in *The Veterans and Active Duty Military Psychotherapy Treatment Planner* (Moore and Jongsma) by John Wiley & Sons, 2009.

C. The veteran/service member has experienced dizziness and a disturbed balance/gait.

D. The veteran/service member has experienced nausea subsequent to his/her head injury.

E. The veteran/service member has experienced fatigue and insomnia subsequent to his/her head injury.

F. As treatment has progressed, the veteran/service member has experienced decreased physical symptoms.

5. Behavioral Symptoms (4)

A. The veteran/service member has displayed behavioral problems subsequent to his/her head injury.

B. The veteran/service member has experienced irritability and emotional/behavioral dysregulation.

C. The veteran/service member has experienced a loss of motivation.

D. The veteran/service member has experienced sleep problems.

E. As treatment has progressed, the veteran/service member has reported decreased behavioral problems, a better sleep pattern, and higher motivation.

6. Negative Impact on Functioning (5)

A. The veteran/service member has identified the effects of the brain injury as having a negative impact on his/her social functioning.

B. The veteran/service member has experienced occupational problems subsequent to his/her head injury.

C. The veteran/service member has struggled academically subsequent to his/her head injury.

D. The veteran/service member reports problems in interpersonal relationships subsequent to his/her head injury.

E. As treatment has progressed, the veteran/service member reports a decreased impact of the brain injury on his/her current functioning.

INTERVENTIONS IMPLEMENTED

1. Assess Extent of Problems (1)*

A. The extent of the veteran's/service member's problems from the mild traumatic brain injury was assessed.

B. The veteran/service member was advised that only mild social, occupational, and interpersonal functioning effects were noted.

C. The veteran/service member was advised that moderate social, occupational, and interpersonal functioning effects were noted.

D. The veteran/service member was advised that significant, social, occupational, and interpersonal functioning effects were noted.

---

*The numbers in parentheses correlate to the number of the Therapeutic Intervention statement in the companion chapter with the same title in *The Veterans and Active Duty Military Psychotherapy Treatment Planner* (Moore and Jongsma) by John Wiley & Sons, 2009.

2. Collect Data about Injury (2)

A. The veteran/service member was asked to review how his/her injury was sustained.

B. Data was collected about the veteran's/service member's level of consciousness during and directly after the head injury.

C. The veteran/service member was assessed for posttraumatic amnesia.

D. The use of drugs and alcohol related to the injury was reviewed.

E. The veteran/service member was forthcoming with significant information about the nature and events about the injury and was supported for this openness.

F. The veteran/service member was unable to provide complete information about the nature of the events regarding the injury, and additional information was sought from other sources.

3. Collect Collateral Information (3)

A. The veteran's/service member's family and friends were sought out to collect collateral information about changes in behavior, personality, or cognitive abilities since the injury.

B. The veteran's/service member's chain of command was consulted regarding changes in behavior, personality, or cognitive abilities since the injury.

C. Sufficient information has been collected regarding the veteran's/service member's changes in behavior, personality, or cognitive abilities since the injury, and treatment should be able to progress.

D. Insufficient information has been provided in regard to the changes in the veteran's/service member's behavior, personality, or cognitive abilities since the injury, and additional sources were sought.

4. Refer to Neurologist (4)

A. The veteran/service member was referred to a neurologist for a neurological examination.

B. The veteran/service member has complied with the referral to a neurologist for a neurological examination, and the results of the examination were reviewed

C. The veteran/service member has not complied with the referral to a neurologist and was reminded to do so.

5. Refer to Neuropsychologist (5)

A. The veteran/service member was referred to a neuropsychologist for a comprehensive evaluation to assess changes in memory, language, motor skills, executive functioning, personality, attention/concentration, and information processing.

B. The veteran/service member has followed through on the referral to the neuropsychologist, and the results of the evaluation were reviewed with him/her.

C. The veteran/service member has not followed through on the referral to a neuropsychologist and was reminded to do so.

6. Review Results of Evaluation (6)

A. The results of the neuropsychological evaluation were reviewed with the veteran/service member.

B. The results of the veteran's/service member's neuropsychological evaluation indicated only mild effects of the brain injury.

C. The results of the veteran's/service member's neuropsychological evaluation indicated moderate effects of the brain injury.

D. The results of the veteran's/service member's neuropsychological evaluation indicated severe effects of the brain injury.

E. The veteran/service member did not appear to be capable of understanding or accepting the results of the neuropsychological evaluation, so they were not reviewed with him/her.

7. Educate about Symptoms (7)

A. The veteran/service member was educated about the typical symptoms of mild traumatic brain injury.

B. The veteran/service member was educated about the length of symptom duration.

C. The veteran/service member was educated about how to minimize the impact of his/her symptoms on daily functioning.

D. The veteran/service member was reinforced for his/her clear understanding of the symptoms, duration, and response for mild traumatic brain injuries.

E. The veteran/service member had a difficult time understanding the symptoms, duration, and how to respond to his/her symptoms and was provided with additional feedback in this area.

8. Provide *Quick Guide* (8)

A. The veteran/service member was provided with the *Quick Guide—Patient/Family: Traumatic Brain Injury* published by the Department of Veterans Affairs.

B. The *Quick Guide—Patient/Family: Traumatic Brain Injury* was reviewed with the veteran/service member.

9. Educate about Minimizing Subsequent Traumatic Brain Injury (9)

A. The veteran/service member was educated about the cumulative negative effects of brain injuries.

B. The veteran/service member was educated about behavior that can minimize the chances of sustaining a subsequent traumatic brain injury.

C. The veteran/service member was advised to wear a seat belt and helmet while riding/driving vehicles, wear a helmet when riding a bicycle/motorcycle, and not drive under the influence of alcohol, drugs, or certain prescription medications.

D. The veteran/service member displayed a clear understanding of the importance of and options available for minimization of the chances of sustaining a subsequent traumatic brain injury and was reinforced for this understanding.

E. The veteran/service member did not seem to understand the necessity or importance of avoiding subsequent traumatic brain injury and was provided with remedial information in this area.

10. Refer to Occupational Therapist (10)

A. The veteran/service member was referred to an occupational therapist for an assessment of functional capacity and cognitive rehabilitation therapy.

B. The veteran/service member has complied with the occupational therapy evaluation, and the results of this evaluation were reviewed with him/her.

C. The veteran/service member was monitored for his/her follow-through on rehabilitation recommendations.

D. The veteran/service member was reinforced for his/her regular follow-through on rehabilitation recommendations.

E. The veteran/service member has failed to follow through on the rehabilitation recommendations and was redirected to do so.

F. The veteran/service member has declined to participate in the assessment of functional capacity and cognitive rehabilitation therapy and was redirected to do so.

11. Assign Organizer/Planner (11)

A. The veteran/service member was taught about the use of an organizer/planner to keep track of medical appointments, work project deadlines, and other important information.

B. The veteran/service member has implemented structured reminders and organizers, and this is noted to be helpful in reducing forgetfulness and enabling him/her to complete necessary tasks.

C. The veteran/service member has not used the structured reminders and continues to forget about daily obligations; he/she was redirected to use these organizers.

12. Encourage Alarm Reminders (12)

A. The veteran/service member was encouraged to use a wristwatch alarm or other small alarm device to remind him/her of important appointments.

B. The veteran/service member has implemented the use of an alarm device to remind him/her of important appointments, and this has been noted to be helpful in reducing forgetfulness and enabling him/her to remember his/her responsibilities.

C. The veteran/service member has not used the alarm reminder technique and continues to forget about important appointments; he/she was redirected to use this technique.

13. Encourage Use of To-Do List (13)

A. The veteran/service member was encouraged to create daily to-do lists and check off each activity/task once it has been completed.

B. The veteran's/service member's use of the to-do list was reviewed, and successes were reinforced.

C. The veteran/service member continues to struggle despite using a to-do list; his/her use of this option was reviewed, and the problem was solved.

D. The veteran/service member has not regularly used the to-do list and was redirected to do so.

14. Emphasize Daily Routine (14)

A. The veteran/service member was taught about using a daily routine in order to decrease his/her confusion.

B. The veteran/service member was assisted in developing a daily routine.

C. The veteran/service member has regularly used the daily routine, and his/her experience of this technique was reviewed and processed.

D. The veteran/service member does not regularly adhere to a daily routine and was redirected to do so.

15. Refer for a Psychopharmacological Intervention (15)

A. Referral to a physician was made for the purpose of evaluation for a prescription of medication to treat the veteran's/service member's attention/concentration deficit concerns.

B. The veteran/service member has followed through on referral to a physician and has been assessed for possible medications, but none was prescribed.

C. Medications to assist in decreasing attention/concentration deficits have been prescribed for the veteran/service member.

D. The physician has followed up on the medication ordered, titrated medication, and monitored side effects.

E. The veteran/service member has not followed up on the referral for medication, and he/she was redirected to do so.

F. The veteran/service member has refused the prescription for medications provided by the physician.

16. Assign Brief Activities (16)

A. The veteran/service member was assigned to create a list of activities that he/she can enjoy in brief increments of time.

B. The veteran/service member was provided with examples of brief activities (e.g., reading or playing video games for 10 minutes at a time).

C. The veteran/service member was encouraged to take breaks during tasks when he/she starts to feel overwhelmed.

D. The veteran's/service member's use of brief activities was reviewed and processed.

E. The veteran/service member has not broken down activities into brief increments of time and was redirected to do so.

17. Gradually Increase Time in Enjoyable Activities (17)

A. The veteran/service member was directed to gradually increase the time he/she spends in enjoyable activities each week.

B. The veteran/service member was directed to maintain a graph of his/her progress in increasing time in activities.

C. The veteran's/service member's gradual increase in activities was reviewed and processed.

D. The veteran/service member has not increased involvement in enjoyable activities and was redirected to do so.

18. Assign Games to Build Attention/Concentration (18)

A. The veteran/service member was assigned to use computer and video games to build his/her attention/concentration.

B. The veteran/service member was urged to use video games that focus on building attention/concentration, such as poker, solitaire, or word puzzles.

C. The veteran's/service member's use of computer/video games that build attention/concentration was reviewed and processed; he/she was reinforced for this use.

D. The veteran/service member has not used computer and video games to increase attention and concentration and was redirected to do so.

19. Solicit Redirection (19)

A. The veteran/service member was encouraged to ask family and friends for redirection when he/she wanders off topic.

B. The veteran/service member was assisted in developing support from family and friends to redirect him/her when he/she is wandering off topic.

C. The use of redirection by family and friends to guide the veteran/service member was processed.

D. The veteran/service member has not solicited help from family and friends to guide him/her when wandering off topic and was redirected to do so.

20. Refer for Medication for Aggressiveness (20)

A. Referral to a physician was made for the purpose of evaluation of the veteran/service member for a prescription of medication to treat aggressiveness.

B. The veteran/service member has followed through on referral to a physician and has been assessed for possible medications, but none was prescribed.

C. Medications to lessen aggression have been prescribed for the veteran/service member.

D. The physician has followed up on the medication ordered, titrated medication, and monitored side effects.

E. The veteran/service member has not followed up on the referral for medication and was redirected to do so.

F. The veteran/service member has refused the prescription for medications provided by the physician.

21. Explore Negative Impact of Aggressive Behavior (21)

A. The veteran/service member was assisted in exploring the negative impact his/her impulsiveness and aggressiveness has had on his/her loved ones.

B. The veteran/service member was assigned the "Plan before Acting" exercise from the *Adult Psychotherapy Homework Planner*, 2nd ed. (Jongsma).

C. The veteran/service member completed the homework assignment, and the content was processed within the session.

D. The veteran/service member was supported as he/she identified the negative impact of his/her impulsive and aggressive behavior on his/her loved ones.

E. The veteran/service member denied any impact of his/her impulsive behavior on his/her loved ones and was provided with concrete examples of these situations.

22. Teach Self-Control Strategies (22)

A. The veteran/service member was taught meditational and self-control strategies to delay gratification and reduce impulsivity.

B. The veteran/service member was instructed to use a "stop, think, react" technique as a way to decrease his/her impulsive acting out.

C. The veteran/service member was assigned the "Impulsive Behavior Journal" exercise from the *Adult Psychotherapy Homework Planner*, 2nd ed. (Jongsma).

D. The veteran/service member completed the homework assignment, and the content was processed within the session.

E. The veteran/service member demonstrated an understanding of the concepts related to self-control strategies that have been taught and found this helpful to control impulses.

F. The veteran/service member has not adequately learned the concepts related to self-control strategies and was provided with additional examples.

23. **Teach Anger Management Techniques (23)**

A. The veteran/service member was assisted in constructing an individualized strategy for managing his/her anger.

B. The veteran/service member was encouraged to use techniques such as counting to 10 before reacting, deep breathing, and monitoring automatic thoughts in order to help manage his/her anger.

C. The veteran/service member was reinforced for his/her acceptance of comprehensive anger management strategies.

D. The veteran/service member was redirected to develop a more comprehensive anger management strategy.

24. **Refer for Medication for Sleep Difficulties (24)**

A. Referral to a physician was made for the purpose of evaluation for a prescription of medication to treat sleeping difficulties.

B. The veteran/service member has followed through on referral to a physician and has been assessed for possible medications, but none was prescribed.

C. Medications to lessen sleeping difficulties have been prescribed for the veteran/service member.

D. The physician has followed up on the medication ordered, titrated medication, and monitored side effects.

E. The veteran/service member has refused the prescription for medications provided by the physician.

F. The veteran/service member has not followed up on the referral for medication and was redirected to do so.

25. **Teach Sleep Hygiene (25)**

A. Basic sleep hygiene techniques (e.g., decreasing stimulants in the evening; having a quiet, comfortable place to sleep; spending time winding down) were reviewed with the veteran/service member.

B. Behavioral strategies to reinforce his/her structured sleep routine were introduced to the veteran/service member.

C. The veteran's/service member's sleep hygiene pattern was reviewed, and he/she was reinforced for positive use of sleep induction techniques.

D. As the veteran/service member has developed more structure to his/her sleep hygiene pattern, he/she has experienced a better pattern of sleep, and this was reviewed.

E. The veteran/service member has not used the sleep hygiene techniques, continues to have poor sleep, and was given additional feedback in this area.

26. Assign Sleep Record (26)

A. The veteran/service member was assigned to keep a record of his/her sleep pattern.

B. The veteran/service member was assigned to complete the "Sleep Pattern Record" exercise from the *Adult Psychotherapy Homework Planner*, 2nd ed. (Jongsma).

C. The veteran/service member has kept a regular record of his/her sleep pattern, and this was reviewed to identify healthy and unhealthy patterns.

D. The veteran/service member has not regularly completed his/her sleep pattern record and was redirected to do so.

27. Refer for Medication to Treat Headaches (27)

A. Referral to a physician was made for the purpose of evaluation for a prescription of medication to treat headaches.

B. The veteran/service member has followed through on referral to a physician and has been assessed for possible medications, but none was prescribed.

C. Medications to lessen headaches have been prescribed for the veteran/service member.

D. The physician has followed up on the medication ordered, titrated medication, and monitored side effects.

E. The veteran/service member has not followed up on the referral for medication and was redirected to do so.

F. The veteran/service member has refused the prescription for medications provided by the physician.

28. Teach Headache Avoidance Strategies (28)

A. The veteran/service member was taught how to recognize and avoid headache triggers.

B. Triggers such as caffeine, dehydration, and intense physical exercise were reviewed with the veteran/service member.

C. As the veteran/service member has regularly monitored himself/herself for headache triggers, his/her pattern of headaches has significantly decreased; this success was reinforced.

D. The veteran/service member has not regularly monitored for headache triggers and was redirected to do so.

29. Arrange for Biofeedback Training (29)

A. The veteran/service member was referred for biofeedback training to help develop more precise relaxation skills, specifically for facial and neck muscles.

B. The veteran/service member was referred for electromyography (EMG) training.

C. The veteran/service member was administered biofeedback training to teach him/her more in-depth relaxation skills.

D. The biofeedback training sessions have been helpful in training the veteran/service member to relax more deeply, which has helped to decrease facial and neck muscle tension.

E. The veteran/service member has not used skills learned in biofeedback training as directed, and this failure was problem-solved.

F. The veteran/service member has not attended biofeedback training and was redirected to do so.

30. Conduct Family Session (30)

A. The veteran's/service member's family was invited for a session to focus on education about mild traumatic brain injury, coping behaviors, and improving existing family supports.

B. The family session was able to teach the veteran's/service member's family about mild traumatic brain injury, coping behaviors, and improving existing family supports.

C. The veteran/service member reports that family support has significantly improved since the family session, and this success was reinforced.

D. The veteran/service member reports that family members continue to provide very limited support, and options for increasing this support were discussed with the veteran/service member.

31. Provide Vocational Rehabilitation Resources (31)

A. The veteran was provided with information about vocational rehabilitation programs provided by the Department of Veterans Affairs.

B. The veteran was referred to this Web site for information about vocational rehabilitation programs: www.vba.va.gov/bln/vrel.

C. The veteran has reviewed information about vocational rehabilitation programs provided by the Department of Veterans Affairs, and his/her reaction was processed.

D. The veteran has not reviewed information about vocational rehabilitation programs and was redirected to do so.

NIGHTMARES

VETERAN/SERVICE MEMBER PRESENTATION

1. Repeated Awakenings Due to Distressing Dreams (1)[*]

A. The veteran/service member reports distress resulting from frequent awakenings during sleep due to emotionally distressing dreams.

B. The veteran/service member described emotionally distressing dreams related to past combat experiences.

C. The veteran/service member reports emotionally distressing dreams containing images of harm to self or loved ones.

D. As the veteran's/service member's daily life external stressors have increased, he/she has experienced repeated awakening and detailed recall of extremely frightening dreams involving threats to himself/herself.

E. As the veteran/service member has resolved his/her experience of combat, his/her incidences of experiencing nightmares have diminished significantly.

F. The veteran/service member reported that he/she no longer experiences frightening dreams.

2. Increased Autonomic Arousal (2)

A. The veteran/service member reports that he/she has experienced abrupt awakening with panic symptoms, followed by intense anxiousness and confusion, and recall of combat-related dream content.

B. As the veteran/service member has begun to resolve his/her concerns related to combat, his/her incidents of panic awakening have decreased.

C. The veteran/service member reported no recent incidents of panic awakening with confusion and disorientation.

3. Fragmented Sleep (3)

A. The veteran/service member reports that he/she finds it difficult to fall asleep within a reasonable period of time.

B. The veteran/service member reported that he/she can fall asleep within a reasonable period of time but often awakens and is unable to return to sleep easily.

C. The veteran/service member reported that he/she wakens at a very early hour and is unable to return to sleep.

D. The veteran/service member reports that his/her sleep is interrupted by distressing dreams.

E. The veteran/service member reported that his/her sleep disturbance has diminished and that he/she is beginning to return to a normal sleep cycle.

F. The veteran/service member reported no longer experiencing sleep disturbance symptoms and is sleeping fairly consistently.

---

[*]The numbers in parentheses correlate to the number of the Behavioral Definition statement in the companion chapter with the same title in *The Veterans and Active Duty Military Psychotherapy Treatment Planner* (Moore and Jongsma) by John Wiley & Sons, 2009.

4. Apprehension about Falling Asleep (4)

A. The veteran/service member believes that he/she will experience nightmares whenever he/she falls asleep.

B. The veteran/service member reports significant apprehension about falling asleep in order to avoid nightmares.

C. The veteran/service member takes an extended period of time to fall asleep.

D. As treatment has progressed, the veteran/service member reports an improvement of being able to fall asleep and the pattern of nightmares has decreased.

E. The veteran/service member reports not experiencing any nightmares and obtaining a regular sleep pattern.

5. Daytime Hypersomnia (5)

A. The veteran/service member reported that he/she feels very sleepy during the day and easily falls asleep, even while sitting in a chair.

B. The veteran/service member reports that he/she has fallen asleep in the presence of others in a social situation on many occasions.

C. The veteran/service member reports that he/she has had difficulty managing his/her daily expectations because of his/her severe sleepiness.

D. The veteran/service member reported that he/she is beginning to feel more rested and alert during the day as his/her sleep pattern is returning to normal.

E. The veteran/service member reported no recent incidents of falling asleep too easily during the day.

6. Anxiety and Dysphoria (6)

A. The veteran/service member reports anxiety and dysphoria during the day, which is directly related to the prior night's nightmare episode.

B. The veteran/service member reports that he/she often obsesses and ruminates about his/her experience of nightmares from the prior night.

C. As the veteran's/service member's pattern of nightmares has decreased, his/her anxiety and dysphoria during the daytime have also decreased.

D. The veteran/service member reports that he/she is no longer anxious or dysphoric during the day.

7. Interpersonal Difficulties Due to Mutual Sleep Period Problems (7)

A. The veteran/service member reports that his/her partner is complaining of his/her excessive and noise during mutual sleep periods.

B. The veteran's/service member's roommate reports that he/she has been frequently awakened due to the veteran's/service member's excessive movement and noise during mutual sleep periods.

C. The veteran/service member engages in kicking, punching, crying, and screaming during mutual sleep periods.

D. As treatment has progressed, the veteran/service member has experienced decreased movement and noise during mutual sleep periods.

INTERVENTIONS IMPLEMENTED

1. Assess Extent of Nightmares (1)[*]

A. The veteran/service member was asked about the frequency, intensity, duration, and history of his/her nightmares.

B. The veteran/service member was asked about the military experiences that may have triggered the nightmares.

C. The veteran/service member asked about the level of emotional distress caused by the nightmares.

D. The assessment of the veteran's/service member's nightmare symptoms indicated that his/her symptoms are extreme and severely interfere with his/her life.

E. The assessment of the veteran's/service member's nightmare symptoms indicated that his/her nightmares are moderate and occasionally affect his/her normal life.

F. The assessment of the veteran's/service member's nightmare symptoms indicated that his/her symptoms are mild and rarely interfere with his/her daily life.

G. The results of the assessment of the veteran's/service member's nightmare symptoms were reviewed with the veteran/service member.

2. Assign Nightmare Log (2)

A. The veteran/service member was requested to maintain a nightmare log for two weeks in order to document times of the night that the nightmares occur as well as the feelings and images.

B. The veteran/service member has regularly maintained a nightmare log, and the results of this log were reviewed and processed with him/her.

C. The veteran/service member has not regularly maintained a nightmare log and was redirected to do so.

3. Assess Sleep Problems (3)

A. The veteran/service member was assessed for sleep problems associated with his/her nightmares.

B. The veteran/service member was assessed in regard to the number of nighttime awakenings, the level of anxiety prior to sleep, bedtime routines, and daytime fatigue.

C. The review of the veteran's/service member's sleep problems indicated severe concerns.

D. The review of the veteran's/service member's sleep problems indicated moderate concerns.

E. The review of the veteran's/service member's sleep problems indicated mild concerns.

4. Compare Symptoms to Normal Reactions (4)

A. An assessment was made to determine if the veteran's/service member's nightmares are consistent with normal reactions after returning from combat deployment.

B. The veteran/service member was advised that his/her reactions are normal after returning from a combat deployment.

---

[*]The numbers in parentheses correlate to the number of the Therapeutic Intervention statement in the companion chapter with the same title in *The Veterans and Active Duty Military Psychotherapy Treatment Planner* (Moore and Jongsma) by John Wiley & Sons, 2009.

C. The veteran/service member was advised that his/her symptoms are more severe than would be typical after returning from combat deployment, and treatment was refocused in this area.

5. Assess for Psychiatric Disorders (5)

A. The veteran/service member was assessed for psychiatric disorders that may be causing the nightmares.

B. The veteran/service member was assessed for posttraumatic stress disorder, autism spectrum disorder, or depression.

C. No psychiatric concerns were identified as a cause for the nightmares, and this was reflected to the veteran/service member.

D. The veteran's/service member's nightmares appear to be directly related to psychiatric concerns, and he/she was referred for appropriate treatment/level of care.

6. Assess Neurological Concerns (6)

A. The veteran/service member was assessed for a history of neurological illness.

B. The veteran/service member was assessed for the history of a traumatic brain injury.

C. The veteran/service member was referred for a history of past exposure to toxins.

D. As specific medical evaluation was indicated, the veteran/service member was referred for such.

E. No specific medical concerns were identified in regard to the veteran's/service member's nightmares, and this was reflected to him/her.

7. Assess Substance Abuse (7)

A. The veteran's/service member's pattern of substance abuse was assessed.

B. The veteran/service member was noted to have a maladaptive pattern of substance abuse.

C. As significant substance abuse concerns were identified, the veteran/service member was referred for substance dependence treatment.

D. The veteran's/service member's pattern of substance abuse indicates no maladaptive patterns.

8. Teach about Connection between Nightmares and Sleep Disturbance (8)

A. The veteran/service member was taught about how fragmented sleep causes sleep problems/nightmares, which in turn promote fragmented, nonrestorative sleep.

B. The veteran/service member was provided with examples about how nightmares and sleep disturbances are self-reinforcing.

C. The veteran/service member displayed a clear understanding of the connection between sleep problems and nightmares and was reinforced for this insight.

D. The veteran/service member struggled to identify how sleep problems and nightmares are connected and was provided with remedial assistance in this area.

9. Teach Importance of Consolidated, Quality Sleep (9)

A. The veteran/service member was taught the concept of how consolidated sleep and quality of sleep is more important than quantity of sleep.

B. The rapid eye movement level of sleep was explained to the veteran/service member.

C. The veteran/service member acknowledged how the best sleep is a deep, consolidated sleep rather than an extended period of time.

10. Instruct on Sleep Hygiene (10)

A. The veteran/service member was instructed on appropriate behavioral practices conducive to good sleep.

B. The veteran/service member was advised about restricting caffeine four hours prior to bedtime.

C. The veteran/service member was encouraged to exercise regularly but not in the evening.

D. The veteran/service member was advised about restricting spicy, late-night snacks and heavy evening meals.

E. The veteran/service member was encouraged to get out of bed if not able to fall asleep within 15 minutes.

F. The veteran/service member was instructed about removing cues that may promote clock watching while in bed.

11. Teach Progressive Muscle Relaxation (11)

A. The veteran/service member was taught progressive muscle relaxation skills.

B. The veteran/service member was assigned to engage in progressive muscle relaxation skills twice per day for 15 minutes each time.

C. The veteran/service member was encouraged to implement the progressive muscle relaxation skills when anxiety or stress rises.

D. The veteran/service member was taught how to apply progressive muscle relaxation skills to his/her daily life.

E. The veteran/service member was provided with feedback about his/her use of progressive muscle relaxation skills.

12. Explain Learned Nature of Nightmares (12)

A. It was explained to the veteran/service member that nightmares can develop into a distinct disorder.

B. The nature of nightmares as a learned behavior similar to insomnia was reviewed with the veteran/service member.

C. An analogy was used to compare nightmares to the concept of a broken record that needs to be reset.

D. The veteran/service member displayed an increased understanding of nightmares as a learned disorder.

E. The veteran/service member had a difficult time understanding nightmares as a learned disorder and was provided with remedial feedback in this area.

13. Explain Nightmares as Imagery (13)

A. The concept of imagery was introduced to the veteran/service member.

B. Nightmares were identified as a form of imagery.

C. The veteran/service member was taught about how he/she is able to direct his/her images when conscious.

D. The veteran/service member displayed a clear understanding of the level of control he/she has over images and therefore nightmares.

14. Select a Moderately Distressing Nightmare (14)

A. The veteran/service member was asked to select a moderately distressing nightmare.

B. The veteran/service member was requested to choose a nightmare that causes a distress level of 50 on a scale of 0 to 100 (0 equals no distress; 100 equals the most distress ever experienced).

C. The veteran/service member was able to select a specific nightmare that causes a moderate level of distress.

D. The veteran/service member needed assistance to identify a moderately distressing nightmare.

15. Differentiate Selected Nightmare from Recurrent Intrusive Thoughts (15)

A. The veteran/service member was requested to select a nightmare that does not occur as a recurrent intrusive thought when awake.

B. The veteran/service member was assisted in differentiating between recurrent intrusive thoughts and his/her nightmares.

C. The veteran/service member was reinforced for selecting a nightmare to work on changing.

16. Restrict Treatment to One Nightmare (16)

A. For the time being, the veteran/service member was instructed to limit his/her treatment interventions to only one nightmare at a time.

B. The veteran/service member was instructed to select only one nightmare at a time to make sure that he/she fully understands the task and to prevent him/her from becoming overwhelmed.

C. The veteran/service member has restricted his/her current treatment interventions to one nightmare.

D. The veteran/service member has struggled to focus on only one nightmare and was provided with additional assistance in this area.

17. Avoid Rehearsal of Nightmare (17)

A. The veteran/service member was instructed that he/she need not rehearse the original nightmare to be changed, since exposure is not necessary for improvement.

B. The veteran/service member displayed understanding that he/she need not rehearse the original nightmare.

C. The veteran/service member continues to rehearse the original nightmare and was redirected in this area.

18. Change Nightmare (18)

A. The veteran/service member was encouraged to change the nightmare in any way that he/she wishes.

B. The veteran/service member was urged to replace a distressing portion of the nightmare with a more positive or adaptive theme/outcome.

C. The veteran/service member was assisted in talking through this changed version of the nightmare.

D. The veteran/service member was reinforced for his/her ability to change the theme of the nightmare.

E. The veteran/service member has not been able to change the theme of the nightmare and was redirected to do so.

19. Direct Regarding Nature of Changed Image (19)

A. Direction was provided to the veteran/service member about a changed dream image, moving from a friend being injured by a roadside bomb to the friend making it through without injury.

B. The veteran/service member was reinforced for his/her understanding of the technique of changing dream themes/outcomes.

C. The veteran/service member continues to struggle with how to change themes/outcomes and was provided with additional feedback in this area.

20. Avoid Direct Dream Theme Changes (20)

A. The veteran/service member was provided with examples of how to complete the dream theme change technique only rather than with suggestions about his/her specific dream changes.

B. The veteran/service member was urged to take ownership and mastery of the dream theme change technique by providing specific examples of his/her own approach in this area.

21. Encourage Dream Rehearsal (21)

A. The veteran/service member was encouraged to rehearse the new dream twice a day for 20 minutes each time until the original nightmare disappears or is no longer distressing.

B. The veteran/service member has rehearsed the new dream on a regular basis, and the benefits of this technique were reviewed and processed.

C. The veteran/service member has not regularly rehearsed the new dream and was redirected to do so.

22. Use Writing to Enhance Imagery (22)

A. The veteran/service member was encouraged to rehearse the new dream in writing, as he/she is not able to use imagery effectively.

B. The veteran/service member has rehearsed the new dream in writing, and the benefits of this technique were reviewed.

C. It was explained to the veteran/service member that his/her rewriting of the dream had been effective.

D. The veteran/service member has not used the writing technique to enhance his/her new dream imagery and was reminded to do so.

23. Select Next Nightmare (23)

A. As the veteran/service member has resolved his/her first selected nightmare, an additional nightmare was selected for resolution.

B. The veteran/service member has selected a second nightmare and was assisted in instituting the reimagining and rewriting of this nightmare.

C. It was reflected to the veteran/service member that he/she appears optimistic about the opportunity to resolve more nightmares.

D. The veteran/service member has not selected an additional nightmare and was redirected to do so.

24. Refer for Medication (24)

A. The veteran/service member was referred to a prescribing clinician in order to assess whether he/she would benefit from an alpha-blocker, antidepressant, or sedative/hypnotic.

B. The veteran/service member has been referred to a prescribing clinician, and medications have been prescribed.

C. The veteran/service member has been referred to a prescribing clinician, but no medication was prescribed.

D. The veteran/service member has not kept an appointment with a prescribing practitioner and was redirected to do so.

25. Review Use of Over-the-Counter Medications (25)

A. The veteran/service member was encouraged to identify any use of self-prescribed, over-the-counter medication.

B. The veteran/service member was asked about use of antihistamines and sleep aids.

C. The veteran/service member has reported use of over-the-counter medications.

D. The veteran/service member reports no use of over-the-counter medications.

26. Monitor Medications (26)

A. The veteran's/service member's progress, compliance, and side effects in regard to prescribed medication were monitored.

B. It was noted that the veteran/service member has displayed adequate progress in his/her use of medication, and this was reported to the prescribing clinician.

C. The veteran/service member has displayed compliance in his/her use of medication, and this was reported to the prescribing clinician.

D. The veteran/service member reports minimal side effects of the prescribed medication, and this was reported to the prescribing clinician.

E. The veteran/service member has had struggles in regard to progress, compliance, and side effects of the prescribed medication, and the details of this were reported to the prescribing clinician.

27. Educate About Side Effects (27)

A. The veteran/service member was educated about the typical side effects of sleep medication.

B. The veteran/service member was educated about drowsiness, agitation, and restlessness that may accompany the use of sleep medication.

C. The service member was assisted in identifying how side effects of sleep medications may interfere with military missions.

D. The veteran/service member was assisted in identifying how the side effects of sleep medications may increase his/her risk of accidents.

E. The veteran/service member displayed a clear understanding of the possible side effects of his/her medications, and he/she was urged to report side effects as needed.

F. The veteran/service member had difficulty understanding the full extent of the side effects of his/her medications and was provided with remedial feedback in this area.

28. Provide Couple's Therapy (28)

A. The veteran/service member was encouraged to utilize couple's therapy to discuss feelings about current situations and the effects of nightmares on the relationship.

B. The veteran/service member and his/her significant other were invited to discuss their feelings and concerns about the current situation.

C. The veteran/service member and his/her partner have discussed their feelings openly, and this has helped to resolve relationship problems stemming from the nightmares.

D. The veteran/service member and his/her partner have not regularly and openly discussed their feelings regarding the nightmares and were redirected to do so.

29. Educate about Nightmares and Sleep Disorders (29)

A. The veteran/service member was provided with educational material on nightmares and sleep disorders.

B. The veteran/service member has reviewed the information on nightmares and sleep disorders, and key topics were reviewed during the session.

C. The veteran/service member has not reviewed the information on sleep disorders and nightmares and was redirected to do so.

OPIOID DEPENDENCE

CLIENT PRESENTATION

1. Impairment or Distress Due to Opioid Use (1)[*]

A. The veteran/service member demonstrates a regular pattern of opioid use.

B. The veteran's/service member's opioid use has led to a pattern of significant impairment.

C. The veteran's/service member's opioid use has created a pattern of distressful symptoms.

D. As treatment has progressed, the veteran's/service member's pattern of opioid use has significantly decreased.

E. The veteran/service member has discontinued use of opioids and reports improved mental and physical status.

2. Increased Tolerance (2)

A. The veteran/service member described a pattern of increasing tolerance for the opioid, as he/she has needed to use more of it to obtain the desired effect.

B. The veteran/service member described a steady increase in the amount and frequency of opioid use as his/her tolerance for it has increased.

3. Physical Withdrawal Symptoms (3)

A. The veteran/service member acknowledged that he/she has experienced physical withdrawal symptoms characteristic of opioid dependence.

B. The veteran's/service member's physical symptoms of withdrawal have eased as he/she has stabilized and maintained abstinence.

C. There is no further evidence of physical withdrawal symptoms.

4. Persistent Desire to Reduce Opioid Use (4)

A. The veteran/service member frequently indicates that he/she would like to decrease or discontinue his/her opioid use.

B. The veteran/service member acknowledged that he/she has frequently attempted to terminate his/her use of opioids but found that he/she has been unable to follow through.

C. The veteran/service member acknowledged that despite the negative consequences and a desire to terminate opioid use, he/she has been unable to do so.

D. As the veteran/service member has participated in a total recovery program, he/she has been able to maintain abstinence from opioid use.

5. Excessive Time Investment (5)

A. The veteran/service member described expending an excessive investment of time and effort in order to obtain, use, or recover from the use of opioids.

---

[*]The numbers in parentheses correlate to the number of the Behavioral Definition statement in the companion chapter with the same title in *The Veterans and Active Duty Military Psychotherapy Treatment Planner* (Moore and Jongsma) by John Wiley & Sons, 2009.

B. The veteran/service member has suspended other important activities in order to participate in opioid use.

C. As the veteran/service member has stabilized in a recovery program, he/she has discovered a large amount of time to give to constructive activities.

6. Suspension of Activities (6)

A. The veteran/service member has suspended his/her involvement in important social, occupational, and recreational activities because of opioid use.

B. The veteran/service member is beginning to recognize that all other aspects of his/her life became secondary to the primary object of obtaining and using opioids.

C. The veteran/service member is resuming his/her social, occupational, and recreational activities as he/she becomes established in the recovery lifestyle.

7. Illegal Activity (7)

A. The veteran/service member frequently engages in illegal activity to support his/her opioid habit.

B. The veteran/service member engages in prostitution in order to financially support his/her opioid habit.

C. The veteran/service member frequently steals in order to finance his/her opioid habit.

D. The veteran/service member engages in illicit drug sales in order to finance his/her own opioid habit.

E. As the veteran/service member has established his/her regular pattern of recovery, his/her involvement in illegal activity has substantially decreased.

8. Persistent Opioid Abuse Despite Problems (8)

A. The veteran/service member has continued to abuse opioids in spite of recurring financial, legal, social, vocational, medical, familial, and self-esteem consequences.

B. The veteran/service member denied that the problems in his/her life are directly caused by opioid use.

C. The veteran/service member acknowledged that opioid use has been the cause of multiple personal problems and verbalized a strong desire to maintain a life free from using opioids.

D. As the veteran/service member has maintained sobriety, the direct negative consequences of his/her opioid use have diminished.

E. The veteran/service member is now able to face resolution of significant problems in his/her life, as he/she has established sobriety.

9. Opioids Used to Manage Pain (9)

A. The veteran/service member reported that he/she has often used opioids in order to manage chronic pain.

B. The veteran/service member began using opioids to manage chronic pain, but as his/her use continued, he/she became addicted to the substance, regardless of physical pain concerns.

C. As treatment has progressed, the veteran/service member has decreased the use of opioids for pain management.

D. The veteran/service member has terminated use of opioids for pain management.

10. Late to Morning Accountability (10)

A. The service member has repeatedly reported late to morning accountability or physical training formations as a result of opioid use.

B. The service member has received official sanction due to repeated lateness to morning accountability and physical training formations.

C. As treatment has progressed, the service member has been more regularly on time for morning accountability or physical training formations.

D. The service member reports being on time regularly for morning accountability or physical training formations.

INTERVENTIONS IMPLEMENTED

1. Refer for Physical Examination (1)*

A. The veteran/service member was referred for a thorough physical evaluation to determine any negative medical affects related to his/her opioid abuse.

B. The veteran/service member was tested for HIV, hepatitis, and sexually transmitted diseases.

C. The veteran/service member has followed through with obtaining a physical examination and was told that his/her opioid use has produced negative medical consequences.

D. The veteran/service member has obtained a physical examination and has been told that there are no significant medical effects of his/her opioid dependence.

E. The physician assessed the veteran/service member for use of methadone and buprenorphine to reduce craving for opioids.

F. The veteran/service member has been prescribed medications to reduce craving for opioids.

G. The veteran/service member has not followed through with obtaining a physical examination, and he/she was redirected to do so.

2. Refer to Maintenance/Withdrawal Program (2)

A. The veteran/service member was referred to a pharmacologically based maintenance/withdrawal program.

B. The veteran/service member was referred to a methadone maintenance program.

C. The veteran/service member was referred to a buprenorphine program.

D. The veteran/service member has entered a pharmacologically based maintenance/withdrawal program, and his/her experience in this program was reviewed.

E. The veteran/service member has not followed through on a pharmacologically based maintenance/withdrawal program and was redirected to do so.

3. Monitor/Titrate Medications (3)

A. The veteran/service member was encouraged to maintain contact with his/her prescribing physician in order to monitor and titrate medications as needed.

B. The effectiveness of medications was reviewed.

---

*The numbers in parentheses correlate to the number of the Therapeutic Intervention statement in the companion chapter with the same title in *The Veterans and Active Duty Military Psychotherapy Treatment Planner* (Moore and Jongsma) by John Wiley & Sons, 2009.

C. The veteran/service member has not maintained contact with his/her prescribing physician and was redirected to do so.

4. Administer Medication (4)

A. Medical staff has administered medications as prescribed.

B. Medical staff assisted the veteran/service member in administering his/her own medications.

C. The veteran/service member refused to accept medications as prescribed.

5. Assess and Monitor Withdrawal (5)

A. During the veteran's/service member's period of withdrawal, he/she was consistently assessed and monitored using a standardized procedure.

B. The Narcotic Withdrawal Scale was used to monitor the veteran's/service member's period of withdrawal.

6. Administer Psychological Instruments (6)

A. The veteran/service member was administered psychological instruments designed to objectively assess the depth of opioid dependence.

B. The Substance Use Disorders Diagnostic Schedule-IV (SUDDS-IV) was administered to the veteran/service member.

C. The Substance Abuse Subtle Screening Inventory-3 (SASSI-3) was administered to the veteran/service member.

D. As the veteran/service member progressed through his/her process of withdrawal, he/she was provided medically appropriate treatment as needed.

E. The veteran/service member did not need any specific medical treatment to complete his/her withdrawal.

F. The veteran/service member has been noted to have completed his/her withdrawal.

7. Obtain Biopsychosocial History (7)

A. A complete family and personal biopsychosocial history was obtained.

B. Specific information from the family and a veteran/service member history was obtained, with a focus on addiction (e.g., family history of addiction and treatment, other substances used, progression of substance abuse, consequences of abuse).

C. The results of the biopsychosocial history were reviewed with the veteran/service member.

8. Assign Didactics Regarding Effects of Chemical Dependence (8)

A. The veteran/service member was assigned to attend a chemical dependence didactic series to increase his/her knowledge of the patterns and effects of chemical dependence.

B. The veteran/service member was asked to identify in writing several key points obtained from the didactic lectures.

C. Key points from the didactic lectures that were noted by the veteran/service member were processed in individual sessions.

D. The veteran/service member has become more open in acknowledging and accepting his/her chemical dependence.

9. Require Chemical Dependence Didactics (9)

A. The veteran/service member was required to attend didactic lectures related to chemical dependence.

B. The veteran/service member was asked to identify in writing several key points obtained from each didactic lecture.

C. Key points from didactic lectures that were noted by the veteran/service member were processed in individual sessions.

10. Assign Addiction Education Material (10)

A. The veteran/service member was asked to read material on addiction to increase his/her awareness of the process of addiction and recovery.

B. The veteran/service member was asked to identify five key points from the material that was assigned on addiction.

C. Key points from the addiction material that was read were discussed.

D. The veteran/service member has not read the assigned reading material on addiction and was redirected to do so.

11. Require Reading *Narcotics Anonymous* (11)

A. The veteran/service member was assigned to read *Narcotics Anonymous*.

B. The veteran/service member was asked to identify five key points from the *Narcotics Anonymous* reading, and these points were processed.

C. The veteran/service member has not completed the assigned reading and was redirected to do so.

12. Refer to Group Therapy (12)

A. It was strongly recommended to the veteran/service member that he/she attend group therapy that is focused on addiction issues.

B. The veteran/service member has followed through with consistent attendance to group therapy and reports that the meetings have been helpful.

C. The veteran/service member has not followed through on regular attendance to group therapy and was redirected to do so.

D. The veteran/service member has attended group therapy meetings, but reports that he/she does not find them helpful, and is resistive to returning to them.

13. Direct Group Therapy (13)

A. Group therapy sessions were provided that facilitated the sharing of, causes for, consequences of, feelings about, and alternatives to addiction.

B. The veteran/service member participated in group therapy sessions, sharing information about the causes, consequences, and feelings about his/her addiction.

C. The veteran/service member has attended group therapy sessions focused on addiction issues but has not actively participated by sharing his/her thoughts and feelings.

D. The veteran/service member has not attended group therapy sessions and was redirected to do so.

14. Assign First-Step Paper (14)

A. The veteran/service member was assigned to complete a NA first-step paper and to share it with his/her group and the therapist.

B. The veteran/service member completed a first-step paper that acknowledged that addictive behavior has dominated his/her life.

C. The veteran/service member has failed to complete the first-step paper and was redirected to do so.

15. List Negative Consequences (15)

A. The veteran/service member was asked to make a list of the ways in which addiction has negatively impacted his/her life and to process this list.

B. The veteran/service member was assigned "Substance Abuse Negative Impact versus Sobriety's Positive Impact" from the *Adult Psychotherapy Homework Planner,* 2nd ed. (Jongsma).

C. The veteran/service member has minimized the negative impact of his/her addictive behavior on his/her life.

D. The veteran/service member has completed his/her list of negative impacts of addictive behaviors on his/her life and has acknowledged the negative consequences he/she has experienced.

E. The veteran/service member has not completed the list of negative impacts upon his/her life and was redirected to do so.

16. Confront Denial (16)

A. The veteran's/service member's use of denial to minimize the severity of his/her opioid abuse was confronted.

B. The veteran/service member was confronted about how he/she has used denial to minimize the severity of the negative consequences of his/her opioid abuse.

C. The veteran/service member was supported as he/she became more open and honest about his/her opioid abuse and the consequences of this abuse.

D. The veteran/service member continues to deny and minimize his/her opioid abuse and the consequences of this abuse; he/she was encouraged to become more open in this area.

17. List Reasons to Stay in Treatment (17)

A. The veteran/service member was assisted in developing a list of reasons why he/she should stay in chemical dependence treatment.

B. The veteran/service member identified several of his/her own reasons for remaining in chemical dependence treatment.

C. The veteran/service member struggled to identify reasons why he/she should remain in treatment, and this was processed within the session.

18. Explore Addiction as an Escape (18)

A. The veteran's/service member's use of opioid abuse as a way to escape stress, emotional pain, and/or boredom was explored.

B. The veteran/service member acknowledged using opioid abuse as a way to escape from stress, emotional pain, and/or boredom.

C. The veteran/service member was confronted for the negative consequences of his/her pattern of escapism.

D. The veteran/service member reported that he/she has decreased his/her opioid abuse as a way to escape stress, emotional pain, and/or boredom.

E. The veteran/service member denied the idea that opioid abuse has been used as an escape from stress.

19. Probe Guilt and Shame Issues (19)

A. The veteran/service member was probed for his/her sense of shame, guilt, and low self-worth that has resulted from opioid abuse and its consequences.

B. The veteran/service member reported significant patterns of shame, guilt, and low self-worth due to his/her opioid abuse and its consequences.

C. The veteran/service member denied any pattern of shame, guilt, and low self-worth.

20. List Reasons for Abstinence (20)

A. The veteran/service member was asked to make a list of at least 10 positive effects that abstinence from opioid abuse could have on his/her life.

B. The veteran/service member was assigned "Making Change Happen" from *The Addiction Treatment Homework Planner,* 4th ed. (Finley and Lenz).

C. The veteran/service member was assigned "A Working Recovery Plan" from *The Addiction Treatment Homework Planner,* 4th ed. (Finley and Lenz).

D. The veteran/service member made a list of positive effects of abstinence from opioid abuse, and this list was processed and reinforced.

E. The veteran/service member was assisted in making a list of positive effects of abstinence from opioid abuse, and this list was processed and reinforced.

F. The veteran/service member has not made a list of positive effects of abstinence from opioid abuse and was redirected to do so.

21. Review Dishonesty and Opioid Abuse/Dependence (21)

A. The veteran/service member was assisted in understanding that dishonesty goes along with opioid abuse, and that honesty is necessary for recovery.

B. The veteran/service member was asked to identify 10 lies that he/she has told to hide opioid abuse.

C. The veteran/service member developed a list of lies that he/she has told to hide opioid abuse, and these were reviewed.

D. The veteran/service member acknowledged his/her own pattern of dishonesty, which has supported his/her opioid abuse behavior, and reported increased honesty during recovery.

E. The veteran/service member denied any pattern of dishonesty to hide opioid abuse.

22. Teach about Honesty (22)

A. The veteran/service member was taught how honesty is essential for real intimacy and how it is crucial to combating interpersonal frustration and loneliness.

B. The veteran/service member was taught that pain and disappointment result when honesty is not given the highest priority in one's life.

C. The veteran/service member was asked to identify situations in which he/she could become more honest and reliable.

D. The veteran/service member was supported as he/she identified ways in which he/she could be more honest and reliable.

E. The veteran/service member was confronted for continuing to engage in dishonesty.

23. Teach about a Higher Power (23)

A. The veteran/service member was presented with information on how faith in a higher power can aid in recovery from opioid abuse and addictive behaviors.

B. The veteran/service member was assisted in processing and clarifying his/her own ideas and feelings about his/her higher power.

C. The veteran/service member was encouraged to describe his/her beliefs about his/her higher power.

D. The veteran/service member was noted to reject the concept of a higher power.

24. Conduct Motivational Interviewing (24)

A. Motivational interviewing techniques were used to help assess the veteran's/service member's preparation for change.

B. The veteran/service member was assisted in identifying his/her stage of change regarding his/her substance abuse concerns.

C. It was reflected to the veteran/service member that he/she is currently building motivation for change.

D. The veteran/service member was assisted in strengthening his/her commitment to change.

E. The veteran/service member was noted to be participating actively in treatment.

25. Assign AA/NA Member Contact (25)

A. The veteran/service member was assigned to meet with an Alcoholics Anonymous/Narcotics Anonymous (AA/NA) member who has been working the 12-step program for several years to find out specifically how the program has helped him/her stay sober.

B. The veteran/service member has followed through on meeting with the AA/NA member and was encouraged about the role that AA/NA can play in maintaining sobriety.

C. The veteran/service member met with the AA/NA member but was not encouraged about the role of self-help groups in maintaining sobriety; his/her experience was processed.

D. The veteran/service member has not followed through on meeting with an AA/NA member and was redirected to do so.

26. Identify Sobriety Expectations (26)

A. The veteran/service member was requested to write out basic expectations that he/she has regarding sobriety.

B. The veteran/service member has identified specific expectations that he/she has regarding sobriety (e.g., physical changes, social changes, emotional needs), and these were processed with the clinician.

C. As the veteran/service member has been assisted in developing a more realistic expectation regarding his/her sobriety, he/she has felt more at ease and willing to work toward sobriety.

D. The veteran/service member has not identified his/her expectations regarding sobriety and was redirected to do so.

27. Encourage Sobriety Despite Relapses (27)

A. Although the veteran/service member has relapsed, he/she was refocused on the need for substance abuse recovery and on the need for sobriety.

B. As the veteran/service member has received continued support for his/her recovery and sobriety despite relapses, he/she has become more confident regarding his/her chances for success.

C. The veteran/service member lacks confidence in his/her ability to obtain recovery and sobriety due to his/her pattern of relapses; this pessimism was challenged and processed.

28. Develop Abstinence Contract (28)

A. The veteran/service member was assisted in developing an abstinence contract regarding the termination of his/her drug.

B. The veteran/service member has developed an abstinence contract to terminate his/her use of drugs, and this contract was reviewed and processed.

C. The veteran/service member was urged to express his/her feelings related to the commitment to discontinue drug use.

D. The veteran/service member reported that he/she felt some sense of relief in breaking emotional ties with his/her drug of choice; the benefits of this progress were reviewed.

E. The veteran/service member has failed to follow through on the abstinence contract to his/her drug of choice and was redirected to do so.

29. Review Negative Peer Influence (29)

A. A review of the veteran's/service member's negative peers was performed, and the influence of these people on his/her substance abuse patterns was identified.

B. The veteran/service member accepted the interpretation that maintaining contact with substance-abusing friends would reduce the probability of successful recovery from his/her chemical dependence.

C. A plan was developed to help the veteran/service member initiate contact with sober people who could exert a positive influence on his/her own recovery (e.g., sobriety buddies).

D. The veteran/service member has begun to reach out socially to sober individuals in order to develop a social network that has a more positive influence on his/her recovery; he/she was reinforced for this progress.

E. The veteran/service member has not attempted to reach out socially to sober individuals in order to develop a social network that has a more positive influence in his/her recovery and was reminded about this important facet of his/her recovery.

30. Plan Social and Recreational Activities (30)

A. A list of social and recreational activities that are free from association with substance abuse was developed.

B. The veteran/service member was verbally reinforced as he/she agreed to begin involvement in new recreational and social activities that will replace substance abuse–related activities.

C. The veteran/service member has begun to make changes in his/her social and/or recreational activities and reports feeling good about this change; the benefits of this progress were reviewed.

D. The veteran/service member was very resistive to any changes in social and recreational activities that have previously been a strong part of his/her life but was encouraged to begin with small changes in this area.

31. Plan Household and Work-Related Activities and Free-Time Projects (31)

A. A list of household, work, and free-time activities that are free from association with substance abuse was developed.

B. The veteran/service member was verbally reinforced as he/she agreed to begin involvement in new activities that will replace substance abuse-related activities.

C. The veteran/service member has begun to make changes in his/her household, work-related, and free-time activities and reports feeling good about this change; the benefits of this progress were reviewed.

D. The veteran/service member was very resistive to any changes in activities that have previously been a strong part of his/her life but was encouraged to begin with small changes in this area.

32. Evaluate Living Situation (32)

A. The veteran's/service member's current living situation was reviewed as to whether it fosters a pattern of chemical dependence.

B. The veteran/service member was supported as he/she agreed that his/her current living situation does encourage continuing substance abuse.

C. The veteran/service member could not see any reason why his/her current living situation would have a negative effect on his/her chemical dependence recovery; he/she was provided with tentative examples in this area.

33. Encourage a Change in Living Situation (33)

A. The veteran/service member was encouraged to develop a plan to find a more positive living situation that will foster his/her chemical dependence recovery.

B. The veteran/service member was reinforced as he/she found a new living situation that is free from the negative influences that the current living situation brings to his/her chemical dependence recovery.

C. The veteran/service member is very resistive to moving from his/her current living situation; he/she was assisted in processing this resistance.

34. Identify Sobriety's Positive Family Effects (34)

A. The veteran/service member was assisted in identifying the positive changes that will occur within family relationships as a result of his/her chemical dependence recovery.

B. The veteran/service member reported that his/her family is enjoying a reduction in stress and increased cooperation since his/her chemical dependence recovery began; his/her reaction to these changes was processed.

C. The veteran/service member was unable to identify any positive changes that have or could occur within family relationships as a result of his/her chemical dependence recovery and was provided with tentative examples in this area.

35. Reinforce Making Amends (35)

A. The negative effects that the veteran's/service member's substance abuse has had on family, friends, and work relationships were identified.

B. A plan for making amends to those who have been negatively affected by the veteran's/service member's substance abuse was developed.

C. The veteran's/service member's implementation of his/her plan to make amends to those who have been hurt by his/her substance abuse was reviewed.

D. The veteran/service member reported feeling good about the fact that he/she has begun to make amends to others who have been hurt by his/her substance abuse; this progress was reinforced.

E. The veteran/service member has not followed through on making amends to others who have been negatively affected by his/her pattern of substance abuse and was reminded to do so.

36. Obtain Commitment Regarding Making Amends (36)

A. The veteran/service member was asked to make a verbal commitment to make amends to key individuals.

B. The veteran/service member was urged to make further amends while working through Steps 8 and 9 of the 12-step program.

C. The veteran/service member was supported as he/she made a verbal commitment to make initial amends now and to make further amends as he/she works through Steps 8 and 9 of the 12-step program.

D. The veteran/service member declined to commit to making amends and was redirected to review the need to make this commitment.

37. Refer for Marital Therapy (37)

A. The couple was referred to a clinician who specializes in behavioral marital therapy.

B. The couple was provided with behavioral marital therapy.

C. The couple was assisted in identifying conflicts that could be addressed using communication, conflict resolution, and/or problem-solving skills.

D. Techniques described by Holzworth-Monroe and Jacobson in "Behavioral Marital Therapy" in *Handbook of Family Therapy* (Gurman and Knickerson) were used to help the couple develop better communication, conflict resolution, and problem-solving skills.

38. Teach about Coping Package (38)

A. The veteran/service member was taught a variety of techniques to help manage urges to use chemical substances.

B. The veteran/service member was taught calming strategies, such as relaxation and breathing techniques.

C. The veteran/service member was taught cognitive techniques, such as thought stopping, positive self-talk, and attention focusing (e.g., distraction from urges, staying focused, behavioral goals of abstinence).

D. The veteran/service member has used his/her coping package techniques to help reduce his/her urges to use chemical substances; this progress was reinforced.

E. The veteran/service member has not used the coping package for managing urges to use chemical substances and was redirected to do so.

39. Explore Schema and Self-Talk (39)

A. The veteran's/service member's schema and self-talk that weaken his/her resolve to remain abstinent were explored.

B. The biases that the veteran/service member entertains regarding his/her schema and self-talk were challenged.

C. The veteran/service member was assisted in generating more realistic self-talk to correct for his/her biases and build resilience.

D. The veteran/service member was provided with positive feedback for his/her replacement of self-talk and biases.

E. The veteran/service member struggled to identify his/her self-talk and biases that weaken his/her resolve to remain abstinent and was provided with tentative examples in this area.

40. Rehearse Replacement of Negative Self-Talk (40)

A. The veteran/service member was assisted in identifying situations in which his/her negative self-talk occurs.

B. The veteran/service member was assisted in generating empowering alternatives to his/her negative self-talk.

C. The veteran/service member was assigned "Journal and Replace Self-Defeating Thoughts" from the *Adult Psychotherapy Homework Planner,* 2nd ed. (Jongsma).

D. The veteran's/service member's success in rehearsing the response to negative self-talk was reviewed and reinforced.

E. The veteran/service member has not done the assigned homework on journaling about self-defeating thoughts and was redirected to do so.

41. Develop Hierarchy of Urge-Producing Cues (41)

A. The veteran/service member was directed to construct a hierarchy of urge-producing cues to use substances.

B. The veteran/service member was assigned "Identifying Relapse Triggers and Cues" from the *Addiction Treatment Homework Planner,* 4th ed. (Finley and Lenz).

C. The veteran/service member was assigned "Relapse Prevention Planning" in the *Addiction Treatment Homework Planner,* 4th ed. (Finley & Lenz).

D. The veteran/service member was assisted in developing a hierarchy of urge-producing cues to use substances.

E. The veteran/service member was helped to identify a variety of cues that prompt his/her use of substances.

F. The veteran/service member has not completed assignments regarding urge-producing cues, and this resistance was processed.

42. Practice Response to Urge-Producing Cues (42)

A. The veteran/service member was assisted in selecting urge-producing cues with which to practice, with a bias toward cues that are likely to result in a successful experience.

B. Behavioral techniques were used to help the veteran/service member cognitively restructure his/her urge-producing cues.

C. The veteran's/service member's use of cognitive restructuring strategies was reviewed and processed.

43. Assess Stress Management Skills (43)

A. The veteran's/service member's current level of skill in managing everyday stressors was assessed.

B. The veteran/service member was assessed in regard to his/her ability to meet role demands for work, social, and family expectations.

C. Behavioral and cognitive restructuring techniques were used to help build social and communication skills to manage everyday challenges.

D. The veteran/service member was provided with positive feedback regarding his/her ability to manage common everyday stressors.

E. The veteran/service member continues to struggle with common everyday stressors and was provided with remedial feedback in this area.

44. Assign Social and Communication Information (44)

A. The veteran/service member was assigned to read about social skills.

B. The veteran/service member was assigned to read about communication skills.

C. The veteran/service member was assigned to read *Your Perfect Right* (Alberti and Emmons).

D. The veteran/service member was assigned to read *Conversationally Speaking* (Garner).

E. The veteran/service member has read the assigned information about social and communication skills, and key points were reviewed.

F. The veteran/service member has not read the assigned information on social and communication skills and was redirected to do so.

45. Explore Pain Level (45)

A. The veteran's/service member's injury-related pain level was assessed in conjunction with his/her pattern of narcotic abuse.

B. The veteran/service member was noted to engage in substance abuse to help manage his/her pain.

C. The veteran/service member was noted to be engaging in substance abuse independent from the pain concerns.

46. Teach Pain Management Skills (46)

A. The veteran/service member was taught about pain management skills in order to have alternatives to substance use for managing pain.

B. The veteran/service member was referred to a pain management program to assist in learning alternative skills for managing pain.

C. The veteran/service member has learned alternative skills for managing pain, his/her use of substances has decreased; this progress was reinforced.

D. The veteran/service member has not utilized pain management opportunities and was redirected to do so.

47. Differentiate between Lapse and Relapse (47)

A. A discussion was held with the veteran/service member regarding the distinction between a lapse and a relapse.

B. A lapse was associated with an initial and reversible return of symptoms or urges to use substances.

C. A relapse was associated with the decision to return to regular use of substances.

D. The veteran/service member was provided with support and encouragement as he/she displayed an understanding of the difference between a lapse and a relapse.

E. The veteran/service member struggled to understand the difference between a lapse and a relapse and was provided with remedial feedback in this area.

48. Discuss Management of Lapse Risk Situations (48)

A. The veteran/service member was assisted in identifying future situations or circumstances in which lapses could occur.

B. The session focused on rehearsing the management of future situations or circumstances in which lapses could occur.

C. The veteran/service member was asked to identify how family and peer conflict contribute to his/her stress levels.

D. The veteran/service member was reinforced for his/her appropriate use of lapse management skills.

E. The veteran/service member was redirected in regard to his/her poor use of lapse management skills.

49. Identify Relapse Triggers (49)

A. The veteran/service member was assisted in developing a list of potential relapse signs and triggers that could lead him/her back to substance abuse.

B. The veteran/service member was requested to complete the "Relapse Triggers" assignment from the *Adult Psychotherapy Homework Planner,* 2nd ed. (Jongsma).

C. The veteran/service member was supported for identifying specific symptoms and how these increase his/her desire for substances.

D. The veteran/service member was assisted in developing a specific strategy for constructively responding to his/her substance abuse relapse triggers.

E. The veteran/service member was reinforced for his/her successful implementation of the coping strategies for the substance abuse relapse triggers.

F. A review was conducted regarding the veteran's/service member's pattern of relapse subsequent to failing to use constructive coping strategies in a trigger situation.

50. Encourage Routine Use of Strategies (50)

A. The veteran/service member was instructed to routinely use the strategies that he/she has learned in therapy (e.g., cognitive restructuring exposure).

B. The veteran/service member was urged to find ways to build his/her new strategies into his/her life as much as possible.

C. The veteran/service member was assigned "Aftercare Plan Components" from the *Adult Psychotherapy Homework Planner*, 2nd ed. (Jongsma).

D. The veteran/service member has not completed the aftercare planning assigned and was redirected to complete this important further step in his/her recovery.

E. The veteran/service member was reinforced as he/she reported ways in which he/she has incorporated coping strategies into his/her life and routine.

F. The veteran/service member was redirected about ways to incorporate his/her new strategies into his/her routine and life.

51. Refer to Supported Employment/Job Coach Program (51)

A. The veteran/service member was referred to a supported employment program to assist him/her in developing independent job skills.

B. The veteran/service member was reinforced for his/her involvement in the supported employment program that has assisted him/her in skill building regarding employment needs.

C. The veteran/service member has not actively participated in the supported employment program and was redirected to do so.

D. The veteran/service member was coached regarding his/her preparation for employment, searching for a job, and maintaining employment.

E. The veteran/service member was assisted in role-playing and rehearsing specific techniques necessary for obtaining and maintaining employment.

F. The veteran/service member was provided with positive feedback regarding his/her increased understanding of issues related to obtaining and maintaining employment.

G. The veteran/service member continues to have a poor understanding of basic concepts related to obtaining and maintaining employment and was provided with additional feedback in this area.

52. Emphasize Positives without Opioids (52)

A. The veteran/service member was taught about how to get good things out of life without using mood-altering substances.

B. The veteran/service member verbalized increased understanding of how to get good things out of life without using mood-altering substances.

C. The veteran/service member denied the concept of getting good things out of life without using mood-altering substances.

53. Assign a List of Pleasurable Activities (53)

A. The veteran/service member was assigned to make a list of pleasurable activities that he/she plans to use in recovery to take the place of opioid abuse.

B. The veteran/service member was assigned "Identify and Schedule Pleasant Activities" from the *Adult Psychotherapy Homework Planner*, 2nd ed. (Jongsma).

C. The veteran/service member completed a list of pleasurable activities to take the place of opioid abuse, and this was processed within the session.

D. The veteran/service member has not developed a list of pleasurable activities to take the place of opioid abuse, and this was worked on within the session.

E. The veteran/service member has not completed a list of pleasurable activities to use during recovery and was redirected to do so.

54. Assign Regular Exercise (54)

A. Based on the veteran's/service member's current physical fitness levels, an exercise routine was developed, and the veteran/service member was assigned to implement it consistently.

B. The veteran/service member has begun to increase his/her exercise level by 10 percent per week.

C. The veteran/service member has sustained his/her exercise level to at least three exercise periods per week, maintaining a training heart rate for at least 20 minutes.

D. The veteran/service member has not followed through on his/her exercise program and was redirected to do so.

55. Assign Step Three Exercise (55)

A. Today's session focused on teaching the veteran/service member about the 12-step recovery program's concept of "turning it over."

B. The veteran/service member was assigned the task of turning problems over to a higher power each day and recording the experiences in a journal.

C. The veteran's/service member's experience of turning problems over to his/her higher power was processed within the session.

D. A decrease in the veteran's/service member's addictive behavior has been noted since he/she has turned peer group negativity problems over to a higher power each day.

E. The veteran/service member struggled with the concept and implementation of turning his/her problems over to a higher power and was provided with remedial feedback in this area.

56. Readminister Psychological Instruments (56)

A. The outcome of treatment was assessed via the readministration of objective tests of opioid dependence.

B. The veteran/service member produced treatment outcome test scores indicating improvement on opioid dependence concerns; this progress was presented to the veteran/service member.

C. The veteran/service member produced treatment outcome test scores indicating lack of improvement on opioid dependence concerns; this lack of progress was presented to the veteran/service member.

PANIC/AGORAPHOBIA

VETERAN/SERVICE MEMBER PRESENTATION

1. Severe Panic Symptoms (1)*

A. The veteran/service member has experienced sudden and unexpected severe panic symptoms that have occurred repeatedly and have resulted in persistent concern about additional attacks.

B. The veteran/service member has significantly modified his/her normal behavior patterns in an effort to avoid panic attacks.

C. The frequency and severity of the veteran's/service member's panic attacks have diminished significantly.

D. The veteran/service member reported that he/she has not experienced any recent panic attack symptoms.

2. Fear of Environmental Situations Triggering Anxiety (2)

A. The veteran/service member described fear of environmental situations that he/she believes may trigger intense anxiety symptoms.

B. The veteran's/service member's fear of environmental situations has resulted in his/her avoidance behavior directed toward those environmental situations.

C. The veteran/service member has a significant fear of leaving home and being in open or crowded public situations.

D. The veteran's/service member's phobic fear has diminished, and he/she has left the home environment without being crippled by anxiety.

E. The veteran/service member is able to leave home normally and function within public environments.

3. Recognition that Fear is Unreasonable (3)

A. The veteran's/service member's phobic fear has persisted in spite of the fact that he/she acknowledges that the fear is unreasonable.

B. The veteran/service member has made many attempts to ignore or overcome his/her unreasonable fear but has been unsuccessful.

4. Concern of Risk (4)

A. The service member is concerned that in emergency situations, he/she will panic and not complete appropriate tasks.

B. The service member identified concerns that panic symptoms will put him/her and others at risk.

C. As treatment has progressed, the service member is much less fearful and is confident that he/she will perform as expected.

---

*The numbers in parentheses correlate to the number of the Behavioral Definition statement in the companion chapter with the same title in *The Veterans and Active Duty Military Psychotherapy Treatment Planner* (Moore and Jongsma) by John Wiley & Sons, 2009.

5. Increasing Isolation (5)

A. The veteran/service member described situations in which he/she has declined involvement with others due to a fear of traveling or leaving a "safe environment," such as his/her home.

B. The veteran/service member reported that he/she has become increasingly isolated due to his/her fear of traveling or leaving a "safe environment."

C. The veteran/service member has severely constricted his/her involvement with others.

D. Although the veteran/service member experiences some symptoms of panic, he/she still feels capable of leaving home.

E. The veteran/service member has been able to leave his/her "safe environment" on a regular basis.

6. Avoids Public Places and Large Groups (6)

A. The veteran/service member avoids public places, such as malls or large stores.

B. The veteran/service member avoids large groups of people.

C. The service member has avoided participation in large military formations.

D. The service member avoids spending time in the dining facilities.

E. The veteran/service member has constricted his/her involvement with others in order to avoid social situations.

F. The veteran/service member has begun to reach out socially and feels more comfortable in public places or with large groups of people.

G. The veteran/service member reported enjoying involvement with large groups of people and feels comfortable going to public places.

INTERVENTIONS IMPLEMENTED

1. Assess Nature of Panic Symptoms (1)*

A. The veteran/service member was asked about the frequency, intensity, duration, and history of his/her panic symptoms, fear, and avoidance.

B. The *Anxiety Disorders Interview Schedule for the DSM-IV* (DiNardo, Brown, and Barlow) was used to assess the veteran's/service member's panic symptoms.

C. The assessment of the veteran's/service member's panic symptoms indicated that his/her symptoms are extreme and severely interfere with his/her life.

D. The assessment of the veteran's/service member's panic symptoms indicates that these symptoms are moderate and occasionally interfere with his/her daily functioning.

E. The results of the assessment of the veteran's/service member's panic symptoms indicate that these symptoms are mild and rarely interfere with his/her daily functioning.

F. The results of the assessment of the veteran's/service member's panic symptoms were reviewed with the veteran/service member.

---

*The numbers in parentheses correlate to the number of the Therapeutic Intervention statement in the companion chapter with the same title in *The Veterans and Active Duty Military Psychotherapy Treatment Planner* (Moore and Jongsma) by John Wiley & Sons, 2009.

2. Explore Panic Stimulus Situations (2)

A. The veteran/service member was assisted in identifying specific stimulus situations that precipitate panic symptoms.

B. The veteran/service member was assigned the homework exercise "Monitoring My Panic Attack Experiences" from the *Adult Psychotherapy Homework Planner,* 2nd ed. (Jongsma).

C. The veteran/service member could not describe any specific stimulus situations that produce panic; he/she was helped to identify that they occur unexpectedly and without any pattern.

D. The veteran/service member was helped to identify that his/her panic symptoms occur when he/she leaves the confines of his/her home environment and enters public situations where there are many people.

3. Assess Impact on Social/Occupational Functioning (3)

A. The impact of the veteran's/service member's panic symptoms on occupational and social functioning were measured through the use of standardized measures.

B. The *OQ-45.2* was used to assess the impact of the panic symptoms on the veteran's/service member's occupational and social functioning.

C. Serial measurement was used for the purpose of assessing progress.

D. The veteran's/service member's level of progress on managing panic symptoms was reviewed with him/her.

4. Assess Supervisor's Concerns (4)

A. Information was sought out from the service member's first-line supervisor to assess the degree the anxiety has impacted this service member's job performance.

B. The service member's first-line supervisor has indicated that the service member's anxiety symptoms have had very little impact on his/her job; this assessment was reflected to the service member.

C. The service member's first-line supervisor has indicated that the service member's anxiety symptoms have had moderate impact on his/her job; this assessment was reflected to the service member.

D. The service member's first-line supervisor has indicated that the service member's anxiety symptoms have had severe impact on his/her job; this assessment was reflected to the service member.

5. Administer Assessments for Agoraphobia Symptoms (5)

A. The veteran/service member was administered psychological instruments designed to objectively assess his/her level of agoraphobia symptoms.

B. The veteran/service member was administered *The Mobility Inventory for Agoraphobia* (Chambless, Coputo, and Gracely).

C. The veteran/service member was provided with feedback regarding the results of the assessment of his/her level of agoraphobia symptoms.

D. The veteran/service member declined to participate in the objective assessment of his/her level of agoraphobia symptoms, and this resistance was processed.

6. Administer Assessments for Anxiety Symptoms (6)

A. The veteran/service member was administered psychological instruments designed to objectively assess his/her level of anxiety symptoms.

B. The veteran/service member was administered *The Anxiety Sensitivity Index* (Reiss, Peterson, and Grusky).

C. The veteran/service member was provided with feedback regarding the results of the assessment of his/her level of anxiety symptoms.

D. The veteran/service member declined to participate in the objective assessment of his/her level of anxiety symptoms, and this resistance was processed.

7. Refer for Medication Evaluation (7)

A. Arrangements were made for the veteran/service member to have a physician evaluation for the purpose of considering psychotropic medication to alleviate phobic symptoms.

B. The veteran/service member has followed through with seeing a physician for an evaluation of any organic causes for the anxiety and the need for psychotropic medication to control the anxiety response.

C. The veteran/service member has not cooperated with the referral to a physician for a medication evaluation and was encouraged to do so.

8. Monitor Medication Compliance (8)

A. The veteran/service member reported that he/she has taken the prescribed medication consistently and that it has helped to control the phobic anxiety; this was relayed to the prescribing clinician.

B. The veteran/service member reported that he/she has not taken the prescribed medication consistently and was encouraged to do so.

C. The veteran/service member reported taking the prescribed medication and stated that he/she has not noted any beneficial effect from it; this was reported to the prescribing clinician.

D. The veteran/service member was evaluated but was not prescribed any psychotropic medication by the physician.

9. Provide Updates to Leadership (9)

A. An update on the service member's condition, potential negative impacts on safety, and occupational limitations was provided to the unit leadership.

B. Recommendations were made to the service member's unit leadership in regard to his/her functioning.

10. Nature of Panic Symptoms (10)

A. A discussion was held about how panic attacks are "false alarms" of danger but are not medically dangerous.

B. A discussion was held about how panic attacks are not a sign of weakness or craziness.

C. The veteran's/service member's panic attacks were discussed, including how they are a common symptom but can lead to unnecessary avoidance, thereby reinforcing the panic attack.

11. Assign Information on Panic Disorders and Agoraphobia (11)

A. The veteran/service member was assigned to read psychoeducational chapters of books or treatment manuals about panic disorders and agoraphobia.

B. The veteran/service member was assigned specific chapters from *Mastery of Your Anxiety and Panic* (Barlow and Craske).

C. The veteran/service member was assigned to read chapters from *Don't Panic: Taking Control of Anxiety Attacks* (Wilson).

D. The veteran/service member was assigned to read *Living with Fear* (Marks).

E. The veteran/service member has read the assigned information on panic disorders and agoraphobia, and key points were discussed.

F. The veteran/service member has not read the assigned information on panic disorders and agoraphobia and was redirected to do so.

12. Discuss Benefits of Exposure (12)

A. The veteran/service member was taught about how exposure can serve as an arena to desensitize learned fear, build confidence, and create success experiences.

B. A discussion was held about the use of exposure to decrease fear, build confidence, and feel safer.

C. The veteran/service member was reinforced as he/she indicated a clear understanding of how exposure can help to conquer panic and agoraphobia symptoms.

D. The veteran/service member did not display understanding about how exposure can help overcome his/her agoraphobia and panic symptoms and was provided with remedial feedback in this area.

13. Discuss Changing Thoughts Effect on Panic Symptoms (13)

A. A discussion was held in regard to how changing thought patterns and eliminating cognitive errors decreases fear reactions and minimizes panic symptoms.

B. The veteran/service member was provided with examples of how cognitive errors cause fear reactions, such as making oneself anxious via self-talk prior to attending a promotion board hearing.

C. The veteran/service member displayed insight into the use of cognitive errors and fear reactions and was reinforced for this.

D. The veteran/service member seemed to struggle with understanding the connection between cognitive errors and panic symptoms and was provided with additional feedback.

14. Train about Coping Strategies (14)

A. The veteran/service member was taught progressive relaxation methods and debriefing exercises.

B. The veteran/service member was trained in the use of coping strategies to manage symptoms of panic attacks.

C. The veteran/service member was taught coping strategies, such as staying focused on behavioral goals, muscular relaxation, evenly paced diaphragmatic breathing, and positive self-talk, in order to manage his/her symptoms.

D. The veteran/service member has become proficient in coping techniques for his/her panic attacks; he/she was reinforced for the regular use of these techniques.

E. The veteran/service member has not regularly used coping techniques for panic attacks and was provided with additional training in this area.

15. Urge External Focus (15)

A. The veteran/service member was urged to keep his/her focus on external stimuli and behavioral responsibilities rather than be preoccupied with internal states and physiological changes.

B. An example was provided of focusing on external stimuli over internal changes (i.e., focusing on breathing or foot placement during running deflects attention from fatigue and pain).

C. The veteran/service member was reinforced as he/she has made a commitment to not allow panic symptoms to take control of his/her life and to not avoid and escape normal responsibilities and activities.

D. The veteran/service member has been successful at turning his/her focus away from internal anxiety states and toward behavioral responsibilities; he/she was reinforced for this progress.

E. The veteran/service member has not maintained an external focus in order to keep panic symptoms from taking control of his/her life and was reminded about this helpful technique.

16. Counteract Panic Myths (16)

A. The veteran/service member was consistently reassured of the fact that there is no connection between panic symptoms and heart attack, loss of control over behavior, or serious mental illness.

B. The veteran/service member was reinforced as he/she verbalized an understanding that panic symptoms do not promote serious physical or mental illness.

17. Utilize Modeling/Behavioral Rehearsal (17)

A. Modeling and behavioral rehearsal were used to train the veteran/service member in positive self-talk that reassured him/her of the ability to work through and endure anxiety symptoms without serious consequences.

B. "Positive Self Talk" from the *Adult Psychotherapy Homework Planner,* 2nd ed. (Jongsma) was assigned to the veteran/service member.

C. The veteran/service member has implemented positive self-talk to reassure himself/herself of the ability to endure anxiety without serious consequences; he/she was reinforced for this progress.

D. The veteran/service member has not used positive self-talk to help endure anxiety and was provided with additional direction in this area.

18. Identify Distorted Thoughts (18)

A. The veteran/service member was assisted in identifying the distorted schemas and related automatic thoughts that mediate anxiety responses.

B. The veteran/service member was taught the role of distorted thinking in precipitating emotional responses.

C. The veteran/service member was reinforced as he/she verbalized an understanding of the cognitive beliefs and messages that mediate his/her anxiety responses.

D. The veteran/service member was assisted in replacing distorted messages with positive, realistic cognitions.

E. The veteran/service member failed to identify his/her distorted thoughts and cognitions and was provided with tentative examples in this area.

19. Explore Beliefs about Battlefield (19)

A. The service member's beliefs about how his/her panic symptoms may cause injury or death of himself/herself or others on the battlefield were explored.

B. The service member was noted to be worried about his/her concerns about being disabled by panic when under fire.

C. Emphasis was provided about how training in combat techniques and how muscle memory take over during combat scenarios.

D. The service member's beliefs and healthy responses to them were processed.

20. Assign Exercises on Self-Talk (20)

A. The veteran/service member was assigned homework exercises in which he/she identifies fearful self-talk and creates reality-based alternatives.

B. The veteran/service member was assigned the homework exercise "Journal and Replace Self-Defeating Thoughts" from the *Adult Psychotherapy Homework Planner*, 2nd ed. (Jongsma).

C. The veteran/service member was directed to do assignments from *10 Simple Solutions to Panic* (Antony and McCabe).

D. The veteran/service member was directed to complete assignments from *Mastery of Your Anxiety and Panic* (Barlow and Craske).

E. The veteran's/service member's replacement of fearful self-talk with reality-based alternatives was critiqued.

F. The veteran/service member was reinforced for his/her successes at replacing fearful self-talk with reality-based alternatives.

G. The veteran/service member was provided with corrective feedback for his/her failures to replace fearful self-talk with reality-based alternatives.

H. The veteran/service member has not completed his/her assigned homework regarding fearful self-talk and was redirected to do so.

21. Teach Sensation Exposure Technique (21)

A. The veteran/service member was taught about sensation exposure techniques.

B. The veteran/service member was taught about generating feared physical sensations through exercise (e.g., breathe rapidly until slightly light-headed) and the use of coping strategies to keep himself/herself calm.

C. The veteran/service member was assigned information about sensation exposure techniques in *10 Simple Solutions to Panic* (Antony and McCabe).

D. The veteran/service member was assigned information about sensation exposure techniques in *Mastery of Your Anxiety and Panic—Therapist's Guide* (Craske, Barlow, and Meadows).

E. The veteran/service member displayed a clear understanding of the sensation exposure technique and was reinforced for his/her understanding.

F. The veteran/service member struggled to understand the sensation exposure technique and was provided with remedial feedback.

22. Assign Homework on Sensation Exposure (22)

A. The veteran/service member was assigned homework exercises to perform sensation exposure and record his/her experience.

B. The veteran/service member was assigned sensation exposure homework from *Mastery of Your Anxiety and Panic* (Barlow and Craske).

C. The veteran/service member was assigned sensation exposure homework from *10 Simple Solutions to Panic* (Antony and McCabe).

D. The veteran's/service member's use of sensation exposure techniques was reviewed and reinforced.

E. The veteran/service member has struggled in his/her implementation of sensation exposure techniques and was provided with corrective feedback.

F. The veteran/service member has not attempted to use the sensation exposure techniques and was redirected to do so.

23. Construct Anxiety Stimuli Hierarchy (23)

A. The veteran/service member was assisted in constructing a hierarchy of anxiety-producing situations associated with his/her phobic fear.

B. It was difficult for the veteran/service member to develop a hierarchy of stimulus situations, as the causes of his/her fear remain quite vague; he/she was assisted in completing the hierarchy.

C. Hierarchy suggestions were offered to the veteran/service member, including holding a rifle, riding in a military vehicle, or going on a combat mission.

D. The veteran/service member was successful at creating a focused hierarchy of specific stimulus situations that provoke anxiety in a gradually increasing manner; this hierarchy was reviewed.

24. Select Initial Exposures (24)

A. Initial exposures were selected from the hierarchy of anxiety-producing situations, with a bias toward likelihood of being successful.

B. A plan was developed with the veteran/service member for managing the symptoms that may occur during the initial exposure.

C. The veteran/service member was assisted in rehearsing the plan for managing the exposure-related symptoms within his/her imagination.

D. Positive feedback was provided for the veteran's/service member's helpful use of symptom management techniques.

E. The veteran/service member was redirected for ways to improve his/her symptom management techniques.

25. Assign Homework on Situational Exposures (25)

A. The veteran/service member was assigned homework exercises to perform situational exposures and record his/her experience.

B. The veteran/service member was assigned the homework exercise "Gradually Reducing Your Phobic Fear" from the *Adult Psychotherapy Homework Planner*, 2nd ed. (Jongsma).

C. The veteran/service member was assigned situational exposures homework from *Mastery of Your Anxiety and Panic* (Barlow and Craske).

D. The veteran/service member was assigned situational exposures homework from *10 Simple Solutions to Panic* (Antony and McCabe).

E. The veteran's/service member's use of situational exposure techniques was reviewed and reinforced.

F. The veteran/service member has struggled in his/her implementation of situational exposure techniques and was provided with corrective feedback.

G. The veteran/service member has not attempted to use the situational exposure techniques and was redirected to do so.

26. Differentiate between Lapse and Relapse (26)

A. A discussion was held with the veteran/service member regarding the distinction between a lapse and a relapse.

B. A lapse was associated with an initial and reversible return of symptoms, fear, or urges to avoid.

C. A relapse was associated with the decision to return to fearful and avoidant patterns.

D. The veteran/service member was provided with support and encouragement as he/she displayed an understanding of the difference between a lapse and a relapse.

E. The veteran/service member struggled to understand the difference between a lapse and a relapse and was provided with remedial feedback in this area.

27. Discuss Management of Lapse Risk Situations (27)

A. The veteran/service member was assisted in identifying future situations or circumstances in which lapses could occur.

B. The session focused on rehearsing the management of future situations or circumstances in which lapses could occur.

C. The veteran/service member was reinforced for his/her appropriate use of lapse management skills.

D. The veteran/service member was redirected in regard to his/her poor use of lapse management skills.

28. Encourage Routine Use of Strategies (28)

A. The veteran/service member was instructed to routinely use the strategies that he/she has learned in therapy (e.g., cognitive restructuring, exposure).

B. The veteran/service member was urged to find ways to build his/her new strategies into his/her life as much as possible.

C. The veteran/service member was reinforced as he/she reported ways in which he/she has incorporated coping strategies into his/her life and routine.

D. The veteran/service member was redirected about ways to incorporate his/her new strategies into his/her routine and life.

29. Develop a "Coping Card" (29)

A. The veteran/service member was provided with a "coping card" on which specific coping strategies were listed.

B. The veteran/service member was assisted in developing his/her "coping card" in order to list helpful coping strategies.

C. The veteran/service member was encouraged to use his/her "coping card" when struggling with anxiety-producing situations.

30. Explore Secondary Gain (30)

A. Secondary gain was identified for the veteran's/service member's panic symptoms because of his/her tendency to escape or avoid certain situations.

B. The veteran/service member denied any role for secondary gain that results from his/her modification of life to accommodate panic; he/she was provided with tentative examples.

C. The veteran/service member was reinforced for accepting the role of secondary gain in promoting and maintaining the panic symptoms and encouraged to overcome this gain through living a more normal life.

D. The veteran/service member was challenged to remain in feared situations and to use coping skills to endure rather than to seek secondary gain.

31. Differentiate Current Fear from Past Pain (31)

A. The veteran/service member was taught to verbalize the separate realities of the current fear and the emotionally painful experience from the past that has been evoked by the phobic stimulus.

B. Caution was taken not to minimize or discount real or potential future threats.

C. The veteran/service member was reinforced when he/she expressed insight into the unresolved fear from the past that is linked to his/her current phobic fear.

D. The irrational nature of the veteran's/service member's current phobic fear was emphasized and clarified.

E. The veteran's/service member's unresolved emotional issue from the past was clarified.

32. Encourage Sharing of Feelings (32)

A. The veteran/service member was encouraged to share the emotionally painful experience from the past that has been evoked by the phobic stimulus.

B. The veteran/service member was taught to separate the realities of the irrationally feared object or situation and the painful experience from his/her past.

33. Provide Posttraumatic Stress Disorder Treatment (33)

A. The veteran/service member was assessed as in need of treatment for posttraumatic stress disorder.

B. Treatment for posttraumatic stress disorder was provided to the veteran/service member.

C. The veteran/service member was referred to treatment for posttraumatic stress disorder.

D. Although treatment for posttraumatic stress disorder appears indicated, the veteran/service member was unwilling to become involved in such treatment; he/she was urged to take advantage of this treatment when able.

34. Support Continued Duties and Activities (34)

A. The service member was supported for following through with military duties.

B. The veteran/service member was encouraged to follow through on family and social activities.

C. The veteran/service member was reminded not to attempt to escape or avoid duties and activities by focusing on the panic.

35. Schedule a "Booster Session" (35)

A. The veteran/service member was scheduled for a "booster session" between one and three months after therapy ends.

B. The veteran/service member was advised to contact the therapist if he/she needs to be seen prior to the "booster session."

C. The veteran's/service member's "booster session" was held, and he/she was reinforced for his/her successful implementation of therapy techniques.

D. The veteran's/service member's "booster session" was held, and he/she was encouraged to attend further treatment, as his/her progress has not been sustained.

36. Identify Mental Health Resources (36)

A. The service member was assisted in identifying mental health resources at the location where he/she will be deployed.

B. The service member was provided with specific information for how to seek mental health services in the area where he/she will be deployed.

C. Contacts were made to assist in the transition for mental health services in the service member's new deployment.

37. Arrange Medication for Deployment Transition (37)

A. The service member was provided with an appropriate amount of medication to get him/her through the deployment transition.

B. Steps were taken to coordinate the service member's ability to access his/her medications through the deployment transition.

PARENTING PROBLEMS RELATED TO DEPLOYMENT

VETERAN/SERVICE MEMBER PRESENTATION

1. Single Parenting (1)*

A. The non-deployed parent reports difficulties with parenting alone while the partner is deployed.

B. The non-deployed parent reports feeling stressed and overwhelmed with the continued difficulties of parenting alone.

C. As treatment has progressed, the non-deployed parent reports less stress and difficulties with managing parenting duties while the partner is deployed.

2. Overwhelmed with Caretaking Responsibilities (2)

A. The non-deployed partner verbalized feelings of increased stress and being overwhelmed with caretaking responsibilities while his/her partner is deployed.

B. The non-deployed partner has experienced stress-related reactions to the overwhelming experience of providing caretaking responsibilities on his/her own, including excessive tiredness, short temper, and anxiousness.

C. As treatment has progressed, the non-deployed partner has identified ways to manage the overwhelming feelings when stressed about caretaking responsibilities.

3. Low Income (3)

A. The non-deployed parent reports insufficient income to adequately provide for the family.

B. Changes in the family income pattern have caused financial difficulties for the non-deployed parent and the rest of the family.

C. As treatment has progressed, the non-deployed parent has developed better resources for managing the family budget.

4. Feelings of Inadequacy (4)

A. The non-deployed partner has indicated feelings of inadequacy as a parent.

B. The deployed partner feels inadequate as a parent, as he/she is not as available to the family.

C. Feelings of inadequacy as a parent have led to overindulgence of the children.

D. As treatment has progressed, the parent has reported an increased sense of adequacy.

5. Guilt over Deployment (5)

A. The deployed parent reports excessive guilt for having to leave his/her child.

B. The deployed parent's excessive guilt has led to a sense of estrangement from his/her family.

C. The service member has identified that his/her guilt for leaving to be deployed is excessive.

D. As treatment has progressed, the service member has reported a decreased sense of guilt.

---

*The numbers in parentheses correlate to the number of the Behavioral Definition statement in the companion chapter with the same title in *The Veterans and Active Duty Military Psychotherapy Treatment Planner* (Moore and Jongsma) by John Wiley & Sons, 2009.

6. Impatience and Hostility (6)

A. The non-deployed parent displays a lack of patience toward the child.

B. The non-deployed parent has displayed hostile feelings toward the child.

C. As treatment has progressed, the non-deployed parent reports increased patience and more positive interactions with the child.

7. Anger and Resentment (7)

A. The non-deployed parent verbalizes feelings of resentment and anger toward the deployed parent.

B. The non-deployed parent feels abandoned by the deployed parent.

C. The non-deployed parent has acknowledged that the spouse's deployment is not the fault of the service member.

D. The non-deployed parent reports decreased feelings of anger and resentment toward the deployed parent.

E. The non-deployed parent is no longer feeling anger and resentment toward the deployed spouse.

8. Lack of Support (8)

A. The non-deployed parent reports a lack of social and community support regarding raising the child.

B. The non-deployed parent reports a lack of military support regarding raising the child.

C. The non-deployed parent reports an increased sense of community and support regarding raising the child.

D. The non-deployed parent expressed being pleased with the social and community support she/he is now receiving in raising the children.

9. Opposition and Defiance (9)

A. The child demonstrates an increase in oppositional and defiant behavior since the service member has been deployed.

B. The child appears to be taking advantage of the decreased level of parenting since the service member has been deployed.

C. The child has gradually improved his/her behavior.

10. Poor Family, Academic, and Social Functioning (10)

A. The child has displayed difficulty in family functioning since the deployed parent has been unavailable.

B. The child's academic functioning has decreased since the service member's deployment.

C. The child's social functioning has decreased since his/her parent has been absent.

D. As treatment has progressed, the child's family, academic, and social functioning has improved.

11. Child Resentment (11)

A. The child demonstrates resentment toward the non-deployed parent.

B. The child demonstrates resentment toward the deployed parent.

C. As treatment has progressed, the child has come to understand the changes in expectations relative to his/her parent's situation and has resolved his/her resentment.

INTERVENTIONS IMPLEMENTED

1. Complete Evaluation (1)*

A. A comprehensive evaluation was completed in regard to the current family situation.

B. The extent of the current family problems was assessed as well as how this has changed since deployment.

C. Information was obtained from the non-deployed parent.

D. Information was obtained from the deployed parent.

2. Encourage Support from Other "Stay-Behind" Parents (2)

A. The non-deployed parent was asked to talk with other "stay-behind" parents.

B. The non-deployed parent was asked to get feedback from other parents about how deployment has affected their families.

C. The non-deployed parent has sought out support and information from other families, and this information was processed.

D. The non-deployed parent has not sought out contact with other stay behind parents and was redirected to do so.

3. Review Expectations (3)

A. The non-deployed parent was asked to describe his/her expectations about being a "single" parent prior to the service member deploying.

B. The non-deployed parent was open about his/her expectations about being a "single" parent, and these expectations were processed.

C. The non-deployed parent struggled to identify his/her expectations about being a "single" parent prior to the service member deploying and was provided with additional, more specific questions in this area.

4. Rank-Order Parenting Problems (4)

A. The non-deployed parent was assigned to create a list of parenting problems that he/she is dealing with.

B. The non-deployed parent was asked to rank his/her list of parenting problems from the most distressing to the least distressing.

C. The non-deployed parent has developed a rank-ordered list of parenting problems, and these were processed within this session.

D. The non-deployed parent has not completed his/her list of parenting problems, and this was completed within the session.

---

*The numbers in parentheses correlate to the number of the Therapeutic Intervention statement in the companion chapter with the same title in *The Veterans and Active Duty Military Psychotherapy Treatment Planner* (Moore and Jongsma) by John Wiley & Sons, 2009.

5. Select Moderately Distressing Problem (5)

A. The non-deployed parent was asked to identify a problem with a moderate level of distress.

B. The non-deployed parent's choice of a moderately distressing problem was reviewed and processed.

6. Use Problem-Solving Technique (6)

A. The non-deployed parent was asked to brainstorm possible solutions to the moderately distressing family problem.

B. The non-deployed parent listed and weighed the pros and cons of each possible solution to the parenting problem.

C. The non-deployed parent was asked to decide on a plan of action for the parenting problem.

D. The non-deployed parent was asked to implement his/her solution to the parenting problem.

E. The non-deployed parent's progress on the parenting problem was monitored, and adjustments were made as necessary.

7. Reinforce Successes (7)

A. The non-deployed parent was assisted in identifying successes in his/her parenting problem resolution.

B. The non-deployed parent's successes in parenting problem resolution were reinforced and celebrated.

C. The non-deployed parent was encouraged to continue solving problems on his/her problem list.

8. Review Finances (8)

A. The non-deployed parent was assigned to create a comprehensive list of expenditures and assets.

B. The non-deployed parent has made a list of expenditures and assets, and this was reviewed in the session.

C. The non-deployed parent was assisted in making distinctions between necessities and luxuries.

D. The non-deployed parent has not developed a comprehensive list of expenditures and assets and was redirected to do so.

9. Encourage Financial Counselor Meeting (9)

A. The non-deployed parent was encouraged to meet with a military financial counselor at the local base/post.

B. The non-deployed parent has met with the military financial counselor, and his/her experience was processed.

C. The non-deployed parent has not met with the military financial counselor and was redirected to do so.

10. Create a Therapeutic Environment (10)

A. The non-deployed parent was engaged through the use of empathy and normalization of his/her struggles with parenting.

B. The non-deployed parent was asked for information regarding the marital relationship, child behavior expectations, and parenting style.

C. The non-deployed parent was provided with positive feedback for being open and honest regarding his/her history of parenting concerns.

D. The non-deployed parent tended to minimize his/her parenting difficulties, and this was reflected to him/her.

11. Normalize Feelings (11)

A. The non-deployed parent's feelings of inadequacy, helplessness, and frustration were normalized by drawing parallels to other military parents' experiences.

B. The non-deployed parent was educated on normal and expected challenges of parenting.

C. The non-deployed parent was reinforced for understanding the normal and expected challenges related to parenting.

D. The non-deployed parent did not display a clear understanding of the normal and unexpected challenges of parenting and was provided with remedial feedback in this area.

12. Encourage Acknowledgment of Resentment (12)

A. The non-deployed parent was encouraged to acknowledge his/her resentment (if any) toward the deployed service member.

B. The non-deployed parent acknowledged that he/she resents the deployed service member's absence, and these emotions were processed.

C. The non-deployed parent acknowledged his/her sense of guilt about resentment toward the deployed service member, and these emotions were processed.

D. The non-deployed parent denied any resentment toward the deployed service member, and this was accepted.

13. Identify Reasons for Resentment (13)

A. The non-deployed parent was assisted in identifying reasons for resentment toward the deployed parent.

B. The non-deployed parent was provided with examples of reasons for resentment toward a deployed parent, including feelings of loneliness, inadequacy, and helplessness.

C. The non-deployed parent acknowledged specific reasons for his/her resentment toward the deployed parent, and these were accepted and processed.

D. The non-deployed parent was unable to identify any reasons for his/her feelings of resentment and was provided with additional support and encouragement in this area.

14. Encourage Nonthreatening Communication of Resentment Feelings (14)

A. The non-deployed parent was encouraged to communicate his/her resentment to the deployed service member in a nonthreatening and nonblaming manner.

B. The non-deployed parent was asked to identify key characteristics of his/her communication about the resentment toward the deployed service member.

C. The non-deployed parent's communication of his/her resentment to the deployed service member was role-played.

D. The nonthreatening and nonblaming manner of the communication between the non-deployed parent and the deployed service member was critiqued and processed.

E. The non-deployed parent has communicated his/her resentment to the deployed service member, and his/her experience was processed.

15. Assign Discussion with Child about Deployment (15)

A. The non-deployed parent was assigned to assist the child in discussing his/her feelings about the other parent being deployed.

B. The non-deployed parent has discussed the other parent's deployment with the child, and the results of this discussion and insights gained were processed.

C. The non-deployed parent has not discussed the child's feeling about the other parent being deployed and was redirected to do so.

16. Assign Reading on Children's Feelings (16)

A. The parents were assigned to read information on children's experience of a parent's deployment.

B. The parents were assigned to read *Off to War: Voices of Soldiers' Children* (Ellis).

C. The parents have read the assigned information about deployment's effect on children, and this information was processed.

D. The parents have not read the assigned information on the effect of a parent's deployment's children and were redirected to do so.

17. Assist in Communication of Guilt Feelings (17)

A. As communication channels exist, the deploying service member was directed to communicate his/her guilt feelings about leaving.

B. The deployed service member has communicated his/her guilt feelings about leaving via mail, e-mail, telephone, or Web cam, and these feelings were processed.

C. As communication options are not available, the non-deployed parent was advised about common guilt feelings for deploying parents.

18. Encourage Contact with Supports in Deployed Setting (18)

A. The deployed service member was encouraged to speak with a behavioral health professional in the deployed setting.

B. The deployed service member was urged to discuss his/her feelings with a chaplain in the deployed setting.

C. The deployed service member was reinforced for his/her use of resources to discuss his/her feelings of guilt related to deployment.

D. The deployed service member has not spoken with the available supports about his/her feelings of guilt about deployment and was reminded to do so.

19. Encourage Active Role Despite Deployment (19)

A. The non-deployed parent was encouraged to talk with the deployed service member regarding taking a more active role in parenting while deployed.

B. Examples were provided of the active role that a deployed parent can still take in the parenting and family decisions, including making joint decisions regarding major parenting issues or increasing parental guidance during routine phone conversations.

C. It was emphasized to the deployed service member that there must be support for the non-deployed parent's decisions.

20. Assign Reading on Child Development (20)

A. The parents were assigned to read information on child development.

B. The parents were assigned to read *Ages and Stages: A Parent's Guide to Normal Childhood Development* (Schaefer and DiGeronimo).

C. The parents have read information regarding child development, and key issues were processed.

D. The parents have not read information regarding child development and were redirected to do so.

21. Teach Parenting Techniques (21)

A. The non-deployed parent was assisted in learning new parenting techniques.

B. The non-deployed parent was taught about the use of positive and negative reinforcement.

C. The non-deployed parent was taught about natural and logical consequences as well as setting clear boundaries.

D. The importance of consistently administering and following through with the consequences was emphasized.

E. The non-deployed parent was taught about time-out techniques.

F. The non-deployed parent displays a clear understanding of proven parenting techniques and was reinforced for this.

G. The non-deployed parent struggled to understand the use of proven parenting techniques and was provided with remedial information in this area.

22. Assign Parenting Training Manuals (22)

A. The parents were directed to read and utilize parenting training manuals.

B. The parents were assigned to read *The Parent's Handbook: Systematic Training for Effective Parenting* (Dinkmeyer, McKay, and Dinkmeyer).

C. The parents have read appropriate parenting training manuals, and key concepts were processed.

D. The parents have not read appropriate training manuals and were redirected to do so.

23. Implement Parenting Techniques (23)

A. The non-deployed parent was assigned to implement parenting techniques and record progress.

B. "Using Reinforcement Principles in Parenting" from the *Adult Psychotherapy Homework Planner*, 2nd ed. (Jongsma) was assigned to the non-deployed parent.

C. The non-deployed parent completed the homework assignment, and the content was processed within the session.

D. The non-deployed parent has implemented parenting techniques, and constructive feedback was provided.

E. The non-deployed parent has not implemented parenting techniques and was redirected to do so.

24. Identify Community Resources (24)

A. The non-deployed parent was directed to identify community resources on and off post/base.

B. The non-deployed parent has identified a variety of community resources, and these were processed.

C. The non-deployed parent was provided with examples of community resources, including church, family resource center, Big Brothers/Big Sisters, and other resources.

D. The non-deployed parent was reinforced when asking for help.

25. Identify Supports (25)

A. The non-deployed parent was assisted in identifying family members and friends who can assist with babysitting, shopping, and other family tasks.

B. The non-deployed parent was reinforced for asking for help.

C. The non-deployed parent has not identified family members or supports that can help with family tasks and was redirected to do so.

26. Coordinate Child Psychological Services (26)

A. Psychological services were coordinated for the child.

B. An appointment was made with a behavioral health professional trained in treating childhood behavior problems.

C. The appointment with a behavioral health professional was kept; the family's experience in this service was processed.

D. Mental health services have not been sought for the child, and the family was redirected to do so.

27. Reinforce Attendance at Family Sessions (27)

A. The non-deployed parent was reinforced for his/her attendance at family therapy sessions when appropriate.

B. The non-deployed parent's experience in attending family therapy sessions was processed.

C. The non-deployed parent has not attended family sessions and was reminded about this important portion of the treatment program.

28. Facilitate Communication with School (28)

A. The non-deployed parent was directed to make an appointment with the child's teacher to provide background information about the child's problem.

B. The non-deployed parent was urged to ask the teacher to keep him/her updated regarding the child's progress and behavior.

C. The non-deployed parent has communicated with the child's teacher, and his/her experience was processed.

D. The non-deployed parent has not communicated with the child's teacher and was reminded to do so.

29. Encourage Stress-Relieving Activities (29)

A. The non-deployed parent was encouraged to engage in activities that he/she can enjoy and that relieve stress.

B. The non-deployed parent was encouraged to exercise, go to the movies, or meet a friend for coffee.

C. The non-deployed parent has regularly engaged in activities that relieve stress, and this progress was reinforced.

D. The non-deployed parent has not used stress-releasing exercises and was redirected to do so.

30. Support New Parenting Strategies (30)

A. Ongoing support and encouragement was provided to the non-deployed parent regarding implementation and follow-through of new parenting strategies.

B. Corrective feedback was provided to the non-deployed parent about new parenting strategies, as needed.

C. The non-deployed parent has not implemented new parenting strategies and was reminded to do so.

31. Schedule a "Booster Session" (31)

A. The non-deployed parent was scheduled for a "booster session" after therapy ended.

B. The non-deployed parent was advised to contact the therapist if he/she needs to be seen prior to the booster session.

C. The non-deployed parent's booster session was held, and he/she was reinforced for his/her successful implementation of therapy techniques.

D. The non-deployed parent's booster session was held, and he/she was coordinated for further treatment as his/her progress has not been sustained.

32. Use Family Session after Service Member's Return (32)

A. A family session was scheduled subsequent to the service member's return from deployment.

B. A family session was held in order to discuss redeployment parenting issues, such as needing to parent as a team.

C. The parents were assigned "Parenting as a Team" from the *Adult Psychotherapy Homework Planner,* 2nd ed. (Jongsma).

D. The parents completed the homework assignment, and the content was processed within the session.

E. The family has adjusted well to the return from deployment, and the parent's teamwork was supported.

F. The family has not adjusted well to the return from deployment, and the spouses are not parenting as a team; additional treatment is needed.

PERFORMANCE-ENHANCING SUPPLEMENT USE

VETERAN/SERVICE MEMBER PRESENTATION

1. Supplement Use Leading to Impairment (1)[*]

A. The veteran/service member acknowledges use of performance-enhancing supplements.

B. The veteran/service member acknowledges that his/her use of performance-enhancing supplements has led to clinically significant impairment.

C. The veteran/service member denies any performance-enhancing supplement use.

D. The veteran/service member denies any impairment due to performance-enhancing supplement use.

E. The veteran/service member has discontinued any performance-enhancing supplement use, due to the clinically significant impairment it causes.

2. Inability to Reduce Stimulant Abuse (2)

A. The veteran/service member acknowledged that he/she has frequently attempted to terminate or reduce his/her use of the performance-enhancing supplements but found that, once begun, he/she has been unable to follow through.

B. The veteran/service member acknowledged that in spite of negative consequences and a desire to reduce or terminate the performance-enhancing substance abuse, he/she has been unable to terminate its use.

C. As the veteran/service member has participated in a total recovery program, and he/she has been able to maintain abstinence from performance-enhancing substances.

3. Agitation Subsequent to Supplement Use (3)

A. The veteran/service member reported that he/she experiences anger, agitation, and aggression subsequent to performance-enhancing supplement use.

B. Members of the veteran's/service member's support network have indicated that the veteran/service member becomes agitated and aggressive subsequent to the use of performance-enhancing supplements.

C. The veteran/service member has displayed an ongoing pattern of anger, agitation, and aggression.

D. The veteran/service member has discontinued his/her performance-enhancing substance use, and his/her pattern of agitation has decreased.

4. Mental Health Symptoms (4)

A. The veteran/service member reports the emergence of anxiety symptoms connected with his/her performance-enhancing supplement use.

B. The veteran/service member reports the emergence of depression connected with his/her performance-enhancing supplement use.

---

[*]The numbers in parentheses correlate to the number of the Behavioral Definition statement in the companion chapter with the same title in *The Veterans and Active Duty Military Psychotherapy Treatment Planner* (Moore and Jongsma) by John Wiley & Sons, 2009.

C. The veteran/service member reports the emergence of psychotic symptoms.

D. As treatment has progressed, the veteran's/service member's anxiety, depression, and psychotic symptoms have reduced as well.

5. Urinalysis Failure (5)

A. The service member reports failing a random urinalysis conducted in his/her unit.

B. The service member is at risk of discipline due to his/her failure on urinalysis screens.

C. The service member has regularly passed urinalysis screens, indicating that he/she is not engaging in any performance-enhancing substance abuse.

INTERVENTIONS IMPLEMENTED

1. Gather Supplement Use History (1)*

A. The veteran/service member was asked to describe his/her performance-enhancing supplement use in terms of the amount and pattern of use, symptoms of abuse, and negative life consequences that have resulted from chemical dependence.

B. The veteran/service member was assessed in regard to anabolic steroids, creatine, and ephedrine.

C. The veteran/service member openly discussed his/her performance-enhancing supplement abuse history and was reinforced as he/she gave complete data regarding its nature and extent.

D. It was reflected to the veteran/service member that he/she was minimizing his/her performance-enhancing supplement abuse and was not giving reliable data regarding the nature and extent of his/her chemical dependence problem.

E. As therapy has progressed, the veteran/service member has become more open in acknowledging the extent and seriousness of his/her performance-enhancing supplement abuse problem.

2. Assess Views about Performance-Enhancing Supplements (2)

A. The veteran/service member was asked to provide his/her opinion about the use of performance-enhancing supplements.

B. The veteran/service member was asked to identify his/her beliefs about health risks or prevalence of use of performance-enhancing supplements.

C. The veteran/service member realistically identified the health risks associated with his/her supplement use.

D. The veteran/service member minimized his/her supplement use and the health risks associated with their use.

E. Active listening was provided as the service member talked about his/her views and opinions about performance-enhancing supplements.

F. The veteran/service member declined to provide much information about his/her views of performance-enhancing supplements and was urged to provide this as he/she is able.

---

*The numbers in parentheses correlate to the number of the Therapeutic Intervention statement in the companion chapter with the same title in *The Veterans and Active Duty Military Psychotherapy Treatment Planner* (Moore and Jongsma) by John Wiley & Sons, 2009.

3. Assess Negative Effects of Supplement Use (3)

A. The veteran/service member was referred to a psychiatric practitioner to evaluate for any negative emotional health consequences associated with performance-enhancing supplement use.

B. The veteran/service member was referred to a medical practitioner to evaluate for any negative physical effects of performance-enhancing supplements.

C. The veteran/service member has complied with evaluations, and mild negative effects were identified in regard to his/her performance-enhancing supplement use.

D. The veteran/service member has complied with evaluations, and moderate negative effects were identified in regard to his/her performance-enhancing supplement use.

E. The veteran/service member has complied with evaluations, and severe negative effects were identified in regard to his/her performance-enhancing supplement use.

4. Monitor Compliance with Recommendations (4)

A. The veteran/service member reported that he/she has complied with medical, psychiatric, or dietary recommendations and that this has helped to control his/her performance-enhancing supplement use and side effects.

B. The veteran/service member reported that he/she has not complied with medical, psychiatric, or dietary recommendations; this was related to the prescribing clinician.

C. The veteran/service member reported that he/she has complied with the medical, psychiatric, or dietary recommendations but does not see any beneficial effect from it; this was related to the medical staff.

D. The veteran/service member was evaluated but was not prescribed any changes in his/her medical, psychiatric, or dietary regime.

5. Educate about Negative Health Consequences of Supplement Use (5)

A. The veteran/service member was educated about the potential negative health consequences of performance-enhancing supplements.

B. The veteran/service member was asked to list the ways in which performance-enhancing supplement use can negatively impact the user.

C. The veteran/service member was supported as he/she has displayed a clear understanding of the negative health consequences of performance-enhancing supplements.

D. The veteran/service member has not displayed a clear understanding of the negative health consequences of performance-enhancing supplements and was provided with additional information in this area.

6. Assign Research on Effects of Supplement Use (6)

A. The veteran/service member was assigned to research the effects of performance-enhancing supplement use.

B. The veteran/service member was directed to review information through reputable Internet sources (i.e., WebMD, National Institutes of Health).

C. The veteran/service member has researched the negative effects of performance-enhancing supplement use, and this information was reviewed and processed.

D. The veteran/service member has not researched the effects of performance-enhancing supplement use and was redirected to do so.

7. Dispose of All Supplements (7)

A. The veteran/service member was assigned to dispose of all performance-enhancing supplements.

B. The veteran/service member was warned and encouraged not to simply give his/her performance-enhancing supplements to a friend or other service member.

C. The veteran/service member was reinforced for disposing of all performance-enhancing supplements.

D. The veteran/service member has not disposed of all performance-enhancing supplements, and the focus of treatment was turned toward this resistance.

8. Develop Reasons for Supplement Use (8)

A. The veteran/service member was assigned to create a list of reasons why he/she used performance-enhancing supplements.

B. The veteran/service member has created a list of reasons why he/she used performance-enhancing supplements, and this was processed within the session.

C. Active listening was used as the veteran/service member identified the reasons behind his/her performance-enhancing supplement use.

D. The veteran/service member has not developed a list of reasons why he/she has used performance-enhancing supplements and was redirected to do so.

9. Identify Temporary Positive Feelings (9)

A. The veteran/service member was directed to identify temporary positive feelings that performance-enhancing supplement use has created.

B. The veteran/service member was assisted in developing a list of temporary positive feelings that performance-enhancing supplement use has created.

C. Active listening was used as the veteran/service member identified the temporary positive feelings that performance-enhancing supplement use has created.

D. The veteran/service member has declined to provide significant feedback about the temporary positive feelings that performance-enhancing supplement use has created and was redirected to do so.

10. Explore Etiology of Supplement Use (10)

A. The veteran/service member was asked to identify how he/she learned about performance-enhancing supplement use.

B. Active listening was used as the veteran/service member identified his/her initial learning about performance-enhancing supplement use.

C. The veteran/service member was assisted in processing his/her early information about performance-enhancing supplement use.

11. Review Win-at-All-Costs Mentality (11)

A. The veteran/service member was educated about the pervasive view in the military and civilian world that strength, power, and beauty should be obtained at any cost.

B. The veteran/service member was assisted in identifying examples of how strength, power, and beauty are sometimes pursued to an unusual degree.

C. It was reflected to the veteran/service member that the pursuit of strength, power, and beauty at any cost is often used as a way to overcome perceived weaknesses.

12. Assign List of Strengths (12)

A. The veteran/service member was asked to identify strengths about himself/herself.

B. The veteran/service member was assisted in reviewing and critiquing his/her list of strengths.

C. The veteran/service member has not followed through on making a list of strengths and was encouraged to do so.

13. Counter Weaknesses by Assigning Environmental Experiments (13)

A. The veteran/service member was assigned environmental experiments to help counter his/her perceived weaknesses.

B. The veteran/service member was asked to do tasks such as asking friends, superiors, or fellow service members if they view him/her as having particular weaknesses.

C. The veteran/service member has engaged in environmental experiments to counter his/her perceived weaknesses, and these results were processed.

D. The veteran/service member has not engaged in environmental experiments to counter his/her perceived weaknesses and was asked to do so.

14. Assign List of Perceived Flaws (14)

A. The veteran/service member was asked to create a list of his/her perceived flaws in stamina, strength, and abilities.

B. The veteran/service member was assisted in creating a list of his/her perceived flaws in stamina, strength, and abilities.

C. The veteran/service member has created a list of his/her perceived flaws in stamina, strength, and abilities, and this was processed within the session.

D. The veteran/service member has not completed a list of his/her perceived flaws in stamina, strength, and abilities and was redirected to do so.

15. Explore Etiology and Maintenance of Perceived Flaws (15)

A. The veteran/service member was assisted in identifying the origins of his/her perceived flaws.

B. The veteran/service member was queried about family history or criticism by superiors as potential etiological factors in his/her perceived flaws.

C. The veteran/service member was assisted in identifying factors that maintain his/her perceived flaws.

D. The veteran/service member was provided with tentative examples of factors that can maintain flawed perceptions, such as maladaptive thoughts or a critical superior.

E. The veteran/service member was reinforced for his/her clear understanding of the origins and maintenance factors of his/her perceived flaws.

F. The veteran/service member has little insight into his/her perceived flaws and was provided with remedial feedback in this area.

16. Build Trust (16)

A. Consistent eye contact, active listening, unconditional positive regard, and warm acceptance were used to help build trust with the veteran/service member.

B. The veteran/service member was encouraged to express his/her feelings of inadequacy and insecurity.

C. The veteran/service member began to express feelings more freely as rapport and trust level increased.

D. The veteran/service member has continued to experience difficulty being open and direct in his/her expression of painful feelings; he/she was encouraged to be more open as he/she feels safer.

17. Challenge Feelings of Inadequacy (17)

A. Challenges were made to the veteran's/service member's feelings of inadequacy and insecurity by creating adaptive cognitions to replace maladaptive ones.

B. The veteran/service member was assigned "Journal and Replace Self-Defeating Thoughts" in the *Adult Psychotherapy Homework Planner*, 2nd ed. (Jongsma).

C. The veteran/service member was able to identify adaptive cognitions to replace his/her maladaptive cognitions.

D. The veteran/service member struggled to identify adaptive cognitions to replace maladaptive ones and was provided with specific examples in this area.

18. Identify Contrary Evidence (18)

A. The veteran/service member was assisted in identifying evidence that does not support his/her views of inadequacy.

B. The veteran/service member was provided with examples of how his/her accomplishments do not support his/her views of inadequacy.

C. The veteran/service member was able to identify that his/her views of inadequacy do not fit with the evidence; this was reinforced and supported.

D. The veteran/service member continues to believe that the evidence shows that he/she is an inadequate individual, and additional feedback was provided in this area.

19. Educate about Peer Pressure (19)

A. The veteran/service member was taught about the significant influence that peer pressure can have on behavior.

B. Examples were provided to the veteran/service member about the significant influence peer pressure can have on behavior.

20. List Peer Pressure Influences (20)

A. The veteran/service member was assigned to list times in his/her life that peer pressure has influenced him/her.

B. The veteran/service member was unable to identify situations in which peer pressure has influenced him/her and was provided with additional questions in this area.

21. Develop Peer Pressure Resistance (21)

A. The veteran/service member was assisted in developing methods to combat peer pressure.

B. The veteran/service member was directed to combat peer pressure in specific ways (e.g., create a new social network; learn to anticipate peer pressure before it happens).

C. The veteran/service member reports that he/she regularly uses methods to combat peer pressure, and these were processed and reinforced.

D. The veteran/service member still succumbs to significant peer pressure and was provided with remedial feedback in this area.

22. Increase Physical Activity (22)

A. The veteran/service member was assigned to engage in physical activity at least five days per week that focuses on aerobic and anaerobic fitness.

B. The veteran/service member has regularly participated in physical activity, and the increased stamina and strength that he/she experiences was reviewed and reinforced.

C. The veteran/service member has not regularly engaged in physical activity and was reminded to do so.

23. Discuss Goals with Chain of Command (23)

A. The service member was encouraged to discuss his/her goals for treatment with his/her chain of command.

B. The service member has discussed his/her goals for treatment with his/her chain of command and received an accepting response; this response was processed.

C. The service member has discussed his/her goals for treatment with his/her chain of command but did not receive an accepting response; this response was processed.

D. The service member has not discussed his/her goals for treatment with his/her chain of command and was reminded to do so.

24. Encourage Updates to Chain of Command (24)

A. The service member was encouraged to keep his/her chain of command updated on his/her progress.

B. The service member was encouraged to ask the chain of command for assistance in remaining abstinent from performance-enhancing supplements.

C. The service member has continuously updated his/her chain of command on his/her progress and needs, and this was reinforced.

D. The service member has not regularly informed his/her chain of command about his/her progress and needs and was redirected to do so.

25. Submit to Urinalysis (25)

A. The veteran/service member was encouraged to submit to random urine testing for the presence of supplements.

B. The veteran's/service member's successful passing of random urinalysis testing was reinforced and celebrated.

C. The veteran/service member has not successfully passed his/her random urinalysis, and his/her treatment was refocused.

PHOBIA

VETERAN/SERVICE MEMBER PRESENTATION

1. Unreasonable Fear of Object/Situation (1)*

A. The veteran/service member described a pattern of persistent and unreasonable phobic fear that promotes avoidance behaviors because an encounter with the phobic stimulus provokes an immediate anxiety response.

B. An object or situation often found or encountered in the military appears to be the stimuli that prompts the veteran's/service member's phobic reaction.

C. The veteran/service member has shown a willingness to begin to encounter the phobic stimulus and endure some of the anxiety response that is precipitated.

D. The veteran/service member has been able to tolerate the previously phobic stimulus without debilitating anxiety.

E. The veteran/service member verbalized that he/she no longer holds fearful beliefs or experiences anxiety during an encounter with the phobic stimulus.

2. Interference with Normal Routines (2)

A. The veteran's/service member's avoidance of phobic stimulus situations is so severe as to interfere with normal functioning.

B. The degree of the veteran's/service member's distrust associated with avoidance behaviors related to phobic experiences is such that he/she is not able to function normally.

C. The veteran/service member is beginning to take on normal responsibilities and function with limited distress.

D. The veteran/service member has returned to normal functioning and reported that he/she is no longer troubled by avoidance behaviors and phobic fears.

3. Avoids Military-Related Stimuli (3)

A. The veteran/service member avoids stimuli specific to military service.

B. The service member avoids specific stimuli that are required for military service (e.g., use of gas mask, fear of flying, fear of being submerged underwater).

C. The service member indicated that his/her functioning in the military has been diminished due to his/her phobic reactions.

D. The veteran/service member has significantly resolved his/her phobic reactions and is capable of doing all expected and required activities.

4. Recognition that Fear Is Unreasonable (4)

A. The veteran's/service member's phobic fear has persisted in spite of the fact that he/she acknowledges that the fear is unreasonable.

---

*The numbers in parentheses correlate to the number of the Behavioral Definition statement in the companion chapter with the same title in *The Veterans and Active Duty Military Psychotherapy Treatment Planner* (Moore and Jongsma) by John Wiley & Sons, 2009.

B. The veteran/service member has made many attempts to ignore or overcome his/her unreasonable fear but has been unsuccessful.

C. The veteran/service member has been successful at overcoming phobic fears that are known to be unreasonable.

5. Negative Self-Concept (5)

A. The veteran/service member reported negative feelings about himself/herself due to inability to overcome fear.

B. Pressure from superiors and fellow service members to overcome his/her fear has created negative self-image for the service member.

C. As the service member has improved his/her ability to overcome fear, he/she has felt better about his/her standing as a member of the military.

6. Phobia without Panic (6)

A. The veteran/service member does not display panic attacks.

B. Although the veteran/service member feels anxious whenever leaving his/her constricted safety zone, he/she does not experience panic symptoms apart from the agoraphobia symptoms.

INTERVENTIONS IMPLEMENTED

1. Assess Phobic Fears (1)[*]

A. The specifics regarding the veteran's/service member's phobic fear were addressed.

B. Military-related phobic fears were reviewed, such as fear of enclosed spaces, flying, and restricted breathing/suffocation.

C. The veteran/service member was helped to verbalize the specific stimuli for his/her phobic fear, the history of the fear, and the degree to which it interferes with his/her life.

2. Administer Fear Survey (2)

A. An objective fear survey was administered to the veteran/service member to assess the depth and breadth of his/her phobic fear, including the focus of the fear, types of avoidance, development, and disability.

B. The *Anxiety Disorders Interview Schedule for the DSM-IV* (DiNardo, Brown, and Barlow) was used to assess the veteran's/service member's phobia concerns.

C. The fear survey results indicate that the veteran's/service member's phobic fear is extreme and severely interferes with his/her life.

D. The fear survey results indicate that the veteran's/service member's phobic fear is moderate and occasionally interferes with his/her daily functioning.

E. The fear survey results indicate that the veteran's/service member's phobic fear is mild and rarely interferes with his/her daily functioning.

F. The results of the fear survey were reviewed with the veteran/service member.

[*]The numbers in parentheses correlate to the number of the Therapeutic Intervention statement in the companion chapter with the same title in *The Veterans and Active Duty Military Psychotherapy Treatment Planner* (Moore and Jongsma) by John Wiley & Sons, 2009.

3. Assess Impact on Social/Occupational Functioning (3)

A. The impact of the veteran's/service member's panic symptoms on occupational and social functioning were assessed through the use of standardized measures.

B. The *OQ-45.2* was used to assess the impact of the panic symptoms on the veteran's/service member's occupational and social functioning.

C. Serial measurement of the veteran's/service member's panic symptoms was used for the purpose of assessing progress.

D. The veteran's/service member's level of progress on managing panic symptoms was reviewed with the veteran/service member.

4. Assess Supervisor's Concerns (4)

A. Information was sought from the service member's first-line supervisor to assess the degree the anxiety has impacted this service member's job performance.

B. The service member's first-line supervisor has indicated that the service member's anxiety symptoms have had very little impact on his/her job; this assessment was reflected to the service member.

C. The service member's first-line supervisor has indicated that the service member's anxiety symptoms have had moderate impact on his/her job; this assessment was reflected to the service member.

D. The service member's first-line supervisor has indicated that the service member's anxiety symptoms have had severe impact on his/her job; this assessment was reflected to the service member.

5. Administer Client-Report Measure (5)

A. A client-report measure was used to further assess the depth and breadth of the veteran's/service member's phobic responses.

B. The *Measures for Specific Phobias* (Antony) was used to assess the depth and breadth of the veteran's/service member's phobic responses.

C. The client-report measures indicated that the veteran's/service member's phobic fear is extreme and severely interferes with his/her life.

D. The client-report measures indicated that the veteran's/service member's phobic fear is moderate and occasionally interferes with his/her life.

E. The client-report measures indicated that the veteran's/service member's phobic fear is mild and rarely interferes with his/her life.

F. The veteran/service member declined to complete the client-report measure, and the focus of treatment was changed to this resistance.

6. Refer for Medication Evaluation (6)

A. As the veteran/service member is unlikely to be compliant with gradual exposure, arrangements were made for him/her to have a physician evaluation for the purpose of considering psychotropic medication to alleviate phobic symptoms.

B. The veteran/service member has followed through with seeing a physician for an evaluation of any organic causes for the anxiety and the need for psychotropic medication to control the anxiety response.

C. The veteran/service member has not cooperated with the referral to a physician for a medication evaluation and was encouraged to do so.

7. Monitor Medication Compliance (7)

A. The veteran/service member reported that he/she has taken the prescribed medication consistently and that it has helped to control the phobic anxiety; this was relayed to the prescribing clinician.

B. The veteran/service member reported that he/she has not taken the prescribed medication consistently and was encouraged to do so.

C. The veteran/service member reported taking the prescribed medication and stated that he/she has not noted any beneficial effect from it; this was reported to the prescribing clinician.

D. The veteran/service member was evaluated but was not prescribed any psychotropic medication by the physician.

8. Provide Updates to Leadership (8)

A. An update on the service member's condition, potential negative impacts on safety, and occupational limitations was provided to the unit leadership.

B. Recommendations were made to the service member's unit leadership in regard to his/her functioning.

9. Normalize Phobias (9)

A. A discussion was held about how phobias are very common.

B. The veteran/service member was taught that phobias are a natural but irrational expression of our fight-or-flight response.

C. It was emphasized to the veteran/service member that phobias are not a sign of weakness but cause unnecessary distress and disability.

D. The veteran/service member was reinforced as he/she displayed a better understanding of the natural facets of phobias.

E. The veteran/service member struggled to understand the natural aspects of phobias and was provided with remedial feedback in this area.

10. Discuss Phobic Cycle (10)

A. The veteran/service member was taught about how phobic fears are maintained by a phobic cycle of unwarranted fear and avoidance that precludes positive, corrective experiences with the feared object or situation.

B. The veteran/service member was taught about how treatment breaks the phobic cycle by encouraging positive, corrective experiences.

C. The veteran/service member was taught information from *Mastery of Your Specific Phobia—Therapist Guide* (Craske, Antony, and Barlow) regarding the phobic cycle.

D. The veteran/service member was taught about the phobic cycle from information in *Specific Phobias* (Bruce and Sanderson).

E. The veteran/service member was reinforced as he/she displayed a better understanding of the phobic cycle of unwarranted fear and avoidance and how treatment breaks the cycle.

F. The veteran/service member displayed a poor understanding of the phobic cycle and was provided with remedial feedback in this area.

11. Assign Reading on Specific Phobias (11)

A. The veteran/service member was assigned to read psychoeducational chapters of books or treatment manuals on specific phobias.

B. The veteran/service member was assigned information from *Mastery of Your Specific Phobia—Client Manual* (Antony, Craske, and Barlow).

C. The veteran/service member was directed to read information about specific phobias from the *Anxiety and Phobia Workbook* (Bourne).

D. The veteran/service member was assigned to read from *Living with Fear* (Marks).

E. The veteran/service member has read the assigned information on phobias, and key points were reviewed.

F. The veteran/service member has not read the assigned information on phobias and was redirected to do so.

12. Discuss Unrealistic Threats, Physical Fear, and Avoidance (12)

A. A discussion was held about how phobias involve perceiving unrealistic threats, bodily expressions of fear, and avoidance of what is threatening that interact to maintain the problem.

B. An example was provided of how someone with a fear of needles may react during the initial inoculation process in basic training.

C. The veteran/service member was taught about factors that interact to maintain the problem phobia from information in *Mastery of Your Specific Phobia—Therapist's Guide* (Craske, Antony, and Barlow).

D. The veteran/service member was taught about factors that interact to maintain phobic fear from information in *Specific Phobias* (Bruce and Sanderson).

E. The veteran/service member displayed a clear understanding about how unrealistic threats, bodily expression of fear, and avoidance combine to maintain the phobic fear; his/her insight was reinforced.

F. Despite specific information about factors that interact to maintain phobic fear, the veteran/service member displayed a poor understanding of these issues; he/she was provided with remedial information in this area.

13. Discuss Changing Thought Patterns (13)

A. A discussion was held about how changing thought patterns and eliminating cognitive barriers decreases phobic reactions and minimizes the severity, recurrence, and impact of the anxiety symptoms.

B. The veteran/service member was provided with examples of how changing thought patterns can decrease phobic reactions.

C. The veteran/service member was asked to identify situations in which he/she has minimized the severity, recurrence, and impact of the anxiety symptoms through elimination of cognitive barriers.

D. The veteran/service member displayed insight into how he/she can change thought patterns and eliminate cognitive barriers and was reinforced for this insight.

E. The veteran/service member struggled to understand the connection between changing thought patterns and decreasing phobic reactions and was provided with additional feedback in this area.

14. Discuss Benefits of Exposure (14)

A. A discussion was held about how exposure serves as an arena to desensitize learned fear, build confidence, and feel safer by building a new history of success experiences.

B. The veteran/service member was taught about the benefits of exposure as described in *Mastery of Your Specific Phobia—Therapist's Guide* (Craske, Antony, and Barlow).

C. The veteran/service member was taught about the benefits of exposure as described in *Specific Phobias* (Bruce and Sanderson).

D. An example was provided about how superiors make subordinates practice in front of mock promotion boards before attending the actual board.

E. The veteran/service member displayed a clear understanding about how exposure serves to desensitize learned fear, build confidence, and feel safer by building a new history of success experiences; his/her insight was reinforced.

F. Despite specific information about how exposure serves to desensitize learned fear, build confidence, and feel safer by building a new history of success experiences, the veteran/service member displayed a poor understanding of these issues; he/she was provided with remedial information in this area.

15. Teach Anxiety Management Skills (15)

A. The veteran/service member was taught anxiety management skills.

B. The veteran/service member was taught about staying focused on behavioral goals and using positive self-talk.

C. Techniques for muscular relaxation and paced diaphragmatic breathing were taught to the veteran/service member.

D. The veteran/service member was reinforced for his/her clear understanding and use of anxiety management skills.

E. The veteran/service member has not used new anxiety management skills and was redirected to do so.

16. Urge External Focus (16)

A. The veteran/service member was urged to keep his/her focus on external stimuli and behavioral responsibilities rather than be preoccupied with internal states and physiological changes.

B. An example was provided of focusing on external stimuli over internal changes (i.e., focusing on breathing or foot placement during running deflects attention from fatigue and pain).

C. The veteran/service member was reinforced as he/she has made a commitment to not allow panic symptoms to take control of his/her life and to not avoid and escape normal responsibilities and activities.

D. The veteran/service member has been successful at turning his/her focus away from internal anxiety states and toward behavioral responsibilities; he/she was reinforced for this progress.

E. The veteran/service member has not maintained an external focus in order to keep panic symptoms from taking control of his/her life and was reminded about this helpful technique.

17. Assign Calming Skills Exercises (17)

A. The veteran/service member was assigned a homework exercise in which he/she practices daily calming skills.

B. The veteran's/service member's use of the exercises for practicing daily calming skills was closely monitored.

C. The veteran's/service member's success at using daily calming skills was reinforced.

D. The veteran/service member was provided with corrective feedback for his/her failures at practicing daily calming skills.

18. Utilize Biofeedback (18)

A. Biofeedback techniques were utilized to facilitate the veteran's/service member's learning of deep muscle relaxation.

B. The veteran/service member has developed a greater depth of relaxation as a result of the biofeedback techniques; he/she was encouraged to continue the regular use of these techniques.

C. The veteran/service member has had difficulty learning to use the biofeedback techniques and was provided with remedial information in this area.

19. Teach Applied Tension Technique (19)

A. The veteran/service member was taught the applied tension technique to help prevent fainting during encounters with phobic objects or situations.

B. The veteran/service member was taught to tense his/her neck and upper torso muscles to curtail blood flow out of the brain to help prevent fainting during encounters with phobic objects or situations involving blood, injection, or injury.

C. The veteran/service member was taught specific applied tension techniques as indicated in "Applied Tension, Exposure in vivo, and Tension-Only in the Treatment of Blood Phobia" in *Behaviour Research and Therapy* (Ost, Fellenius, and Sterner).

D. The veteran/service member was provided with positive feedback for his/her use of the applied tension technique.

E. The veteran/service member has struggled to appropriately use the applied tension technique and was provided with remedial feedback in this area.

20. Assign Daily Applied Tension Practice (20)

A. The veteran/service member was assigned a homework exercise in which he/she practices daily use of the applied tension skills.

B. The veteran's/service member's daily use of the applied tension technique was reviewed.

C. The veteran/service member was reinforced for his/her success at using daily applied tension skills.

D. The veteran/service member was provided with corrective feedback for his/her failure to appropriately use daily applied tension skills.

21. Identify Distorted Thoughts (21)

A. The veteran/service member was assisted in identifying the distorted schemas and related automatic thoughts that mediate anxiety responses.

B. The veteran/service member was taught the role of distorted thinking in precipitating emotional responses.

C. The veteran/service member was reinforced as he/she verbalized an understanding of the cognitive beliefs and messages that mediate his/her anxiety responses.

D. The veteran/service member was assisted in replacing distorted messages with positive, realistic cognitions.

E. The veteran/service member failed to identify his/her distorted thoughts and cognitions and was provided with tentative examples in this area.

22. Assign Homework on Cognitive Restructuring/Self-Talk (22)

A. The veteran/service member was assigned homework exercises to identify fearful self-talk and to create reality-based alternatives and record his/her experience.

B. The veteran/service member was assigned "Journal and Replace Self-Defeating Thoughts" from the *Adult Psychotherapy Homework Planner*, 2nd ed. (Jongsma).

C. The veteran/service member completed the homework assignment, and the content was processed within the session.

D. The veteran's/service member's use of cognitive restructuring techniques was reviewed and reinforced.

E. The veteran/service member has struggled in his/her implementation of cognitive restructuring techniques and was provided with corrective feedback.

F. The veteran/service member has not attempted to use the self-talk techniques and was redirected to do so.

23. Utilize Modeling/Behavioral Rehearsal (23)

A. Modeling and behavioral rehearsal were used to train the veteran/service member in positive self-talk that reassured him/her of the ability to work through and endure anxiety symptoms without serious consequences.

B. The veteran/service member was assigned "Positive Self-Talk" from the *Adult Psychotherapy Homework Planner*, 2nd ed. (Jongsma).

C. The veteran/service member completed the homework assignment, and the content was processed within the session.

D. The veteran/service member has implemented positive self-talk to reassure himself/herself of the ability to endure anxiety without serious consequences; he/she was reinforced for this progress.

E. The veteran/service member has not used positive self-talk to help endure anxiety and was provided with additional direction in this area .

24. Construct Anxiety Stimuli Hierarchy (24)

A. The veteran/service member was assisted in constructing a hierarchy of anxiety-producing situations associated with his/her phobic fear.

B. It was difficult for the veteran/service member to develop a hierarchy of stimulus situations, as the causes of his/her fear remain quite vague; he/she was assisted in completing the hierarchy.

C. The veteran/service member was provided with hierarchy suggestions, including wearing a gas mask without the hood or wearing it for only a few seconds at a time, then gradually increasing time worn.

D. The veteran/service member was provided with an example of an anxiety-producing hierarchy, such as sitting in a helicopter while it is running but not taking off.

E. The veteran/service member was successful at creating a focused hierarchy of specific stimulus situations that provoke anxiety in a gradually increasing manner; this hierarchy was reviewed.

25. Select Initial Exposures (25)

A. Initial exposures were selected from the hierarchy of anxiety-producing situations, with a bias toward likelihood of being successful.

B. A plan was developed with the veteran/service member for managing the symptoms that may occur during the initial exposure.

C. The veteran/service member was assisted in rehearsing the plan for managing the exposure-related symptoms within his/her imagination.

D. Positive feedback was provided for the veteran's/service member's helpful use of symptom management techniques.

E. The veteran/service member was redirected for ways to improve his/her symptom management techniques.

26. Assign Homework on Situational Exposures (26)

A. The veteran/service member was assigned homework exercises to perform situational exposures and record his/her experience.

B. The veteran/service member was assigned "Gradually Reducing Your Phobic Fear" from the *Adult Psychotherapy Homework Plann*er, 2nd ed. (Jongsma).

C. The veteran/service member was assigned situational exposures homework from *Mastery of Your Specific Phobia—Client Manual* (Antony, Craske, and Barlow).

D. The veteran/service member was assigned situational exposures homework from *Living with Fear* (Marks).

E. The veteran's/service member's use of situational exposure techniques was reviewed and reinforced.

F. The veteran/service member has struggled in his/her implementation of situational exposure techniques and was provided with corrective feedback.

G. The veteran/service member has not attempted to use the situational exposure techniques and was redirected to do so.

27. Differentiate between Lapse and Relapse (27)

A. A discussion was held with the veteran/service member regarding the distinction between a lapse and a relapse.

B. A lapse was associated with a temporary and reversible return of symptoms, fear, or urges to avoid.

C. A relapse was associated with the decision to return to fearful and avoidant patterns.

D. The veteran/service member was provided with support and encouragement as he/she displayed an understanding of the difference between a lapse and a relapse.

E. The veteran/service member struggled to understand the difference between a lapse and a relapse and was provided with remedial feedback in this area.

28. Discuss Management of Lapse Risk Situations (28)

A. The veteran/service member was assisted in identifying future situations or circumstances in which lapses could occur.

B. The veteran's/service member's plan for managing lapses was reviewed.

C. The session focused on rehearsing the management of future situations or circumstances in which lapses could occur.

D. The veteran/service member was reinforced for his/her appropriate use of lapse management skills.

E. The veteran/service member was redirected in regard to his/her poor use of lapse management skills.

29. Encourage Routine Use of Strategies (29)

A. The veteran/service member was instructed to routinely use the strategies that he/she has learned in therapy (e.g., cognitive restructuring, exposure).

B. The veteran/service member was urged to find ways to build his/her new strategies into his/her life as much as possible.

C. The veteran/service member was reinforced as he/she reported ways in which he/she has incorporated coping strategies into his/her life and routine.

30. Develop a "Coping Card" (30)

A. The veteran/service member was provided with a "coping card" on which specific coping strategies were listed.

B. The veteran/service member was assisted in developing a "coping card" in order to list his/her helpful coping strategies.

C. The veteran/service member was encouraged to use his/her "coping card" when struggling with anxiety-producing situations.

31. Explore Secondary Gain (31)

A. Secondary gain was identified for the veteran's/service member's panic symptoms because of his/her tendency to escape or avoid certain situations.

B. The veteran/service member was provided with examples of secondary gain that may reinforce phobic actions, such as not having to go on combat missions or ensuring disability benefits are not denied.

C. The veteran/service member denied any role for secondary gain that results from his/her modification of life to accommodate panic; he/she was provided with tentative examples.

D. The veteran/service member was reinforced for accepting the role of secondary gain in promoting and maintaining the panic symptoms and encouraged to overcome this gain through living a more normal life.

32. Differentiate Current Fear from Past Pain (32)

A. The veteran/service member was taught to verbalize the separate realities of the current fear and the emotionally painful experience from the past that has been evoked by the phobic stimulus.

B. Care was taken not to minimize real potential future threats.

C. The veteran/service member was reinforced when he/she expressed insight into the unresolved fear from the past that is linked to his/her current phobic fear.

D. The irrational nature of the veteran's/service member's current phobic fear was emphasized and clarified.

E. The veteran's/service member's unresolved emotional issue from the past was clarified.

33. Encourage Sharing of Feelings (33)

A. The veteran/service member was encouraged to share the emotionally painful experience from the past that has been evoked by the phobic stimulus.

B. The veteran/service member was taught to separate the realities of the irrationally feared object or situation and the painful experience from his/her past.

34. Support Continued Duties and Activities (34)

A. The service member was supported for following through with military duties.

B. The veteran/service member was encouraged to follow through on family and social activities.

C. The veteran/service member was reminded not to attempt to escape or avoid duties and activities by focusing on the panic.

35. List Expectations for Improvement (35)

A. The veteran/service member was asked to list several ways that his/her life will become more satisfying or fulfilling as he/she manages his/her symptoms of panic and continues normal responsibilities.

B. The veteran/service member identified many ways in which his/her life will be more satisfying as his/her symptoms are managed, and these changes were supported and reinforced.

C. The veteran/service member has struggled to identify ways in which his/her life may become more satisfying and fulfilling as he/she manages his/her symptoms of panic and was provided with tentative examples in this area.

36. Schedule a "Booster Session" (36)

A. The veteran/service member was scheduled for a "booster session" between one and three months after therapy ends.

B. The veteran/service member was advised to contact the therapist if he/she needs to be seen prior to the "booster session."

C. The veteran's/service member's "booster session" was held, and he/she was reinforced for his/her successful implementation of therapy techniques.

D. The veteran's/service member's "booster session" was held, and he/she was coordinated for further treatment, as his/her progress has not been sustained.

37. Identify Mental Health Resources (37)

A. The service member was assisted in identifying mental health resources at the location where he/she will be deployed.

B. The service member was provided with specific information for how to seek mental health services in the area where he/she will be deployed.

C. Contacts were made to assist in the transition for mental health services in the service member's new deployment.

38. Arrange Medication for Deployment Transition (38)

A. The service member was provided with an appropriate amount of medication to get him/her through the deployment transition.

B. Steps were taken to coordinate the service member's ability to access his/her medications through the deployment transition.

PHYSIOLOGICAL STRESS RESPONSE—ACUTE

VETERAN/SERVICE MEMBER PRESENTATION

1. Excessive Physiological Arousal (1)*

A. The veteran/service member experiences excessive physiological reactivity associated with the presence of an unidentified trigger.

B. The veteran/service member experiences excessive physiological reactivity regardless of internal or external cues being present.

C. The veteran's/service member's physiological reactivity has diminished.

D. The veteran/service member reports no longer experiencing excessive physiological arousal.

2. Exaggerated Startle Response (2)

A. The veteran/service member described having experienced an exaggerated startle response.

B. The veteran's/service member's exaggerated startle response has diminished.

C. The veteran/service member no longer experiences an exaggerated startle response.

3. Agitation/Irritability (3)

A. The veteran/service member described a pattern of irritability that was not present before the traumatic event occurred.

B. The veteran/service member reported incidents of becoming angry and losing his/her temper easily, resulting in explosive outbursts.

C. The veteran's/service member's irritability has diminished somewhat and the intensity of the explosive outbursts has lessened.

D. The veteran/service member reported no recent incidents of explosive, angry outbursts.

4. Sleep Disturbance (4)

A. Since the traumatic event occurred, the veteran/service member has experienced a desire to sleep much more than normal.

B. Since the traumatic event occurred, the veteran/service member has found it very difficult to initiate and maintain sleep.

C. Since the traumatic event occurred, the veteran/service member has had a fear of sleeping.

D. The veteran's/service member's sleep disturbance has terminated, and he/she has returned to a normal sleep pattern.

5. Sensory Sensitivity (5)

A. The veteran/service member described a pattern of increased sensory sensitivity.

B. The veteran/service member reported exaggerated behaviors intended to detect threats.

C. The veteran's/service member's hypervigilant pattern has diminished.

---

*The numbers in parentheses correlate to the number of the Behavioral Definition statement in the companion chapter with the same title in *The Veterans and Active Duty Military Psychotherapy Treatment Planner* (Moore and Jongsma) by John Wiley & Sons, 2009.

D. The veteran/service member reports no longer experiencing increased sensory activity or exaggerated behaviors to detect threats.

6. Constant Threat Assessment (6)

A. The veteran/service member reports a constant pattern of monitoring/scanning the environment to detect potential threats.

B. The veteran/service member often engages in unnecessary behavior in order to search out potential threats.

C. The veteran/service member displays hypervigilance even in very safe situations.

D. The veteran/service member reported a decreased pattern of monitoring or scanning the environment to detect threats.

7. Lack of Concentration (7)

A. The veteran/service member described a pattern of lack of concentration that began with the exposure to the traumatic event.

B. The veteran/service member reported that he/she is now able to focus more clearly on cognitive processing.

C. The veteran's/service member's ability to concentrate has returned to normal levels.

8. Exhaustion after Arousal (8)

A. The veteran/service member reported periods of exhaustion following long periods of hypervigilant arousal.

B. As the veteran's/service member's pattern of increased arousal has diminished, his/her complaints of exhaustion have diminished as well.

C. The veteran/service member reports an appropriate pattern of arousal and no significant exhaustion.

9. Medical Problems (9)

A. The veteran/service member reports a pattern of chronic stress.

B. The veteran/service member reported that his/her stress has been so persistent for so long as to cause medical problems.

C. The veteran/service member has medical concerns related to ulcers, poor sleep, and other stress-related difficulties.

D. The veteran/service member reported that as his/her pattern of chronic stress has decreased, his/her medical problems have improved.

INTERVENTIONS IMPLEMENTED

1. Assess Level of Physiological Stress Response Symptoms (1)[*]

A. The veteran/service member was asked about the frequency, intensity, duration, and history of his/her hyperarousal symptoms.

---

[*]The numbers in parentheses correlate to the number of the Therapeutic Intervention statement in the companion chapter with the same title in *The Veterans and Active Duty Military Psychotherapy Treatment Planner* (Moore and Jongsma) by John Wiley & Sons, 2009.

B. The assessment of the veteran's/service member's hyperarousal symptoms indicated that his/her symptoms are extreme and severely interfere with his/her life.

C. The assessment of the veteran's/service member's hyperarousal symptoms indicates that these symptoms are moderate and occasionally interfere with his/her daily functioning.

D. The results of the assessment of the veteran's/service member's hyperarousal symptoms indicate that these symptoms are mild and rarely interfere with his/her daily functioning.

E. The results of the assessment of the veteran's/service member's hyperarousal symptoms were reviewed with the client.

2. Assess Supervisor's Concerns (2)

A. Information was sought out from the service member's first-line supervisor to assess the degree the hyperarousal symptoms have impacted the service member's job performance.

B. The service member's first-line supervisor has indicated that the service member's hyperarousal symptoms have had very little impact on his/her work performance; this assessment was reflected to the service member.

C. The service member's first-line supervisor has indicated that the service member's hyperarousal symptoms have had a moderate impact on his/her job; this assessment was reflected to the service member.

D. The service member's first-line supervisor has indicated that the service member's hyperarousal symptoms have had severe impact on his/her job; this assessment was reflected to the service member.

3. Administer Self-Report Measures (3)

A. Self-report measures were used to assist with differential diagnosis.

B. The veteran/service member was assessed with the Minnesota Multiphasic Personality Inventory, 2nd ed. (MMPI-2).

C. The PTSD—Military version was used to assess the veteran/service member.

D. The veteran/service member has completed the self-report measures, and a differential diagnosis was able to be made.

E. The results of the self-report measures were shared with the veteran/service member.

4. Provide Feedback about Testing (4)

A. The veteran/service member was provided with feedback regarding his/her testing results.

B. The testing results reflected rather limited concerns related to physiological stress response problems, and this was reflected to the veteran/service member.

C. The testing results reflected rather moderate concerns related to physiological stress response problems, and this was reflected to the veteran/service member.

D. The testing results reflected rather severe concerns related to physiological stress response problems, and this was reflected to the veteran/service member.

5. Refer for Medication Evaluation (5)

A. Arrangements were made for the veteran/service member to have a physician evaluation for the purpose of considering psychotropic medication to alleviate hyperarousal symptoms.

B. The veteran/service member has followed through with seeing a physician for an evaluation of any organic causes for the anxiety and the need for psychotropic medication to control the hyperarousal response.

C. The veteran/service member has not cooperated with the referral to a physician for a medication evaluation and was encouraged to do so.

6. Monitor Medication Compliance (6)

A. The veteran/service member reported that he/she has taken the prescribed medication consistently and that it has helped to control the hyperarousal symptoms; this was relayed to the prescribing clinician.

B. The veteran/service member reported that he/she has not taken the prescribed medication consistently and was encouraged to do so.

C. The veteran/service member reported taking the prescribed medication and stated that he/she has not noted any beneficial effect from it; this was reported to the prescribing clinician.

D. The veteran/service member was evaluated but was not prescribed any psychotropic medication by the physician.

7. Provide Updates to Leadership (7)

A. An update on the service member's condition, potential negative impacts on safety, and occupational limitations was provided to the unit leadership.

B. Recommendations were made to the service member's unit leadership in regard to the service member's functioning.

8. Encourage Physician Assessment for Physical Health Effects (8)

A. The veteran/service member was encouraged to see a physician in order to assess any negative impact that stress has had on his/her physical health.

B. The veteran/service member was assessed for high blood pressure and/or arrhythmias.

C. The veteran/service member has followed through on the physical assessment, and significant physical health concerns were identified; the impact of these concerns was processed.

D. The veteran/service member has followed through on a physician assessment, but no significant concerns were identified.

E. The veteran/service member has not followed through on a physician's assessment but was reminded to do so.

9. Assess Substance Abuse (9)

A. The veteran's/service member's pattern of substance abuse was assessed.

B. The veteran/service member was noted to have a maladaptive pattern of substance abuse.

C. The veteran's/service member's pattern of substance use indicates no maladaptive patterns.

10. Refer for a Chemical Dependency Treatment (10)

A. The veteran/service member was referred for chemical dependency treatment.

B. The veteran/service member has utilized chemical dependency treatment, and his/her progress was noted.

C. Despite encouragement, the veteran/service member has not utilized chemical dependency treatment and was reminded to do so.

11. Encourage 12-Step Program Attendance (11)

A. The veteran/service member was encouraged to attend a 12-step program at least three times a week for three months.

B. The veteran/service member was directed to attend Alcoholics Anonymous.

C. The veteran/service member has attended the 12-step program, and his/her progress was reviewed.

D. The veteran/service member has not attended a 12-step program and was reminded to do so.

12. Explore Facts of Traumatic Event (12)

A. The veteran/service member was gently encouraged to tell the entire story of the traumatic event.

B. The veteran/service member was assigned "Describe the Trauma" from the *Adult Psychotherapy Homework Planner*, 2nd ed. (Jongsma).

C. The veteran/service member completed the homework assignment, and the content was processed within the session.

D. The veteran/service member was given the opportunity to share what he/she recalls about the traumatic event.

E. Today's therapy session explored the sequence of events before, during, and after the traumatic event.

13. Educate about Reactions to Trauma (13)

A. The veteran/service member was educated about the common reactions after exposure to a traumatic event.

B. The veteran/service member was educated about increased startle response, insomnia, nightmares, and mood changes.

C. The veteran/service member displayed an adequate understanding of the likely response to trauma, and this was reinforced.

D. The veteran/service member displayed a poor understanding of the common responses to trauma and was provided with remedial information in this area.

14. Normalize Experience and Symptoms (14)

A. The veteran/service member was advised about how his/her symptoms appear to be a normal response to an unusual experience.

B. As the veteran's/service member's symptoms have not remitted, he/she was referred to a higher level of care.

C. As the veteran's/service member's symptoms are causing clinically significant distress in functioning, he/she was referred to a higher level of care.

15. Explain Connection between Thoughts, Feelings, and Behavior (15)

A. The veteran/service member was taught how thoughts impact our feelings and behavior.

B. The specific role that the thoughts play in maintaining fear and reinforcing avoidance of perceived threats was reviewed.

C. The veteran/service member was provided with an example that relates to his/her situation of how thoughts impact feelings and behavior.

D. The veteran/service member was reinforced for his/her understanding about how thoughts impact behavior.

E. The veteran/service member struggled to understand how thoughts impact feelings and behavior and was provided with remedial assistance in this area.

16. Develop Awareness of Automatic Thoughts (16)

A. The veteran/service member was assisted in developing an awareness of his/her automatic thoughts that are consistent with a hostile worldview.

B. The veteran/service member was assisted in identifying how his/her automatic thoughts may lead to the belief that injury and death is inevitable.

C. The veteran/service member was supported for making the connection between his/her automatic thoughts and a hostile and dangerous worldview.

D. The veteran/service member struggled to connect his/her automatic thoughts to his/her worldview and was provided with remedial feedback in this area.

17. Assign Dysfunctional Thinking Journal (17)

A. The veteran/service member was requested to keep a daily journal that lists each situation associated with anxious feelings and the dysfunctional thinking that triggered the hyperarousal symptoms.

B. The veteran/service member was directed to complete the "Negative Thoughts Trigger Negative Feelings" assignment from the *Adult Psychotherapy Homework Planner*, 2nd ed. (Jongsma).

C. The veteran/service member completed the homework assignment, and the content was processed within the session.

D. The Socratic method was used to challenge the veteran's/service member's dysfunctional thoughts and to replace them with positive, reality-based thoughts.

E. The veteran/service member was reinforced for instances of successful replacement of negative thoughts with more realistic positive thinking.

F. The veteran/service member has not kept a record of his/her automatic thoughts and was redirected to do so.

18. Reinforce Positive Self-Talk (18)

A. The veteran/service member was reinforced for any successful replacement of distorted negative thinking with positive, reality-based cognitive messages.

B. It was noted that the veteran/service member has been engaging in positive, reality-based thinking that has enhanced his/her self-confidence and increased adaptive action.

C. The veteran/service member was assigned to complete the "Positive Self-Talk" assignment from the *Adult Psychotherapy Homework Planner*, 2nd ed. (Jongsma).

D. The veteran/service member completed the homework assignment, and the content was processed within the session.

19. Teach Diaphragmatic Breathing (19)

A. The veteran/service member was taught diaphragmatic breathing skills.

B. The veteran/service member was assigned to engage in deep diaphragmatic breathing twice per day for 10 minutes each time.

C. The veteran/service member was encouraged to implement the diaphragmatic breathing techniques when anxiety or stress rises.

D. The veteran/service member was taught how to apply diaphragmatic breathing techniques to his/her daily life.

E. The veteran/service member was provided with feedback about his/her use of diaphragmatic breathing skills.

20. Teach Progressive Muscle Relaxation (20)

A. The veteran/service member was taught progressive muscle relaxation skills.

B. The veteran/service member was assigned to engage in progressive muscle relaxation skills twice per day for 15 minutes each time.

C. The veteran/service member was encouraged to implement the progressive muscle relaxation skills when anxiety or stress rises.

D. The veteran/service member was taught how to apply progressive muscle relaxation skills to his/her daily life.

E. The veteran/service member was provided with feedback about his/her use of progressive muscle relaxation skills.

21. Construct Anxiety Stimuli Hierarchy (21)

A. The veteran/service member was assisted in constructing a hierarchy of anxiety-producing situations associated with his/her hyperarousal symptoms.

B. It was difficult for the veteran/service member to develop a hierarchy of stimulus situations, as the causes of his/her hyperarousal symptoms remain quite vague; he/she was assisted in completing the hierarchy.

C. The veteran/service member was provided with hierarchy suggestions, such as wearing a gas mask without the hood or wearing it for only a few seconds at a time, then gradually increasing time worn, etc.

D. The veteran/service member was provided with an example of an anxiety-producing hierarchy, such as sitting in a helicopter while it is running but not taking off.

E. The veteran/service member was successful at creating a focused hierarchy of specific stimulus situations that provoke anxiety in a gradually increasing manner; this hierarchy was reviewed.

22. Select Initial Exposures (22)

A. Initial exposures were selected from the hierarchy of arousal-producing situations, with a bias toward likelihood of being successful.

B. A plan was developed with the veteran/service member for managing the hyperarousal symptoms that may occur during the initial exposure.

C. The veteran/service member was assisted in rehearsing the plan for managing the exposure-related symptoms within his/her imagination.

D. Positive feedback was provided for the veteran's/service member's helpful use of symptom management techniques.

E. The veteran/service member was redirected for ways to improve his/her symptom management techniques.

23. Assign Homework on Situational Exposures (23)

A. The veteran/service member was assigned homework exercises to perform situational exposures and record his/her experience.

B. The veteran/service member was assigned "Gradually Reducing Your Phobic Fear" from the *Adult Psychotherapy Homework Planner*, 2nd ed. (Jongsma).

C. The veteran/service member completed the homework assignment, and the content was processed within the session.

D. The veteran's/service member's use of situational exposure techniques was reviewed and reinforced.

E. The veteran/service member has struggled in his/her implementation of situational exposure techniques and was provided with corrective feedback.

F. The veteran/service member has not attempted to use the situational exposure techniques and was redirected to do so.

24. Educate about Arousal and Insomnia (24)

A. The veteran/service member was educated about how increased levels of arousal promote insomnia.

B. The veteran/service member acknowledged that he/she has difficulty sleeping when arousal has increased, and this experience was normalized.

C. The veteran/service member struggled to make a connection between arousal and insomnia and was provided with remedial examples in this area.

25. Instruct on Behavioral Practices (25)

A. The veteran/service member was instructed on appropriate behavioral practices conducive to good sleep.

B. The veteran/service member was advised about restricting caffeine four hours prior to bedtime.

C. The veteran/service member was encouraged to exercise regularly but not in the evening.

D. The veteran/service member was advised about restricting spicy late-night snacks and heavy evening meals.

E. The veteran/service member was instructed about removing cues to time that may promote "clock watching" while in bed.

26. Assign Sleep Record (26)

A. The veteran/service member was assigned to keep a record of his/her sleep pattern.

B. The veteran/service member was assigned the "Sleep Pattern Record" exercise from the *Adult Psychotherapy Homework Planner,* 2nd ed. (Jongsma).

C. The veteran/service member completed the homework assignment, and the content was processed within the session.

D. The veteran's/service member's record of his/her sleep pattern was reviewed and processed.

E. The veteran/service member has not completed the sleep pattern record and was redirected to do so.

27. Educate about Co-occurring Conditions (27)

A. The veteran/service member was educated about how other conditions can make an individual more sensitive and aware of arousal levels, which can lead to greater distress.

B. The veteran/service member was provided with examples of coexisting disorders/conditions that can exacerbate distress levels, including panic and pain problems.

C. The veteran/service member displayed an understanding of the connection between co-occurring disorders and greater arousal/distress; this insight was reinforced.

D. The veteran/service member struggled to identify the connection between co-occurring disorders and increased arousal/distress and was provided with specific examples in this area.

28. Provided Panic Treatment (28)

A. The veteran/service member was provided with treatment for panic disorder symptoms.

B. The veteran/service member was provided with treatment to help decrease his/her pattern of panic attacks.

C. The veteran/service member has responded well to treatment for panic symptoms, decreasing his/her pattern of physiological response.

D. The veteran/service member has not participated in panic disorder treatment and was redirected to do so.

29. Provide Pain Symptoms Treatment (29)

A. The veteran/service member was provided with treatment related to his/her pain symptoms.

B. The veteran/service member has responded well to treatment for pain symptoms and was reinforced for this progress.

C. The veteran/service member has not engaged in treatment for pain symptoms and was reminded to do so.

POST-DEPLOYMENT REINTEGRATION PROBLEMS

SERVICE MEMBER PRESENTATION

1. Difficulty Adjusting to Return from Deployment (1)*

A. The service member reported difficulty adjusting subsequent to his/her return from deployment.

B. The service member reported that he/she has experienced feelings of loneliness and lack of meaning in life subsequent to his/her return from deployment.

C. The service member reported a sense of lost identity now that he/she is no longer deployed.

D. The service member reported significant changes in his/her lifestyle from prior to deployment.

E. As treatment has progressed, the service member has now appropriately adjusted to the changes resulting from returning from deployment.

2. Overwhelmed with Responsibilities (2)

A. The service member reports feeling overwhelmed with family, social, and occupational responsibilities.

B. The service member has had difficulty adjusting to his/her prior responsibilities.

C. The service member reports that he/she has begun to cope with the demands of family, social, and occupational responsibilities.

D. The service member reports that he/she is very much enjoying fulfilling his/her family, social, and occupational responsibilities.

3. Increased Conflict with Significant Other (3)

A. The service member reported frequent or continual arguing with his/her significant other.

B. The frequency of conflict between the partners has diminished.

C. The service member reported implementation of conflict resolution skills.

D. The service member reported that his/her relationship with the partner has improved significantly and arguing has become very infrequent.

4. Disconnection from Family and Friends (4)

A. The service member reports a sense of disconnection from family and friends.

B. The service member reports that family and friends do not appear to understand his/her experiences.

C. The service member reports that he/she feels more connected to former comrades than to family and friends.

D. The service member reports that his/her sense of connection with family and friends has improved.

---

*The numbers in parentheses correlate to the number of the Behavioral Definition statement in the companion chapter with the same title in *The Veterans and Active Duty Military Psychotherapy Treatment Planner* (Moore and Jongsma) by John Wiley & Sons, 2009.

5. Anger (5)

A. The service member presented with verbalizations of anger as well as tense, rigid muscles, and glaring facial expressions.

B. The service member expressed his/her irritability with bodily signs of muscle tension, clenched fists, and refusal to make eye contact.

C. The service member has been reported to be increasing his/her aggressiveness toward family friends and strangers.

D. The service member appeared more relaxed, less angry, and did not exhibit physical signs of aggression.

E. The service member's family reported that he/she has been more relaxed within the home setting and has not shown glaring looks or pounded his/her fist on the table.

6. Irritability (5)

A. The service member described a history of reacting too angrily to rather insignificant irritants in his/her daily life.

B. The service member indicated that he/she recognizes that he/she becomes too angry in the face of rather minor frustrations and irritants.

C. Minor irritants in the service member's life have resulted in explosive, angry outbursts that have led to destruction of property and/or striking out physically at others.

D. The service member has made significant progress at increasing frustration tolerance and reducing explosive overreactivity to minor irritants.

E. There have no reports of angry outbursts recently as the service member is feeling more calm and at peace.

7. Ambivalence about Home versus Deployment (6)

A. The service member reports ambivalent feelings regarding remaining at home versus a desire to return to the deployed setting.

B. The service member sees positive and negative aspects about being home.

C. The service member sees positive and negative aspects about returning to the deployed setting.

D. As treatment has progressed, the service member has become more certain about his/her desired future setting.

E. The service member reports that he/she feels confident and at ease with being home.

F. The service member reports a desire to return to the deployed setting.

8. Financial Stress (7)

A. The service member reports increased financial stress subsequent to his/her return from deployment.

B. While deployed, the service member's financial situation has deteriorated.

C. The service member reports a feeling of hopelessness and low self-esteem associated with the lack of sufficient income to cover the cost of living.

D. As treatment has progressed, the service member has become more optimistic about his/her financial capabilities.

E. The service member reports that his/her financial concerns have dissipated significantly, and he/she feels more capable of maintaining financial stability.

9. Sleep Disturbance (8)

A. The service member reported periods of inability to sleep and other periods of sleeping for many hours without the desire to get out of bed.

B. The service member's problem with sleep interference has diminished as the depression has lifted.

C. Medication has improved the service member's problems with sleep disturbance.

10. Mood Disturbance (8)

A. The service member reported that he/she feels deeply sad and has periods of tearfulness on an almost daily basis.

B. The service member's depressed affect was clearly evident within the session as tears were shed on more than one occasion.

C. The service member described periods of significant mood fluctuation.

D. The service member reported that he/she has begun to feel less sad and can experience periods of joy.

E. The service member appeared to be happier within the session, and there is no evidence of tearfulness.

INTERVENTIONS IMPLEMENTED

1. Build Trust (1)*

A. Consistent eye contact, active listening, unconditional positive regard, and warm acceptance were used to help build trust with the service member.

B. A sense of understanding about the challenges service members deal with after deployment was communicated to the service member.

C. The service member began to express feelings more freely as rapport and the trust level were emphasized.

D. The service member has continued to experience difficulty being open and direct in his/her expression of painful feelings; he/she was encouraged to take advantage of this trustworthy environment.

2. Assess Post-Deployment Concerns (2)

A. The service member's type, intensity, and frequency of post-deployment concerns were assessed.

B. The impact of the service member's post-deployment concerns on his/her social functioning was assessed.

C. The impact of the service member's post-deployment concerns on his/her occupational functioning was assessed.

---

*The numbers in parentheses correlate to the number of the Therapeutic Intervention statement in the companion chapter with the same title in *The Veterans and Active Duty Military Psychotherapy Treatment Planner* (Moore and Jongsma) by John Wiley & Sons, 2009.

D. The impact of the service member's post-deployment concerns on his/her interpersonal functioning was assessed.

E. The effect of the service member's post-deployment concerns was reflected to him/her to assure accuracy.

3. Encourage Attendance at Post-Deployment Briefings/Evaluations (3)

A. The service member was encouraged to attend required unit post-deployment briefings and evaluations.

B. The service member was directed to attend the chaplain's briefing subsequent to post-deployment.

C. The service member was encouraged to attend the combat stress control/mental health briefing subsequent to deployment.

D. The service member was directed to attend the post-deployment health assessment.

E. The service member was assisted in processing his/her reaction to his/her post-deployment briefings and evaluations.

F. The service member has not attended the expected post-deployment briefings and evaluations and was redirected to follow up on these helpful services.

4. Assist in Maintaining Positive Attitude (4)

A. The service member was assisted in maintaining a positive attitude about required briefings and evaluations.

B. The use of briefings and evaluations to assist with post-deployment reintegration was emphasized.

C. The prevention of social and emotional problems and the increase in life satisfaction associated with post-deployment briefings was emphasized.

D. The service member reported a more positive attitude about the required briefings subsequent to the emphasis on how they improve his/her life satisfaction and emotional well-being.

E. Despite support for the positive aspects of required briefings and evaluations, the service member has a negative attitude about them; he/she was encouraged to be open to the use of these briefings.

5. Explain Benefit of Post-Deployment Evaluations (5)

A. The service member was directed to answer thoughtfully and honestly during post-deployment evaluations.

B. The benefits of honesty during evaluations was emphasized, including how it helps to identify current and potential problems and will document service-connected problems/disabilities.

C. The service member acknowledged the importance of answering thoughtfully and honestly during post-deployment evaluations; he/she was supported for this honesty.

D. The service member minimizes any benefit from post-deployment evaluations and was encouraged to be open and honest despite his/her lack of understanding in this area.

6. Encourage Patience (6)

A. The service member was encouraged to take his/her time with regard to becoming reacquainted to his/her redeployment life.

B. The problems that occur by attempting to adjust too quickly were reviewed.

C. The service member was warned about burning himself/herself out in his/her rapid readjustment.

D. The problems with alienating others as he/she adjusts too quickly to post-deployment were pointed out.

7. Develop Priorities (7)

A. The service member was assisted in creating a to-do list.

B. The service member was assisted in prioritizing his/her needs based on importance and difficulty.

C. The service member was encouraged to start with issues with greater a chance of successful completion and ease in order to build confidence.

D. The service member has developed a prioritized list of responsibilities, and this was processed with him/her.

E. The service member has resisted developing a list of priorities and was redirected to do so.

8. Encourage Empathy for Significant Other (8)

A. The service member was encouraged to have empathy for his/her significant other in regard to how responsibilities change.

B. The service member was directed to be patient and maintain awareness of his/her significant other's feelings when reassuming household and family responsibilities.

C. The service member has acknowledged the need to empathize with his/her significant other and was reinforced for this.

D. The service member does not appear to be displaying much empathy for his/her significant other and was provided with additional feedback in this area.

9. Discuss Disruption and Stress (9)

A. A discussion was held with the service member about how abrupt disruption and change can worsen family problems, even when a high level of stress was preexisting.

B. The service member was supported as he/she acknowledged the problems that abrupt changes can create and has tried to be slower in making changes in the family.

C. The service member continues to make significant abrupt changes, creating higher levels of stress in his/her family, and he/she was provided with additional feedback in this area.

10. Hold Couple's Session about Responsibilities (10)

A. The service member's significant other was invited for a couple's session.

B. There was evidence of significant disagreement and conflict surrounding the issue of the division of household and family responsibilities.

C. An agreement about household responsibilities was developed within the couple's session.

D. The couple was reinforced for developing an agreement that describes individual and joint duties.

11. Encourage Setting Limits (11)

A. The service member was encouraged to set limits with his/her extended family and friends.

B. The service member was encouraged to have a primary focus on his/her immediate family.

C. The service member has limited time and access of his/her extended family and friends as a means of focusing on immediate family members, and he/she was reinforced for this.

D. The service member has struggled to set limits with extended family and friends and was redirected in this area.

12. **Educate about Alcohol and Family Stress (12)**

A. The service member was educated about how alcohol can worsen personal and family stress.

B. The many problems that can develop from increased alcohol use were processed.

C. The service member's decreased coping abilities when drinking were emphasized.

D. The service member has put strict limits on his/her alcohol use subsequent to deployment, and this was reinforced.

E. The service member has not limited his/her drinking subsequent to deployment and was redirected to do so.

13. **Refer for Substance Abuse Evaluation (13)**

A. The service member was assessed for the presence of chemical dependence.

B. The service member was referred for an evaluation for the presence of chemical dependence.

C. The need for chemical dependence treatment was presented to the service member.

D. Chemical dependence treatment was arranged for the service member.

E. The service member declined any referral to a chemical dependence program.

F. The service member was assessed for the presence of a chemical dependence problem, but no such problem was found.

14. **Discuss Partner's Greater Independence (14)**

A. A discussion was held in regard to the service member's partner's increase in independence as a result of taking on more responsibilities and new roles while the service member was deployed.

B. The service member was supported as he/she identified how his/her partner's increased independence has occurred.

C. The service member was supported as he/she processed fears and anxieties related to the changes in his/her partner's level of independence.

D. The service member denied any fear of anxiety related to his/her partner's potential independence and was encouraged to identify these feelings if they occur.

15. **Encourage Discussion about Relationship Changes (15)**

A. The service member was instructed to discuss with his/her significant other ways in which the significant other has changed or grown during the service member's absence.

B. The service member was assigned to work with his/her partner on "How Can We Meet Each Other's Needs and Desires?" from the *Adult Psychotherapy Homework Planner*, 2nd ed. (Jongsma).

C. The service member was assigned to work with his/her partner on "Positive and Negative Contributions to the Relationship: Mine and Yours?" from the *Adult Psychotherapy Homework Planner*, 2nd ed. (Jongsma).

D. The service member completed the homework assignment, and the content was processed within the session.

E. The service member has completed a discussion with his/her significant other about changes in growth during the service member's absence, and his/her experience was processed.

F. The service member has not had a discussion about the changes in growth that occurred during his/her absence and was reminded to do so.

16. Compare Children's Development (16)

A. The service member was directed to create a comparison list of where his/her children were developmentally when he/she left and where they are now.

B. The service member was assisted in creating a comparison list of his/her children's developmental changes.

C. The service member has developed a list of developmental changes for his/her children, and this was processed.

D. The service member has not developed a comparison list of developmental changes for his/her children and was redirected to do so.

17. Assign Child Development Reading (17)

A. The service member was assigned to read material on child development.

B. The service member was directed to read *Ages and Stages: A Parent's Guide to Normal Childhood Development* (Schaefer and DiGeronimo).

C. The service member was directed to read *Your Child's Growing Mind: Brain Development and Learning from Birth to Adolescence* (Healy).

D. The service member has read the assigned material on child development, and key points were processed.

E. The service member had many questions about childhood development issues, and these were answered.

F. The service member has not read the assigned information on child development and was redirected to do so.

18. Assign Reading on Child Rearing (18)

A. The service member was assigned to read material on effective child-rearing techniques.

B. The service member was directed to read *The Parent's Handbook: Systematic Training for Effective Parenting* (Dinkmeyer, McKay, and Dinkmeyer).

C. The service member was directed to read *Parenting with Love and Logic* (Klein and Fey).

D. The service member has read the assigned information on parenting, and key points were processed.

E. The service member has not read the assigned information on parenting and was redirected to do so.

19. Explain Changes in Parenting Styles (19)

A. The service member was advised about different parenting styles (e.g., indulgent versus authoritarian).

B. The service member was assisted in identifying how parenting styles may change due to being the only parent available while the service member was deployed.

C. The service member was taught about how parenting style changes due to developmental needs of the children.

D. The service member displayed an understanding of the potential for changing parenting styles and was reinforced for this insight.

E. The service member had poor understanding of the changes that can happen in parenting style and was provided with remedial feedback in this area.

20. Encourage Flexibility in Parenting Styles (20)

A. The service member was encouraged to be flexible in his/her parenting style.

B. The service member was taught about negotiating parenting roles and responsibilities in the family.

C. The service member was assigned to complete "Learning to Parent as a Team" from the *Adult Psychotherapy Homework Planner*, 2nd ed. (Jongsma).

D. The service member completed the homework assignment, and the content was processed within the session.

E. A couple's session was held in order to help negotiate parental roles.

21. Compare Income (21)

A. The service member was asked to compare net income while deployed versus current net income.

B. A review was made about expenses that will need to be cut in order to balance with current income.

22. List Expenses (22)

A. The service member was asked to list expenses.

B. The service member was assisted in identifying expenses that he/she has now that he/she did not have while deployed.

C. The service member was assisted in planning as to how to budget for expenses.

D. The service member was assigned "Plan a Budget" from the *Adult Psychotherapy Homework Planner*, 2nd ed. (Jongsma).

E. The service member completed the homework assignment, and the content was processed within the session.

F. The service member has reviewed expenses and budgeting, and this was reviewed within the session.

G. The service member has not completed a budget and was redirected to do so.

23. Refer to Financial Assistance Program (23)

A. The service member was referred to a financial assistance program at his/her local base/post for a loan or assistance with food, clothing, or household items.

B. The service member described ambivalence in regard to seeking out assistance, and this was accepted and processed.

C. The service member has followed up on the referral to a financial assistance program, and he/she was reinforced for accessing these helpful services.

D. The service member has not followed up on the referral to a financial assistance program and was reminded about this resource.

24. Discourage Immediate Decisions (24)

A. The service member was encouraged to postpone discussion about career changes until the stress level in the family has decreased.

B. The service member was directed to hold off making decisions about leaving the military or moving to a different base/post.

C. The service member agreed that he/she should wait for major decisions until his/her stress level has decreased and routines have returned to normal.

25. Educate about Road Rage and Adjustment (25)

A. The service member was educated about road rage.

B. The service member was advised about the challenges that may occur while driving in a nonhostile environment.

C. The service member was instructed to initially allow his/her significant other to drive when possible.

26. Review Positives about Return (26)

A. The service member was directed to create a list of positive aspects of returning from deployment.

B. The service member was assisting in developing a list of positive aspects of returning from deployment (e.g., more time with family, out of harm's way, less restriction of travel).

C. The service member has developed a list of positive aspects about returning from deployment, and this was processed.

D. The service member has not developed a list of positive aspects about returning from deployment and was redirected to do so.

27. Coordinate Contact with Military OneSource (27)

A. The service member was provided with information about how to contact the Military OneSource for free, confidential counseling from a civilian behavioral health care provider.

B. The service member was provided with the Military OneSource toll-free number: 1-800-342-9647.

C. The service member has contacted the Military OneSource for free, confidential counseling from a civilian behavioral health care provider; his/her experience with this resource was reviewed.

D. The service member has not contacted Military OneSource and was reminded about this helpful resource.

POSTTRAUMATIC STRESS DISORDER (PTSD)

VETERAN/SERVICE MEMBER PRESENTATION

1. Exposure to Traumatic Events (1)[*]

A. The veteran/service member reports that he/she was exposed to a traumatic event involving actual or perceived threat of death or serious injury.

B. The veteran/service member has been exposed to a traumatic event in which others were seriously injured or died.

C. The veteran's/service member's intense emotional response to the traumatic event has gradually diminished.

D. The veteran/service member can now recall the traumatic event associated with death and injury without an intense emotional response.

2. Strong Emotional Response to Traumatic Event (2)

A. The veteran/service member reports feelings of intense fear and horror in response to the traumatic event.

B. The veteran/service member emphasizes his/her sense of helplessness related to the traumatic event.

C. The veteran/service member is easily overwhelmed by his/her emotional response to the traumatic event.

D. As treatment has progressed, the veteran's/service member's emotional response to the traumatic event has become more manageable.

E. The veteran/service member reports that his/her intense fear, horror, and helplessness have diminished to manageable levels.

3. Intrusive Thoughts (3)

A. The veteran/service member described experiencing intrusive, distressing thoughts or images that recall the traumatic event and its associated intense emotional response.

B. The veteran/service member reported experiencing fewer intrusive, distressing thoughts of the traumatic event.

C. The veteran/service member reported no longer experiencing intrusive, distressing thoughts of the traumatic event.

4. Disturbing Dreams (4)

A. The veteran/service member described disturbing dreams that he/she experiences and are associated with the traumatic event.

B. The frequency and intensity of the veteran's/service member's disturbing dreams associated with the traumatic event have decreased.

---

[*]The numbers in parentheses correlate to the number of the Behavioral Definition statement in the companion chapter with the same title in *The Veterans and Active Duty Military Psychotherapy Treatment Planner* (Moore and Jongsma) by John Wiley & Sons, 2009.

C. The veteran/service member reported no longer experiencing disturbing dreams associated with the traumatic event.

5. Flashbacks (5)

A. The veteran/service member reported experiencing illusions about or flashbacks to the traumatic event.

B. The frequency and intensity of the veteran's/service member's flashback experiences have diminished.

C. The veteran/service member reported no longer experiencing flashbacks to the traumatic event.

6. Distressful Reminders (6)

A. The veteran/service member experienced intense distress when exposed to reminders of the traumatic event.

B. The veteran/service member reported having been exposed to some reminders of the traumatic event without experiencing overwhelming distress.

7. Physiological Reactivity (6)

A. The veteran/service member experiences physiological reactivity associated with fear and anger when he/she is exposed to the internal or external cues that symbolize the traumatic event.

B. The veteran's/service member's physiological reactivity has diminished when he/she is exposed to internal or external cues of the traumatic event.

C. The veteran/service member reported no longer experiencing physiological reactivity when exposed to internal or external cues of the traumatic event.

8. Thought/Feeling/Conversation Avoidance (7)

A. The veteran/service member described trying to avoid thinking, feeling, or talking about the traumatic event because of the associated negative emotional response.

B. The veteran/service member is making less effort to avoid thoughts, feelings, or conversations about the traumatic event.

C. The veteran/service member reported that he/she is now able to talk or think about the traumatic event without feeling overwhelmed with negative emotions.

9. Place/People Avoidance (8)

A. The veteran/service member reported a pattern of avoidance of activity, places, or people associated with the traumatic event because he/she is fearful of the negative emotions that may be triggered.

B. The veteran/service member is able to tolerate contact with people, places, or activities associated with the traumatic event without feeling overwhelmed.

10. Blocked Recall (9)

A. The veteran/service member stated that he/she has an inability to recall some important aspect of the traumatic event.

B. The veteran's/service member's amnesia regarding some important aspects of the traumatic event has begun to lessen.

C. The veteran/service member can now recall almost all of the important aspects of the traumatic event, as his/her amnesia has terminated.

11. Lack of Interest (10)

A. The veteran/service member has developed a lack of interest and a pattern of lack of participation in activities that previously had been rewarding and pleasurable.

B. The veteran/service member has begun to show some interest in participation in previously rewarding activities.

C. The veteran/service member is now showing a normal interest in participation in rewarding activities.

12. Detachment (11)

A. The veteran/service member described feeling a sense of detachment from others.

B. The veteran/service member reported regaining a sense of attachment in participation with others.

C. The veteran/service member reported that he/she no longer feels alienated from others and is able to participate in social and intimate interactions.

13. Blunted Emotions (12)

A. The veteran/service member reported an inability to experience the full range of emotions, including love.

B. The veteran/service member reported beginning to be in touch with his/her feelings again.

C. The veteran/service member is able to experience the full range of emotions.

14. Pessimistic/Fatalistic (13)

A. Since the traumatic event occurred, the veteran/service member has had a pessimistic and fatalistic attitude regarding the future.

B. The veteran/service member sees his/her future as foreshortened.

C. The veteran/service member is beginning to experience a somewhat hopeful attitude regarding the future.

D. The veteran's/service member's pessimistic, fatalistic attitude regarding the future has terminated and he/she has begun to make plans and talk about the future with a more hopeful attitude.

15. Sleep Disturbance (14)

A. Since the traumatic event occurred, the veteran/service member has experienced a desire to sleep much more than normal.

B. Since the traumatic event occurred, the veteran/service member has found it very difficult to initiate and maintain sleep.

C. Since the traumatic event occurred, the veteran/service member has had a fear of sleeping.

D. The veteran's/service member's sleep disturbance has terminated, and he/she has returned to a normal sleep pattern.

16. Irritability (15)

A. The veteran/service member described a pattern of irritability that was not present before the traumatic event occurred.

B. The veteran/service member reported incidents of becoming angry and losing his/her temper easily, resulting in explosive outbursts.

C. The veteran's/service member's irritability has diminished somewhat and the intensity of the explosive outbursts has lessened.

D. The veteran/service member reported no recent incidents of explosive, angry outbursts.

17. Lack of Concentration (16)

A. The veteran/service member described a pattern of lack of concentration that began with the exposure to the traumatic event.

B. The veteran/service member reported that he/she is now able to focus more clearly on cognitive processing.

C. The veteran's/service member's ability to concentrate has returned to normal levels.

18. Hypervigilance (17)

A. The veteran/service member described a pattern of hypervigilance.

B. The veteran/service member described having experienced an exaggerated startle response.

C. The veteran's/service member's exaggerated startle response has diminished.

D. The veteran/service member no longer experiences an exaggerated startle response.

E. The veteran's/service member's hypervigilant pattern has diminished.

F. The veteran/service member reported no longer experiencing hypervigilance.

19. Refuses to Participate in Missions (18)

A. The service member has refused to participate in training missions.

B. The service member has refused to participate in combat missions.

C. Despite direct ultimatums, the service member has refused to participate in expected combat or training missions.

D. The service member has agreed to participate in combat and training missions.

E. The service member has successfully participated in additional training and combat missions.

20. Alcohol/Drug Abuse (19)

A. Since the traumatic experience, the veteran/service member has engaged in a pattern of alcohol and/or drug abuse as a maladaptive coping mechanism.

B. The veteran's/service member's alcohol and/or drug abuse has diminished as he/she has worked through the traumatic event.

C. The veteran/service member reported no longer engaging in any alcohol or drug abuse.

21. Desires Separation from Military (20)

A. The service member reports a desire to separate from the military.

B. The veteran indicated that he/she separated from the military because of his/her posttraumatic stress disorder concerns.

C. The service member has specific plans to separate from the military.

D. As treatment has progressed, the service member reports being more at ease with remaining in the military.

E. The service member has made a final decision as to his/her military status.

22. Letting Others Down (21)

A. The veteran/service member reports a sense that he/she let his comrades and his/her unit down.

B. The veteran/service member reports that he/she feels as if he/she did not do his/her duty for his/her country.

C. As treatment has progressed, the veteran/service member has identified that he/she has done what was expected of him/her as a soldier.

D. The veteran/service member is more at peace with his/her actions in the field.

23. Marital and Family Conflicts (22)

A. The veteran/service member described a pattern of interpersonal conflict with family members.

B. The veteran/service member described that he/she has been having significant primary relationship problems.

C. The veteran's/service member's partner reports that he/she is irritable, withdrawn, and preoccupied with the traumatic event.

D. As the veteran/service member has worked through his/her reaction to the traumatic event, there has been less conflict within personal relationships.

E. The veteran/service member and his/her partner reported increased communication satisfaction within the interpersonal relationship.

24. Interpersonal Conflict (23)

A. The veteran/service member described a pattern of interpersonal conflict, especially in regard to friends, fellow comrades, and superiors.

B. The veteran's/service member's friends, comrades, and superiors have reported that he/she is irritable, withdrawn, and preoccupied with the traumatic event.

C. As the veteran/service member has worked through his/her reaction to the traumatic event, there has been less conflict within personal relationships.

D. The veteran/service member reported increased communication and satisfaction with interpersonal relationships.

25. Suicidal/Homicidal Thoughts (24)

A. The veteran/service member reported experiencing suicidal/homicidal thoughts since the onset of PTSD.

B. The veteran's/service member's suicidal/homicidal thoughts have become less intense and less frequent.

C. The veteran/service member reported no longer experiencing any suicidal/homicidal thoughts.

26. Interpersonal Conflict (25)

A. The veteran/service member described a pattern of interpersonal conflict, especially in regard to intimate relationships.

B. As the veteran/service member has worked through his/her reaction to the traumatic event, there has been less conflict within personal relationships.

C. The veteran's/service member's partner reported that he/she is irritable, withdrawn, and preoccupied with the traumatic event.

D. The veteran/service member and his/her partner reported increased communication and satisfaction with their interpersonal relationship.

INTERVENTIONS IMPLEMENTED

1. Develop Trust (1)*

A. Today's clinical contact focused on building the level of trust with the veteran/service member through consistent eye contact, active listening, unconditional positive regard, and warm acceptance.

B. Empathy and support were provided for the veteran's/service member's expression of thoughts and feelings during today's clinical contact.

C. The veteran/service member was asked about the frequency, intensity, duration, and history of his/her anxiety symptoms, fear, and avoidance.

D. The veteran/service member was assigned the "How the Trauma Affects Me" portion of the *Adult Psychotherapy Homework Planner,* 2nd ed. (Jongsma).

E. The veteran/service member was provided with support and feedback as he/she described his/her maladaptive pattern of anxiety.

F. As the veteran/service member has remained mistrustful and reluctant to share his/her underlying thoughts and feelings, he/she was provided with additional reassurance.

G. The veteran/service member verbally recognized that he/she has difficulty establishing trust because he/she has often felt let down by others in the past, and he/she was accepted for this insight.

2. Talk with Supervisor (2)

A. A discussion was held with the service member's first-line supervisor to assess the degree the PTSD symptoms have impacted the service member's job performance.

B. The service member's squad leader, platoon sergeant, or first sergeant was consulted in regard to the impact of the PTSD symptoms on the service member's job performance.

C. The service member's first-line supervisor indicated mild concerns in regard to the service member's job performance.

D. The service member's first-line supervisor indicated moderate concerns in regard to the service member's job performance.

E. The service member's first-line supervisor indicated severe concerns in regard to the service member's job performance.

---

*The numbers in parentheses correlate to the number of the Therapeutic Intervention statement in the companion chapter with the same title in *The Veterans and Active Duty Military Psychotherapy Treatment Planner* (Moore and Jongsma) by John Wiley & Sons, 2009.

3. Refer/Conduct Psychological Testing (3)

A. Psychological testing was administered to assess for the presence and strength of the PTSD symptoms.

B. The PTSD Checklist—Military Version was administered to the veteran/service member.

C. The psychological testing confirmed the presence of significant PTSD symptoms.

D. The psychological testing confirmed mild PTSD symptoms.

E. The psychological testing revealed that there are no significant PTSD symptoms present.

F. The results of the psychological testing were presented to the veteran/service member.

4. Provide Testing Feedback (4)

A. The veteran/service member was provided with feedback regarding his/her psychological test results.

B. The veteran/service member was advised that his/her psychological test results reflected only mild PTSD symptoms.

C. The veteran/service member was advised that his/her psychological test results reflected moderate PTSD symptoms.

D. The veteran/service member was advised that his/her psychological test results reflected severe PTSD symptoms.

5. Assess Chemical Dependence (5)

A. The veteran/service member was asked to describe his/her use of alcohol and/or drugs as a means of escape from negative emotions.

B. The veteran/service member was supported as he/she acknowledged that he/she has abused alcohol and/or drugs as a means of coping with the negative consequences associated with the traumatic event.

C. The veteran/service member was quite defensive about giving information regarding his/her substance abuse history and minimized any such behavior; this was reflected to him/her, and he/she was urged to be more open.

6. Refer to Chemical Dependence Treatment (6)

A. The veteran/service member was referred for chemical dependence treatment.

B. The veteran/service member consented to chemical dependence treatment referral, as he/she has acknowledged that substance abuse is a significant problem.

C. The veteran/service member refused to accept a referral for chemical dependence treatment and continued to deny that substance abuse is a problem.

D. The veteran/service member was reinforced for following through on obtaining chemical dependence treatment.

E. The veteran's/service member's treatment focus was switched to his/her chemical dependence problem.

7. Refer for Medication Evaluation (7)

A. The veteran/service member was referred for a medication evaluation to help stabilize his/her moods and decrease the intensity of his/her feelings.

B. The veteran/service member was reinforced as he/she agreed to follow through with the medication evaluation.

C. The veteran/service member was strongly opposed to being placed on medication to help stabilize his/her moods and reduce emotional distress; his/her objections were processed.

8. Monitor Medication (8)

A. The veteran's/service member's response to the medication was discussed in today's therapy session.

B. The veteran/service member reported that the medication has helped to stabilize his/her moods and decrease the intensity of his/her feelings; he/she was directed to share this information with the prescribing clinician.

C. The veteran/service member reports little to no improvement in his/her moods or anger control since being placed on the medication; he/she was directed to share this information with the prescribing clinician.

D. The veteran/service member was reinforced for consistently taking the medication as prescribed.

E. The veteran/service member has failed to comply with taking the medication as prescribed; he/she was encouraged to take the medication as prescribed.

9. Provide Update to Leadership (9)

A. An update was provided to the service member's unit leadership on his/her condition, potential negative impacts on safety, and any occupational limitations while taking medication.

B. The service member's unit leadership was advised about the service member's use of medication.

C. Periodic updates were provided to the service member's unit leadership about his/her medication treatment and progress.

10. Explore Facts of Traumatic Event (10)

A. The veteran/service member was gently encouraged to tell the entire story of the (most) traumatic event.

B. The veteran/service member was encouraged to express the details of the traumatic event, focusing on how he/she felt before, during, and after the traumatic event.

C. Today's therapy session explored the sequence of events before, during, and after the veteran's/service member's traumatic event, including his/her most memorable portions, sights, smells, and other stimuli.

D. The veteran's/service member's emotions associated with the trauma were processed.

E. The veteran/service member was encouraged to tell the story of the event as often as necessary as a form of exposure therapy.

11. Educate about PTSD (11)

A. The veteran/service member was educated about posttraumatic stress disorder, including symptoms, causes, prognosis, and available treatments.

B. The veteran/service member was directed to information in the Web site www.ncptsd.va.gov.

C. The veteran's/service member's questions in regard to PTSD symptoms, causes, prognosis, and treatment were reviewed and answered.

12. **Differentiate between PTSD and Combat Stress Reaction (12)**

   A. The veteran/service member was educated about the differences between PTSD and combat stress reaction.

   B. PTSD was identified for the veteran/service member as a collection of specific, often chronic symptoms that significantly impact social and occupational functioning and that requires treatment.

   C. Combat stress reaction was defined for the veteran/service member as brief emotional, behavioral, and/or physical reactions to a combat stressor that are expected to resolve on their own or with minimal intervention.

   D. The veteran/service member was assisted in gaining a greater understanding of how his/her symptoms fit PTSD or combat stress reaction categories.

   E. The veteran/service member was reinforced for his/her clear understanding of the difference between PTSD and combat stress reactions.

   F. The veteran/service member struggled to understand how his/her symptoms fit into PTSD versus combat stress reaction and was provided with additional information in this area.

13. **Teach about Effective Treatments (13)**

   A. The veteran/service member was taught about effective treatments for PTSD.

   B. The veteran/service member was taught about virtual reality and in vivo exposure techniques to desensitize his/her fears.

   C. The veteran/service member was taught about cognitive restructuring to assist him/her in viewing the world in a much less dangerous manner.

   D. The veteran/service member was reinforced for his/her clear understanding of the expectations of treatment for PTSD.

   E. The veteran/service member seemed to struggle to understand how effective treatment for PTSD may work and was provided with remedial information in this area.

14. **Assign Reading on PTSD (14)**

   A. The veteran/service member was assigned to read about cognitive restructuring, exposure therapy, and relaxation training in chapters of books or treatment manuals on PTSD.

   B. The veteran/service member was assigned specific chapters from *Reclaiming Your Life from a Traumatic Experience: A Prolonged Exposure Treatment Program Workbook* (Rothbaum, Foa, and Hembre).

   C. The veteran/service member has read the assigned information on PTSD; key concepts were reviewed.

   D. The veteran/service member has not read the assigned information on PTSD and was redirected to do so.

15. **Teach Diaphragmatic Breathing (15)**

   A. The veteran/service member was taught diaphragmatic breathing skills.

B. The veteran/service member was assigned to engage in deep diaphragmatic breathing twice per day for 10 minutes each time.

C. The veteran/service member was encouraged to implement the diaphragmatic breathing techniques when anxiety or stress rises.

D. The veteran/service member was taught how to apply diaphragmatic breathing techniques to his/her daily life.

E. The veteran/service member was provided with feedback about his/her use of diaphragmatic breathing skills.

16. Teach Progressive Muscle Relaxation (16)

A. The veteran/service member was taught progressive muscle relaxation skills.

B. The veteran/service member was assigned to engage in progressive muscle relaxation skills twice per day for 15 minutes each time.

C. The veteran/service member was encouraged to implement the progressive muscle relaxation skills when anxiety or stress rises.

D. The veteran/service member was taught how to apply progressive muscle relaxation skills to his/her daily life.

E. The veteran/service member was provided with feedback about his/her use of progressive muscle relaxation skills.

17. Explain Connection between Thoughts, Feelings, and Behavior (17)

A. The veteran/service member was taught how thoughts impact our feelings and behavior.

B. The specific role that the thoughts play in maintaining fear and reinforcing avoidance of perceived threats was reviewed.

C. The veteran/service member was provided with an example that relates to his/her situation of how thoughts impact feelings and behavior.

D. The veteran/service member was reinforced for his/her display of understanding about how thoughts impact behavior.

E. The veteran/service member struggled to adopt the concepts of how thoughts impact feelings and behavior and was provided with remedial assistance in this area.

18. Develop Awareness of Automatic Thoughts (18)

A. The veteran/service member was assisted in developing an awareness of his/her automatic thoughts that are consistent with a hostile worldview.

B. The veteran/service member was assisted in identifying how his/her automatic thoughts may lead to the belief that injury and death is inevitable.

C. The veteran/service member was supported for making the connection between his/her automatic thoughts and a hostile and dangerous worldview.

D. The veteran/service member struggled to connect his/her automatic thoughts to his/her worldview and was provided with remedial feedback in this area.

19. Assign Dysfunctional Thinking Journal (19)

A. The veteran/service member was requested to keep a daily journal that lists each situation associated with depressed feelings and the dysfunctional thinking that triggered the depression.

B. The veteran/service member was directed to complete the "Negative Thoughts Trigger Negative Feelings" assignment from the *Adult Psychotherapy Homework Planner,* 2nd ed. (Jongsma).

C. The Socratic method was used to challenge the veteran's/service member's dysfunctional thoughts and to replace them with positive, reality-based thoughts.

D. The veteran/service member was reinforced for instances of successful replacement of negative thoughts with more realistic positive thinking.

E. The veteran/service member has not kept a record of his/her automatic thoughts and was redirected to do so.

20. Reinforce Positive Self-Talk (20)

A. The veteran/service member was reinforced for any successful replacement of distorted negative thinking with positive, reality-based cognitive messages.

B. It was noted that the veteran/service member has been engaging in positive, reality-based thinking that has enhanced his/her self-confidence and increased adaptive action.

C. The veteran/service member was assigned to complete the "Positive Self-Talk" assignment from the *Adult Psychotherapy Homework Planner,* 2nd ed. (Jongsma).

21. Discuss PTSD Symptoms (21)

A. A discussion was held with the veteran/service member about how PTSD results from exposure to trauma and leads to intrusive recollections, unwarranted fears, anxiety, and a vulnerability to other negative emotions.

B. The veteran/service member was provided with specific examples of how PTSD symptoms occur and affect individuals.

C. The veteran/service member displayed a clear understanding of the dynamics of PTSD and was provided with positive feedback.

D. The veteran/service member has struggled to understand the dynamics of PTSD and was provided with remedial feedback in this area.

22. Use Imaginal Exposure (22)

A. The veteran/service member was asked to describe the traumatic experience at an increasing, but self-managed level of detail.

B. Virtual reality techniques were used to help the veteran/service member recount/relive the emotional experience for an ever-increasing period of time.

C. The veteran/service member was asked to continue to describe his/her traumatic experience at his/her own chosen level of detail until the associated anxiety reduces and stabilizes.

D. The veteran/service member was encouraged to continue recounting the emotional experiences until he/she can do this for an extended period of time (e.g., 60–90 minutes).

E. The veteran/service member was directed to do imaginal exposures as described in *Prolonged Exposure Therapy for PTSD: Emotional Processing of Traumatic Experience— Therapist Guide* (Foa, Hembre, and Rothbaum).

F. The veteran/service member was reinforced for his/her progress in imaginal exposure.

G. The veteran/service member was assisted in problem-solving obstacles to his/her imaginal exposure success.

23. Use in Vivo Exposure (23)

A. The veteran/service member was asked to gradually expose himself/herself to objects, situations, and places that create significant anxiety.

B. The veteran/service member was supported and encouraged as he/she gradually exposed himself/herself to objects, situations, and places that create significant anxiety.

C. The veteran's/service member's increased ability to have in-person exposure to objects, situations, and places that had created significant anxiety was celebrated and applauded.

D. The veteran/service member has struggled to expose himself/herself to objects, situations, and places that have created anxiety and was provided with additional feedback and support.

24. Provide Ongoing Treatment (24)

A. The veteran/service member was provided with psychoeducation one to two times per week for up to three months.

B. The veteran/service member was provided with exposure treatment once or twice per week for three months.

C. The veteran/service member was provided with cognitive treatment once or twice per week for three months.

D. The veteran/service member has utilized his/her treatment to reach acceptable level of symptom remission.

E. The veteran/service member was provided with follow-up "booster" sessions on an as-needed basis.

25. Teach Thought Stopping (25)

A. The veteran/service member was taught a thought-stopping technique.

B. The veteran/service member was taught to internally voice the word STOP immediately upon noticing unwanted trauma or otherwise negative unwanted thoughts.

C. The veteran/service member was taught to imagine something representing the concept of stopping (e.g., a stop sign or stoplight) immediately upon noticing unwanted trauma or otherwise negative unwanted thoughts.

D. The veteran/service member was assisted in reviewing his/her use of thought-stopping techniques and was provided with positive feedback for his/her appropriate use of this technique.

E. Redirection was provided, as the veteran/service member has not learned to use the thought-stopping technique.

26. Employ EMDR Technique (26)

A. The veteran/service member was trained in the use of the eye movement desensitization and reprocessing (EMDR) technique to reduce his/her emotional reactivity to the traumatic event.

B. The veteran/service member reported that the EMDR technique has been helpful in reducing his/her emotional reactivity to the traumatic event.

C. The veteran/service member reported partial success with the use of the EMDR technique to reduce emotional distress.

D. The veteran/service member reported little to no improvement with the use of the EMDR technique to decrease his/her emotional reactivity to the traumatic event.

27. Discuss Lapse versus Relapse (27)

A. The veteran/service member was assisted in differentiating between a lapse and a relapse.

B. A lapse was defined for the veteran/service member as the initial and reversible return of symptoms, fear, or urges to avoid.

C. A relapse was defined for the veteran/service member as the return to fearful and avoidant patterns.

D. The veteran/service member was reinforced for his/her ability to respond to a lapse without relapsing.

28. Identify and Rehearse Response to Lapse Situations (28)

A. The veteran/service member was asked to identify future situations or circumstances in which lapses could occur.

B. The veteran/service member was asked to rehearse the management of his/her potential lapse situations.

C. The veteran/service member was reinforced as he/she identified and rehearsed how to cope with potential lapse situations.

D. The veteran/service member was provided with helpful feedback about how to best manage potential lapse situations.

E. The veteran/service member declined to identify or rehearse the management of potential lapse situations, and this resistance was redirected.

29. Encourage Use of Therapy Strategies (29)

A. The veteran/service member was encouraged to routinely employ strategies used in therapy.

B. The veteran/service member was urged to use cognitive restructuring, social skills, and exposure techniques while building social interactions and relationships.

C. The veteran/service member was reinforced for his/her regular use of therapy techniques within social interactions and relationships.

D. The veteran/service member was unable to identify many situations in which he/she has used therapy techniques to help build social interactions and social relationships and was redirected to seek these situations out.

30. Develop a "Coping Card" (30)

A. The veteran/service member was provided with a "coping card" on which specific coping strategies were listed.

B. The veteran/service member was assisted in developing his/her "coping card" in order to list helpful coping strategies.

C. The veteran/service member was encouraged to use his/her "coping card" when struggling with anxiety-producing situations.

31. Use Writing as Exposure (31)

A. The veteran/service member was instructed to utilize writing about the trauma as a method of exposure.

B. The veteran/service member was assigned "Share the Painful Memory" from the *Adult Psychotherapy Homework Planner,* 2nd ed. (Jongsma).

C. The veteran/service member has used writing as a way to have exposure to his/her painful memories, as exposure approaches were too difficult for him/her; his/her experience was processed.

D. The veteran/service member has not completed the assignments regarding writing about the trauma and was redirected to do so.

32. Use Imagery Rehearsal Therapy (32)

A. Imagery rehearsal therapy was used as an adjunctive treatment for nightmares.

B. The veteran/service member has identified a decrease in his/ her nightmares due to the use of imagery rehearsal therapy, and this progress was reviewed and plotted.

C. The veteran/service member has struggled to engage in the imagery rehearsal therapy and was provided with remedial feedback in this area.

33. Instruct on Sleep Hygiene (33)

A. The veteran/service member was encouraged to engage in behavioral practices conducive to good sleep.

B. The veteran/service member was urged to avoid caffeine and spicy meals/snacks prior to sleep.

C. The veteran/service member was encouraged to exercise each morning.

D. The veteran/service member was encouraged to get out of bed if he/she is not able to fall asleep within 15 minutes.

E. The veteran/service member was encouraged to remove used timepieces that may promote "clock watching."

F. The veteran/service member was reinforced for his/her improved sleep hygiene practices.

G. The veteran/service member continues to struggle with sleep problems and was provided with remedial ideas in this area.

34. Refer for Group Therapy (34)

A. The veteran/service member was referred for group therapy to help him/her share and work through his/her feelings about the trauma with other individuals who have experienced traumatic incidents.

B. The veteran/service member was given the directive to self-disclose at least once during the group therapy session about his/her traumatic experience.

C. It was emphasized to the veteran/service member that his/her involvement in group therapy has helped him/her realize that he/she is not alone in experiencing painful emotions surrounding a traumatic event.

D. It was reflected to the veteran/service member that his/her active participation in group therapy has helped him/her share and work through many of his/her emotions pertaining to the traumatic event.

E. The veteran/service member has not made productive use of the group therapy sessions and has been reluctant to share his/her feelings about the traumatic event; he/she was encouraged to use this helpful technique.

35. Conduct Family/Conjoint Session (35)

A. A conjoint session was held to facilitate healing the hurt that the veteran's/service member's PTSD symptoms have caused to others.

B. The veteran/service member was supported while apologizing to significant others for the irritability, withdrawal, and angry outbursts that are part of his/her PTSD symptom pattern.

C. Support was provided as the veteran's/service member's significant others verbalized the negative impact that the veteran's/service member's PTSD symptoms have had on their lives.

D. Significant others indicated support for the veteran/service member and accepted apologies for previous hurts that his/her behavior caused; the benefits of this progress were highlighted.

36. Encourage Physical Exercise (36)

A. The veteran/service member was assisted in developing a physical exercise routine as a means of coping with stress and developing an improved sense of well-being.

B. The veteran/service member was reinforced for following through on implementing a regular exercise regimen as a stress release technique.

C. The veteran/service member has failed to consistently implement a physical exercise routine and was encouraged to do so.

37. Encourage Medical Separation Appointments (37)

A. The service member was encouraged to attend all medical separation appointments.

B. The service member was reinforced for his/her attendance at all medical separation appointments.

C. The service member was redirected as he/she has not attended all medical separation appointments.

38. Explore Appeal Opportunities (38)

A. The service member does not agree with the medical separation finding and was provided with options for appeal.

B. The service member was urged to request a second opinion.

C. Consultation with judge advocate general or a civilian attorney was suggested to the service member.

39. Facilitate Veterans Affairs Representative Meeting (39)

A. A Veterans Affairs representative from the appropriate geographical region was contacted.

B. The veteran has been coordinated with the appropriate Veterans Affairs representative.

40. Provide Veterans Affairs Benefits Information (40)

A. The veteran was provided with the appropriate information in regard to his/her Veterans Affairs benefits.

B. The veteran was referred to a Web site for Veterans Affairs: www.vba.va.gov/vba.

41. Emphasize Importance of Veterans Affairs Meetings (41)

A. The importance of attending all Veterans Affairs medical appointments was stressed to the veteran.

B. The importance of attending compensation evaluations was stressed to the veteran.

C. The importance of attending regular health care appointments was stressed to the veteran.

D. The veteran has attended all scheduled appointments and was provided with positive feedback in this area.

E. The veteran has not attended all scheduled appointments and was reminded to do so.

PRE-DEPLOYMENT STRESS

SERVICE MEMBER PRESENTATION

1. Overwhelmed with Preparation (1)*

A. The service member complains of feeling overwhelmed with the amount of preparation involved prior to deployment.

B. The service member has been unable to juggle the variety of preparations necessary for deployment.

C. As treatment has progressed, the service member feels more capable of preparing for his/her deployment.

2. Emotional Withdrawal (2)

A. The service member reports uncharacteristic emotional withdrawal from his/her loved ones prior to deployment.

B. The service member has struggled to express his/her emotions to his/her loved ones.

C. The service member tends to isolate himself/herself from others.

D. As treatment has progressed, the service member has been more emotionally available to his/her loved ones.

3. Decreased Communication (3)

A. The service member reports declining communication with loved ones.

B. The service member has found it difficult to express his/her emotions to his/her loved ones.

C. The service member has improved his/her communication with loved ones as he/she prepares to deploy.

4. Decreased Intimacy (4)

A. Although the service member is able to communicate with his/her loved ones, his/her thoughts and feelings are very surface oriented.

B. The service member has struggled to express feelings of intimacy toward his/her loved ones.

C. The service member finds it hard to tell others that he/she loves them.

D. As treatment has progressed, the service member has expressed his/her intimate feelings toward loved ones.

5. Anxiety about Injury (5)

A. The service member noted that he/she has become anxious and fearful about being injured or killed during deployment.

B. The service member feels paralyzed by his/her pattern of anxiety and fear.

C. As treatment has progressed, the service member's level of anxiety has greatly decreased, and he/she is more at ease with deployment.

---

*The numbers in parentheses correlate to the number of the Behavioral Definition statement in the companion chapter with the same title in *The Veterans and Active Duty Military Psychotherapy Treatment Planner* (Moore and Jongsma) by John Wiley & Sons, 2009.

6. Anxiety about "Unknown" Nature of Deployment (6)

A. The service member reports that he/she has many uncertainties about his/her deployment.

B. The service member has not been advised about specific aspects of his/her deployment.

C. The service member reports anxiety about what will occur during his/her deployment.

D. As treatment has progressed, the service member has become more at ease with the uncertainties of the upcoming deployment.

7. Financial Worries (7)

A. The service member complains of significant worries related to finances while deployed.

B. The service member is uncertain about how his/her loved ones will be able to cope financially during his/her deployment.

C. As treatment has progressed, the service member feels more at ease with how financial needs will be met.

8. Guilt about Leaving (8)

A. The service member reports a sense of guilt about leaving loved ones behind.

B. The service member reflected that he/she wishes he/she did not have to leave his/her loved ones.

C. As treatment has progressed, the service member has come to see leaving loved ones behind as a necessary part of his/her service.

INTERVENTIONS IMPLEMENTED

1. Assess Pre-Deployment Stress (1)[*]

A. The service member's level of pre-deployment stress was assessed.

B. The service member was asked to gauge his/her stress on a scale of 1 (no stress) to 100 (complete stress).

C. The factors that seem to increase and decrease the service member's stress were assessed.

D. Active listening was used as the service member described the extent and nature of his/her stress.

E. The service member struggled to identify specifics about his/her stress and probing questions were asked to help provide clarity.

2. Prioritize Stressors (2)

A. The service member was asked to create a list of all pre-deployment stressors that he/she must take care of.

B. The service member was assisted with identifying examples of possible pre-deployment stressors, including financial concerns, insecurity regarding loss of an intimate relationship, fear of injury or death, etc.

C. The service member was assisted in rating his/her stressors from the most to the least stressful.

---

[*]The numbers in parentheses correlate to the number of the Therapeutic Intervention statement in the companion chapter with the same title in *The Veterans and Active Duty Military Psychotherapy Treatment Planner* (Moore and Jongsma) by John Wiley & Sons, 2009.

D. The service member was supported as he/she identified and rated his/her stressors.

E. The service member was defensive about identifying stressors and was urged to do so as he/she is able.

3. Apply Military Problem-Solving Process (3)

A. The service member was taught problem-solving skills that involve identifying the problem, brainstorming solutions, evaluating options, implementing action, and evaluating results.

B. The service member was assigned "Applying Problem-Solving to Interpersonal Conflict" in the *Adult Psychotherapy Homework Planner,* 2nd ed. (Jongsma).

C. The service member was reinforced as he/she verbalized an understanding of the problem-solving skill techniques.

D. Role-playing was used to help the service member apply problem-solving techniques to daily problems in his/her life.

E. The service member has not internalized the problem-solving skills and was provided with remedial assistance in this area.

4. Assess Pre-Deployment Anxiety (4)

A. The service member's level of anxiety related to deployment was assessed.

B. The service member was asked to identify his/her anxiety symptoms in regard to the pre-deployment phase.

C. The service member was asked about his/her pre-deployment anxiety in regard to apprehension about being injured, being away from loved ones for an extended period of time, or the loss of privacy.

D. Active listening was provided as the service member talked about his/her level of anxiety.

E. The service member was noted to have a low degree of anxiety regarding pre-deployment matters.

F. The service member was noted to have a high degree of anxiety regarding pre-deployment matters.

5. Normalize Fears (5)

A. The service member was reassured that most service members feel fearful at some point prior to deployment.

B. The service member was reinforced as he/she commented on the normal level of concern that he/she is experiencing.

C. As the service member sees his/her level of anxiety to be much more than typical, the focus of the treatment was switched to his/her general anxiety symptoms.

6. Assign Conversation with Other Service Members (6)

A. The service member was assigned to talk to other service members preparing for deployment about these feelings.

B. The service member was assigned to talk to service members who have returned from deployment about these feelings.

C. The service member has talked with other service members, and his/her findings were reviewed and processed.

D. The service member has not yet talked with other service members about pre-deployment stress and was redirected to do so.

7. Assign Talk with Chaplain (7)

A. The service member was assigned to talk with his/her chaplain to address any spiritual concerns he/she may be having about the deployment.

B. The service member has talked with his/her chaplain about spiritual matters related to the deployment and reported that this has been helpful; his/her experience was processed.

C. The service member has talked with his/her chaplain about spiritual concerns but did not find this to be helpful; he/she was urged to try again with the option of going to a different chaplain.

D. The service member has not talked to a chaplain about spiritual matters related to the deployment and was redirected to do so.

8. Link to Community Resources (8)

A. The service member was linked to community resources that can help the family during difficult times.

B. The service member was encouraged to use community resources to assist the family in difficult times.

C. The service member was reminded that he/she has helped to support community resources (i.e., through taxes or United Way donations, etc).

D. The service member was reinforced for his/her courage in asking for help when needed.

E. The service member has declined to utilize community resources and was reminded about their availability if he/she sees the need in the future.

9. Refer to Military OneSource (9)

A. The service member was provided with the phone number for Military OneSource: 1-888-342-9647.

B. The service member was encouraged to provide the Military OneSource number to his/her loved ones.

10. Create a Budget (10)

A. The service member was referred to a financial counselor at his/her local base/post to assist with creating a budget.

B. The service member was assigned "Plan a Budget" from the *Adult Psychotherapy Homework Planner,* 2nd ed. (Jongsma).

C. The service member was reinforced for his/her budget planning.

D. The service member was reinforced for adherence to his/her identified budget.

E. The service member has not planned and maintained a budget and was reminded to do so.

11. Include Significant Other in Financial Planning (11)

A. The service member was encouraged to include his/her significant other in the financial planning.

B. The service member was reminded to make sure that he/she gets support from his/her significant other in regard to the budget plans.

C. Contingencies for financial hardships were identified as an important aspect of the budget process.

D. The service member was reinforced for his/her comprehensive budget plan that was developed with his/her significant other.

E. The service member was provided with additional encouragement, as he/she has not developed a budget plan that can be supported by his/her significant other and one that allows for unexpected financial hardships.

12. Use and Maintain Budget (12)

A. The service member was encouraged to adhere to the budget by making it part of his/her daily routine prior to deployment.

B. The service member was assigned to review his/her budget with his/her significant other weekly for the first few months of deployment.

C. The service member was reinforced for adhering to the budget.

D. The service member has not adhered to the budget and was encouraged to do so.

13. Educate about Servicemembers Civil Relief Act (13)

A. The service member was educated about the Servicemembers Civil Relief Act (SCRA).

B. The service member was encouraged to identify whether he/she may qualify for reduced interest payments and payment deferments.

C. The service member was reinforced for his/her use of the Servicemembers Civil Relief Act.

D. The service member has not utilized the Servicemembers Civil Relief Act and was reminded about this helpful policy.

14. Discourage Time Away from Family (14)

A. The service member was encouraged to avoid the temptation to spend free time with friends or on activities that only he/she enjoys.

B. The service member was encouraged to spend time with family members prior to deployment.

C. The service member was reinforced for his/her use of free time with family.

D. The service member was noted to be spending most of his/her free time away from family and was encouraged to develop greater balance in this area.

15. Assign Whole-Family Activities (15)

A. The service member was encouraged to participate in activities that involved the entire family (i.e., going to the beach or spending time at the park).

B. The service member was assigned "When Can We Be Together?" in the *Brief Family Therapy Homework Planner* (Bevilacqua and Dattilio).

C. The service member has developed whole-family activities and was reinforced for this.

D. The service member continues to struggle to incorporate the entire family into activities, and was provided with remedial feedback in this area.

16. Assist with Boundary Setting (16)

A. The service member was encouraged to set clear boundaries with extended family and friends regarding visiting and social obligations in the weeks leading up to deployment.

B. The service member role-played how to set clear boundaries with extended family and friends regarding visiting and social obligations in the weeks leading up to deployment.

C. The service member was reinforced for setting clear rules regarding social obligations in the weeks leading up to deployment.

D. The service member has not set clear boundaries for social obligations in the weeks leading up to deployment and was reminded to do so.

17. Explore Unresolved Relationship Problems (17)

A. The service member was assisted in resolving unresolved marital/relationship problems that may resurface during the deployment.

B. The service member was assigned "How Can We Meet Each Other's Needs and Desires?" in the *Adult Psychotherapy Homework Planner*, 2nd ed. (Jongsma).

C. The service member has identified unresolved marital/relationship issues and was reinforced for working to resolve these concerns.

D. The service member denies any unresolved marital/relationship problems, and he/she was reminded to deal with these concerns as they may appear.

18. Conduct Couple's/Marital Session (18)

A. A couple's/marital session was conducted for the purpose of resolving indentified problems.

B. The couple's therapy was quite focused, keeping in mind that the number of meetings may be limited.

C. The couple's session was more directive in nature, due to the limited time available to resolving these concerns.

D. The couple was reinforced for working to resolve marital concerns.

19. Encourage Increased Affection (19)

A. The service member was encouraged to increase levels of verbal and physical affection during the weeks preceding deployment.

B. The service member was reinforced for his/her increased verbal and physical affection during the weeks preceding deployment.

C. The service member has not significantly increased levels of verbal and physical affection during the weeks preceding deployment and was reminded to do so.

20. Encourage Reassurance of Commitment and Love (20)

A. The service member was encouraged to ensure his/her significant other of his/her commitment and love of him/her.

B. The service member was reinforced for increased communication with loved ones as a means to strengthen intimacy.

C. The service member has not increased his/her communication with loved ones and was reminded how this can strengthen intimacy.

21. Educate about Alcohol Use (21)

A. The service member was educated on how alcohol use can increase anxiety and stress, disrupt sleep, decrease sexual performance, and create anger and resentment from loved ones in the family.

B. The service member's alcohol use was monitored for concerns related to abuse.

C. The service member was reinforced for his/her decreased alcohol intake.

D. The service member has not decreased his/her alcohol intake and was reminded to do so.

22. Assign Research on Communication Modes Available (22)

A. The service member was assigned to research the availability and primary modes of communication used in his/her deployment site.

B. The service member was encouraged to review the level of Internet and telephone access.

C. The service member has obtained information about communication modes available and was encouraged to inform the family of these opportunities.

D. The service member has not sought out information about available communication modes in his/her deployment site and was reminded to obtain this information.

23. Create Communication Calendar (23)

A. The service member was instructed to create a communication calendar, in collaboration with his/her family.

B. The service member has developed a detailed list of basic times that he/she can call, e-mail, or write.

C. Loved ones were reminded that communication times may change due to unforeseen circumstances.

D. The service member has not created a communication calendar and was reminded to do so.

24. Explain about Communication Lapses (24)

A. The service member was directed to explain to his/her family that if he/she is not heard from for a period of time, this does not mean that he/she has been injured or killed but is most likely due to communication blackouts or downed networks.

B. The service member has talked to family members about communication patterns and the possibility of periods of inability to communicate.

C. The service member has not talked to family about communication lapses and was reminded to do so.

25. Preplan for Special Occasions (25)

A. The service member was encouraged to preplan for special occasions.

B. The service member was encouraged to preorder gifts and flowers for special occasions, such as a child's birthday, wedding anniversary, etc.

C. The service member has preordered items for delivery to his/her loved ones while deployed and was reinforced for this display of planning.

D. The service member has not preplanned for special occasions and was reminded to do so.

26. Educate about Children's Understanding (26)

A. The service member was educated about how young children may not understand the concept of the length of time of a deployment.

B. The service member displayed understanding that children may need different opportunities to understand the length of deployment.

C. The service member has a clear understanding of how his/her child(ren) will understand the concept of the length of his/her deployment.

27. Create Visual Aids to Track Length of Deployment (27)

A. The service member was assisted in brainstorming visual aids that will assist his/her child in keeping track of when the service member will return home.

B. The service member was provided with examples of tracking the length of time until a parent returns (e.g., placing 365 pieces of candy in a jar, allowing one piece to be taken out every day for a one-year deployment).

C. The service member has created a visual aid that will assist his/her child in keeping track of when the service member will return; this visual aid was reviewed and reinforced.

D. The service member has not created a helpful, age-appropriate visual aid to assist his/her child in understanding the length of time until the service member returns and was reminded to do so.

28. Visit Military Legal Department (28)

A. The service member was directed to visit the military legal department (i.e., judge advocate general) at his/her local base/post to review and update documents.

B. The service member was encouraged to review and update his/her will and/or power of attorney.

C. The service member was encouraged to include his/her spouse/legal guardian in this process.

D. The service member has updated his/her proper documents and was reinforced for this.

E. The service member has avoided updating his/her proper documents and was reminded about this necessary task.

29. Consider Limited Power of Attorney (29)

A. The service member was advised about options regarding a limited power of attorney that would provide him/her with greater protection in the event of a separation, divorce, or other extreme situation.

B. The service member was advised about how a limited power of attorney can give some rights but not others (i.e., pay certain bills or sell a vehicle but not sell a house).

C. The pros and cons of different levels of power of attorney were reviewed with the service member.

D. The service member was assisted in deciding the degree of power of attorney he/she was willing to grant.

30. Encourage Decisions on Continuing Types of Contracts (30)

A. The service member was directed to review the continuing types of contracts he/she currently has and whether these should continue during deployment.

B. The service member was directed to review specific types of continuing contracts, such as an apartment lease or a cellular telephone contract.

C. The service member was assisted in deciding what to do about continuing contracts during a deployment.

D. The service member has not made decisions about continuing contracts and was reminded about taking care of responsibilities.

31. Copy Important Documents (31)

A. The service member was instructed to copy important documents to take on his/her deployment.

B. The service member was encouraged to provide a copy of important documents to his/her spouse or legal representative.

C. The service member was encouraged to consider specific documents that should be reviewed or copied, including birth certificates, immunizations, medical records, passports, etc.

D. The service member has made arrangements in regard to his/her important documents and was reinforced for this.

E. The service member has not made arrangements for his/her important documents and was reminded to do so.

32. Coordinate Transitional Medications (32)

A. The service member was directed to coordinate for his/her medications that may be necessary during the transition from his/her stateside unit until settling into the deployment location.

B. The service member has coordinated for his/her medications during the transition into deployment and was reinforced for taking care of these types of details.

C. The service member has not coordinated for his/her transition medications and was reminded to do so.

33. Provide American Red Cross Information (33)

A. The service member was provided with information about the American Red Cross in order to facilitate family contact in an emergency.

B. The service member was directed to provide information about the American Red Cross to his/her family.

SEPARATION AND DIVORCE

VETERAN/SERVICE MEMBER PRESENTATION

1. Thoughts of Ending the Relationship (1)[*]

A. One partner reported having thoughts about ending the relationship.

B. Both partners reported having thoughts about wanting to end the relationship.

C. The partners reported having strong thoughts about ending the relationship but have not taken any specific steps to do so.

D. As treatment has progressed, thoughts about ending the relationship have ceased.

2. Separation (2)

A. One partner is planning to move out of the home to establish separate living arrangements, due to dissatisfaction with the relationship.

B. One partner has moved out of the home and has established separate living arrangements, due to dissatisfaction with the relationship.

C. The partners have become less connected with each other since the separation began.

D. The partners expressed feelings of hurt, disappointment, anxiety, and depression related to the separation.

E. The partners have become more motivated to resolve differences since the separation began.

F. The partners have begun living together again.

3. Legal Proceedings (3)

A. One partner has filed a divorce petition.

B. Child custody proceedings have been initiated.

C. The partners expressed feelings of sadness surrounding the legal proceedings related to the divorce.

D. The partners expressed feelings of anger and resentment over the legal proceedings.

E. The partners tend to blame each other for the legal complications related to the divorce.

F. As the partners have resolved conflicts, legal proceedings have been discontinued.

4. Confusion about Children (4)

A. The partners expressed confusion about how to best deal with the feelings that the children are experiencing about the marital crisis.

B. The estranged partners have radically different ideas about how to deal with the children's emotional struggles.

C. The partners often criticize each other for how each deals with the children's feelings.

D. The partners continue to be on the path of separation and divorce but feel more competent about how to cope with the children's feelings.

[*]The numbers in parentheses correlate to the number of the Behavioral Definition statement in the companion chapter with the same title in *The Veterans and Active Duty Military Psychotherapy Treatment Planner* (Moore and Jongsma) by John Wiley & Sons, 2009.

E. The partners have developed a mutually agreeable plan for dealing with the children's feelings and behavior.

5. Emotional Reaction to Loss of Relationship (5)

A. One partner identified feelings of anger, hurt, and fear about the breakup of the relationship.

B. Both partners reported feelings of anger, hurt, and fear due to the breakup of the relationship.

C. The partners have reported having fears of having to face life as a single person.

D. The partners tend to blame each other for the emotions that result from the breakup of the relationship.

E. As the relationship has improved, there is less anger, hurt, and fear expressed.

F. The partners continue on the path of separation and divorce but have less of an emotional reaction to the loss of the relationship.

6. Spiritual Conflict (6)

A. One partner has identified experiencing spiritual conflict due to the breaking of the marriage vows.

B. Both partners describe spiritual conflict regarding breaking of the marriage vows.

C. The partners have resolved their spiritual conflict by resolving the problems within the marriage.

D. The partners' spiritual conflict has lessened.

7. Grief (7)

A. One partner described feelings of depression as part of the grief process related to the loss of the relationship.

B. Both partners described feelings of depression as part of the grief process related to the loss of the relationship.

C. One partner displayed evidence of social withdrawal as part of the grief process related to loss of the relationship.

D. As the veteran/service member has worked through the grief related to the loss of the relationship, depression and social withdrawal have decreased.

8. Uncertainty about Remaining in Military (8)

A. The service member indicated that he/she has an impending change of duty station move.

B. The service member indicated concern that he/she will be separated from his/her children and/or partner as a result of a change of duty station move.

C. The service member is uncertain about whether he/she should remain in the military due to the risk of being separated from his/her partner and/or children.

D. The service member has come to terms with the nature of his/her military career and the potential for being separated from his/her family members.

E. The service member has indicated that he/she is not willing to risk the potential of being separated from his/her family and expects to terminate his/her military service.

INTERVENTIONS IMPLEMENTED

1. Assess for Extramarital Problems (1)*

A. Each partner's emotional health was assessed.

B. Each partner's physical health was assessed.

C. Each partner's vocational stability was assessed.

D. Each partner's religious conflict over divorce issues was assessed.

E. Extramarital concerns were noted to exist.

F. No extramarital concerns appear to be affecting the current relationship.

2. Postpone Separation until Extramarital Problems Resolved (2)

A. The couple was identified as experiencing significant problems unrelated to the marriage.

B. Each partner was encouraged to postpone any decision about separation until problems unrelated to the marriage have been addressed.

C. The partners were supported for agreeing to postpone any decisions about separation until after problems unrelated to the marriage have been addressed.

D. The partners are pursuing significant changes with the marriage despite needing to resolve extramarital problems and were encouraged to change this focus.

3. Establish Type of Treatment (3)

A. The partners identified that they wanted to work together to try to resolve the marriage problems and were advised to begin conjoint marital therapy.

B. The partners identified individual issues that needed to be treated in order to resolve the marital issues and were referred for individual treatment.

C. The partners indicated no interest in conjoint or individual counseling to improve the marriage and were advised to begin predivorce treatment.

D. The partners were uncertain about the commitment to the relationship and the type of treatment that might be necessary; this was selected as the focus of current sessions.

4. Assess Steps toward Divorce (4)

A. Each partner was assessed for the steps that have been taken toward divorce.

B. Each partner was administered the Marital Status Inventory (Weiss and Cerreto).

C. Each partner was interviewed about his or her sense of hope and vision of the future for the relationship.

5. Assess Developmental Stage of Marriage (5)

A. The partners were assessed for what developmental stage of marriage they are in.

B. The partners were noted to be in the early-marriage stage.

C. The partners were noted to be in the couple-with-young-children stage.

D. The partners were noted to be in the long-term-marriage stage.

E. The developmental stage of the marriage was reflected to the couple.

---

*The numbers in parentheses correlate to the number of the Therapeutic Intervention statement in the companion chapter with the same title in *The Veterans and Active Duty Military Psychotherapy Treatment Planner* (Moore and Jongsma) by John Wiley & Sons, 2009.

6. Assess History of the Marriage (6)

A. The recent history of the marriage was assessed.

B. As the history of the marriage was assessed, changes in the respective partners' happiness were noted.

C. As the history of the marriage was assessed, the timing of changes regarding the expectations for the marriage was noted.

D. As the history of the marriage was assessed, the timing of thoughts about divorce was noted.

E. The changes occurring during the history of the marriage were reflected to the partners.

7. Assess Current Satisfaction (7)

A. The partners' current satisfaction with the marital relationship was assessed.

B. The partners were administered self-report instruments to assess their current satisfaction with the marital relationship (e.g., Relationship Satisfaction Questionnaire [Burnes]; Marital Adjustment Test [Locke and Wallace]; or Dyadic Adjustment Scale [Spanier]).

C. The partners' current satisfaction with the marital relationship was reflected to the couple.

D. The partners have not completed the self-report instruments regarding marital satisfaction and were redirected to do so.

8. Assess for Affairs (8)

A. Each partner was asked about involvement in an affair.

B. The partners were questioned about their suspicion of extramarital affairs.

C. There is a strong suspicion about extramarital affairs, and this was brought out into the open.

D. It was noted that the partners acknowledged a history of extramarital affairs.

E. It was reflected to the partners that there are no indications of presence or suspicion of extramarital affairs.

9. Assess for Violence/Intimidation (9)

A. In individual sessions, the partners were assessed for the experience of violence or intimidation in the relationship.

B. Violence and intimidation were identified as existing within the relationship, and the partners were advised about the appropriate treatment for these concerns.

C. It was reflected to the partners that there was no evidence of violence or intimidation within the relationship.

10. Review Extended Family History (10)

A. Each partner's extended family history was reviewed with regard to the incidence of divorce.

B. Each partner was asked to verbalize how the extended family history may be affecting the decision to divorce.

C. The review of the extended family history indicated strong prohibitions about divorce, and the effects of this expectation were noted.

D. The review of the extended family history indicated multiple divorces and little expectation for marriage to last, and this was reflected to the partners.

11. Identify Subcultural Influence (11)

A. Each partner was asked about subcultural identification (e.g., ethnicity, religious affiliation).

B. Discussion was held about the influence of the subcultural identification on attitudes about divorce.

C. A conflict between behavior and beliefs was identified, and the partners were assisted in facilitating a resolution of this conflict.

D. The partners denied any influence of the subculture identification on the attitudes toward divorce and were encouraged to monitor this area.

12. Identify Impact of Military (12)

A. Each partner was asked to describe how the military has impacted the marriage/relationship.

B. Active listening was used as each partner described the impact of military involvement on the marriage.

C. The partners were helped to process the content of how the military has impacted the relationship considering each other's prospective.

D. The partners were assisted in using problem-solving problems techniques to address the impact of military service on the relationship.

13. Identify Personal Responsibility (13)

A. Each partner was asked to turn to the other and identify his or her own personal contributions to the downfall of the relationship.

B. Each partner was asked to turn to the other and express personal attempts to make the relationship work.

C. Each partner was reinforced for taking significant responsibility for the relationship.

D. The partners tended to take varying levels of responsibility for the relationship, and this was reflected to them.

E. Both partners take very little responsibility for the relationship, and this was reflected to them.

14. Verbalize Pros and Cons (14)

A. Each partner was asked to verbalize his/her point of view on the pros and cons of preserving the relationship.

B. Each partner was asked to verbalize his/her point of view on the pros and cons of separation or divorce.

C. As the pros and cons of preserving the relationship versus divorce were reviewed, the partners' views were noted to be quite congruent.

D. As the pros and cons of preserving the relationship versus divorce were reviewed, the partners' views were noted to be incongruent in their assessment.

15. Review Implications of Divorce (15)

A. Each partner was asked to verbalize the emotional implications of divorce.

B. Each partner was asked to identify the implications of divorce for the rest of the family (including children).

C. Each partner was asked to identify the religious implications of divorce.

D. Each partner was asked to identify the social implications of divorce.

E. As each partner reviewed the implications of divorce, the other partner was asked to paraphrase the first person's statements in each area to increase understanding and empathy between the two partners.

F. Paraphrasing of each partner's identified implications of divorce was verified for accuracy with the partner.

16. Sensitize to Effects on Children (16)

A. The partners were directed to discuss the anticipated effects of separation and divorce on their children.

B. The upheaval that divorce causes for children was highlighted as the partners discussed the anticipated effects on their children.

C. The partners tended to minimize the effects of separation and divorce on the children and were provided with additional feedback in this area.

17. Assign Reading Regarding Children and Divorce (17)

A. The parents were assigned to read information about children and divorce.

B. The following texts were recommended to the parents: *How to Help Your Child Overcome Your Divorce* (Benedek and Brown), *The Parent's Book about Divorce* (Gardener), and *Mom's House, Dad's House* (Ricci).

C. The partners have read the information on children and divorce, and the salient points were reviewed.

D. The partners have not done any reading regarding children and divorce and were redirected to do so.

18. Emphasize Children's Best Interest (18)

A. The partners were asked to verbally contract with each other and the therapist that all decisions in the divorce and separation process will be made with the best interests of the children as the paramount concern.

B. The partners were supported for verbally contracting with each other and the therapist that all decisions in the divorce and separation process will be made with the best interests of the children as the paramount concern.

C. As the separation and divorce process has unfolded, the partners were provided with positive feedback about keeping the best interests of the children as the paramount concern.

D. The partners were confronted when they deviated from the best interests of the children as the paramount concern in the divorce and separation process.

19. Role-Play Informing the Children (19)

A. Role-playing techniques were used to help the partners rehearse telling the children together about the impending divorce.

B. The partners were prompted to include the following elements as they tell the children about the decision to divorce: They both love the children; they plan to divorce; the divorce is not the children's fault; there is nothing that the children can do to get the parents back together; and they will continue to love and see the children.

C. As the partners role-played how to tell the children about the divorce, they were provided with feedback and redirection.

20. Review the Telling of the Children (20)

A. The experience of the partners telling the children about the divorce or separation was reviewed.

B. Probing questions were used to identify the need for further explanation or support for the children.

C. The partners were pressed for an agreement on the further needs that the children have regarding explanation or support.

21. Describe Destructive Anger (21)

A. Each partner was asked to describe times when his/her own anger was destructive to the other partner.

B. Support and feedback were provided as the partners reviewed destructive anger experiences.

22. Clarify Therapist's Role (22)

A. The therapist's role was clarified to the partners, with an emphasis on aiding the family in making the separation or divorce transition and helping both partners deal with the turbulent emotions experienced during this process.

B. An emphasis was placed on the therapist's role as serving the best interest of all family members.

C. It was emphasized to the partners that the therapist would not be a mediator or judge.

D. The partners were assessed for their understanding of the therapist's role.

E. As the partners have attempted to place the therapist in the role of mediator or judge, they were redirected.

23. Recognize Gradations of Anger (23)

A. The partners were taught to recognize the gradations of anger.

B. The partners were taught about when they need to take steps to cool down before self-control becomes eroded.

C. The partners were taught cool-down techniques (e.g., relaxation and deep breathing exercises, take time-out for 15 minutes, go for a walk).

D. The partners were assessed for their understanding of the gradations of anger and when they need to take steps to cool down.

E. Feedback was provided to the partners regarding their use of cool-down techniques when becoming too angry.

24. Identify "Hot Topic" Responses (24)

A. Each partner was asked to identify topics that seem to be "hot" and cause increased emotional responses.

B. After identifying "hot topics," the partners were directed to practice in-session cognitive rehearsal about how to cope with such topics adaptively.

C. Support and feedback were provided as the partners practiced how to deal with "hot topics."

D. As the partners reviewed their adaptive attempts to deal with "hot topics," they were provided with additional feedback and reinforcement.

25. Practice the Time-out Technique (25)

A. The partners were directed to practice using time-out (agree to pause in the conversation when anger begins to elevate) while discussing an emotional topic in session.

B. Support and feedback were provided to the partners as they practiced using time-out.

C. The partners' ongoing use of time-out during emotional discussions was reviewed and processed.

26. Facilitate Discussion of Separation (26)

A. The partners were advised to obtain legal advice before agreeing to a separation.

B. The discussion regarding a separation was facilitated.

C. The partners were assisted in making a decision about when one partner will move out of the house.

D. Because the partners do not have the financial ability to maintain two homes, the details of an in-house separation were negotiated.

27. Facilitate Agreement about Acceptable Contact (27)

A. The partners were assisted in developing an agreement about what forms of contact are acceptable and prohibited.

B. The partners were supported as they identified typical types of contact that are acceptable during the separation and divorce (e.g., planning around children's activities).

C. The partners were assisted as they identified typical prohibited activities during the separation and divorce (e.g., affection displays, sexual intimacy).

D. The partners were assessed for their adherence to the contract regarding acceptable and prohibited types of contact.

28. Refer for Individual Therapy for Anger and Planning (28)

A. Individual sessions were used on an as-needed basis to allow each partner to express anger, disappointment, and disapproval about what has happened during the separation and divorce.

B. The expressions of hurt were balanced with an elicitation of each partner's goals for coping with short-term and long-term situations with the other partner and children.

C. The partners were provided with feedback regarding emotional expression and goals for coping.

29. Educate about Marriage Dissolution Choices (29)

A. The partners were informed about the choices available for dissolving the marriage.

B. The partners were taught about litigation, which is an adversarial legal process.

C. The partners were taught about arbitration, involving a third party chosen by both partners, who makes decisions regarding property and custody.

D. The partners were taught about mediation, in which the partners come to their own agreement with the help of a trained mediator.

E. The partners displayed an understanding of the options for dissolution of the marriage and have selected a specific option.

30. Facilitate Coparenting Agreement (30)

A. The partners were assisted in developing a coparenting agreement.

B. The partners' coparenting agreement was formulated to include a pledge that the children's primary residence will be established in their best interests.

C. The partner's coparenting agreement was formulated to include a pledge that neither parent will belittle the other parent or that parent's family members in front of the children.

D. The partner's coparenting agreement was formulated to include promises that the parents will avoid placing the children in loyalty conflicts.

E. The coparenting agreement that was facilitated included an agreement regarding the terms of financial support for the children.

F. The partners have not come to an agreement on coparenting and were provided with additional assistance and feedback in this area.

31. Assist in Social Network Development (31)

A. Using individual sessions, each partner was assisted in developing a varied social network.

B. The partners were assisted in developing skills for asking others to socialize; beginning or increasing involvement in club, community, volunteer, and/or church activities; and dating.

C. Each partner was reinforced for developing a more varied social network.

D. Remedial assistance was provided for the partner who has struggled to develop a varied social network.

32. Ensure Attendance to Children's Emotional Needs (32)

A. A parent-child session was used to ensure that the children's emotional needs are being attended to.

B. The parents were reinforced for giving appropriate attention to the children's emotional needs.

C. Gaps in attending to the children's emotional needs were identified, and the parents were assisted in attending to these needs.

33. Encourage Support Group (33)

A. The partners were encouraged to attend a local divorce support group.

B. The partners were encouraged to attend a self-help group (e.g., Parents Without Partners).

C. One partner was directed to attend a local divorce support group.

D. One partner was directed to attend a self-help group (e.g., Parents Without Partners).

E. The use of group support options was processed.

34. Assess Affect on Religious/Spiritual Connections (34)

A. The affect of the divorce on either partner's religious and spiritual connections was assessed.

B. As one partner has identified problems with religious or spiritual connection due to the divorce, assistance was provided in problem solving how to reestablish these connections (e.g., switching parishes, investigating congregations that welcome divorced members).

C. The partners were supported for maintaining healthy religious and spiritual connections.

35. Encourage Decision about Remaining in Military (35)

A. The partners were encouraged to decide whether they see remaining in the military as an acceptable option.

B. The partners were asked to assess whether the strain that being in the military entails is acceptable.

C. The partners have decided that remaining in the military is the best option, and they were supported for this decision.

D. The partners have decided that leaving the military is the best option, and they were supported in this decision.

E. The partners are still uncertain about whether to remain in the military and were urged to make a more definite decision in this area.

SEXUAL ASSAULT BY ANOTHER SERVICE MEMBER

SERVICE MEMBER PRESENTATION

1. Thoughts Dominated by the Sexual Assault (1)[*]

A. The service member described experiencing intrusive, distressing thoughts or images that recall the sexual assault and its associated intense emotional response.

B. The service member reported experiencing an inability to manage the thoughts about the sexual assault.

C. The service member reported experiencing less difficulty with intrusive, distressing thoughts of the traumatic event.

D. The service member reported no longer experiencing intrusive, distressing thoughts of the traumatic event.

2. Extreme Emotional Response (2)

A. The service member described a pattern of extreme emotional reactivity when thinking or talking about the sexual assault.

B. The service member described a pattern of irritability that was not present before the sexual assault.

C. The service member reported incidents of becoming angry and losing his/her temper easily, resulting in explosive outbursts.

D. The service member's emotional reactivity has diminished somewhat as the intensity of the emotions have lessened.

E. The service member reported no recent incidents of emotional reactivity when thinking or talking about the sexual assault.

3. Sense of Betrayal (3)

A. The service member reports a sense of betrayal by his/her fellow service members.

B. The service member believes that other service members could have assisted in stopping or intervening on the sexual assault but that they choose not to do so.

C. As treatment has progressed, the service member has gained a realistic outlook about the level of trust toward other service members.

4. General Distrust of All Service Members (4)

A. The service member reports a general pattern of distrust for all individuals associated with the military.

B. The service member reported that his/her distrust extends beyond those who were directly or indirectly involved in the sexual assault incident.

---

[*]The numbers in parentheses correlate to the number of the Behavioral Definition statement in the companion chapter with the same title in *The Veterans and Active Duty Military Psychotherapy Treatment Planner* (Moore and Jongsma) by John Wiley & Sons, 2009.

C. As treatment has progressed, the service member has come to understand how to differentiate those service members who can be trusted from those who cannot be trusted.

D. The service member displayed a more realistic point of view regarding trust versus distrust of other service members.

5. Anger and Resentment (5)

A. The service member reports a pattern of anger and resentment toward his/her unit and superiors.

B. The service member reports a pattern of anger and resentment toward the military.

C. As treatment has progressed, the service member has been able to focus his/her anger toward the party responsible for the assault.

D. The service member has learned to manage his/her pattern of anger and resentment in a healthy manner.

6. Intimacy Problems (6)

A. The service member has a pattern of extreme difficulty in forming intimate relationships with others.

B. As the service member begins to form intimate relationships with others, he/she experiences feelings of anxiety and avoidance.

C. As the service member has begun to work through his/her experiences of abuse, he/she reported less anxiety associated with current intimate relationships.

D. The service member no longer experiences anxiety and avoidance in current intimate relationships.

7. Sexual Dysfunction (7)

A. The service member reported an inability to enjoy sexual contact with a desired partner.

B. The service member experiences feelings of anxiety and tension when sexual contact with a desired partner is initiated.

C. The service member reported that he/she had successful and enjoyable sexual contact with a desired partner.

D. The service member no longer experiences feelings of anxiety during sexual contact with a desired partner and reports satisfaction in this area.

INTERVENTIONS IMPLEMENTED

1. Explore Sexual Assault History (1)[*]

A. The service member was encouraged to tell as much of the details of the assault as he/she is comfortable with.

B. The nature of the sexual assault on the service member was assessed, including recency, connection to the perpetrator, criminal investigation, avoidance behaviors, and overall psychological health.

---

[*]The numbers in parentheses correlate to the number of the Therapeutic Intervention statement in the companion chapter with the same title in *The Veterans and Active Duty Military Psychotherapy Treatment Planner* (Moore and Jongsma) by John Wiley & Sons, 2009.

C. The service member was assigned "Picturing the Place of Abuse" from the *Adult Psychotherapy Homework Planner,* 2nd ed. (Jongsma).

D. The service member was overwhelmed by feelings of sadness and shame as he/she talked about his/her sexual assault; direct support was provided.

E. It was reflected to the service member that he/she is not able to talk about the assault without becoming emotionally overwhelmed.

F. The service member was urged to share the specifics of the abuse as he/she feels safe in doing so.

2. Assess Assault Impact (2)

A. An assessment was completed of the impact the sexual assault has had on the service member's social, occupational, and interpersonal functioning.

B. The impact of the sexual assault on the service member's social, occupational, and interpersonal function was noted to be fairly mild, and this was reflected to the service member.

C. The impact of the sexual assault on the service member's social, occupational, and interpersonal function was noted to be moderate, and this was reflected to the service member.

D. The impact of the sexual assault on the service member's social, occupational, and interpersonal function was noted to be severe, and this was reflected to the service member.

3. Refer for Medication Evaluation (3)

A. The service member was referred for a medication evaluation to assist with sleep onset and maintenance.

B. The service member was referred for a medication evaluation to assist with depression or anxiety symptoms.

C. The service member was reinforced as he/she agreed to follow through on the medication evaluation.

D. The service member was strongly opposed to being placed on medication to help stabilize his/her moods and emotional distress; his/her objections were processed.

4. Monitor Medications (4)

A. The service member's response to the psychotropic medication was discussed in today's therapy session.

B. The service member has reported that the medication has helped to stabilize his/her moods and decrease the intensity of his/her feelings; he/she was directed to share this information with the prescribing clinician.

C. The service member reports little to no improvement in his/her moods or anger control since being on the medication; he/she was directed to share this information with the prescribing clinician.

D. The service member was reinforced for consistently taking the psychotropic medication as prescribed.

E. The service member has failed to comply with taking the medication as prescribed; he/she was encouraged to take the medication as prescribed.

5. Contact Supports (5)

A. The service member was assisted in identifying and contacting community supports who could assist him/her in recovery from the sexual assault.

B. The service member was assisted in identifying and contacting family supports who could assist him/her in recovery from the sexual assault.

C. The service member has sought out support from others, and their reaction to his/her request was processed.

D. The service member's courage for asking for support was reinforced.

E. The service member has not sought out community and family supports for coping with the sexual assault and was urged to do so.

6. Contact Victim's Advocate (6)

A. The service member was urged to make contact with his/her military sexual assault victim's advocate.

B. At the service member's request, the military's sexual assault victim's advocate was talked to and directed to contact the service member.

C. During the session today, the service member was assisted in making direct contact with the military's sexual assault victim's advocate.

D. The service member has made contact with the military's sexual assault victim's advocate, and his/her experience with this contact was reviewed.

E. The service member has not made contact with the military's sexual assault victim's advocate and was redirected to do so.

7. Direct to Chaplain (7)

A. The service member was encouraged to talk with his/her unit chaplain for spiritual guidance and comfort.

B. The service member was assisted in making contact with his/her unit chaplain.

C. The service member has made contact with his/her unit chaplain, and his/her experience of spiritual guidance and comfort was reviewed and processed.

D. The service member has not sought out contact with his/her unit chaplain and was redirected to do so.

8. Locate Support Group (8)

A. The service member was provided with assistance in locating a support group of other service members who have been sexually assaulted.

B. The service member was assisted in contacting an online support group of other service members who have been sexually assaulted.

C. The service member has contacted a support group, and his/her experience was processed.

D. The service member has not contacted a support group and was redirected to do so.

9. Coordinate Contact with Military OneSource (9)

A. The service member was provided with information about how to contact the Military OneSource for free, confidential counseling from a civilian behavioral health care provider.

B. The service member was provided with the Military OneSource toll-free number: 1-800-342-9647.

C. The service member has contacted the Military OneSource for free, confidential counseling from a civilian behavioral health care provider; his/her experience with this resource was reviewed.

D. The service member has not contacted Military OneSource and was reminded about this helpful resource.

10. Develop a Supportive Environment (10)

A. Today's session focused on building a level of trust with the service member through consistent eye contact, active listening, unconditional positive regard, and warm acceptance.

B. Empathy and support were provided for the service member's expression of thoughts and feelings during today's session.

C. The service member was provided with support and feedback as he/she described his/her sexual assault.

D. Specific awareness of personal feelings that may be construed as judgmental was maintained throughout this session.

E. As the service member has remained distrustful and reluctant to share his/her underlying thoughts and feelings, he/she was provided with additional reassurance.

F. The service member verbally recognized that his/she has difficulty establishing trust because he/she has often felt let down by others in the past, and he/she was accepted for this insight.

11. Process Perpetrator Service Membership (11)

A. The service member was encouraged to discuss how the perpetrator being a fellow service member influences his/her reaction to the sexual assault.

B. Relevant concerns from the service member's reaction to the perpetrator's military status were reviewed and processed.

C. The service member was supported as he/she identified the ways in which the perpetrator's service membership affects his/her reaction to the sexual assault.

D. The service member does not see any relevant factors in regard to the perpetrator's service membership, and this was accepted at face value.

12. Assign Reading on Guilt and Shame (12)

A. The service member was assigned to read literature on guilt and shame.

B. The service member was assigned to read *Healing the Shame that Binds You* (Bradshaw).

C. The service member was assigned to read *The Gift of Guilt: Ten Steps to Freedom from Guilt Forever* (Miller).

D. The service member has read the literature on dealing with guilt and shame, and important material was processed.

E. The service member has not read the information on dealing with guilt and shame and was redirected to do so.

13. Identify Self-Blame Thoughts (13)

A. The service member was assisted in identifying any beliefs held related to self-blame for the sexual assault.

B. The service member was challenged as he/she identified feelings of self-blame for the sexual assault.

C. The beliefs of self-blame for the sexual assault were compassionately and respectfully challenged.

D. The service member does not hold any beliefs regarding self-blame for the sexual assault, and this was reinforced and supported.

14. Identify Gender Bias in Blaming within the Military (14)

A. The service member was assisted in identifying and discussing how the military culture may unknowingly blame the female victim for the sexual assault.

B. Specific examples of how the military culture may indirectly blame the female victim for the sexual assault were provided (e.g., "Women don't belong in the military"; "It's her fault for wanting to be around men all the time").

C. The service member identified his/her own experience of gender bias/blame within the military, and this was processed.

D. The service member denied any role for direct or indirect gender bias in regard to the blame for the sexual assault.

15. Assign Letter to Perpetrator (15)

A. The service member was assigned to write a letter to the perpetrator that expressed his/her feelings about the abuse.

B. The service member was assigned "A Blaming Letter and a Forgiving Letter to Perpetrator" in the *Adult Psychotherapy Homework Planner,* 2nd edition (Jongsma).

C. The service member has followed through with writing a letter to the perpetrator of the abuse and processed the confrontational letter within the session.

D. The service member has decided to send the confrontational letter to the perpetrator of the abuse; his/her expectations were processed.

E. The service member has decided to confront the perpetrator in person with the contents of the letter he/she had written; his/her expectations were processed.

F. The service member has decided against confronting the perpetrator with the contents of the letter, and this was accepted.

16. Assist with Face-to-Face Meeting (16)

A. The service member has decided to confront his/her perpetrator in a face-to-face meeting, and he/she was assisted in making plans for this meeting.

B. Chain of command was contacted about the service member's desire for a face-to-face meeting with the perpetrator.

C. The service member's expectations of a face-to-face meeting were processed.

D. The service member's experience of the face-to-face meeting was processed.

17. Use Empty-Chair Technique (17)

A. Utilizing the empty-chair technique, confrontation of the perpetrator was role-played until the service member felt comfortable with the process.

B. The service member's experience of the empty-chair technique was processed.

C. The service member has used the empty-chair technique to become more at ease with the confrontation of the perpetrator, and this progress was reinforced.

D. The service member continues to struggle with how to confront the perpetrator and was supported in this struggle.

18. Encourage Increased Contact with Others (18)

A. The service member was urged to gradually increase his/her contact with others.

B. As the service member has become comfortable with others, he/she was encouraged to share intimate details about himself/herself with the person.

C. The service member was encouraged to gradually increase the sharing of his/her personal information as the other person has been determined to be trustworthy.

D. The service member has not felt that the other person is trustworthy enough for his/her intimate personal information and was encouraged to share this only as he/she feels comfortable doing so.

19. List Positive Interactions (19)

A. The service member was urged to create a list of all positive interactions with other service members that he/she can recall.

B. The service member was assisted in developing a list of positive interactions with other service members.

C. The service member has completed his/her list of positive interactions with other service members, and this was processed.

D. The service member has not completed a list of positive interactions with service members and was redirected to do so.

20. Increase Social Interactions with the Opposite Sex (20)

A. The service member was urged to gradually become more involved in social interactions with service members of the opposite sex.

B. The service member's concerns about increased contact with service members of the opposite sex were processed and problem-solved.

C. The service member has gradually become more involved with social interactions with the opposite sex, and this progress was reinforced.

D. The service member has not become more involved in social interactions with service members of the opposite sex and was reminded to do this as he/she feels capable of doing so.

21. Teach Relaxation Techniques (21)

A. The service member was taught relaxation techniques such as imagery or progressive muscle relaxation.

B. The service member was assigned to use the relaxation techniques to relax twice a day for 10 to 20 minutes.

C. The service member was directed to use the relaxation techniques prior to and during social interactions.

D. The service member reported that regular use of the relaxation techniques has led to decreased anxiety in social situations; he/she was encouraged to continue these techniques.

E. The service member has not implemented the relaxation techniques in social situations and continues to feel quite distressed; he/she was redirected to do so.

22. Encourage Sharing Positive Feelings (22)

A. The service member was encouraged to share his/her positive feelings about an individual with that particular person.

B. The service member has shared his/her positive feelings about an individual with that person, and his/her experience was processed.

C. The service member has not shared his/her positive feelings about an individual with that person, and this resistance was processed.

23. Encourage Sharing Sexual Assault Information (23)

A. The service member was asked to select a trusted individual with whom he/she can share the intimate details of the sexual assault.

B. The service member has shared the intimate details about the sexual assault with a trusted individual; his/her experience of this exercise was processed within the session.

C. The service member has not shared the intimate details of the sexual assault with a trusted individual and was encouraged to do so as he/she feels capable.

24. Encourage Sharing about Sexual Intimacy Concerns (24)

A. The service member was assisted in identifying his/her concerns about sexual intimacy.

B. The service member was encouraged to discuss his/her concerns about sexual intimacy with his/her partner.

C. The service member was supported while talking about sexual intimacy concerns with his/her partner.

D. The service member has discussed the concerns about sexual intimacy with his/her partner, and this interaction was processed.

E. The service member has not discussed the concerns about sexual intimacy with his/her partner and was urged to do so as he/she feels capable.

25. Gradually Increase Sexual Contact with Partner (25)

A. The service member was encouraged to gradually increase the level of sexual contact with his/her partner as he/she feels comfortable.

B. The service member was urged to start with simple affection, such as hugging, then gradually move on to more intimate sexual contact.

C. The service member has gradually increased the level of sexual contact with his/her partner, and his/her experience in this area was processed.

D. The service member has not gradually increased the level of sexual contact with his/her partner, and his/her reluctance to do so was processed.

26. Educate about Criminal Investigation Process (26)

A. The service member was educated about the criminal investigation process.

B. The service member was encouraged to cooperate fully with the investigation.

C. The service member was supported through the criminal investigation process.

27. Keep Superiors Informed (27)

A. The service member was encouraged to keep his/her chain of command informed of the status and progress of the criminal investigation process.

B. At appropriate intervals, the service member was reminded to keep the chain of command informed about the progress and status of the criminal investigation.

28. Review Continued Service (28)

A. The service member was assigned to develop a pro and con list regarding continued military service.

B. The service member has completed a pro and con list regarding continued military service, which was processed within the session.

C. The service member has not created a pro and con list regarding continued military service and was redirected to do so.

D. The service member has decided to remain within the military, and this choice was honored.

E. The service member has decided to separate from the military, and this decision was honored.

29. Reinforce Self-Efficacy (29)

A. The service member's views, statements, and behaviors that are consistent with self-efficacy theory were reinforced.

B. The service member was reinforced for statements that reflect a sense of capability in performing in a manner that is conducive to obtaining goals.

C. The service member was noted to be increasing his/her self-efficacious statements and behaviors.

D. It was noted that the service member has not increased his/her self-efficacious statements.

30. Reinforce Survivor Viewpoint (30)

A. The service member was reinforced when he/she displayed a greater sense of control by viewing himself/herself as a survivor.

B. The service member's comments indicative of being a survivor (versus a victim) were reinforced.

C. It was reflected to the service member that he/she has a survivor mentality rather than a victim mentality.

SHIFT WORK SLEEP DISORDER

VETERAN/SERVICE MEMBER PRESENTATION

1. Difficulty Adjusting to Shift Rotation/Night Shifts (1)[*]

A. The veteran/service member has frequent changes in his/her shift pattern due to frequent shift rotations.

B. The veteran/service member frequently works night shifts, causing sleep problems.

C. Due to a reversal in the veteran's/service member's normal sleep/wake schedule, he/she has experienced difficulty in staying asleep.

D. The veteran/service member is beginning to adapt to the reverse sleep/wake schedule and obtain the necessary sleep required.

E. The veteran/service member has not adapted to the reversal in his/her sleep/wake schedule and has changed his/her situation to be able to return to a normal sleep schedule.

2. Sleep Debt (2)

A. The veteran/service member complains of an inability to sleep during the day when not working.

B. The veteran's/service member's difficulty sleeping has gradually increased, creating a cycle of tiredness and poor sleep.

C. The veteran/service member reports not feeling rested even after he/she sleeps.

D. The veteran/service member reports that he/she has adjusted to sleeping at a time other than his/her customary sleep pattern.

3. Daytime Sleepiness (3)

A. The veteran/service member reported that he/she feels very sleepy during the day and easily falls asleep, even while sitting in a chair.

B. The veteran/service member reported that he/she has fallen asleep in a chair in the presence of others or in a social situation on many occasions.

C. The veteran/service member reported that he/she is beginning to feel more rested and alert during the day as his/her sleep pattern is returning to normal.

D. The veteran/service member reported no recent incidents of falling asleep too easily during the day.

4. Poor Concentration (4)

A. Due to the excessive sleepiness and fatigue, the veteran/service member has difficulty concentrating.

B. The veteran/service member complains about situations in which he/she has been unable to maintain focus due to his/her high level of sleepiness and fatigue.

---

[*]The numbers in parentheses correlate to the number of the Behavioral Definition statement in the companion chapter with the same title in *The Veterans and Active Duty Military Psychotherapy Treatment Planner* (Moore and Jongsma) by John Wiley & Sons, 2009.

C. As treatment has progressed, the veteran/service member has improved on his/her pattern of sleep, and his/her concentration has improved as well.

5. Decreased Energy/Motivation (5)

A. The veteran/service member reports a decrease in energy and motivation due to his/her sleep deprivation.

B. The veteran/service member reports that he/she is less interested in his/her previous activities.

C. As treatment has progressed, the veteran's/service member's sleep pattern has improved, and this has improved his/her energy and motivation.

6. Errors, Accidents, and Discipline (6)

A. The veteran/service member described an increased pattern of errors and/or accidents in his/her work.

B. The veteran/service member noted that he/she has had more accidents due to his/her difficulty with fatigue and lack of sleep.

C. The veteran/service member has received disciplinary action due to his/her poor performance.

D. As treatment has progressed, the veteran/service member has gained a better sleep pattern and reports decreased errors and accidents.

7. "Sick Call" (7)

A. The service member reports an increased utilization of "sick call."

B. The service member often does not feel capable of performing his/her duties.

C. As treatment has progressed, the service member's sleep pattern has improved, and his/her use of "sick call" has decreased.

INTERVENTIONS IMPLEMENTED

1. Assess Sleep Disturbance (1)[*]

A. The exact nature of the veteran's/service member's sleep disturbance was assessed, including his/her bedtime routine, activity level while awake, nutritional habits, napping practice, actual sleep time, rhythm of time for being awake versus sleeping, and so on.

B. The assessment of the veteran's/service member's sleep disturbance found a chronic history of this problem, which becomes exacerbated at times of high stress.

C. The assessment of the veteran's/service member's sleep disturbance found that the veteran/service member does not practice behavioral habits that are conducive to a good sleep-wake routine.

2. Assess Bedtime Routine and Hygiene (2)

A. The veteran's/service member's pattern of bedtime routine activities was reviewed and assessed.

---

[*]The numbers in parentheses correlate to the number of the Therapeutic Intervention statement in the companion chapter with the same title in *The Veterans and Active Duty Military Psychotherapy Treatment Planner* (Moore and Jongsma) by John Wiley & Sons, 2009.

B. The veteran's/service member's sleep hygiene behaviors were reviewed and assessed.

C. The veteran's/service member's nutritional and health habits as they relate to his/her sleep difficulties were assessed.

D. It was reflected to the veteran/service member that his/her bedtime routine, sleep hygiene behaviors, and nutritional health habits do not indicate significant concerns for his/her sleep pattern.

E. It was reflected to the veteran/service member that his/her sleep pattern, bedtime routine, sleep hygiene behaviors, and nutritional/health habits have a significant impact on his/her sleep pattern.

3. Assign a Sleep Journal (3)

A. The veteran/service member was asked to keep a journal of his/her nightly sleep pattern and routine.

B. The veteran/service member has followed through on keeping a sleep journal, and this information was processed within the session.

C. The veteran/service member acknowledged that his/her sleep disturbance seemed clearly to be related to specific sleep routine factors; he/she was reinforced for this insight.

D. The veteran/service member has not kept a regular sleep journal and was redirected to do so.

4. Obtain Collateral Information (4)

A. Collateral sources of information were interviewed (e.g., superiors, coworkers, family members) to verify the impact of the shift work and related sleep disturbances.

B. Focus on the negative impact on occupational and social functioning was provided as collateral sources of information were reviewed.

C. The discrepancies between the veteran's/service member's information and the collateral sources information was reviewed and resolved.

5. Assess Substance Abuse (5)

A. The degree of the veteran's/service member's substance abuse and its relationship to his/her sleep disorder were assessed.

B. The veteran/service member was reinforced for acknowledging a relationship between his/her substance abuse and his/her sleep disturbance.

C. The veteran/service member was referred to treatment that was focused on substance abuse, which would secondarily improve his/her sleep.

D. The veteran/service member acknowledged that his/her sleep disturbance seemed related to a medication change, and he/she was referred to his/her physician for an evaluation of this relationship.

6. Educate about Negative Effects of Substances (6)

A. The veteran/service member was educated about the negative effects that substances can have on an individual's sleep patterns and sleep architecture.

B. The veteran/service member was supported as he/she displayed a clear understanding of the effects of substances on his/her sleep.

C. The veteran/service member struggled to understand the full effects of substances on his/her sleep pattern and was redirected in this area.

7. Discontinue Nonprescribed Substance Use (7)

A. The veteran/service member was directed to discontinue all nonprescribed substance use until he/she is evaluated by a medical health care provider.

B. The veteran/service member was encouraged to be evaluated by a medical health care provider in order to identify the usefulness or side effects of his/her substance use.

C. The veteran/service member was supported as he/she has discontinued all nonprescribed substance use.

D. The veteran/service member has continued his/her nonprescribed substance use, and the focus of treatment was turned toward these concerns.

8. Assess Mental Health (8)

A. The impact of the veteran's/service member's sleep deprivation on his/her mental health and vice versa was assessed.

B. The veteran/service member was assessed for depression/mood disorders, anxiety, and psychotic symptoms.

C. Subsequent to assessment, the minimal impact of the veteran's/service member's sleep deprivation on his/her mental health was reflected to him/her.

D. The significant effect of the veteran's/service member's sleep deprivation on his/her mental health was reflected to him/her.

9. Emphasize Fewer Night Shifts (9)

A. It was explained to the veteran/service member that decreasing the number of night shifts worked in a row can help to minimize disruptions in sleep.

B. A discussion was held with the veteran/service member about how he/she might change the number of night shifts worked in a row.

C. The veteran/service member has changed his/her pattern of night shift work, and the benefits of this change were reviewed.

D. The veteran/service member has not changed his/her pattern of night shift work and was reminded about how this can be helpful.

10. Encourage Review with Supervisor (10)

A. The veteran/service member was encouraged to review alternate work schedule arrangements with his/her supervisor.

B. The veteran's/service member's supervisor was contacted in regard to making alternative work schedule arrangements.

C. The veteran's/service member's supervisor has made alternate work schedule arrangements, and the benefits of this were reviewed.

D. The veteran's/service member's supervisor has not made alternative work schedule arrangements, and this was processed with the veteran/service member.

11. Refer for Physician Evaluation (11)

A. The veteran/service member was referred to his/her physician to rule out any physical and/or pharmacological causes for his/her sleep disturbance.

B. The veteran/service member was referred to his/her physician to evaluate whether psychotropic medications might be helpful to induce sleep.

C. The veteran/service member was referred for sleep lab studies.

D. The physician has indicated that physical organic causes for the veteran's/service member's sleep disturbance have been found, and a regimen of treatment for these problems has been initiated.

E. The physician ruled out any physical/organic or medication side effect as the cause for the veteran's/service member's sleep disturbance.

F. The physician has ordered psychotropic medications to help the veteran/service member return to a normal sleep pattern.

G. The veteran/service member has not followed through on the referral to his/her physician and was redirected to complete this task.

12. Monitor Medication Compliance (12)

A. The veteran/service member was noted to be consistently taking the psychotropic medication and stated that it was effective at increasing normal sleep routines.

B. The veteran/service member reported taking the psychotropic medication on a consistent basis but has not noted any positive effect on his/her sleep; he/she was directed to review this with the prescribing clinician.

C. The veteran/service member reported not consistently taking his/her psychotropic prescription and was encouraged to do so.

13. Instruct on Sleep Hygiene (13)

A. The veteran/service member was instructed on appropriate sleep hygiene practices.

B. The veteran/service member was advised about restricting excessive liquid intake, spicy late-night snacks, or heavy evening meals.

C. The veteran/service member was encouraged to exercise regularly but not directly before bedtime.

D. The veteran/service member was taught about minimizing or avoiding caffeine, alcohol, tobacco, and other stimulant intake.

E. The veteran/service member was reinforced for his/her regular use of sleep hygiene techniques.

F. The veteran/service member has not regularly used sleep hygiene practices and was redirected to do so.

14. Assign a Sleep Record (14)

A. The veteran/service member was assigned the "Sleep Pattern Record" exercise from the *Adult Psychotherapy Homework Planner,* 2nd ed. (Jongsma).

B. The veteran/service member has completed the sleep pattern record, and his/her experience was processed.

C. The veteran/service member has not completed the sleep pattern record exercise and was redirected to do so.

15. Teach Stimulus Control Techniques (15)

A. The veteran/service member was taught stimulus control techniques.

B. The veteran/service member was taught to lie down to sleep only when sleepy and to use the bed only for sleep or sexual activity.

C. The veteran/service member was taught to get out of bed if sleep does not arrive soon after retiring and then lie back down when sleepy.

D. The veteran/service member was taught to set an alarm to the same wake-up time every morning, regardless of sleep time or quality, and not to nap during the day.

E. The veteran/service member has regularly used stimulus control techniques and was reinforced for using these helpful techniques.

F. The veteran/service member has not used stimulus control techniques on a regular basis and was redirected to do so.

16. Develop Stimulus Control Plan (16)

A. The veteran/service member was assisted in developing a plan for implementation of stimulus control techniques.

B. The obstacles for the service member's stimulus control plan were identified, such as decreased time given for sleep, crowded and noisy barracks, etc.

C. The veteran's/service member's compliance with his/her stimulus control plan was monitored.

D. The veteran/service member was supported for his/her progress.

E. The veteran/service member was assisted in making changes to his/her stimulus control plan.

17. Teach Relaxation Skills (17)

A. The veteran/service member was trained in deep muscle relaxation and deep breathing exercises with and without the use of audiotape instruction.

B. The veteran/service member has implemented the deep muscle relaxation skills that were taught and has reported successful initiation of sleep; he/she was directed to continue the use of this helpful skill.

C. The veteran/service member has not implemented the relaxation training skill on a consistent basis and was encouraged to do so.

18. Refer for Biofeedback (18)

A. The veteran/service member was administered biofeedback to reinforce successful relaxation responses.

B. The veteran's/service member's ability to relax has increased as a result of the biofeedback training.

C. As the veteran/service member has increased his/her relaxation skills, he/she has slept better; his/her progress was reinforced.

D. The veteran/service member has not regularly used biofeedback techniques and was reminded to use these helpful techniques.

19. Explore and Replace Distorted Self-Talk (19)

A. The veteran/service member was assisted in exploring his/her schema and self-talk that mediate his/her emotional responses counterproductive to sleep (e.g., fears, worries of sleeplessness).

B. The veteran's/service member's self-talk biases were challenged, and he/she was assisted in replacing the distorted messages with reality-based alternatives.

C. The veteran/service member was assisted in developing positive self-talk that will increase the likelihood of establishing a sound sleep pattern.

20. Assign Self-Talk Homework (20)

A. The veteran/service member was assigned a homework exercise in which he/she identifies targeted self-talk and created reality-based alternatives.

B. The veteran/service member was assigned "Negative Thoughts Trigger Negative Feelings" in the *Adult Psychotherapy Homework Planner,* 2nd ed. (Jongsma).

C. The veteran's/service member's use of self-talk techniques was reviewed and reinforced for successes.

D. The veteran/service member was provided with corrective feedback toward improvement of his/her use of self-talk techniques.

21. Assign Thought-Stopping Techniques (21)

A. The veteran/service member was assigned to implement thought-stopping techniques on a daily basis in between sessions.

B. The veteran/service member was assigned "Making Use of the Thought-Stopping Technique" in the *Adult Psychotherapy Homework Planner,* 2nd ed. (Jongsma).

C. The veteran's/service member's use of thought-stopping techniques was reviewed, and his/her failures in this area were redirected.

22. Prepare for Shift Change (22)

A. The veteran/service member was instructed to prepare for an approaching shift change by gradually shifting his/her bedtime and wake time back by one to two hours, several days to a week before the change.

B. The veteran's/service member's use of the gradual shift technique for his/her approaching shift change was reviewed and processed.

C. The veteran/service member has regularly used the gradual shift technique; the benefits of this technique were reviewed.

D. The veteran/service member has not used the gradual shift technique and was redirected to do so.

23. Assign Sunglasses (23)

A. The veteran/service member was encouraged to wear wraparound sunglasses during his/her drive home from work during the day, in order to minimize the impact that daylight has on circadian rhythm while driving home.

B. The veteran/service member has regularly used wraparound sunglasses to decrease the impact of daylight on his/her circadian rhythm, and the benefits of this were monitored.

C. The veteran/service member has not used the sunglasses technique to manage his/her circadian rhythm and was reminded about this useful technique.

24. Encourage Specific Scheduling of Personal Errands and Responsibilities (24)

A. The veteran/service member was encouraged to attend to personal errands and responsibilities during specified times during the day.

B. The veteran/service member was encouraged to keep errands to a minimum on his/her days of work and to take care of most of these on his/her day off.

C. The veteran/service member was reinforced for setting consistent times to complete personal errands.

D. The veteran/service member has not set a consistent time to complete personal errands and was redirected to do so.

25. Discourage Reversion to Nighttime Sleep Schedule (25)

A. The veteran/service member was encouraged not to revert to a nighttime sleep schedule over the weekend or on a night off.

B. The problems that reverting back and forth between sleep shifts can cause were reviewed with the veteran/service member.

26. Create a Light-Free Sleeping Environment (26)

A. The veteran/service member was instructed to create a light-free sleeping environment.

B. The veteran/service member was given ideas about blacking out windows and ceiling door cracks, and wearing a night mask.

C. The veteran/service member has worked to create a light-free sleeping environment, and the benefits of these changes were reviewed.

D. The veteran/service member has not developed a light-free sleeping environment and was redirected to do so.

27. Decrease Noise/Disruption (27)

A. The veteran/service member was encouraged to minimize noise and disruptions during sleep times.

B. The veteran/service member was provided with ideas to decrease noise and disruptions during sleep times, such as turning off the telephone ringer, asking family members to be quiet, removing pets from the immediate area, etc.

C. The veteran/service member has developed a quieter sleeping area, and the benefits of this were reviewed.

D. The veteran/service member has not initiated steps to decrease noise and disruptions and was reminded to do so.

28. Moderate Caffeine Use (28)

A. The veteran/service member was encouraged to use moderate amounts of caffeine to promote wakefulness.

B. The veteran/service member has been able to manage his/her caffeine intake in order to promote wakefulness without creating difficulty sleeping.

C. The veteran/service member continues to use an inappropriate amount of caffeine and was redirected in this area.

29. Advise about Brief Naps (29)

A. The veteran/service member was encouraged to take brief naps during breaks or lunch periods, if allowed.

B. The veteran/service member has utilized "power naps" to help increase alertness during work hours, and the benefits of this technique were reviewed.

C. The veteran/service member has not utilized naps during breaks or lunch periods, and was instructed about the usefulness of this technique.

30. Maintain Metabolism through Consistent Caloric Intake (30)

A. The veteran/service member was instructed to maintain a consistent caloric intake.

B. The veteran/service member reports that his/her consistent caloric intake has helped to keep his/her metabolism steady and improved his/her sleep/wake functioning.

C. The veteran/service member has not used the consistent caloric intake method as a way to manage his/her metabolism and was redirected to do so.

31. Encourage Physical Activity through Work (31)

A. The veteran/service member was encouraged to engage in some sort of physical activity during his/her night work shift hours.

B. The veteran/service member was encouraged to take brief walks through the night.

C. The veteran/service member has used the technique of engaging in brief physical activity during his/her work hours, and the benefits of this were reviewed.

D. The veteran/service member has not used the brief physical activity technique and was redirected to do so.

SOCIAL DISCOMFORT

VETERAN/SERVICE MEMBER PRESENTATION

1. Social Anxiety/Shyness (1)*

A. The veteran/service member described a pattern of social anxiety and shyness that presents itself in almost any interpersonal situation.

B. The veteran's/service member's social anxiety presents itself whenever he/she has to interact with people whom he/she does not know or must interact in a group situation.

C. The veteran's/service member's social anxiety has diminished, and he/she is more confident in social situations.

D. The veteran/service member has begun to overcome his/her shyness and can initiate social contact with some degree of comfort and confidence.

E. The veteran/service member reported that he/she no longer experiences feelings of social anxiety or shyness when having to interact with new people or group situations.

2. Disapproval/Hypersensitivity (2)

A. The veteran/service member described a pattern of hypersensitivity to the criticism or disapproval of others.

B. The veteran's/service member's insecurity and lack of confidence has resulted in an extreme sensitivity to any hint of disapproval from others.

C. The veteran/service member has acknowledged that his/her sensitivity to criticism or disapproval is extreme and has begun to take steps to overcome it.

D. The veteran/service member reported increased tolerance for incidents of criticism or disapproval.

3. Social Isolation (3)

A. The veteran/service member has no close friends or confidants outside of first-degree relatives.

B. The veteran's/service member's social anxiety has prevented him/her from building and maintaining a social network of friends and acquaintances.

C. The veteran/service member has begun to reach out socially and to respond favorably to the overtures of others.

D. The veteran/service member reported enjoying contact with friends and sharing personal information with them.

4. Social Avoidance (4)

A. The veteran/service member reported a pattern of avoiding situations that require a degree of interpersonal contact

---

*The numbers in parentheses correlate to the number of the Behavioral Definition statement in the companion chapter with the same title in *The Veterans and Active Duty Military Psychotherapy Treatment Planner* (Moore and Jongsma) by John Wiley & Sons, 2009.

B. The veteran's/service member's social anxiety has caused him/her to avoid social situations within work, family, and neighborhood settings.

C. The veteran/service member has shown some willingness to interact socially as he/she has overcome some of the social anxiety that was formerly present.

D. The veteran/service member indicated that he/she feels free now to interact socially and does not go out of his/her way to avoid such situations.

5. Fear of Social Mistakes (5)

A. The veteran/service member reported resisting involvement in social situations because of a fear of saying or doing something foolish or embarrassing in front of others.

B. The veteran/service member has been reluctant to involve himself/herself in social situations because he/she is fearful of his/her social anxiety becoming apparent to others.

C. The veteran/service member has become more confident of his/her social skills and has begun to interact with more comfort.

D. The veteran/service member reported being able to interact socially without showing signs of social anxiety that would embarrass him/her.

6. Performance Anxiety (6)

A. The veteran/service member reported experiencing debilitating performance anxiety when expected to participate in required social performance demands.

B. The veteran/service member described himself/herself as unable to function when expected to complete typical social performance demands.

C. The veteran/service member avoids required social performance demands.

D. As treatment has progressed, the veteran/service member has become more at ease with typical social performance demands.

E. The veteran/service member reports no struggles with performance anxiety.

7. Physiological Anxiety Symptoms (7)

A. The veteran/service member has an increased heart rate and experiences sweating, dry mouth, muscle tension, and shakiness in most social situations.

B. As the veteran/service member has learned new social skills and developed more confidence in himself/herself, the intensity and frequency of physiological anxiety symptoms has diminished.

C. The veteran/service member reported engaging in social activities without experiencing any physiological anxiety symptoms.

8. Loss of Promotion (8)

A. The service member complains of being passed over for promotion due to poor performance during promotion board interviews.

B. The service member believes that his/her poor performance during promotion board interviews is related to his/her high anxiety and social discomfort.

C. As treatment has progressed, the service member described decreased anxiety related to promotion board interviews.

D. The service member has been able to participate in promotion board interviews with limited anxiety.

E. The service member has been given a promotion.

INTERVENTIONS IMPLEMENTED

1. Build Rapport (1)*

A. Consistent eye contact, active listening, unconditional positive regard, and warm acceptance were used to build rapport with the veteran/service member.

B. The veteran/service member began to express feelings more freely as rapport and trust levels increased.

C. The veteran/service member has continued to experience difficulty being open and direct in his/her expression of painful feelings; he/she was encouraged to be more open as he/she feels safer.

2. Assess Nature of Social Discomfort Symptoms (2)

A. The veteran/service member was asked about the frequency, intensity, duration, and history of his/her social discomfort symptoms, fear, and avoidance.

B. The *Anxiety Disorders Interview Schedule for DSM-IV* (DiNardo, Brown, and Barlow) was used to assess the veteran's/service member's social discomfort symptoms.

C. The assessment of the veteran's/service member's social discomfort symptoms indicated that his/her symptoms are extreme and severely interfere with his/her life.

D. The assessment of the veteran's/service member's social discomfort symptoms indicates that these symptoms are moderate and occasionally interfere with his/her daily functioning.

E. The results of the assessment of the veteran's/service member's social discomfort symptoms indicate that these symptoms are mild and rarely interfere with his/her daily functioning.

F. The results of the assessment of the veteran's/service member's social discomfort symptoms were reviewed with him/her.

3. Explore Social Discomfort Stimulus Situations (3)

A. The veteran/service member was assisted in identifying specific stimulus situations that precipitate social discomfort symptoms.

B. The veteran/service member was assigned "Monitoring My Panic Attack Experiences" from the *Adult Psychotherapy Homework Planner,* 2nd ed. (Jongsma).

C. The veteran/service member could not identify any specific stimulus situations that produce social discomfort; he/she was helped to identify that they occur unexpectedly and without any pattern.

D. The veteran/service member was helped to identify his/her social discomfort symptoms that occur when he/she is expected to perform basic social interaction expectations.

---

*The numbers in parentheses correlate to the number of the Therapeutic Intervention statement in the companion chapter with the same title in *The Veterans and Active Duty Military Psychotherapy Treatment Planner* (Moore and Jongsma) by John Wiley & Sons, 2009.

4. Administer Social Anxiety Assessment (4)

A. The veteran/service member was administered a measure of social anxiety to further assess the depth and breadth of his/her social fears and avoidance.

B. The veteran/service member was administered the Social Interaction Anxiety Scale and/or Social Phobia Scale (Mattick and Clarke).

C. The result of the assessment of the social anxiety indicated a high level of social fears and avoidance; this was reflected to the veteran/service member.

D. The result of the assessment of the social anxiety indicated a medium level of social fears and avoidance; this was reflected to the veteran/service member.

E. The result of the assessment of the social anxiety indicated a low level of social fears and avoidance; this was reflected to the veteran/service member.

F. The veteran/service member declined to participate in an assessment of social anxiety; the focus of treatment was turned to this resistance.

5. Refer for Medication Evaluation (5)

A. Arrangements were made for the veteran/service member to have a physician evaluation for the purpose of considering psychotropic medication to alleviate social discomfort symptoms.

B. The veteran/service member has followed through with seeing a physician for an evaluation of any organic causes for the anxiety and the need for psychotropic medication to control the anxiety response.

C. The veteran/service member has not cooperated with the referral to a physician for a medication evaluation and was encouraged to do so.

6. Monitor Medication Compliance (6)

A. The veteran/service member reported that he/she has taken the prescribed medication consistently and that it has helped to control the anxiety; this was reported to the prescribing clinician.

B. The veteran/service member reported that he/she has not taken the prescribed medication consistently and was encouraged to do so.

C. The veteran/service member reported taking the prescribed medication and stated that he/she has not noted any beneficial effect from it; this was reported to the prescribing clinician.

D. The veteran/service member was evaluated but was not prescribed any psychotropic medication by the physician.

7. Refer to Group Therapy (7)

A. The veteran/service member was referred to a small (closed enrollment) group for social anxiety.

B. The veteran/service member was enrolled in a social anxiety group as defined in *The Group Therapy Treatment Planner,* 2nd ed. (Paleg and Jongsma).

C. The veteran/service member was enrolled in a social anxiety group as defined in *Social Anxiety Disorder* (Turk, Heimberg, and Hope) and *Clinical Handbook of Psychological Disorders* (Barlow).

D. The veteran/service member has participated in the group therapy for social anxiety; his/her experience was reviewed and processed.

E. The veteran/service member has not been involved in group therapy for social anxiety concerns and was redirected to do so.

8. Discuss Cognitive Biases (8)

A. A discussion was held regarding how social anxiety derives from cognitive biases that overestimate negative evaluation by others, undervalue the self, increase distress, and often lead to unnecessary avoidance.

B. The veteran/service member was provided with examples of cognitive biases that support social anxiety symptoms.

C. The veteran/service member was reinforced as he/she identified his/her own cognitive biases.

D. The veteran/service member was unable to identify any cognitive biases that support his/her anxiety symptoms and was provided with tentative examples in this area.

9. Assign Information on Social Anxiety, Avoidance, and Treatment (9)

A. The veteran/service member was assigned to read information on social anxiety that explains the cycle of social anxiety and avoidance and provides a rationale for treatment.

B. The veteran/service member was assigned information about social anxiety, avoidance, and treatment from *Overcoming Shyness and Social Phobia* (Rapee).

C. The veteran/service member was assigned information about social anxiety, avoidance, and treatment from *Overcoming Social Anxiety and Shyness* (Butler).

D. The veteran/service member was assigned to read information from *The Shyness and Social Anxiety Workbook* (Antony and Swinson).

E. The veteran/service member has read the information on social anxiety, avoidance, and treatment, and key concepts were reviewed.

F. The veteran/service member has not read the assigned material on social anxiety, avoidance, and treatment and was redirected to do so.

10. Discuss Cognitive Restructuring (10)

A. A discussion was held about how cognitive restructuring and exposure serve as an arena to desensitize learned fear, build social skills and confidence, and reality-test biased thoughts.

B. The veteran/service member was reinforced as he/she displayed a clear understanding of the use of cognitive restructuring and exposure to desensitize learned fear, build social skills and confidence, and reality-test biased thoughts.

C. The veteran/service member did not display a clear understanding of the use of cognitive restructuring and exposure and was provided with remedial feedback in this area.

11. Teach Anxiety Management Skills (11)

A. The veteran/service member was taught anxiety management skills.

B. The veteran/service member was taught about staying focused on behavioral goals and riding the wave of anxiety.

C. Techniques for muscular relaxation and paced diaphragmatic breathing were taught to the veteran/service member.

D. The veteran/service member was reinforced for his/her clear understanding and use of anxiety management skills.

E. The veteran/service member has not used his/her new anxiety management skills and was redirected to do so.

12. Identify Distorted Thoughts (12)

A. The veteran/service member was assisted in identifying the distorted schemas and related automatic thoughts that mediate social anxiety responses.

B. The veteran/service member was assigned "Journal and Replace Self-Defeating Thoughts" from the *Adult Psychotherapy Homework Planner,* 2nd ed. (Jongsma).

C. The service member completed the homework assignment, and the content was processed within the session.

D. The veteran/service member was taught the role of distorted thinking in precipitating emotional responses.

E. The veteran/service member was reinforced as he/she verbalized an understanding of the cognitive beliefs and messages that mediate his/her anxiety responses.

F. The veteran/service member was assisted in replacing distorted messages with positive, realistic cognitions.

G. The veteran/service member failed to identify his/her distorted thoughts and cognitions and was provided with tentative examples in this area.

13. Assign Exercises on Self-Talk (13)

A. The veteran/service member was assigned homework exercises in which he/she identifies fearful self-talk and creates reality-based alternatives.

B. The veteran/service member was assigned "Restoring Socialization Comfort" from the *Adult Psychotherapy Homework Planner,* 2nd ed. (Jongsma).

C. The veteran/service member was directed to do assignments from *The Shyness and Social Anxiety Workbook* (Antony and Swinson).

D. The veteran/service member was directed to complete assignments from *Overcoming Shyness and Social Phobia* (Rapee).

E. The veteran's/service member's replacement of fearful self-talk with reality-based alternatives was critiqued.

F. The veteran/service member was reinforced for his/her successes at replacing fearful self-talk with reality-based alternatives.

G. The veteran/service member was provided with corrective feedback for his/her failures to replace fearful self-talk with reality-based alternatives.

H. The veteran/service member has not completed his/her assigned homework regarding fearful self-talk and was redirected to do so.

14. Construct Anxiety Stimuli Hierarchy (14)

A. The veteran/service member was assisted in constructing a hierarchy of anxiety-producing situations associated with his/her phobic fear.

B. It was difficult for the veteran/service member to develop a hierarchy of stimulus situations, as the causes of his/her fear remain quite vague; he/she was assisted in completing the hierarchy.

C. The service member was asked to include the expectation of being reviewed by a promotion board as a portion of his/her hierarchy of anxiety-producing situations associated with his/her phobic fear.

D. The veteran/service member was successful at completing a focused hierarchy of specific stimulus situations that provoke anxiety in a gradually increasing manner; this hierarchy was reviewed.

15. Select Exposures that Are Likely to Succeed (15)

A. Initial in vivo or role-played exposures were selected, with a bias toward those that have a high likelihood of being a successful experience for the veteran/service member.

B. Cognitive restructuring was done during and after the exposure using behavioral strategies (e.g., modeling, rehearsal, social reinforcement).

C. In vivo or role-played exposures were patterned after those in "Social Anxiety Disorder" by Turk, Heimberg, and Hope in *Clinical Handbook of Psychological Disorders* (Barlow).

D. A review was conducted with the veteran/service member about his/her use of in vivo or role-played exposures.

E. The veteran/service member was provided with positive feedback regarding his/her use of exposures.

F. The veteran/service member has not used in vivo or role-played exposures and was redirected to do so.

16. Assign Homework on Exposure (16)

A. The veteran/service member was assigned homework exercises to perform sensation exposure and record his/her experience.

B. The veteran/service member was assigned "Gradually Reducing Your Phobic Fear" from the *Adult Psychotherapy Homework Planner,* 2nd ed. (Jongsma).

C. The veteran/service member was assigned sensation exposures homework from *The Shyness and Social Anxiety Workbook* (Antony and Swinson).

D. The veteran/service member was directed to complete assignments from *Overcoming Shyness and Social Phobia* (Rapee).

E. The veteran's/service member's use of sensation exposure techniques was reviewed and reinforced.

F. The veteran/service member has struggled in his/her implementation of sensation exposure techniques and was provided with corrective feedback.

G. The veteran/service member has not attempted to use the sensation exposure techniques and was redirected to do so.

17. Build Social and Communication Skills (17)

A. Instruction, modeling, and role-playing were used to build the veteran's/service member's general social and communication skills.

B. Techniques from *Social Effectiveness Therapy* (Turner, Beidel, and Cooley) were used to teach social and communication skills.

C. Positive feedback was provided to the veteran/service member for his/her use of increased use of social and communication skills.

D. Despite the instruction, modeling, and role-playing about social and communication skills, the veteran/service member continues to struggle with these techniques and was provided with additional feedback in this area.

18. Assign Information on Social and Communication Skills (18)

A. The veteran/service member was assigned to read about general social and/or communication skills in books or treatment manuals on building social skills.

B. The veteran/service member was assigned to read *Your Perfect Right* (Alberti and Emmons).

C. The veteran/service member was assigned to read *Conversationally Speaking* (Garner).

D. The veteran/service member has read the assigned information on social and communication skills, and key points were reviewed.

E. The veteran/service member has not read the information on social and communication skills and was redirected to do so.

19. Differentiate between Lapse and Relapse (19)

A. A discussion was held with the veteran/service member regarding the distinction between a lapse and a relapse.

B. A lapse was associated with an initial and reversible return of symptoms, fear, or urges to avoid.

C. A relapse was associated with the decision to return to fearful and avoidant patterns.

D. The veteran/service member was provided with support and encouragement as he/she displayed an understanding of the difference between a lapse and a relapse.

E. The veteran/service member struggled to understand the difference between a lapse and a relapse and was provided with remedial feedback in this area.

20. Discuss Management of Lapse Risk Situations (20)

A. The veteran/service member was assisted in identifying future situations or circumstances in which lapses could occur.

B. The session focused on rehearsing the management of future situations or circumstances in which lapses could occur.

C. The veteran/service member was reinforced for his/her appropriate use of lapse management skills.

D. The veteran/service member was redirected in regard to his/her poor use of lapse management skills.

21. Encourage Routine Use of Strategies (21)

A. The veteran/service member was instructed to routinely use the strategies that he/she has learned in therapy (e.g., cognitive restructuring, exposure).

B. The veteran/service member was urged to find ways to build his/her new strategies into his/her life as much as possible.

C. The veteran/service member was reinforced as he/she reported ways in which he/she has incorporated coping strategies into his/her life and routine.

D. The veteran/service member was redirected about ways to incorporate his/her new strategies into his/her routine and life.

22. Develop a "Coping Card" (22)

A. The veteran/service member was provided with a "coping card" on which specific coping strategies were listed.

B. The veteran/service member was assisted in developing his/her "coping card" in order to list helpful coping strategies.

C. The veteran/service member was encouraged to use his/her "coping card" when struggling with anxiety-producing situations.

23. Explore Rejection Experiences (23)

A. The veteran/service member was asked to identify childhood and adolescent experiences of social rejection and neglect that have contributed to his/her current feelings of social anxiety.

B. Active listening was provided as the veteran/service member described in detail many incidents of feeling rejected by peers, which has led to social anxiety and social withdrawal.

C. The veteran/service member denied any history of rejection experiences and was urged to speak about these if he/she should recall them in the future.

24. Assign Books on Shame (24)

A. The veteran/service member was directed to read books on shame.

B. It was recommended to the veteran/service member that he/she read *Healing the Shame that Binds You* (Bradshaw) and *Facing Shame* (Fossum and Mason).

C. The veteran/service member has read the assigned books on shame and can now better identify how shame has affected his/her relating to others; key points from the reading material were reviewed.

D. As the veteran/service member has overcome his/her feelings of shame, he/she was asked to initiate one social contact per day for increasing lengths of time.

E. The veteran/service member has failed to follow through on reading the recommended materials on shame and was urged to do so.

25. Identify Defense Mechanisms (25)

A. The veteran/service member was assisted in identifying the defense mechanisms that he/she uses to avoid close relationships.

B. The veteran/service member was assisted in reducing his/her defensiveness so as to be able to build social relationships and not alienate himself/herself from others.

26. Schedule a "Booster Session" (26)

A. The veteran/service member was scheduled for a "booster session" between one and three months after therapy ends.

B. The veteran/service member was advised to contact the therapist if he/she needs to be seen prior to the "booster session."

C. The veteran's/service member's "booster session" was held, and he/she was reinforced for his/her successful implementation of therapy techniques.

D. The veteran's/service member's "booster session" was held, and he/she was coordinated for further treatment, as his/her progress has not been sustained.

SPIRITUAL AND RELIGIOUS ISSUES

VETERAN/SERVICE MEMBER PRESENTATION

1. **Conflict between Religious Beliefs and Military Service (1)**[*]
   A. The veteran/service member reports serious spiritual and moral conflicts between his/her religious beliefs and the expectations of his/her military service.
   B. The veteran/service member reflected that he/she has been asked to engage in activities that are contrary to his/her religious beliefs.
   C. The veteran/service member feels immobilized by the conflicts between his/her religious beliefs and military service.
   D. The veteran/service member reported greater understanding of how to integrate his/her religious beliefs with the expectations of military service.
   E. The veteran/service member has resolved the conflicts between his/her religious beliefs and military service.

2. **Feelings of Emptiness (2)**
   A. The veteran/service member verbalized a feeling of emptiness and lack of direction to his/her life as if some important part were missing.
   B. The veteran/service member verbalized the lack of meaning that life has but recognized that he/she needs to give more attention to his/her spiritual journey.
   C. The veteran/service member has begun to explore spiritual beliefs and to engage in faith practices that have reduced the feeling of emptiness and meaninglessness.

3. **Desire for Higher Power Relationship (3)**
   A. The veteran/service member verbalized a desire for a closer relationship with God.
   B. The veteran/service member stated that he/she has not felt a close relationship with a higher power and would like to develop this in his/her life.
   C. The veteran/service member has begun to engage in spiritual practices that have increased a sense of relationship with God.
   D. The veteran/service member reported feeling more in touch with, understood by, and supported by a higher power.

4. **Lack of Religious Training (4)**
   A. The veteran/service member complained about having no religious education or training during childhood and now feels lost as to how to begin to understand the role of God in his/her life.
   B. The veteran/service member has begun to explore religious belief systems and to engage in faith practices in order to deepen spiritual focus.

---

[*]The numbers in parentheses correlate to the number of the Behavioral Definition statement in the companion chapter with the same title in *The Veterans and Active Duty Military Psychotherapy Treatment Planner* (Moore and Jongsma) by John Wiley & Sons, 2009.

C. The veteran/service member reported that a new sense of meaning has entered his/her life as he/she engages in spiritual growth experiences.

5. Denies God's Existence (5)

A. The veteran/service member expresses a belief that there is no God due to past hurt, rejection, and/or childhood traumas.

B. The veteran/service member professes to be an atheist or agnostic.

C. The veteran/service member has begun to entertain alternative views about his/her past hurt and God's role in his/her life.

D. The veteran/service member has reconciled his/her past hurt, rejection, and childhood traumas with a loving and caring God.

6. Religious Discrimination (6)

A. The veteran/service member believes that he/she has been discriminated against by the military due to his/her spiritual/religious beliefs.

B. The veteran/service member has had difficulty practicing his/her spiritual/religious beliefs within the structure of the military.

C. The veteran/service member has sought out and developed opportunities for practice of his/her spiritual/religious beliefs.

D. The veteran/service member has taken steps to resolve his/her perceived discrimination due to his/her spiritual/religious beliefs.

E. The veteran/service member has become more accepting of the expectations of the military and his/her spiritual/religious beliefs and no longer feels discriminated against.

INTERVENTIONS IMPLEMENTED

1. Develop Trust (1)*

A. Today's clinical contact focused on building a level of trust within the therapeutic relationship through consistent eye contact, active listening, unconditional positive regard, and warm acceptance.

B. Empathy and support were provided for the veteran/service member's expression of thoughts and feelings during today's clinical contact.

C. The veteran/service member was provided with support and feedback as he/she described his/her feelings of survivor guilt.

D. As the veteran/service member has remained mistrustful and reluctant to share his/her underlying thoughts and feelings, he/she was provided with additional reassurance.

E. The veteran/service member verbally acknowledged that he/she has difficulty establishing trust, and this was accepted by the therapist.

2. Assess Spiritual Concerns (2)

A. The veteran's/service member's type, intensity, and frequency of spiritual/religious concerns were assessed.

---

*The numbers in parentheses correlate to the number of the Therapeutic Intervention statement in the companion chapter with the same title in *The Veterans and Active Duty Military Psychotherapy Treatment Planner* (Moore and Jongsma) by John Wiley & Sons, 2009.

B. The impact of the veteran's/service member's spiritual/religious concerns on his/her social, occupational, and interpersonal functioning was assessed.

C. The level of impact of the veteran's/service member's spiritual/religious concerns was rated as mild.

D. The level of concern and the impact of the veteran's/service member's spiritual/religious concerns was rated as moderate.

E. The level of concerns and impact of the veteran's/service member's spiritual/religious concerns was rated as severe.

3. Review Spiritual Beliefs System (3)

A. The veteran/service member was asked to describe his/her spiritual belief system.

B. The veteran/service member was assisted in identifying how his/her spiritual belief system compares and contrasts with traditional religious systems.

C. The veteran/service member was supported as he/she reviewed his/her spiritual belief system.

4. Identify Influence on Current Beliefs (4)

A. The veteran/service member was assisted in identifying factors that influenced his/her current beliefs.

B. The veteran/service member was provided with examples of how family, friends, television, school, worship, and other factors can influence current beliefs.

C. The veteran/service member was supported as he/she identified influences on his/her current beliefs.

D. The veteran/service member struggled to identify the influences on his/her current beliefs and was provided remedial feedback in this area.

5. Process Emotional Reaction to Spiritual Discussion (5)

A. The veteran/service member has experienced significant emotional reaction in discussing his/her spiritual belief system, and these emotions were processed.

B. The veteran/service member has become less emotionally reactive related to his/her spiritual concerns.

C. The veteran/service member did not display any significant emotional reactions when discussing his/her spiritual concerns.

6. Refer to Military Chaplain (6)

A. The service member was urged to talk with a military chaplain to help identify the rationale behind the conflict between his/her beliefs system and serving in the military.

B. The service member has talked with a military chaplain and has been able to resolve some of the conflicts between his/her belief system and serving in the military.

C. Despite contacting a military chaplain, the service member has been unable to resolve the conflicts between his/her beliefs system and serving in the military.

D. The service member has not contacted a military chaplain and was redirected to do so.

7. Encourage Additional Chaplain Support (7)

A. The service member was directed to seek out a second military chaplain because his/her questions were not initially answered or appreciated.

B. The service member acknowledged that seeing a second military chaplain has been more helpful.

C. The service member has sought out help from a second military chaplain but has not benefited from that contact.

D. The service member has not sought out a second military chaplain was redirected to do so.

8. Discuss Importance of Religion during Wartime (8)

A. A discussion was held with the service member about the importance that religion has played in the military during times of war.

B. The service member was provided with specific examples of how religion has been a significant asset during times of war.

9. Assign a Written Spiritual Journey (9)

A. The veteran/service member was asked to write out a history of his/her spiritual quest and to bring the story to a later session for processing.

B. The veteran/service member was encouraged to summarize the highlights of his/her spiritual journey up to this date.

C. The veteran/service member was assigned "My History of Spirituality" from the *Adult Psychotherapy Homework* Planner, 2nd ed. (Jongsma).

D. The veteran/service member has followed through on the assignment of writing about his/her spiritual journey, and the content of this journaling was processed.

E. Active listening was provided as the veteran/service member listed several experiences within his/her life that have caused alienation from God.

10. Identify Inconsistent Beliefs (10)

A. The veteran/service member was directed to develop a list of beliefs that are no longer consistent with his/her current beliefs.

B. The veteran/service member has developed a list of beliefs that are no longer consistent with his/her current beliefs, and this list was processed.

C. The veteran/service member has not completed a list of beliefs that are no longer consistent with his/her current beliefs and was redirected to do so.

11. Challenge Validity and Usefulness of Beliefs (11)

A. The veteran/service member was assisted in challenging the validity and/or usefulness of his/her current religious views.

B. Negative experiences that have affected the veteran's/service member's current religious views were identified and reviewed for validity and usefulness.

C. Care was taken simply to reflect and organize the veteran's/service member's religious views while discussing the usefulness of his/her current views rather than entering into a debate.

D. The veteran/service member was provided with emotional support as he/she identified the level of validity and usefulness of his/her current views about religion and faith.

12. Encourage Forgiveness (12)

A. The veteran/service member was assisted in identifying how others have instilled fear and conditioned him/her to view religion as critical, judgmental, and punitive.

B. The veteran/service member was encouraged to forgive those that have instilled fear in him/her regarding religion.

C. The veteran/service member was supported as he/she applied his/her forgiveness of others for conditioning him/her to view religion as critical, judgmental, or punitive.

D. The veteran/service member struggled to forgive others for conditioning him to view religion as critical, judgmental, and punitive and was provided with additional encouragement and feedback in this area.

13. Educate about Differences between Religion, Spirituality, and a Higher Power (13)

A. The veteran/service member was educated about the differences between religion, spirituality, and a higher power.

B. The veteran/service member was referred to administrator/chaplain for help in differentiating between religion, spirituality, and a higher power.

C. The veteran/service member has been able to identify differences between religion, spirituality, and a higher power, and the concepts were reviewed and reinforced.

D. The veteran/service member continues to have difficulty understanding the difference between religion, spirituality, and a higher power and was provided with additional feedback in this area.

14. Identify Application of Main Principles (14)

A. The veteran/service member was assisted in identifying the main principles of his/her chosen belief system.

B. The veteran/service member was directed to identify how the main principles of his/her chosen belief system apply to his/her everyday life.

C. The veteran/service member was assisted in identifying and applying his/her belief system principles.

D. The veteran/service member has struggled to identify the main principles for his/her chosen belief system or how they apply to his/her everyday life, and was provided with remedial feedback in this area.

15. Encourage Discussion of Conflicts (15)

A. The veteran/service member was encouraged to create a list of those aspects of his/her belief system that conflict with his/her view of life.

B. The veteran/service member was encouraged to create a list of those aspects of his/her belief system that conflict with his/her service in the military.

C. The veteran/service member was encouraged to discuss his/her religious conflicts with a spiritual/religious leader.

D. The veteran/service member was encouraged to discuss his/her religious conflicts with an individual whose spiritual/religious values he/she respects.

E. The veteran/service member has discussed conflicts with respected individuals/religious leaders, and his/her experience was processed.

F. The veteran/service member has not discussed his/her conflicts with a spiritual/religious leader or others he/she respects and was redirected to do so.

16. Assign Narrative Statement (16)

A. The veteran/service member was assigned to write a narrative statement regarding how he/she believes his/her life has a void and lacks meaning and purpose.

B. The veteran/service member completed a narrative statement regarding issues related to meaning and purpose, and this was processed within the session.

C. The veteran/service member has not completed the narrative statement regarding meaning and purpose and was assisted in completing this assignment.

D. The veteran/service member has not completed the narrative statement regarding meaning and purpose and was redirected to do so.

17. Assign Response to Narrative Statement (17)

A. The veteran/service member was assigned to write a narrative statement addressing how including spirituality and religion in his/her life will fill his/her sense of void and lack of meaning.

B. The veteran/service member was encouraged to be very specific about how his/her spirituality will give him/her meaning.

C. The veteran/service member has completed the response to his/her concerns about meaning and purpose, and this was reviewed within the session.

D. The veteran/service member has not completed any response to his/her concerns about meaning and purpose and was redirected to do so.

18. Explore Faith (18)

A. The meaning of faith was explored with the veteran/service member.

B. The connection of faith and religion was reviewed with the veteran/service member.

19. Review Use of Faith (19)

A. The veteran/service member was asked to identify other areas of his/her life where he/she has used faith.

B. The veteran/service member has identified ways in which he/she uses faith within other areas of his/her life, and these were processed within the session.

C. The veteran/service member struggled to identify other situations in which he/she uses faith and was provided with specific examples.

20. Recommend Prayer/Meditation (20)

A. The veteran/service member was encouraged to pray on a daily basis.

B. The veteran/service member was recommended to meditate on a daily basis.

C. The veteran/service member has engaged in daily devotional practices, and his/her experience was processed.

D. The veteran/service member has not used prayer or meditation on a regular basis and was redirected to do so.

21. Recommend *The Purpose-Driven Life* (21)

A. As the veteran/service member is Protestant, *The Purpose-Driven Life* (Warren) was recommended.

B. The veteran/service member has read *The Purpose-Driven Life,* and key components were reviewed.

C. The veteran/service member has not read *The Purpose-Driven Life* and was redirected to do so.

22. Encourage Religious Services (22)

A. The veteran/service member was encouraged to attend a worship service on a weekly basis.

B. The veteran/service member was asked to assess how his/her worship experience fit with his/her beliefs.

C. The veteran/service member has regularly attended worship services, and this was reinforced.

D. The veteran/service member has not regularly attended worship services and was redirected to do so.

23. Maintain Church Diary (23)

A. The veteran/service member was encouraged to maintain a "church diary" in which to write reflections and make notes about lessons learned during sermons.

B. The veteran/service member has maintained a "church diary," and his/her experience was reviewed.

C. The veteran/service member was encouraged to review the "church diary" throughout the week.

D. The veteran/service member has not completed a "church diary" and was redirected to do so.

24. Increase Services (24)

A. The veteran/service member was encouraged to attend worship/prayer services as frequently as he/she feels comfortable.

B. The veteran/service member has increased his/her involvement in worship/prayer services, and this was positively reinforced.

25. Identify Community Activities (25)

A. The veteran/service member was assisted in identifying religious-based community groups and activities.

B. The veteran/service member was encouraged to attend religious training classes.

C. The veteran/service member was encouraged to engage in church social activities.

D. The veteran/service member was encouraged for his/her regular attendance in religious-based community groups and activities.

E. The veteran/service member has not increased his/her involvement in religious-based groups and activity and was redirected to do so.

26. Encourage Talk with Respected Service Member (26)

A. The service member was assisted in identifying a fellow comrade whose spiritual/religious beliefs he/she respects.

B. The veteran/service member was encouraged to talk with a respected service member about his/her own struggles with religion.

C. The service member was encouraged to talk with the respected service member about experiences related to ridicule and discrimination.

D. The service member has talked with another service member about experiences related to conflict, ridicule, and discrimination, and this experience was processed.

E. The service member has not followed up with talking with another service member about struggles with religion and was redirected to do so.

SUBSTANCE ABUSE/DEPENDENCE

VETERAN/SERVICE MEMBER PRESENTATION

1. Increased Tolerance and Withdrawal (1)*

A. The veteran/service member displayed a maladaptive pattern of substance use, manifested by increased tolerance and withdrawal.

B. The veteran/service member reported that he/she must use greater amounts of substances due to an increased pattern of tolerance of the mood-altering chemicals.

C. The veteran/service member described that he/she experiences significant physical withdrawal symptoms when he/she goes without the substances for any long period of time.

D. As the veteran/service member has worked on his/her recovery, his/her maladaptive pattern of substance use has been discontinued.

2. Inability to Reduce Alcohol and/or Drug Abuse (2)

A. The veteran/service member acknowledged that he/she frequently has attempted to terminate or reduce his/her use of the mood-altering drug, but found that once use has begun, he/she has been unable to follow through.

B. The veteran/service member acknowledged that despite the negative consequences and a desire to reduce or terminate mood-altering drug abuse, he/she has been unable to do so.

C. As the veteran/service member has participated in a total recovery program, he/she has been able to maintain abstinence from mood-altering drug use.

3. Negative Blood Effects (3)

A. The veteran's/service member's blood work results reflected a pattern of heavy substance abuse (e.g., liver enzymes are elevated, electrolytes are imbalanced).

B. The veteran's/service member's blood work results indicate that mood-altering drugs have been used.

C. As the veteran/service member has participated in the recovery program and has been able to maintain abstinence from mood-altering drugs, his/her blood work has shown improved status and has come back to within normal limits.

4. Physical Indicators (3)

A. The veteran's/service member's physical evaluation results reflect a pattern of heavy substance abuse (e.g., elevated blood pressure, stomach pain, malnutrition).

B. As the veteran/service member has participated in the recovery program and has been able to maintain abstinence from mood-altering drugs, his/her physical status has shown improvement.

C. The veteran's/service member's physical status and lab results have returned to normal.

---

*The numbers in parentheses correlate to the number of the Behavioral Definition statement in the companion chapter with the same title in *The Veterans and Active Duty Military Psychotherapy Treatment Planner* (Moore and Jongsma) by John Wiley & Sons, 2009.

5. Denial (4)

A. The veteran/service member presented with denial regarding the negative consequences of his/her substance abuse, in spite of direct feedback about its negative effect.

B. The veteran's/service member's denial is beginning to break down as he/she is acknowledging that substance abuse has created problems in his/her life.

C. The veteran/service member now openly admits to the severe negative consequences in which substance abuse has resulted.

6. Amnesiac Blackouts (5)

A. The veteran/service member has experienced blackouts during alcohol abuse, which have resulted in memory loss for periods of time in which the veteran/service member was still functional.

B. The veteran/service member stated that his/her first blackout occurred at a young age and that he/she has experienced many of them over the years of his/her alcohol abuse.

C. The veteran/service member acknowledged only one or two incidents of amnesiac blackouts.

D. The veteran/service member has not had any recent experience of blackouts, as he/she has been able to maintain sobriety.

7. Persistent Alcohol and/or Drug Abuse despite Problems (6)

A. The veteran/service member has continued to abuse alcohol/drugs in spite of recurring physical, legal, vocational, social, or relationship problems that were directly caused by the substance use.

B. The veteran/service member denied that many problems in his/her life are directly caused by alcohol or drug abuse.

C. The veteran/service member acknowledged that alcohol or drug abuse has been the cause of multiple problems in his/her life and verbalized a strong desire to maintain a life free from using all mood-altering substances.

D. As the veteran/service member has maintained sobriety, some of the direct negative consequences of substance abuse have diminished.

E. The veteran/service member is now able to face resolution of significant problems in his/her life as he/she is able to establish sobriety.

8. Increased Tolerance (7)

A. The veteran/service member described a pattern of increasing tolerance for the mood-altering substance, as he/she needed to use more of it to obtain the desired effect.

B. The veteran/service member described the steady increase in the amount and frequency of the substance abuse, as his/her tolerance for it has increased.

9. Physical Withdrawal Symptoms (8)

A. The veteran/service member acknowledged that he/she has experienced physical withdrawal symptoms (e.g., shaking, seizures, nausea, headaches, sweating, insomnia) as he/she withdrew from the substance abuse.

B. The veteran's/service member's physical symptoms of withdrawal have eased as he/she has stabilized and maintained abstinence from the mood-altering substance.

C. There is no further evidence of physical withdrawal symptoms.

10. Addiction-Related Arrests (9)

A. The veteran/service member indicated that he/she has been arrested for addiction-related offenses (e.g., driving under the influence, minor in possession, uttering and publishing, assault, possession and/or delivery of a controlled substance, shoplifting, breaking and entering).

B. The veteran/service member has had altercations with the military police due to his/her substance-related behavior.

C. The veteran/service member has recognized the connection between his/her addiction problems and his/her legal concerns.

D. The veteran/service member reported incarceration related to his/her pattern of illegal behavior when intoxicated or substance abusing.

E. As the veteran/service member has decreased his/her use of mood-altering substances, he/she reports a decrease in legal problems.

11. Late to Morning Accountability (10)

A. The service member has repeatedly reported late to morning accountability or physical training formations as a result of substance abuse.

B. The service member has received official sanction due to his/her repeated lateness to morning accountability and physical training formations.

C. As treatment has progressed, the service member has been more regularly on time for morning accountability and physical training formations.

D. The service member reports being on time regularly for morning accountability and physical training formations.

INTERVENTIONS IMPLEMENTED

1. Refer for Physical Examination (1)[*]

A. The veteran/service member was referred for a thorough physical examination to determine any negative medical effects related to his/her chemical dependence.

B. The veteran/service member has followed through with obtaining a physical examination and was told that his/her chemical dependence has produced negative medical consequences.

C. The veteran/service member has obtained a physical examination from a physician and has been told that there are no significant medical effects of his/her chemical dependence.

D. The veteran/service member has been prescribed medications.

E. Specific treatment orders have been written by the physician.

F. The veteran/service member has not followed through with obtaining a physical examination, and he/she was again directed to do so.

---

[*]The numbers in parentheses correlate to the number of the Therapeutic Intervention statement in the companion chapter with the same title in *The Veterans and Active Duty Military Psychotherapy Treatment Planner* (Moore and Jongsma) by John Wiley & Sons, 2009.

2. Refer to Treatment Recovery Program (2)

A. The veteran/service member was referred to a pharmacologically based treatment/recovery program

B. The veteran/service member was referred for acamprosate or naltrexone treatment.

C. The veteran/service member has complied with the referral to a pharmacologically based treatment/recovery program, and his/her progress was reviewed.

D. The veteran/service member has not complied with the referral to a pharmacologically based treatment/recovery program and was redirected to do so.

3. Titrate Medication (3)

A. The veteran/service member was encouraged to maintain contact with his/her physician in order to monitor and titrate medications as needed.

B. The veteran's/service member's medications have been titrated, and this has produced increased effectiveness and decreased side effects.

C. The veteran/service member has not maintained contact with his/her physician, and he/she was redirected to do so.

4. Administer/Monitor Medications (4)

A. Medical staff administered medications as prescribed.

B. Medical staff assisted the veteran/service member in administering his/her own medications.

C. The veteran/service member refused to accept medication as prescribed.

D. As the veteran/service member has taken the medication prescribed by his/her physician, the effectiveness and side effects of the medication were monitored.

E. The veteran/service member reported that the medication has been beneficial in reducing substance abuse/dependence symptoms, and this was relayed to the prescribing clinician.

F. The veteran/service member reported that the medication has not been helpful, and this was relayed to the prescribing clinician.

G. The veteran/service member has not consistently taken the medication, and he/she was redirected to do so.

5. Assess and Monitor Withdrawal (5)

A. During the veteran's/service member's period of withdrawal, he/she was consistently assessed and monitored using a standardized procedure.

B. As the veteran/service member progressed through his/her process of withdrawal, he/she was provided medically appropriate treatment as needed.

C. The veteran/service member did not require any specific medical treatment to complete his/her withdrawal.

D. The veteran/service member has been noted to complete his/her withdrawal.

6. Administer Assessment for Substance Abuse/Dependence Traits (6)

A. The veteran/service member was administered psychological instruments designed to objectively assess the strength of substance abuse/dependence.

B. The Substance Abuse Subtle Screening Inventory-3 (SASSI-3) was administered to the client.

C. The Substance Use Disorders Diagnostic Schedule-IV (SUDDS-IV) was administered to the client.

D. The veteran/service member has completed the assessment of substance abuse/dependence, and minimal concerns were identified; these results were reported to the veteran/service member.

E. The veteran/service member has completed the assessment of substance abuse/dependence, and significant concerns were identified; these results were reported to the veteran/service member.

F. The veteran/service member refused to participate in psychological assessment of substance abuse/dependence, and the focus of treatment was turned toward this defensiveness.

7. Gather Drug and/or Alcohol History (7)

A. The veteran/service member was asked to describe his/her alcohol and/or drug use in terms of the amount and pattern of use, symptoms of abuse, and negative life consequences that have resulted from chemical dependence.

B. A complete psychosocial history was taken, with a focus on the personal and family history of addiction.

C. It was reflected to the veteran/service member that he/she has minimized his/her substance abuse and did not give reliable data regarding the nature and extent of his/her chemical dependence problem or family history.

D. As therapy has progressed, the veteran/service member has become more open in acknowledging the extent and seriousness of his/her substance abuse problems; this progress has been reinforced.

8. Assign Didactics Regarding Effects of Chemical Dependence (8)

A. The veteran/service member was assigned to attend a chemical dependence didactic series to increase his/her knowledge of the patterns and effects of chemical dependence.

B. The veteran/service member was asked to identify in writing several key points obtained from each didactic lecture.

C. Key points from didactic lectures that were noted by the veteran/service member were processed in individual sessions.

D. It was reflected to the veteran/service member that he/she has become more open in acknowledging and accepting his/her chemical dependence.

9. Assign Readings on Addiction Recovery (9)

A. The veteran/service member was assigned to read evidence-based material regarding addiction recovery (e.g., *Overcoming Your Alcohol or Drug Problem,* 2nd ed. [Daley and Marlatt]).

B. The veteran/service member was asked to process with the therapist five key points that were gained from the reading of substance abuse literature.

C. The veteran/service member has read the assigned substance abuse literature and processed it within the session.

D. The veteran/service member has not read the assigned substance abuse literature and was redirected to do so.

10. Assign Readings on Addiction (10)

A. The veteran/service member was assigned to read material on addiction.

B. The veteran/service member was assigned *Willpower's Not Enough* (Washton).

C. The veteran/service member was assigned *The Addiction Workbook* (Fanning).

D. The veteran/service member was assigned readings from Alcoholics Anonymous.

E. The veteran/service member was asked to process with the therapist five key points that were gained from the reading on addiction.

F. The veteran/service member has read the assigned addiction literature and processed it within the session.

G. The veteran/service member has not read the assigned addiction literature and was redirected to do so.

11. Require Reading *Narcotics Anonymous* (11)

A. The veteran/service member was assigned to read material on the process of becoming addicted in *Narcotics Anonymous.*

B. The veteran/service member was asked to identify five key points from *Narcotics Anonymous* reading and process them with the therapist.

C. The veteran/service member has not completed the assigned reading and was redirected to do so.

12. Refer to Group Therapy (12)

A. It was strongly recommended to the veteran/service member that he/she attend group therapy that is focused on addiction issues.

B. The veteran/service member has followed through with consistent attendance to group therapy and reports that the meetings have been helpful.

C. The veteran/service member has not followed through on regular attendance to group therapy, and he/she was redirected to do so.

D. The veteran/service member has attended group therapy meetings but reports that he/she does not find them helpful and is resistive to returning to them; he/she was urged to try this helpful component again.

13. Direct Group Therapy (13)

A. Group therapy sessions were provided that facilitated the sharing of, causes for, consequences of, feelings about, and alternatives to addiction.

B. The veteran/service member participated in group therapy sessions, sharing information about his/her causes, consequences, and feelings about his/her addiction.

C. The veteran/service member has attended group therapy sessions focused on addiction issues but has not actively participated by sharing his/her thoughts and feelings.

D. The veteran/service member has not attended group therapy sessions and was redirected to do so.

14. Assign First-Step Paper (14)

A. The veteran/service member was assigned to complete an NA first-step paper and to share it with his/her group and the therapist.

B. The veteran/service member was assigned the Step One exercise from the *Alcoholism and Drug Abuse Patient Workbook* (Perkinson).

C. The veteran/service member completed a first-step paper and in it acknowledged that addictive behavior has dominated his/her life; this insight was reinforced.

D. The veteran/service member has failed to complete the first-step paper and was redirected to do so.

15. Confront Denial (15)

A. The veteran's/service member's pattern of denial was identified and reflected to him/her.

B. Confrontation was used to prompt the veteran/service member to honestly identify the severity and negative consequences of his/her substance abuse.

C. The veteran/service member has been confronted about his/her substance abuse severity and negative consequences; he/she has become more realistic about these concerns.

D. The veteran/service member has become more defensive as he/she has been confronted about the use, severity, and consequences of his/her substance abuse.

16. List Negative Consequences (16)

A. The veteran/service member was asked to make a list of the ways in which addiction has negatively impacted his/her life and to process this list.

B. The veteran/service member was assigned "Substance Abuse Negative Impact vs. Sobriety's Positive Impact" from the *Adult Psychotherapy Homework Planner*, 2nd ed. (Jongsma).

C. The veteran/service member completed the homework assignment, and the content was processed within the session.

D. It was reflected to the veteran/service member that he/she has minimized the negative impact of his/her addictive behavior on his/her life.

E. The veteran/service member has completed his/her list of negative impacts of addictive behaviors on his/her life and acknowledged the negative consequences he/she has experienced; this insight was processed.

F. The veteran/service member has not completed the list of negative impacts upon his/her life and was redirected to do so.

17. Explore Addiction as an Escape (17)

A. The veteran's/service member's use of substance abuse as a way to escape stress, emotional pain, and/or boredom was explored.

B. The veteran/service member acknowledged using substance abuse as a way to escape from stress, emotional pain, and/or boredom; this insight was reinforced.

C. The veteran/service member was confronted for the negative consequences of his/her pattern of escapism.

D. The veteran/service member reported that he/she has decreased his/her substance abuse as a way to escape stress, emotional pain, and/or boredom; this progress was reinforced.

E. The veteran/service member denied the idea that substance abuse has been used as an escape from stress and was provided with additional feedback in this area.

18. Probe Guilt and Shame Issues (18)

A. The veteran/service member was probed for his/her sense of shame, guilt, and low self-worth that has resulted from substance abuse and its consequences.

B. The veteran/service member reported significant patterns of shame, guilt, and low self-worth due to his/her substance abuse and its consequences, which was processed.

C. The veteran/service member denied any pattern of shame, guilt, and low self-worth and was provided with examples of how this can occur.

19. List Reasons to Stay Abstinent (19)

A. The veteran/service member was assisted in developing a list of reasons why he/she should stay abstinent from substances.

B. The veteran/service member was assigned "Making Change Happen" from the *Addiction Treatment Homework Planner*, 4th ed. (Finley and Lenz).

C. The veteran/service member was assigned "A Working Recovery Plan" from the *Addiction Treatment Homework Planner*, 4th ed. (Finley and Lenz).

D. The veteran/service member completed the homework assignment, and the content was processed within the session.

E. The veteran/service member identified several of his/her own reasons for remaining abstinent from substances; this list was processed.

F. The veteran/service member struggled to identify reasons why he/she should remain abstinent, and this was processed within the session.

20. Review Dishonesty and Substance Abuse/Dependence (20)

A. The veteran/service member was assisted in understanding that dishonesty goes along with substance abuse, and that honesty is necessary for recovery.

B. The veteran/service member was asked to identify 10 lies that he/she has told to hide substance abuse.

C. The veteran/service member developed a list of lies that he/she has told to hide substance abuse, and these were reviewed.

D. The veteran/service member acknowledged his/her pattern of dishonesty, which has supported his/her substance abuse behavior, and reported increased honesty during recovery; this insight was highlighted.

E. The veteran/service member denied any pattern of dishonesty to hide substance abuse and was provided with examples of how this occurs.

21. Teach about Honesty (21)

A. The veteran/service member was taught about why honesty is essential to recovery.

B. The veteran/service member was provided with several examples of how honesty is an important part of recovery.

C. The veteran/service member was asked to identify his/her own understanding of how honesty is essential to recovery.

22. Teach about a Higher Power (22)

A. The veteran/service member was presented with information on how faith in a higher power can aid in recovery from substance abuse and addictive behaviors.

B. The veteran/service member was assisted in processing and clarifying his/her own ideas and feelings about his/her higher power.

C. The veteran/service member was encouraged to describe his/her beliefs about his/her higher power.

D. The veteran/service member rejected the concept of a higher power and was urged to remain open to this concept.

23. Conduct Motivational Interviewing (23)

A. Motivational interviewing techniques were used to help assess the veteran's/service member's preparation for change.

B. The veteran/service member was assisted in identifying his/her stage of change regarding his/her substance abuse concerns.

C. It was reflected to the veteran/service member that he/she is currently building motivation for change.

D. The veteran/service member was assisted in strengthening his/her commitment to change.

E. The veteran/service member was noted to be participating actively in treatment.

24. Assign AA/NA Member Contact (24)

A. The veteran/service member was assigned to meet with an Alcoholics Anonymous/Narcotics Anonymous (AA/NA) member who has been working the 12-step program for several years to find out specifically how the program has helped him/her stay sober.

B. The veteran/service member has followed through on meeting with the AA/NA member and was encouraged about the role that AA/NA can play in maintaining sobriety.

C. The veteran/service member met with the AA/NA member but was not encouraged about the role of self-help groups in maintaining sobriety; his/her experience was processed.

D. The veteran/service member has not followed through on meeting with an AA/NA member and was redirected to do so.

25. Identify Sobriety Expectations (25)

A. The veteran/service member was asked to write out basic expectations that he/she has regarding sobriety.

B. The veteran/service member has identified specific expectations that he/she has regarding sobriety (e.g., physical changes, social changes, emotional needs), and these were processed with the clinician.

C. As the veteran/service member has been assisted in developing a more realistic expectation regarding his/her sobriety, he/she has felt more at ease and willing to work toward sobriety.

D. The veteran/service member has not identified his/her expectations regarding sobriety and was redirected to do so.

26. Encourage Sobriety Despite Relapses (26)

A. Although the veteran/service member has relapsed, he/she was refocused on the need for substance abuse recovery and on the need for sobriety.

B. As the veteran/service member has received continued support for his/her recovery and sobriety despite his/her relapses, he/she has become more confident regarding his/her chances for success.

C. The veteran/service member lacks confidence in his/her ability to obtain recovery and sobriety due to his/her pattern of relapses; this pessimism was challenged and processed.

27. Assign Abstinence Contract (27)

A. The veteran/service member was assigned to write an abstinence contract for his/her drug of choice as a means of terminating his/her emotional and cognitive involvement with that drug.

B. The veteran/service member has followed through with writing the abstinence contract for his/her drug of choice, and the contents of it were processed.

C. The veteran's/service member's feelings about writing an abstinence contract were processed.

D. The veteran/service member reported that he/she felt some sense of relief at breaking emotional ties with his/her drug of choice; the benefits of this progress were reviewed.

E. The veteran/service member failed to follow through on the assigned abstinence contract for his/her drug of choice and was redirected to do so.

28. Review Negative Peer Influence (28)

A. A review of the veteran's/service member's negative peers was performed, and the influence of these people on his/her substance abuse patterns was identified.

B. The veteran/service member accepted the interpretation that maintaining contact with substance-abusing friends would reduce the probability of successful recovery from his/her chemical dependence.

C. A plan was developed to help the veteran/service member initiate contact with sober people who could exert a positive influence on his/her own recovery (e.g., sobriety buddies).

D. The veteran/service member has begun to reach out socially to sober individuals in order to develop a social network that has a more positive influence on his/her recovery; he/she was reinforced for this progress.

E. The veteran/service member has not attempted to reach out socially to sober individuals in order to develop a social network that has a more positive influence in his/her recovery and was reminded about this important facet of his/her recovery.

29. Identify Sobriety's Positive Family Effects (29)

A. The veteran/service member was assisted in identifying the positive changes that will occur within family relationships as a result of his/her chemical dependence recovery.

B. The veteran/service member reported that his/her family is enjoying a reduction in stress and increased cooperation since his/her chemical dependence recovery began; his/her reaction to these changes was processed.

C. The veteran/service member was unable to identify any positive changes that have or could occur within family relationships as a result of his/her chemical dependence recovery and was provided with tentative examples in this area.

30. Reinforce Making Amends (30)

A. The negative effects that the veteran's/service member's substance abuse has had on family, friends, and work relationships were identified.

B. A plan for making amends to those who have been negatively affected by the veteran's/service member's substance abuse was developed.

C. The veteran's/service member's implementation of his/her plan to make amends to those who have been hurt by his/her substance abuse was reviewed.

D. The veteran/service member reported feeling good about the fact that he/she has begun to make amends to others who have been hurt by his/her substance abuse; this progress was reinforced.

E. The veteran/service member has not followed through on making amends to others who have been negatively affected by his/her pattern of substance abuse and was reminded to do so.

31. Obtain Commitment Regarding Making Amends (31)

A. The veteran/service member was asked to make a verbal commitment to make amends to key individuals.

B. The veteran/service member was urged to make further amends while working through Steps 8 and 9 of a 12-step program.

C. The veteran/service member was supported as he/she made a verbal commitment to make initial amends now and to make further amends as he/she works through Steps 8 and 9 of the 12-step program.

D. The veteran/service member declined to commit to making amends and was redirected to review the need to make this commitment.

32. Refer for Marital Therapy (32)

A. The couple was referred to a clinician who specializes in behavioral marital therapy.

B. The couple was provided with behavioral marital therapy.

C. The couple was assisted in identifying conflicts that could be addressed using communication, conflict-resolution, and/or problem-solving skills.

D. Techniques described by Holzworth-Monroe and Jacobson in "Behavioral Marital Therapy" in *Handbook of Family Therapy* (Gurman and Knickerson) were used to help the couple develop better communication, conflict-resolution, and problem-solving skills.

33. Teach about Coping Strategies (33)

A. The veteran/service member was taught a variety of calming and coping techniques to help manage urges to use chemical substances.

B. The veteran/service member was taught calming strategies, such as relaxation and breathing techniques.

C. The veteran/service member was taught cognitive techniques, such as thought-stopping, positive self-talk, and attention-focusing skills (e.g., distraction from urges, staying focused, behavioral goals of abstinence).

D. The veteran/service member has used his/her calming and coping strategies to help reduce his/her urges to use chemical substances; this progress was reinforced.

E. The veteran/service member has not used the calming and coping strategies for managing urges to use chemical substances and was redirected to do so.

34. Explore Schema and Self-Talk (34)

A. The veteran's/service member's schema and self-talk that weaken his/her resolve to remain abstinent were explored.

B. The biases that the veteran/service member entertains regarding his/her schema and self-talk were challenged.

C. The veteran/service member was assisted in generating more realistic self-talk to correct for his/her biases and build resilience.

D. The veteran/service member was provided with positive feedback for his/her replacement of self-talk and biases.

E. The veteran/service member struggled to identify his/her self-talk and biases that weaken his/her resolve to remain abstinent and was provided with tentative examples in this area.

35. Rehearse Replacement of Negative Self-Talk (35)

A. The veteran/service member was assisted in identifying situations in which his/her negative self-talk occurs.

B. The veteran/service member was assisted in generating empowering alternatives to his/her negative self-talk.

C. The veteran/service member was assigned "Journal and Replace Self-Defeating Thoughts" from the *Adult Psychotherapy Homework Planner*, 2nd ed. (Jongsma).

D. The veteran/service member completed the homework assignment, and the content was processed within the session.

E. The veteran's/service member's success in rehearsing the response to negative self-talk was reviewed and reinforced.

36. Develop Hierarchy of Urge-Producing Cues (36)

A. The veteran/service member was directed to construct a hierarchy of urge-producing cues to use substances.

B. The veteran/service member was assisted in developing a hierarchy of urge-producing cues to use substances.

C. The veteran/service member was assigned "Identifying Relapse Triggers and Cues" from the *Addiction Treatment Homework Planner,* 4th ed. (Finley and Lenz).

D. The veteran/service member was assigned "Relapse Prevention Planning" from the *Addiction Treatment Homework Planner,* 4th ed. (Finley and Lenz).

E. The veteran/service member completed the homework assignment, and the content was processed within the session.

F. The veteran/service member was helped to identify a variety of cues that prompt his/her use of substances.

G. The veteran/service member has failed to identify a hierarchy of urge-producing cues and was assisted in developing this task.

37. Practice Response to Urge-Producing Cues (37)

A. The veteran/service member was assisted in selecting urge-producing cues with which to practice, with a bias toward cues that are likely to result in a successful experience.

B. Behavioral techniques were used to help the veteran/service member cognitively restructure his/her urge-producing cues.

C. The veteran's/service member's use of cognitive-restructuring strategies was reviewed and processed.

38. Assess Stress-Management Skills (38)

A. The veteran's/service member's current level of skill in managing everyday stressors was assessed.

B. The veteran/service member was assessed in regard to his/her ability to meet role demands for work, social, and family expectations.

C. Behavioral and cognitive-restructuring techniques were used to help build social and communication skills to manage everyday challenges.

D. The veteran/service member was provided with positive feedback regarding his/her ability to manage common everyday stressors.

E. The veteran/service member continues to struggle with common everyday stressors and was provided with remedial feedback in this area.

39. Assign Social and Communication Information (39)

A. The veteran/service member was assigned to read about social skills.

B. The veteran/service member was assigned to read about communication skills.

C. The veteran/service member was assigned to read *Your Perfect Right* (Alberti and Emmons).

D. The veteran/service member was assigned to read *Conversationally Speaking* (Garner).

E. The veteran/service member has read the assigned information about social and communication skills, and key points were reviewed.

F. The veteran/service member has not read the assigned information on social and communication skills and was redirected to do so.

40. Teach Pain Management (40)

A. The veteran/service member was taught about pain management in order to learn alternatives to substance use for managing pain.

B. The veteran/service member was referred to a pain management program to learn alternatives to substance use for managing pain.

C. As the veteran/service member has gained better control over his/her pain, it was noted that he/she has gained greater control over substance use.

41. Differentiate between Lapse and Relapse (41)

A. A discussion was held with the veteran/service member regarding the distinction between a lapse and a relapse.

B. A lapse was associated with an initial and reversible return of symptoms or urges to use substances.

C. A relapse was associated with the decision to return to regular use of substances.

D. The veteran/service member was provided with support and encouragement as he/she displayed an understanding of the difference between a lapse and a relapse.

E. The veteran/service member struggled to understand the difference between a lapse and a relapse and was provided with remedial feedback in this area.

42. Uncover Triggers for Relapse (42)

A. A 12-step recovery program relapse prevention exercise was used to help the veteran/service member uncover his/her triggers for relapse.

B. Through the use of the 12-step recovery program relapse prevention exercise, the veteran/service member has gained a significant amount of insight into his/her triggers for relapse.

C. The veteran/service member struggled to identify his/her triggers for relapse and was provided with remedial assistance in this area.

43. Discuss Management of Lapse Risk Situations (43)

A. The veteran/service member was assisted in identifying future situations or circumstances in which lapses could occur.

B. The session focused on rehearsing the management of future situations or circumstances in which lapses could occur.

C. The veteran/service member was asked to identify how family and peer conflict contribute to his/her stress levels.

D. The veteran/service member was reinforced for his/her appropriate use of lapse management skills.

E. The veteran/service member was redirected in regard to his/her poor use of lapse management skills.

44. Identify Relapse Triggers (44)

A. The veteran/service member was assisted in developing a list of potential relapse signs and triggers that could lead him/her back to substance abuse.

B. The veteran/service member was asked to identify specific primary psychotic symptoms that affect his/her desire for substances.

C. The veteran/service member was assigned "Relapse Triggers" from the *Adult Psychotherapy Homework Planner*, 2nd ed. (Jongsma).

D. The veteran/service member completed the homework assignment, and the content was processed within the session.

E. The veteran/service member was supported for identifying specific primary psychotic symptoms and how these increase his/her desire for substances.

F. The veteran/service member was assisted in developing a specific strategy for constructively responding to his/her substance abuse relapse triggers.

G. The veteran/service member was reinforced for his/her successful implementation of the coping strategies for the substance abuse relapse triggers.

H. A review was conducted regarding the veteran's/service member's pattern of relapse subsequent to failing to use constructive coping strategies in a trigger situation.

45. Encourage Routine Use of Strategies (45)

A. The veteran/service member was instructed to routinely use the strategies that he/she has learned in therapy (e.g., cognitive restructuring exposure).

B. The veteran/service member was assigned "Aftercare Plan Components" from the *Adult Psychotherapy Homework Planner*, 2nd ed. (Jongsma).

C. The veteran/service member completed the homework assignment, and the content was processed within the session.

D. The veteran/service member was urged to find ways to build his/her new strategies into his/her life as much as possible.

E. The veteran/service member was reinforced as he/she reported ways in which he/she has incorporated coping strategies into his/her life and routine.

F. The veteran/service member was redirected about ways to incorporate his/her new strategies into his/her routine and life.

46. Teach about Life's Pleasures (46)

A. The veteran/service member was taught about the importance of getting pleasure out of life without using mood-altering substances.

B. The veteran/service member was reminded that the benefits obtained from using mood-altering substances can be developed through the use of alternative, nonsubstance means in order to develop pleasure in his/her life.

C. The veteran/service member reflected his/her understanding of how he/she can get pleasure out of life without using mood-altering substances.

D. The veteran/service member does not appear to understand how life's pleasures can be developed without using mood-altering substances and was provided with remedial feedback in this area.

47. List Pleasurable Activities (47)

A. The veteran/service member was asked to develop a list of pleasurable activities.

B. The veteran/service member was assigned the *Inventory of Rewarding Activities* (Birchler and Weiss).

C. The veteran/service member was assigned to engage in selected activities on a daily basis.

D. The veteran's/service member's use of pleasurable activities was reviewed.

E. The veteran/service member has not developed a regular practice of engaging in pleasurable activities and was redirected to do so.

48. Recommend Daily Routine of Physical Exercise (48)

A. The veteran/service member was recommended to develop a daily routine of physical exercise to assist in building body stamina and self-esteem and to reduce depression.

B. The veteran/service member was encouraged to read *Exercising Your Way to Better Mental Health* (Leith) to introduce him/her to the concept of combating stress, depression, and anxiety with exercise.

C. The veteran/service member has followed through with reading the recommended book on exercise and mental health and reported that it was beneficial; key points were reviewed.

D. The veteran/service member has implemented a regular exercise regimen as a depression reduction technique and reported successful results; he/she was verbally reinforced for this progress.

E. The veteran/service member has not followed through with reading the recommended material on the effect of exercise on mental health and was encouraged to do so.

49. Review Current Level of Fitness with Leadership (49)

A. The service member was instructed to discuss his/her current level of fitness with his/her platoon sergeant, first sergeant, or other leadership.

B. The service member was encouraged to work with his/her sergeant to develop a regular physical fitness regimen.

C. The service member was reinforced for his/her improved physical fitness training.

D. The service member has not developed an improved physical fitness regimen and was redirected to do so.

50. Teach about "Turning It Over" (50)

A. The veteran/service member was taught about the concept of turning problems over to a higher power every day.

B. The veteran/service member was asked to reflect upon his/her opportunities to turn his/her problems over to a higher power and how this would be beneficial.

C. The veteran/service member was reinforced for his/her use of a higher power.

D. The veteran/service member has not turned problems over to a higher power and was provided with examples of how others have used this option.

SUICIDAL IDEATION

VETERAN/SERVICE MEMBER PRESENTATION

1. Suicidal Ideation without Plan (1)*

A. The veteran/service member reported experiencing recurrent suicidal ideation but denied having any specific plan to implement suicidal urges.

B. The frequency and intensity of the veteran's/service member's suicidal urges have diminished.

C. The veteran/service member stated that he/she has not experienced any recent suicidal ideation.

D. The veteran/service member stated that he/she no longer has interest in causing harm to himself/herself.

2. Death Preoccupation (1)

A. The veteran/service member reported recurrent thoughts of his/her own death.

B. The intensity and frequency of the recurrent thoughts of death have diminished.

C. The veteran/service member reported no longer having thoughts of his/her own death.

3. Suicide Intent (2)

A. The veteran/service member reported that his/her thoughts about suicide have grown to the point of an intention of committing suicide.

B. The veteran/service member presents as an individual planning to commit suicide.

C. The frequency and intensity of suicidal urges have diminished.

D. The veteran/service member denies any recent suicidal ideation.

E. The veteran/service member stated that he/she no longer has any intent to harm himself/herself.

4. Suicidal Ideation with Plan (3)

A. The veteran/service member reported experiencing ongoing suicidal ideation and has developed a specific plan for suicide.

B. Although the veteran/service member acknowledged that he/she has developed a suicide plan, he/she indicated that the suicidal urge is controllable and promised not to implement such a plan.

C. Because the veteran/service member had a specific suicide plan and strong suicidal urges, he/she was willingly admitted to a supervised psychiatric facility and more intensive treatment.

D. The veteran/service member stated that his/her suicidal urges have diminished and he/she has no interest in implementing any specific suicide plan.

E. The veteran/service member reported no suicidal urges.

---

*The numbers in parentheses correlate to the number of the Behavioral Definition statement in the companion chapter with the same title in *The Veterans and Active Duty Military Psychotherapy Treatment Planner* (Moore and Jongsma) by John Wiley & Sons, 2009.

5. Hopelessness/Emptiness (4)

A. The veteran/service member displayed a bleak, hopeless attitude regarding life, linked to recent stressful experiences that are overwhelming him/her.

B. The veteran/service member described a hopeless attitude related to a recent divorce proceeding.

C. The veteran/service member described a sense of emptiness.

D. The veteran/service member displayed a hopeless attitude related to the death of a family member.

E. The veteran's/service member's hopeless attitude about life has diminished and he/she has begun to make more hopeful statements about the future.

F. The veteran/service member no longer has a hopeless attitude about life and has demonstrated a normal attitude of hope and planning for the future.

6. Past Suicide Attempts/Gestures (5)

A. The veteran/service member reported a history of suicide attempts that have not been recent but did require professional and/or family/friend intervention to guarantee safety.

B. The veteran/service member described a history of suicide gestures without any specific intent of actually killing himself/herself.

C. The veteran/service member minimized his/her history of suicide attempts and treated the experience lightly.

D. The veteran/service member acknowledged the history of suicide attempts with appropriate affect and explained the depth of his/her depression at the time of the attempt.

E. The veteran/service member indicated no current interest in or thoughts about suicidal behavior.

7. Risky/Dangerous Behavior in Combat (6)

A. The service member has been engaging in self-destructive or dangerous behavior that appears to invite death.

B. The service member has engaged in dangerous behavior during combat missions (e.g., entering a house without backup).

C. The service member has been increasing self-destructive or dangerous behaviors.

D. The service member's pattern of self-destructive behavior has significantly diminished.

E. As treatment has progressed, the service member has discontinued his/her pattern of self-destructive and dangerous behavior.

8. Close Connection to Completed Suicide (7)

A. The veteran/service member reported that a family member has committed suicide.

B. The veteran/service member reported that a close friend has committed suicide.

C. The veteran/service member acknowledged the family/social history of depression/suicide and indicated the negative impact of this on him/her.

9. Lethargy/Apathy (8)

A. The veteran/service member reported no longer having the energy for or the interest in activities that he/she formerly found challenging and rewarding.

B. The veteran/service member reported a pattern of engaging in little or no constructive activity and often just sitting or lying around the house.

C. The veteran/service member has begun to demonstrate increased energy and interest in activity.

D. The veteran/service member has returned to normal levels of energy and has also shown renewed interest in enjoyable and challenging activities.

10. Akathisia (9)

A. The veteran/service member displays akathisia (motor restlessness).

B. The veteran's/service member's long history of prescription medication use has resulted in akathisia.

C. The veteran's/service member's use of illicit drugs has resulted in akathisia.

D. The veteran/service member has shown a calmer, more relaxed demeanor recently.

E. The veteran/service member shows no evidence of akathisia any longer.

11. Lack of Future Orientation (10)

A. The veteran/service member displays a lack of future orientation.

B. The veteran/service member does not identify any future plans.

C. The veteran/service member appears hopeless about the future.

D. As treatment has progressed, the veteran/service member has become more hopeful and focused on his/her future.

12. Giving Away Meaningful Possessions (11)

A. The veteran/service member has recently been giving away personal and meaningful possessions to friends, family, or strangers.

B. The veteran/service member acknowledged that his/her hopelessness about the future has resulted in his/her giving away possessions.

C. As treatment has progressed, the veteran/service member has become more hopeful.

13. Uncharacteristic Hostility (12)

A. The veteran/service member displays a recent onset of uncharacteristic disrespectful and hostile behavior toward superiors.

B. The veteran/service member has become hostile toward his/her superiors.

C. As treatment has progressed, the veteran/service member has returned to his/her typical positive relationship with superiors.

INTERVENTIONS IMPLEMENTED

1. Assess Suicidal Ideation (1)[*]

A. The veteran/service member was asked to describe the frequency and intensity of his/her suicidal ideation, the details of any existing suicide plan, the history of any previous suicide attempts, and any family history of depression or suicide.

---

[*]The numbers in parentheses correlate to the number of the Therapeutic Intervention statement in the companion chapter with the same title in *The Veterans and Active Duty Military Psychotherapy Treatment Planner* (Moore and Jongsma) by John Wiley & Sons, 2009.

B. The veteran/service member was encouraged to be forthright regarding the current strength of his/her suicidal feelings and the ability to control such suicidal urges.

C. The veteran/service member was assessed as being at a high risk for committing suicide.

D. The veteran/service member was assessed as being at a moderate risk for committing suicide.

E. The veteran/service member was assessed as being at a low risk for committing suicide.

2. Administer Psychological Testing (2)

A. Psychological testing was administered to the veteran/service member to evaluate the depth of his/her depression and the degree of suicide risk.

B. The Beck Depression Inventory, 2nd ed. (BDI-II) was administered.

C. The Beck Hopelessness Scale (BHS) was administered.

D. The Suicide Probability Scale (SPS) was administered.

E. The psychological test results indicate that the veteran's/service member's depression is severe and the suicide risk is high.

F. The psychological test results indicate that the veteran's/service member's depression is moderate and the suicide risk is mild.

G. The psychological test results indicate that the veteran's/service member's depression level has decreased significantly and the suicide risk is minimal.

3. Notify Significant Others (3)

A. Significant others were notified of the veteran's/service member's suicidal ideation, and they were asked to form a 24-hour suicide watch until the veteran's/service member's crisis subsides.

B. The service member's chain of command was advised about his/her suicide potential.

C. The follow-through of significant others in providing supervision of the veteran/service member during this suicide crisis was monitored.

D. Significant others were contacted to make sure that the veteran/service member was receiving adequate supervision.

4. Identify Immediate Help (4)

A. The veteran/service member was asked to identify a clear plan for seeking help if he/she feels suicidal prior to the next appointment.

B. The veteran/service member was directed to contact his/her immediate supervisor, relative, or friend if his/her suicide thoughts become overwhelming.

C. The veteran/service member committed to specific options for seeking help if he/she feels suicidal prior to the next appointment, and this support was reinforced.

5. Schedule Follow-up Appointment (5)

A. A follow-up appointment was scheduled for the veteran/service member.

B. The veteran/service member was reminded about the importance of the follow-up appointment due to the concern about suicide.

C. The veteran/service member has attended his/her follow-up appointment.

D. The veteran/service member has not attended his/her follow-up appointment, and steps were taken to contact him/her.

6. Develop Suicide Prevention/No Harm Contract (6)

A. A suicide prevention contract/no harm was developed with the veteran/service member that stipulated what he/she will and will not do when experiencing suicidal thoughts or impulses.

B. The veteran/service member was asked to make a commitment to agree to the terms of the suicide prevention contract and did make such a commitment.

C. The veteran/service member declined to sign a suicide prevention contract, and more specific steps to maintain his/her safety from self-injurious behavior were initiated.

7. Review No-Harm Contract (7)

A. The no-harm contract was reviewed on a session-by-session basis, as needed.

B. The veteran/service member was reminded about his/her commitment to the no-harm contract.

C. The veteran/service member was reinforced for his/her recommitment to the no-harm contract.

D. The veteran/service member was not able to recommit to the no-harm contract, and more specific steps were taken to provide for his/her safety.

8. Develop Commitment to Treatment (8)

A. The contract between clinician and the veteran/service member was discussed.

B. A written commitment to treatment contract was developed for the veteran/service member to sign.

C. The veteran/service member has signed the written commitment to treatment contract, and this progress was reinforced.

D. The veteran/service member made a verbal agreement to the treatment contract.

E. The veteran/service member has not committed to the treatment contract, and additional steps were taken to engage him/her in treatment.

9. Notify Significant Others to Make Home Safe (9)

A. Significant others were notified of the veteran's/service member's suicidal ideation, and they were asked to form a 24-hour suicide watch until his/her crisis subsides.

B. The follow-through of significant others in providing supervision of the veteran/service member during this suicide crisis was monitored.

C. Significant others were contacted to make sure that the veteran/service member was receiving adequate supervision.

D. Significant others were encouraged to remove firearms and other potentially lethal means of suicide from the veteran's/service member's easy access.

E. Contact was made with significant others within the veteran's/service member's life to monitor his/her behavior and to remove potential means of suicide.

10. Inform Chain of Command (10)

A. The service member's chain of command was notified of his/her suicidal ideation and was asked to form a 24-hour suicide watch until the service member's crisis subsides.

B. The service member's chain of command was contacted to make sure that he/she is receiving adequate supervision.

C. The chain of command was assisted in making the work environment safer by restricting access to weapons and limiting the service member to low-risk training.

11. Arrange for Hospitalization (11)

A. Because the veteran/service member was judged to be uncontrollably harmful to himself/herself, arrangements were made for psychiatric hospitalization.

B. The veteran/service member cooperated voluntarily with admission to a psychiatric hospital.

C. The veteran/service member refused to cooperate voluntarily with admission to a psychiatric facility, and therefore commitment procedures were initiated.

12. Inform about Hospitalization (12)

A. The veteran's/service member's family members were informed about his/her required hospitalization.

B. The veteran's/service member's chain of command was informed about his/her required hospitalization.

13. Develop Safety Plan (13)

A. A safety plan was developed with the service member's chain of command.

B. A 24-hour-per-day shadow program was developed.

C. The service member was expected to be in sight of a peer 24 hours a day.

D. The service member has been compliant with the safety plan as developed.

E. The service member has not been compliant with the safety plan and was reminded to continue this for his/her own safety.

F. The service member has not been compliant with the safety plan, and a more restrictive setting was initiated.

14. Meet with Significant Others (14)

A. The veteran's/service member's significant others were invited to receive information about his/her suicidal ideation, how they can help, and what behaviors may be counterproductive.

B. The veteran's/service member's significant others indicated support for him/her and understood the information related to suicidal ideation, helpfulness, and counterproductive behaviors.

C. The veteran's/service member's significant others declined to meet to obtain more information about his/her situation and were encouraged to utilize this opportunity as they see fit.

15. Promote Family Communication (15)

A. A family therapy session was held to promote communication of the veteran's/service member's feelings of sadness, hurt, and anger.

B. The family members were encouraged to communicate their respect for and understanding of the veteran's/service member's feelings.

C. Family members were encouraged to process the conflicts and feelings between them so as to find a resolution and to express a commitment to an ongoing relationship.

16. Explore Emotional Pain Sources (16)

A. The veteran/service member was asked to explore and identify life factors that preceded the suicidal ideation.

B. The veteran/service member was supported as he/she identified the sources of emotional pain and hopelessness that precipitated the suicidal crisis.

C. The veteran/service member was reluctant to identify the sources of emotional pain and hopelessness that precipitated the suicidal crisis and was provided with tentative examples of how these occur.

D. The veteran/service member was assisted in developing coping strategies to manage his/her stressors.

17. Review Past Suicidal Ideation (17)

A. A discussion was held with the veteran/service member regarding past episodes of suicidal ideation.

B. The veteran/service member was assisted in identifying triggers for his/her past suicidal ideation.

C. The veteran/service member was open and forthcoming with his/her history of suicidal ideation and triggers, and this information was processed.

D. The veteran/service member seemed reluctant to provide information about his/her past suicidal ideation and triggers, and additional assistance was provided.

18. Highlight Past Successes in Overcoming Suicidal Ideation (18)

A. The veteran/service member was asked to identify previous situations in which he/she has overcome suicidal ideation.

B. The veteran/service member was assisted in identifying his/her past experience for overcoming suicidal ideation.

C. The veteran/service member was unable to identify how he/she has overcome suicidal ideation in the past, and was asked questions to explore this further.

19. Refer for Medication Evaluation (19)

A. An assessment was made about the veteran's/service member's need for antidepressant medication, and arrangements were made for a prescription.

B. The veteran/service member cooperated with a referral to a physician who evaluated him/her for antidepressant medication and provided a prescription for this medication.

C. The veteran/service member agreed to accept a prescription for antidepressant medication.

D. The veteran/service member refused to accept a prescription for antidepressant medication.

E. The veteran/service member has not followed through on the referral for medication and was redirected to do so.

20. Follow Up on Missed Medication Appointment (20)

A. The veteran/service member was asked to identify why he/she missed the scheduled medication appointment.

B. The veteran's/service member's family members were contacted about his/her failure to attend the scheduled medication appointment.

C. The veteran's/service member's chain of command was contacted in regard to his/her failure to attend the scheduled appointment.

D. The veteran/service member has attended all scheduled medication appointments, and this consistency was reinforced.

21. Monitor Medication Compliance (21)

A. The veteran/service member has been monitored for compliance with the prescribed antidepressant medication, and the effects of that medication were assessed.

B. The veteran/service member has been noted to be taking the medication as prescribed and reports that it has produced a reduction in the depth of depression and suicidal ideation.

C. The veteran/service member has not been taking the antidepressant medication consistently and was urged to do so.

D. The veteran/service member reported taking the antidepressant medication consistently but said that no positive effects from this medication have been noted; this was communicated to the prescribing clinician.

E. The veteran's/service member's prescribing physician has been contacted regarding the veteran's/service member's medication compliance and the effect of the medication on the depression and suicidal ideation.

22. Promote Hopeful Attitude (22)

A. The veteran/service member was assisted in identifying positive and hopeful things in his/her life at the present time.

B. The veteran/service member identified positive aspects, relationships, and achievements in his/her life, and these positive things were supported and reinforced.

C. The veteran/service member was supported as he/she reported and demonstrated an increased sense of hope for himself/herself and the future.

D. When the veteran/service member displayed a more pessimistic attitude, he/she was encouraged to have a more positive outlook.

23. Identify Distorted Cognitions (23)

A. The veteran/service member was assisted in developing an awareness of the negative and distorted cognitive messages that reinforce helplessness and hopelessness.

B. The veteran/service member was assigned the homework exercise "Negative Thoughts Trigger Negative Feelings" in the *Adult Psychotherapy Homework Planner*, 2nd ed. (Jongsma).

C. The veteran/service member has identified several distorted self-talk messages that he/she has engaged in that are counterproductive and precipitate feelings of low self-esteem, hopelessness, and helplessness; these were processed.

D. The veteran/service member struggled to identify distorted cognitions and was provided with tentative examples in this area (e.g., I am worthless, I am not worthy of love).

24. Teach Awareness of Automatic Thoughts (24)

A. The veteran/service member was taught about how to become more aware of automatic thoughts.

B. The veteran/service member was directed to maintain a daily journal of automatic thoughts.

C. The veteran/service member was assigned the homework exercise "Journal of Distorted, Negative Thoughts" in the *Adult Psychotherapy Homework Planner*, 2nd ed. (Jongsma).

D. The veteran/service member identified his/her automatic thoughts, and these were processed within the session.

E. The veteran/service member struggled to identify distorted, negative thoughts and was provided with additional examples in this area.

25. Use Cognitive Restructuring Techniques (25)

A. The veteran/service member was taught cognitive restructuring techniques to revise distorted negative core schemas.

B. The veteran/service member was provided with examples of maladaptive distortions (e.g., all-or-nothing thinking, overgeneralization, magnification).

C. The veteran/service member was reinforced for modifying his/her negative automatic thoughts and replacing them with more realistic positive thoughts that produce feelings of hope and empowerment.

D. The veteran/service member was redirected when he/she did not use the cognitive restructuring techniques.

26. Continue Queries about Suicidal Ideation (26)

A. The veteran/service member was asked about possible suicidal ideation despite the apparent resolution of the suicide crisis.

B. The veteran/service member indicated no further suicidal ideation, and this was reinforced.

C. The veteran/service member identified some level of suicidal ideation, and treatment was focused again on resolving this suicide crisis.

27. Explore Spiritual Support System (27)

A. The veteran's/service member's spiritual belief system was explored to discover whether it could be a source of reassurance, support, and peace.

B. The veteran/service member was assigned the homework exercise "The Aftermath of Suicide" from the *Adult Psychotherapy Homework Planner,* 2nd ed. (Jongsma).

C. The veteran/service member was encouraged to engage in the faith practices that nurture and strengthen his/her spiritual belief system.

D. The veteran/service member was reinforced for verbalizing the feeling of support that results from his/her spiritual faith.

E. The veteran/service member has not explored the use of a spiritual support system for his/her concerns and was encouraged to investigate this helpful resource.

28. Refer to Spiritual Leader (28)

A. The veteran/service member was encouraged to meet with his/her identified spiritual leader to obtain support, encouragement, and strengthening of spiritual tenets.

B. The veteran/service member was directed to meet with his/her unit chaplain.

C. The veteran's/service member's meeting with his/her spiritual leader was processed, and support for continued involvement in his/her faith network was encouraged.

D. The veteran/service member has not sought out a spiritual leader and was redirected to do so.

29. Identify Mental Health Resources (29)

A. The service member was assisted in identifying mental health resources at the location where he/she will be deployed.

B. The service member was provided with specific information for how to seek mental health services in the area where he/she will be deployed.

C. Contacts were made to assist in the transition for mental health services in the service member's new deployment.

30. Arrange Medication for Deployment Transition (30)

A. The service member was provided with an appropriate amount of medication to get him/her through the deployment transition.

B. Steps were taken to coordinate the service member's ability to access his/her medications through the deployment transition.

SURVIVOR'S GUILT

VETERAN/SERVICE MEMBER PRESENTATION

1. Feelings of Guilt (1)[*]

A. The veteran/service member verbalized guilt over his/her survival when a fellow comrade was killed or seriously injured.

B. The veteran/service member acknowledged that although he/she has been injured, he/she experiences guilt because others were more seriously injured or died.

C. The veteran/service member verbalized an unreasonable belief of having contributed to the death of his/her comrade(s).

D. The veteran's/service member's feelings of guilt have diminished.

E. The veteran/service member reported that he/she no longer experiences guilt related to his/her loss.

2. Self-Blame for Loss (2)

A. The veteran/service member reported a sense of blame for a comrade's loss of life.

B. The veteran/service member made unreasonable statements about how he/she was responsible for his/her comrade's death.

C. The veteran/service member acknowledged a partial responsibility for the loss of a comrade.

D. The veteran/service member reports a reduced sense of blame for his/her comrade's death.

E. The veteran/service member reported that he/she no longer experiences a sense of blame for the loss of his/her comrade's life.

3. Preoccupation about Failure to Prevent Loss/Injury (3)

A. The veteran/service member reports constant thoughts about how he/she did not do enough to prevent a comrade's loss of life.

B. The veteran/service member often thinks that he/she could have minimized his/her comrade's injuries if he/she had acted in a different manner.

C. The veteran/service member reports that his/her thoughts about his/her role in a comrade's loss of life or injury have become more manageable.

D. The veteran/service member has acknowledged a more realistic understanding of his/her role in his/her comrade's loss of life or injury.

4. Worthlessness and Self-Loathing (4)

A. The veteran/service member had experienced feelings of worthlessness and self-loathing that began subsequent to his/her comrade's death or injury.

B. The veteran/service member often makes comments about his/her worthlessness and failure as a soldier.

---

[*]The numbers in parentheses correlate to the number of the Behavioral Definition statement in the companion chapter with the same title in *The Veterans and Active Duty Military Psychotherapy Treatment Planner* (Moore and Jongsma) by John Wiley & Sons, 2009.

C. The veteran's/service member's feelings of worthlessness and self-loathing have diminished as he/she has gained greater perspective on his/her comrade's loss/injury.

D. The veteran/service member has expressed positive feelings about himself/herself and affirmations of his/her own self-worth.

5. Death Preoccupations (5)

A. The veteran/service member reported recurrent thoughts about his/her own death.

B. The veteran/service member expresses a desire to die or suffer the same fate of his/her comrade.

C. The intensity and frequency of the veteran's/service member's recurrent thoughts of death have diminished.

D. The veteran/service member reported no longer having thoughts of his/her own death or injury.

6. Self-Destructive Behaviors (6)

A. The veteran/service member has been engaging in self-destructive or dangerous behaviors that appear to invite death.

B. The veteran/service member has increased his/her pattern of fighting and other self-destructive behavior.

C. The veteran's/service member's drug and alcohol use has dramatically increased since his/her comrade's death/injury.

D. The veteran/service member has been increasing self-destructive or dangerous behaviors.

E. The veteran/service member has begun to decrease his/her self-destructive or dangerous behaviors.

F. As treatment has progressed, the veteran/service member has discontinued his/her pattern of self-destructive and dangerous behaviors.

INTERVENTIONS IMPLEMENTED

1. Develop Trust (1)[*]

A. Today's clinical contact focused on building a level of trust within the therapeutic relationship through consistent eye contact, active listening, unconditional positive regard, and warm acceptance.

B. Empathy and support were provided for the veteran's/service member's expression of thoughts and feelings during today's clinical contact.

C. The veteran/service member was provided with support and feedback as he/she described his/her pattern of survivor guilt.

D. As the veteran/service member has remained mistrustful and reluctant to share his/her underlying thoughts and feelings, he/she was provided with additional reassurance.

E. The veteran/service member verbally acknowledged that he/she has difficulty establishing trust, and this was accepted by the therapist.

---

[*]The numbers in parentheses correlate to the number of the Therapeutic Intervention statement in the companion chapter with the same title in *The Veterans and Active Duty Military Psychotherapy Treatment Planner* (Moore and Jongsma) by John Wiley & Sons, 2009.

2. Explore Facts of Traumatic Incident (2)

A. The veteran/service member was gently encouraged to tell the entire story of the traumatic event.

B. The veteran/service member was given the opportunity to share what he/she recalls about the traumatic event.

C. The veteran/service member was allowed to talk about his/her guilt-inducing traumatic experience in as much detail as he/she felt capable of providing.

D. Today's therapy session explored the sequence of events before, during, and after the guilt-inducing traumatic event.

3. Assess Severity and Impact of Guilt (3)

A. The depth of the veteran's/service member's guilt was assessed.

B. The level of intensity and the frequency with which the veteran/service member experiences guilt was assessed.

C. The veteran/service member was assisted in identifying the social, occupational, and interpersonal functioning impact of his/her guilt feelings.

D. The veteran/service member was supported as he/she reviewed the impact of his/her guilt concerns.

E. The veteran/service member seemed to be cautious about providing much information regarding his/her guilt concerns and was urged to do so as he/she feels capable.

4. Arrange for Psychiatric Evaluation (4)

A. The veteran/service member was referred for a medication evaluation to determine if antidepressant, anxiolitic, or hypnotic medication is needed to relieve more significant mood or anxiety symptoms and/or sleep disturbances.

B. The veteran/service member was reinforced as he/she agreed to follow through with the medication evaluation.

C. The veteran/service member was strongly opposed to being placed on medication to help stabilize his/her mood and anxiety symptoms; his/her objections were processed.

D. The veteran/service member was assessed for psychiatric medication, and a prescription was provided by the prescribing clinician.

E. The veteran/service member was assessed for possible medication to assist in treating his/her more significant mood, anxiety, and sleep disturbance systems, but no medication was prescribed.

5. Monitor Effects of Medication (5)

A. The veteran's/service member's response to the medication was discussed in today's therapy session.

B. The veteran/service member reported that the medication has helped to stabilize his/her moods and decrease the intensity of his/her feelings; he/she was directed to share this information with the prescribing clinician.

C. The veteran/service member reports little to no improvement in his/her moods or anger control since being placed on the medication; he/she was directed to share this information with the prescribing clinician.

D. The veteran/service member was reinforced for consistently taking the medication as prescribed.

E. The veteran/service member has failed to comply with taking the medication as prescribed; he/she was encouraged to take the medication as prescribed.

F. Consistent contact was kept with the veteran's/service member's prescribing professional in regard to the veteran's/service member's medication compliance, side effects, and efficacy.

6. Encourage Telling Story of Loss (6)

A. The veteran/service member was treated with empathy and compassion as he/she was encouraged to tell the story of his/her recent loss in detail.

B. The veteran/service member was supported as he/she told the story of his/her recent loss.

C. The veteran/service member was reinforced for telling the entire story of the recent loss.

D. The veteran/service member has been guarded about telling the entire story of his/her recent loss and was encouraged to do this in a trusting environment.

E. The veteran/service member was assisted in processing the most relevant material from his/her experience of the loss.

7. Convey Caring, Empathy, and Respect (7)

A. Basic counseling techniques were used to convey caring, empathy, and respect.

B. Reflection and empathic responding were used to convey caring, empathy, and respect.

C. It was noted that the veteran/service member seemed to be more at ease as the clinician conveyed caring, empathy, and respect.

8. Educate about Importance of Strong Emotions (8)

A. The veteran/service member was educated about the importance of acknowledging and connecting with strong emotions.

B. The veteran/service member was encouraged to experience emotional catharsis related to the loss.

C. The veteran/service member was reinforced for his/her acceptance of his/her strong emotions related to the loss.

9. Normalize Emotions (9)

A. The veteran/service member was educated about how experiencing shame, self-blame, and self-loathing is common in response to this type of event.

B. The veteran/service member was provided with examples of how other veteran/service members have experienced shame, self-blame, and self-loathing after this type of event.

C. The veteran/service member was supported and reinforced as he/she has indicated acceptance of the normal nature of his/her emotions.

D. The veteran/service member has not accepted the natural experience of his/her emotions and was provided with additional feedback in this area.

10. Educate about Atypical Symptoms (10)

A. The veteran/service member was educated about emotional and behavioral symptoms that are not typical for survivor reaction.

B. The veteran/service member was urged to monitor himself/herself for symptoms of suicide ideation, increased substance abuse, or domestic violence.

C. The veteran/service member was provided with feedback about how he/she might respond to atypical symptoms.

11. Explore Impediments to Recovery (11)

A. The veteran/service member was urged to explore any impediments to his/her adapting a view of self as "survivor."

B. The veteran/service member was provided with examples of how some dynamics can be an impediment to recovery (e.g., getting sympathy from others).

C. The veteran/service member was supported as he/she identified impediments for accepting the view of self as "survivor."

D. The veteran/service member denied any specific impediments that seemed to keep him/her from developing a "survivor" identity, and this was accepted.

12. Educate about Benefits of Survivor Identity (12)

A. The veteran/service member was educated about how those who see themselves as "survivors" are able to gain a sense of self-control and self-determination.

B. Examples were used from the veteran's/service member's military training and career to illustrate the benefit of a survivor mentality.

C. The veteran/service member was supported as he/she identified his/her benefits for being a "survivor."

D. The veteran/service member was supported as he/she identified an increase in control and self-determination by having a "survivor" mentality.

E. The veteran/service member has struggled to see any benefit from a survivor mentality and was provided with redirection in this area.

13. Assign Support for the Event as Misfortune (13)

A. The veteran/service member was assigned to create a list of reasons supporting the idea that the event was related to misfortune and events outside of his/her control.

B. The veteran/service member was asked to develop a list of reasons why the event was simply a misfortune, regardless of whether he/she completely believes in them.

C. The veteran/service member has completed a list of reasons supporting the idea that the event was related to misfortune; the list was processed.

D. As the veteran/service member has reviewed his/her list of reasons supporting the idea that the event was outside of his/her control, he/she has felt less guilty.

E. The veteran/service member has declined to create a list of reasons supporting the idea that the event was outside of his/her control, and this reticence was processed.

14. Challenge Maladaptive Thoughts (14)

A. The veteran/service member was assisted in identifying maladaptive thoughts that promote misplaced self-blame.

B. The veteran's/service member's maladaptive thoughts that promote misplaced self-blame were challenged.

C. The veteran/service member was assisted in replacing his/her maladaptive thoughts that promote misplaced self-blame.

D. As the veteran's/service member's misplaced self-blame thoughts were identified, challenged, and replaced, he/she reports decreased guilt about the loss.

E. The veteran/service member has failed to accept any challenge to his/her thoughts that promote misplaced self-blame and was provided with additional feedback in this area.

15. Emphasize Effects of Chaos in Combat (15)

A. It was noted that the events related to the veteran's/service member's actions or lack of actions related to the loss was a chaotic combat situation.

B. A discussion was held about the accidents that happen during the stress and chaos of combat.

C. It was reflected to the veteran/service member that the extreme circumstances of combat can negatively impact decision making.

D. The veteran/service member was assisted in processing the issues related to how the stress and chaos affected his/her actions or lack of actions.

16. Emphasize Routine (16)

A. The veteran/service member was educated about how following a routine promotes familiarity, contentment, and predictability.

B. The veteran/service member was encouraged to follow a routine regularly in order to restore a sense of safety and stability.

17. Instruct about Daily Work and Exercise (17)

A. The veteran/service member was instructed to attend work on a daily basis, missing only due to sickness or other extreme circumstances.

B. The veteran/service member was encouraged to exercise on a regular basis, regardless of his/her sense of giving up.

C. The veteran/service member was reinforced for his/her regular work and exercise schedule.

D. The veteran/service member has not worked and exercised on a regular basis and was redirected to do so.

18. Facilitate Closure (18)

A. The veteran/service member was encouraged to facilitate closure by acknowledging the loss and discussing the impact of the loss on his/her life.

B. The veteran/service member was encouraged to say goodbye by participating in a ritual in order to grieve the loss of the comrade.

C. The veteran/service member was encouraged to attend a funeral/memorial service or visit the burial site.

D. The veteran/service member was encouraged to write a farewell letter or talk to a picture as a ritual for grieving the loss of his/her comrade.

E. The veteran/service member was supported as he/she has taken specific steps to grieve the loss of his/her comrade.

F. The veteran/service member has not taken specific steps to grieve the loss of his/her comrade and was redirected to do so.

19. Assign Visit with Others in Grief (19)

A. The veteran/service member was directed to visit with someone else who knew the fellow comrade and share pleasant memories of the deceased.

B. The veteran/service member was asked to list the most positive aspects of and memories about the relationship with the lost comrade.

C. The veteran's/service member's contact with others grieving the deceased was processed.

D. The veteran/service member has not coordinated to visit with someone else who knew his/her fallen comrade(s) and was redirected to do so.

20. Encourage Annual Memorial Service (20)

A. The veteran/service member was encouraged to plan an annual memorial service honoring the fellow comrade(s).

B. The veteran/service member was assisted in developing a ritual/memorial service that will allow him/her to celebrate the memorable aspects of the lost comrade and the blessings from the comrade's life.

C. The veteran/service member has followed through on developing and implementing an annual memorial/ritual to commemorate the memory of the lost comrade; this experience was processed.

D. The veteran/service member has not followed through on developing an annual memorial service honoring the fallen comrade and was redirected to do so.

21. Emphasize the Joy of Life (21)

A. The veteran/service member was instructed to make a list of why it is good to be alive.

B. The veteran/service member has completed a list of why he/she sees it as good to be alive, and this was processed within the session.

C. The veteran/service member has not completed a list of why it is good to be alive, and his/her reluctance was processed.

22. Emphasize Strengths (22)

A. The veteran/service member was instructed to compile a list of his/her personal, emotional, and social strengths and assets that have helped him/her through difficult times in the past.

B. The veteran/service member was provided with specific examples of his/her strengths from the past that have helped him/her through difficult times.

C. The veteran/service member has completed a list of his/her personal, emotional, and social strengths and assets that have helped him/her through difficult times in the past, and he/she was helped to apply this to his/her current struggles.

D. The veteran/service member has not completed a list of strengths and was redirected to do so.

23. Emphasize Relative Benefit of Inner Resolve and Fortitude (23)

A. The veteran/service member was reminded that his/her situation would be worse if it were not for his/her inner resolve and fortitude.

B. The veteran/service member was assisted in identifying ways in which his/her inner resolve and fortitude have already helped him/her recover.

C. The veteran/service member was unable to identify ways in which his/her inner resolve and fortitude have been beneficial to him/her and was provided with remedial feedback in this area.

24. Explore the Meaning of Life (24)

A. The veteran/service member was encouraged to explore his/her meaning of life and his/her purpose on earth.

B. The veteran/service member was supported as he/she identified his/her beliefs of the meaning of life and his/her purpose on earth.

C. The veteran/service member seemed to have difficulty developing and understanding of meaning-of-life issues and was provided with common examples.

25. Encourage Mentor Contact (25)

A. The veteran/service member was encouraged to talk to someone with more wisdom and experience who is able to share his/her philosophy of life and death.

B. The veteran/service member was encouraged to search for and find a mentor to guide his/her spiritual development.

C. The veteran/service member was reinforced for seeking wisdom and experience from a respected person of spiritual depth.

D. The veteran's/service member's experience with his/her mentor was processed.

E. The veteran/service member has not sought out a spiritual mentor and was redirected to do so.

26. Encourage Connection with Others Experiencing Loss (26)

A. The veteran/service member was encouraged to talk with a veteran or fellow service member who has experienced the same type of loss and feelings.

B. The veteran's/service member's contact with others who have experienced the same type of loss and feelings was reinforced and processed.

C. The veteran/service member has not attempted to coordinate support from another veteran or fellow service member who has experienced the same type of loss and feelings and was redirected to do so.

27. Meet with Chaplain (27)

A. The veteran/service member was encouraged to meet with a military chaplain to discuss his/her emotional and spiritual conflicts about the loss.

B. The veteran/service member was provided with specific information about how to seek out or locate a military chaplain who fits his/her spiritual beliefs.

C. The veteran/service member has met with a military chaplain, and this experience was processed.

D. The veteran/service member has not met with the military chaplain and was redirected to do so.

28. Refer to Grief Support Group (28)

A. The veteran/service member was encouraged to attend a grief/loss support group.

B. The veteran/service member has followed through on attending a grief/loss support group, and his/her positive experience was processed.

C. The veteran/service member has followed through on attending a grief/loss support group, and his/her negative experience was processed.

D. The veteran/service member has not followed through on attending the recommended grief/loss support group and was encouraged to do so.

29. Assess and Encourage Recovery and Cleanup Efforts (29)

A. The service member was assessed to ensure that he/she is psychologically and physically ready to participate in cleanup and recovery activities.

B. The service member was encouraged to participate in cleanup and recovery activities.

C. The service member was discouraged from participating in cleanup and recovery activities.

D. The service member's experience of involvement in cleanup and recovery efforts was processed.

TOBACCO USE

VETERAN/SERVICE MEMBER PRESENTATION

1. Consistent Tobacco Use (1)[*]

A. The veteran/service member described a history of consistent tobacco use manifested by increased use, tolerance, and withdrawal.

B. The veteran/service member acknowledged that he/she has consistently used tobacco, with an inability to successfully discontinue use.

C. The veteran/service member has committed himself/herself to a plan of abstinence from tobacco use.

D. The veteran/service member has maintained total abstinence from nicotine use, which is confirmed by others.

2. Exhibits Decreased Physical Fitness (2)

A. The veteran/service member acknowledged that he/she has become less physically fit because of his/her use of tobacco.

B. The veteran/service member displayed physical indicators that reflect the results of heavy tobacco use (e.g., decreased lung capacity, decreased stamina).

C. The veteran/service member acknowledged that his/her physical problems are related to his/her pattern of heavy tobacco use.

D. As the veteran/service member has participated in the recovery program and has been able to maintain abstinence from tobacco, his/her physical status has improved.

3. Increased Tobacco Use (3)

A. The veteran's/service member's frequency of tobacco use is increasing.

B. Despite the veteran's/service member's attempts at decreasing tobacco use, he/she has continued to increase tobacco use.

4. Inability to Terminate or Reduce Tobacco Use (4)

A. The veteran/service member acknowledged that he/she frequently has attempted to terminate or reduce use of tobacco but found that he/she has been unable to follow through.

B. The veteran/service member acknowledged that, in spite of negative consequences and a desire to terminate tobacco use, he/she has been unable to do so.

C. As the veteran/service member has participated in a total recovery program, he/she has been able to maintain abstinence from nicotine.

5. Physical Withdrawal Symptoms (5)

A. The veteran/service member acknowledged that he/she has experienced physical withdrawal symptoms (e.g., tobacco craving, anxiety, insomnia, irritability, depression) when going without nicotine for any length of time.

[*]The numbers in parentheses correlate to the number of the Behavioral Definition statement in the companion chapter with the same title in *The Veterans and Active Duty Military Psychotherapy Treatment Planner* (Moore and Jongsma) by John Wiley & Sons, 2009.

B. The veteran's/service member's physical symptoms of withdrawal have eased as he/she has stabilized in maintaining abstinence from tobacco products.

6. Social Dissatisfaction Due to Tobacco Use (6)

A. The veteran/service member complained of discolored teeth, bad breath, and/or foul-smelling clothes due to tobacco use.

B. The veteran/service member identified significant social dissatisfaction and alienation due to the personal hygiene effects of his/her tobacco use.

C. As the veteran's/service member's tobacco use has decreased, his/her personal hygiene has improved, along with his/her social satisfaction.

7. Intense Cravings (7)

A. The veteran/service member identified intense nicotine cravings after awakening in the morning.

B. The veteran/service member reported intense nicotine cravings when he/she is unable to use tobacco for several hours at a time.

C. The veteran/service member reported that his/her performance has been affected by his/her intense cravings for nicotine.

D. As the veteran's/service member's tobacco use has decreased, his/her nicotine cravings have gradually decreased as well.

8. Lying (8)

A. The veteran/service member has lied to family and/or friends in order to hide his/her tobacco use.

B. The veteran/service member reports a sense of guilt for his/her untruthfulness to family and friends regarding tobacco use.

C. The veteran/service member has become more honest about his/her tobacco use.

9. Tobacco Use Despite Losses (9)

A. The veteran/service member has continued to use tobacco despite having someone close die from tobacco-related cancer or pulmonary disease.

B. The veteran/service member tends to minimize the contribution tobacco had on his/her loved one's death.

C. As the veteran/service member has become more accepting that his/her loved one died due to tobacco-related causes, his/her motivation for decreasing tobacco use increased.

10. Failure of Physical Training Tests (10)

A. The service member has failed required physical training tests due to decreased lung capacity.

B. The service member is at risk for restriction or sanction due to his/her failure at required physical training tasks.

C. As the service member's tobacco use has decreased, his/her capability on required physical training tests has improved.

INTERVENTIONS IMPLEMENTED

1. Gather Addictive Behavior History (1)*

A. The veteran/service member was asked to describe his/her pattern of nicotine use and other addictions in terms of the amount and pattern of use, symptoms of abuse, and negative life consequences that have resulted from addictive behaviors.

B. Active listening was provided as the veteran/service member openly discussed his/her addictive behavior history and gave complete data regarding its nature and extent.

C. It was reflected to the veteran/service member that he/she was minimizing his/her pattern of addictive behaviors and did not give reliable data regarding the nature and extent of his/her addiction problems.

D. As therapy has progressed, the veteran/service member has become more open in acknowledging the extent and seriousness of his/her nicotine dependence and addiction problems.

2. List Negative Consequences (2)

A. The veteran/service member was asked to make a list of the ways in which nicotine dependence has negatively impacted his/her physical, occupational, social, and interpersonal functioning and to process this list.

B. It was reflected to the veteran/service member that he/she has minimized the negative impact of his/her nicotine dependence on his/her physical, occupational, social, and interpersonal functioning.

C. The veteran/service member completed his/her list of negative impacts of nicotine dependence on his/her physical, occupational, social, and interpersonal functioning and was noted to acknowledge the negative consequences that he/she has experienced.

D. The veteran/service member has not completed the list of negative impacts on his/her physical, occupational, social, and interpersonal functioning and was redirected to do so.

3. Explain the Five Stages of Change (3)

A. The five stages of change were explained to the veteran/service member.

B. Information from *The Transtheoretical Approach: Crossing Traditional Boundaries of Therapy* (Prochaska and DiClemente) was used to explain the five stages of change to the veteran/service member.

C. The veteran/service member was instructed about pre-contemplation, contemplation, preparation, action, and maintenance.

D. The veteran/service member was reinforced for his/her understanding of the five stages of change.

E. The veteran/service member did not display significant understanding about the five stages of change and was provided with remedial information in this area.

4. Assess Contemplation Stage (4)

A. The veteran/service member was assessed to as to whether he/she verbalizes a desire to stop using tobacco.

---

*The numbers in parentheses correlate to the number of the Therapeutic Intervention statement in the companion chapter with the same title in *The Veterans and Active Duty Military Psychotherapy Treatment Planner* (Moore and Jongsma) by John Wiley & Sons, 2009

B. The veteran's/service member's level of contemplation to change was assessed.

C. The veteran/service member was assessed to be in the contemplation stage of change.

D. The veteran/service member was assessed to still be in the pre-contemplation stage of change.

5. Refer for Physical Examination (5)

A. The veteran/service member was referred for a thorough physical examination to determine any negative effects related to his/her nicotine dependence.

B. The veteran/service member has followed through with obtaining a physical examination and was told that his/her nicotine dependence has produced negative medical consequences.

C. The veteran/service member has obtained a physical examination from a physician and has been told that there are no significant medical effects of his/her nicotine dependence.

D. The veteran's/service member's physician has ordered medications that facilitate withdrawal from nicotine and assist in maintaining abstinence.

E. The veteran/service member has not followed through with obtaining a physical examination and was again directed to do so.

6. Educate about Health Risks (6)

A. The veteran/service member was educated about nicotine dependence and the negative effects of nicotine.

B. The veteran/service member was asked to identify several key points learned from the information about using tobacco.

C. Key points were processed with the veteran/service member.

D. The veteran/service member has become more open and acknowledging and accepting of his/her nicotine dependence; this progress was reinforced.

7. Assign Readings on Health Hazards of Smoking (7)

A. The veteran/service member was assigned to read material on nicotine dependence and its negative social, emotional, and medical consequences and to select several key ideas to discuss at a later session.

B. The veteran/service member was assigned to read information from these web links: www.cancer.gov/cancertopics/factsheet/tobacco/cancer; www.cancer.org.

C. The veteran/service member has read the information provided on nicotine dependency, etiology, and consequences, and key ideas were processed.

D. As a result of his/her reading assignment information on nicotine dependence, the veteran/service member has demonstrated an increased understanding of nicotine dependence and the process of recovery.

E. The veteran/service member has not followed through on reading the assigned material on nicotine dependence and was redirected to do so.

8. List Limits/Effects on Functioning (8)

A. The veteran/service member was asked to make a list of ways in which nicotine dependence has negatively impacted his/her life and to process this list.

B. The veteran/service member was directed to identify how his/her physical functioning has been changed due tobacco use (e.g., failing a physical training test).

C. The veteran/service member was directed to identify how his/her social functioning has been affected by tobacco use (e.g., boyfriend/girlfriend left due to tobacco use).

D. It was reflected to the veteran/service member that he/she has minimized the negative impact of nicotine dependence on his/her life.

E. The veteran/service member completed the list of negative impacts of nicotine dependence on his/her life and was noted to acknowledge the negative consequences that he/she experienced.

F. The veteran/service member has not completed the list of negative impacts on his/her life and was redirected to do so.

9. List Improvements from Tobacco Cessation (9)

A. The veteran/service member was instructed to create a list of how his/her life will be better if he/she quits using tobacco.

B. The veteran/service member was provided with examples of how he/she may benefit from quitting tobacco (e.g., more dates, save more money, clothes won't smell, run faster on physical training tests).

C. The veteran/service member has completed a list of how his/her life will be better if he/she quits using tobacco, and this list was reviewed and processed.

D. The veteran/service member has not completed his/her list of benefits from quitting tobacco and was redirected to do so.

10. Set Date for Tobacco Cessation (10)

A. The veteran/service member was instructed to set a specific date to stop using tobacco.

B. The veteran/service member has moved into the preparation stage of change.

C. The veteran/service member was reinforced for setting a specific date to stop using tobacco.

D. The veteran/service member has not set a specific date for his/her cessation of tobacco and was reminded to do so.

11. Remove Tobacco Paraphernalia (11)

A. The veteran/service member was instructed to remove all tobacco paraphernalia from his/her home, office, and car as a way to prevent temptation and limit impulsive tobacco use.

B. The veteran/service member was directed to remove cigarette lighters, unused packs of cigarettes, cans of smokeless tobacco, and ashtrays.

C. The veteran/service member was reinforced for his/her disposal of all tobacco paraphernalia.

D. The veteran/service member has not disposed of tobacco paraphernalia and was reminded to do so.

12. Educate about Multimodal Approaches (12)

A. The veteran/service member was educated about the use of multiple approaches to create the greatest chance of success in the cessation of tobacco use.

B. The veteran/service member was educated about combining pharmacological therapy and cognitive-behavioral therapy.

C. The veteran/service member displayed a clear understanding of the use of a combination of treatment approaches.

13. Discuss Benefits, Limitations, and Risks of Treatment (13)

A. The veteran/service member was provided with information about the benefits and limitations of treatment for smoking cessation.

B. The veteran/service member was advised about the risks of pharmacological therapy and cognitive-behavioral therapy.

C. Concerns that the veteran/service member had regarding the benefits, limitations, and risks of treatment were identified and addressed.

D. The veteran/service member displays a clear understanding of the benefits, risks, and limitations of treatment.

14. Refer for Prescription (14)

A. The veteran/service member was referred to a prescribing practitioner for an evaluation for nicotine replacement therapy (e.g., nicotine patch and/or gum).

B. The veteran/service member was referred to a prescribing practitioner for medication to assist in his/her smoking cessation efforts (i.e., Wellbutrin/Zyban or Chantix).

C. The veteran/service member has been assessed for the use of nicotine replacement therapy, and a prescription was provided.

D. The veteran/service member has been assessed for the use of medication to assist in his/her nicotine cessation, and a prescription was provided.

E. The veteran/service member has been assessed for nicotine replacement, therapy and/or medication, but none was provided.

F. The veteran/service member has not attended the evaluation for nicotine replacement therapy or medication and was redirected to do so.

15. Provide Educational Material on Pharmacology (15)

A. Educational material was provided to the veteran/service member in regard to the various pharmacological treatments available.

B. The veteran/service member was provided with information about common and rare side effects for pharmacological treatments.

C. The veteran/service member was provided with information about the length of time needed to see benefit from pharmacological treatments and how the treatment will need to be used.

D. The veteran/service member was reinforced for his/her clear understanding of the information related to pharmacological treatments.

E. The veteran/service member displayed a poor understanding of the information related to pharmacological treatments and was provided with remedial information in this area.

16. Review of Medications by Program Staff (16)

A. The medications were reviewed by staff to monitor effectiveness and side effects.

B. Medication was titrated as necessary.

C. The veteran/service member has been compliant to the appointments and medication changes ordered by the physician.

D. The veteran/service member has not maintained contact with the staff, and was redirected to do so.

17. Refer to a Nicotine Dependence Recovery Group (17)

A. The veteran/service member was assigned to attend a nicotine dependence recovery group on a frequent and regular basis in order to gain support for his/her recovery.

B. The veteran/service member has maintained consistent attendance at nicotine dependence recovery meetings and has reported that the meetings have been helpful; this progress was highlighted.

C. The veteran/service member has not followed through with regular attendance at nicotine dependence group meetings and was redirected to do so.

D. The veteran/service member has attended nicotine dependence recovery group meetings but reported that he/she does not find them helpful and is resistive to returning to them; his/her experience was processed.

18. Instruct about Consistent Use of Techniques (18)

A. Instructions were given to the veteran/service member about consistently practicing cognitive techniques learned in group.

B. The veteran/service member was reinforced for his/her regular use of cognitive techniques learned in group.

C. The veteran/service member has not regularly used cognitive techniques learned in group, and was reminded to do so.

D. The veteran/service member was reminded to use cognitive rehearsal in high-risk situations and to review throughout the day the top five reasons why it is important to quit.

19. Instruct about Behavioral Practice (19)

A. Instructions were given to the veteran/service member about consistently practicing behavioral techniques learned in group.

B. The veteran/service member was reminded to use delaying, fading, and aversion techniques.

C. The veteran/service member has regularly used behavioral techniques and was reinforced for this progress.

D. It was noted that the veteran/service member has not been regularly using his/her behavioral techniques, and he/she was redirected to do so.

20. Reinforce Use of Cognitive Behavioral Techniques (20)

A. The veteran/service member has regularly used cognitive-behavioral techniques, and his/her use was verbally reinforced.

B. The veteran's/service member's use of cognitive-behavioral techniques was highlighted as integral to his/her success.

C. The veteran's/service member's partial use of cognitive behavioral techniques was reinforced, and he/she was reminded about the more regular use of these techniques.

21. Educate about Common Triggers (21)

A. Common triggers for the use of tobacco were identified for the veteran/service member.

B. The veteran/service member was assisted in identifying his/her own triggers for tobacco use.

C. The veteran/service member displayed an increased understanding that triggers increase cravings and create risk for tobacco use.

D. The veteran/service member has struggled to understand how triggers increase cravings and was provided with remedial information in this area.

22. **Identify Internal Triggers (22)**

A. Internal triggers that increase the likelihood of tobacco use were identified with the veteran/service member.

B. The veteran/service member was asked to create a list of internal triggers that increased the likelihood of tobacco use.

C. The veteran/service member was provided with examples of internal triggers that may increase the likelihood of tobacco use (e.g., feeling angry or sad, lack of sleep, anxiety).

D. The veteran/service member was reinforced for his/her identification of internal triggers that increased the likelihood of tobacco use.

E. The veteran/service member struggled to identify internal triggers that increase his/her likelihood of tobacco use and was provided with remedial information in this area.

23. **Identify External Triggers (23)**

A. External triggers that increase the likelihood of tobacco use were identified with the veteran/service member.

B. The veteran/service member was asked to create a list of external triggers that increased likelihood of tobacco use.

C. The veteran/service member was provided with examples of external triggers that may increase the likelihood of tobacco use (e.g., alcohol use, being around others who smoke, going to a bar).

D. The veteran/service member was reinforced for his/her identification of external triggers that increased the likelihood of tobacco use.

E. The veteran/service member struggled to identify external triggers that increase his/her likelihood of tobacco use and was provided with remedial information in this area.

24. **Teach Relaxation Techniques (24)**

A. The veteran/service member was taught relaxation techniques (e.g., progressive relaxation, guided imagery, biofeedback).

B. The veteran/service member was assigned to relax twice a day for 10 to 20 minutes.

C. The veteran/service member reported regular use of relaxation techniques, which has been noted to lead to decreased tobacco use and to decreased urges to engage in other addictive behaviors.

D. The veteran/service member has not implemented relaxation techniques and continues to feel quite stressed, using tobacco to relax; he/she was redirected to use the relaxation techniques.

25. **Assign Regular Exercise (25)**

A. Based on the veteran's/service member's current physical fitness levels, an exercise routine was developed, and the veteran/service member was assigned to implement it consistently.

B. The veteran/service member was reinforced as he/she has begun to increase his/her exercise level by 10 percent per week.

C. The veteran/service member has sustained his/her exercise level to at least three exercise periods per week, maintaining a training heart rate for at least 20 minutes; positive feedback was provided.

D. The veteran/service member has not followed through on his/her exercise program and was redirected to do so.

26. Explore Tobacco Use as an Escape (26)

A. Today's session focused on how tobacco was used to escape from stress, physical or emotional pain, and/or boredom.

B. Active listening was provided as the veteran/service member identified his/her use of tobacco as a way to escape from stress, physical or emotional pain, and/or boredom.

C. The veteran/service member was assigned "Learning to Self-Soothe" from the *Addiction Treatment Homework Planner,* 4th ed. (Finley and Lenz).

D. The veteran/service member was confronted about the negative consequences of his/her pattern of using tobacco as an escape.

E. The veteran/service member displayed an increased understanding of the negative consequences of using tobacco as an escape; this insight was highlighted.

F. The veteran/service member rejected the idea of his/her using tobacco as an escape; he/she was asked to monitor this dynamic.

27. Develop a Written Coping Plan (27)

A. The veteran/service member was assisted is developing a written coping plan for each high-risk situation, using behavioral and cognitive techniques.

B. The veteran/service member was assisted in developing a written coping plan for high-risk situations.

C. The veteran/service member was assigned "Avoiding Nicotine Relapse Triggers" from the *Addiction Treatment Homework Planner*, 4th ed. (Finley and Lenz).

D. The veteran/service member has completed the assignments regarding relapse triggers, and his/her plan was reviewed and reinforced.

E. The veteran/service member has not completed the written plan to cope with high-risk situations and was redirected to do so.

28. Replace Smoking Habit (28)

A. The veteran/service member was encouraged to replace the habit of smoking with more healthy strategies.

B. The veteran/service member was directed to eat carrot sticks or sugar-free candy, do relaxation exercise, increase water intake, or chew on a toothpick as an alternative to the habit of smoking.

C. The veteran/service member was reinforced for his/her use of alternative habits for smoking.

D. The veteran/service member has not utilized alternative habits for smoking and was redirected to do so.

29. Increase Physical Activity (29)

A. The veteran/service member was encouraged to increase his/her level of physical activity.

B. The veteran/service member was taught about the benefits of exercise when attempting to stop using tobacco (e.g., control weight, improve mood, and relieve restlessness and anxiety).

C. The veteran/service member has increased his/her level of physical activity, and this was reinforced.

D. The veteran/service member has not increased his/her level of physical activity and was reminded to do so.

30. Design a Behavior Modification Program (30)

A. The veteran/service member was assisted in designing a behavior modification program that targets tobacco abuse and reinforces periods of abstinence.

B. The veteran/service member identified an understanding of the identified techniques used in a behavior modification program that targets tobacco abuse and reinforces periods of abstinence.

C. The veteran/service member struggled to identify the concepts related to a behavior modification program and was provided with additional ideas.

31. Implement a Behavior Modification Program (31)

A. The veteran/service member was assigned to implement a behavior modification program that stipulates rewards for nicotine abstinence and agreed to follow through with it.

B. The veteran/service member was reinforced as he/she reported implementation of a behavior modification program and said that it has been successful.

C. The veteran/service member has not begun to use the behavior modification program and was redirected to do so.

32. Use Money Saved for a Substantial Purchase (32)

A. The veteran/service member was encouraged to calculate the amount of money spent on tobacco products each year.

B. The veteran/service member was encouraged to save the money spent on tobacco products and buy a substantial purchase as a reward.

C. The veteran/service member has rewarded himself/herself with a substantial purchase, and his/her response to this was reviewed.

D. The veteran/service member has not rewarded himself/herself with a substantial purchase that is possible because of his/her savings from not purchasing tobacco products and was reminded about this option.